The Loss of the
Trades Increase

THE LOSS
OF THE
TRADES INCREASE

An Early Modern Maritime Catastrophe

RICHMOND BARBOUR

PENN

UNIVERSITY OF PENNSYLVANIA PRESS

PHILADELPHIA

HANEY FOUNDATION SERIES

A volume in the Haney Foundation Series, established in 1961
with the generous support of Dr. John Louis Haney.

Published by
University of Pennsylvania Press
Philadelphia, Pennsylvania 19104-4112
www.upenn.edu/pennpress

Printed in the United States of America on acid-free paper
1 3 5 7 9 10 8 6 4 2

A Catalogue record for this book is available
from the Library of Congress
ISBN 978-0-8122-5277-4

CONTENTS

A NOTE ON THE TITLE

This book modernizes the spelling and punctuation of early modern texts. A salient exception is the ship's name, the *Trades Increase*, which, to retain its functional ambiguity, appears as originally inscribed. It reads either as a possessive phrase, "the trade's increase" or a declaration: "the trades are increasing." The possessive form holds alternate subjective and objective readings: the expansion of commerce itself and the capital gains that such expansion brings. To read "the trades increase" as a sentence is to apprehend a widespread quickening of transoceanic commerce that England finds itself compelled to join. In this nexus of variant meanings, the great ship so named both embodies the extant expansion of the nation's trade and constitutes a principal agent and pledge of further increase. Its christening announces the East India Company's defining commitment to growth.

ABBREVIATIONS OF MAJOR PRIMARY SOURCES

D   Journal of Nicholas Downton, 19 April 1610–19 November 1613. BL (British Library) IOR L/MAR/A/11

D in P   Downton's journal in Purchas, 3:194–304

G   Journal of Benjamin Greene, 15 November 1610–22 December 1612. BL IOR L/MAR/A/12

J   Sir William Foster, ed., *The Journal of John Jourdain, 1608–1617* (Cambridge: Hakluyt Society, 1905)

LR   Frederick Charles Danvers and Sir William Foster, eds., *Letters Received by the East India Company from Its Servants in the East*, 6 vols., 1602–17 (London: Sampson Low, 1896-1902)

M in P   Sir Henry Middleton's journal in Purchas, 3:115–93

ODNB   *Oxford Dictionary of National Biography* (online edition)

P   Samuel Purchas, *Hakluytus Posthumus, or Purchas His Pilgrimes*, 20 vols. (Glasgow: MacLehose and Sons, 1905-7)

S   Journal of John Saris on the *Clove*, 3 April 1611–17 November 1613. BL IOR L/MAR/A/14

S in P   Saris's journal in Purchas, 3:357–519

The Charter Generation of the London East India Company

Established in 1602, the London East India Company's first residence or "factory" overseas—a home, warehouse, and sales outlet for "factors," mercantile agents posted abroad—was located in a great port city on Java's northwest tip: Bantam. This was a place where Englishmen went to die. Located along a wide shallow bay some fifty miles west of Jakarta, the city occupied a region rife with waterborne diseases, like dysentery, malaria, cholera, and typhoid, that overtaxed the ressistance of many voyagers. Plague was endemic there as well. The longevity of an Englishman in Bantam was often less than one year. Their ships, mobile incubators of disease, suffered from worms and other marine parasites that bored through wooden hulls. Copper sheathing had not yet been devised, and wood-destroying organisms thrived in tropical waters. The hull of an English ship that survived the passage to Bantam in the early seventeenth century was likely to have become dangerously porous, requiring extensive repairs before the surviving mariners, and their Chinese, Javan, and Indian shipmates hired on the spot to replace the dead, could hope to sail homeward with the pepper, cloves, silks, China dishes, and other exotica that drew London's investors to the East Indies.

In late December 1612, almost three years to the day after its public launch at Deptford, the greatest English merchant vessel of the Jacobean age anchored in the bay of Bantam. Named by an optimistic King James I, the massive *Trades Increase* was the flagship of the East India Company's Sixth Voyage (1610–13), the costliest of the Company's opening decade: an expedition whose bold ambitions tested, with tragic force, the limits of the founding generation. Arriving at Bantam, the ship's interim commander Nicholas Downton felt a strange queasiness: "We were encountered with most noisome smells." Early modern Europeans credited miasmic theories of contagion— foul smells spread disease—and Downton found Bantam's stench ominous: it would be "hard and doubtful for any newcomers to continue their health" in such a place, he surmised.[1] He had sound cause for concern. Three years constituted an inordinately long passage from England to Java. Numerous crewmen had died at sea or deserted in India, others suffered from scurvy and other afflictions, many having contracted wasting fevers during their recent stay in Sumatra. The great ship itself was compromised not only by the expected damage from marine parasites but more acutely from repeated groundings, a hazard of its unusually deep draft. The most alarming such incident, striking a rock off Sumatra, had required their return to Tiku for urgent repairs of dubious integrity. The mariners recognized that neither the vessel nor its crew would reach England in this condition.

The East India Company's other custom-built ship of 1609, a smaller vessel christened the *Peppercorn* by the Prince of Wales at the same Deptford ceremony—Lieutenant General Downton's usual command—made the passage. Duly outfitted for the journey, it sailed from Bantam for London with rich cargo in February 1613. Two weeks later, the fleet's third ship, the small *Darling*, departed for the Moluccas in quest of cloves, mace, and other spices more lucrative than Bantam's abundant pepper, a commodity that already glutted England. Remaining with his flagship, the fleet's commanding general Sir Henry Middleton beached it to clean and resheathe the hull. The repairs, however, surpassed the reach of his dwindling crew and the Chinese laborers hired to replace them. Workers died in large numbers at the contagious site. Lacking a drydock in which to perform the repairs, the process required them to roll the ship by the keel over onto its side, with ballast strategically arranged inside and on deck, while pulling at ropes and pulleys tied to the masts. They managed to treat one side of the hull. But in the struggle to roll it over to the other side, the mainmast broke. The vessel was too broad of beam for this indispensable repair: too big *not* to fail. Sick at heart, before succumbing in May 1613 to the disease and despair that wiped out his crew, Middleton watched his once-glorious vessel, a proud platform for cross-cultural performances of English dignity throughout the East Indies, rot in the mud. The hulk became a repeated target of arson by persons unknown—Javan agents, survivors speculated, presumably to prevent the construction of an English fort from the timbers. The charred ruin was eventually burned to the waterline. Thus, outward bound on its sole voyage, the *Trades Increase*, together with most of its crew, perished wretchedly on the far side of the world. In the meantime, Downton sailed home with handsome earnings for the shareholders in London. The loss of the great ship and its crew ignited rancorous controversy there. But the Company's magnates defended their interests determinedly. Their fleets sailed on.

The full story of this expedition has not been told before. Earlier generations of archivists and editors, comprehending British imperialism as a force for moral and economic improvement in the world, sifted the past for intimations of empire, and they marginalized this epic failure. "Looking back," John Darwin observes, "we can see that, as long as empires remained the great fact of the present, and the likely shape of the future, they cast a large shadow over how the past was conceived" (Darwin, 33). The prolific Sir George Birdwood (1832–1917), Sir Clements Markham (1830–1916), and Sir William Foster (1863–1951), major East India Company archivists, evidently viewed the Sixth Voyage as a regrettable episode, a valiant sacrifice on the high road of imperial achievement. They summarized it but did not dwell on it, concentrating their editorial energies on more heartening accounts of English voyaging. When publishing Sixth Voyage journals, they produced abstracts, redactions, and tellingly selective editions. The Company's first and greatest editor-publisher, Samuel Purchas (bap. 1577, d. 1626), was an avowed friend, apologist, and beneficiary of the East India Company. He has long been notorious for his cuts. To juxtapose the redactions he published to their surviving sources, as I do in this study, discloses editorial decisions generally compatible with his agenda as a foundational promoter of English expansionism.

Reading back from an era of British hegemony, finding teleological momentum in initiatives that could well have eventuated otherwise, the editors of the great majority of printed East India Company papers downplayed and effaced dysfunctions that haunted and ultimately unraveled the British Empire—incapacities and breakdowns like those Linda Colley anatomizes in *Captives*. Offering a postmortem of a forgotten piece of late seventeenth-century history, she observes, for example, that the failure of England's colony at Tangiers, "reveals . . . stresses and vulnerabilities that proved persistent" in British imperialism (Colley, 33). Consulting original manuscripts where possible, *The Loss of the "Trades Increase"* redirects Colley's framing of imperial history onto corporate history, to a catastrophic yet still profitable venture pivotal to the onset of global capitalism. The sun has set on the British Empire—yet not on the financial empires of London, New York,

Tokyo, and other global centers of banking and investment. Joint-stock corporations, which formerly quickened the emergence of nation-based imperialism, continue to evolve. Warping the political discourses of the nations that license them, they now propel transnational economies whose exponential payoffs to elites derive from human and environmental degradations of an unsustainable planetary magnitude.

A ruling premise of this book is that the story it tells—a microhistory of catastrophic loss producing selective, intensely controversial gain—matters at least as much now as it did in 1615, when vituperative debates erupted over the demise of the *Trades Increase*. To examine the Sixth Voyage and the controversies it engendered, I submit, exposes the genealogical origins of powers, methods, incentives, structures of exploitation, and vulnerabilities integral to the corporate economies and attendant discourses that continue to build, and to destabilize, our material and financial worlds. The conflicts inherent in the East India Company from the outset—between national and corporate interests, executive and common shareholders, shareholders and wage earners, personal and corporate enrichment, plunder and ongoing trade, short-term profits and institutional sustainability—have perpetuated and elaborated themselves, igniting recurrent volatility in global markets. The work of the Company's founding generation remains pertinent not only because it established preconditions for a lengthy interval of British imperial dominion but more importantly now, because it expressed and propagated, in a stark and sometimes brutal manner, global appetites, cultural and material logistics, methods of governance, conflicts of interest, patterns of exploitation, and vulnerabilities that persist in profit-seeking multinational corporations.

To study the origins of these globe-bestriding bodies is to understand them as contingent and responsive organizations, not as preordained and constant powers, and to discern possible points of leverage upon them. Though possessed of legal personhood, practical immortality, and the wealth of nations, these commercial entities coexist with other public institutions and corporate groups capable of challenging them.[2] It is worth noting that Queen Elizabeth I's 1600 charter assumed that a joint-stock body like the East India Company cultivated its monopolistic privileges solely at the Crown's pleasure. In its projection of power overseas, of course, the East India Company moved beyond the orbit of the territorial state that sanctioned it and came to exercise internally the supervisory, disciplinary, and political functions of an independent state or commonwealth.[3] Nevertheless, at home, it remained answerable to the monarch, Parliament, public opinion, and the vicissitudes of ready capital. To recognize that, from the outset, tensions and ambiguities of jurisdiction vexed relations between the nascent English nation-state, whose emergent powers were porous and inchoate in the early modern period, and London's globally ambitious trading companies, casts important light on the evolving struggles between corporate and civic authority, neocolonial ideologies and genuine public interest, across the world today.

The Queen's Charter

Late in her reign, when Queen Elizabeth I granted the London East India Company its charter, the new joint-stock body was an unlikely candidate for imperial dominion in Asia. That the Company managed to outlive its founders is an achievement worth interrogating. The English were emulous late-comers to the Indian Ocean, and their fleets were small. While their determination to enter the eastern trade was firm, their plans remained flexible, opportunistic, and abrogable. After nearly a hundred years of sporadic attempts toward eastern waters, London's merchants finally bestirred themselves to create their own East India Company at the return of a Dutch fleet from the Indian Ocean by the Cape of Good Hope, the route Vasco da Gama pioneered for Portugal (1497–99). Seeking direct access to the silks and spices enriching their European rivals, for several decades the English tried and failed to reach Cathay (northeast China), their ultimate target, by the frozen seas to the northeast and northwest. England's first joint-stock company, the Russia Company, came together in 1553 in pursuit of that dream. London's merchants did not abandon the search for a northern passage to claim for England. But in 1598, a major book exposing Portuguese decadence in India, *The Voyage of John Huyghen van Linschoten to the East Indies*, appeared in English. The next year, the Dutch fleet's return galvanized London's mercantile elite, whose privateering-enriched maritime industry dominated those of Britain's other port cities.[4] Perhaps the southern seas were open after all. If so, London's magnates wanted maximal shares of the action.

A meeting of principal merchants on 25 September 1599 reported, "The Dutchmen prepare for a new voyage, and to that end have bought diverse ships here in England." Alarmed that English bottoms would earn Dutch profits, and "stirred up with no less affection to advance the trade of their native country than the Dutch merchants were to benefit their Commonwealth," they petitioned the queen and Privy Council to grant them exclusive

English rights to trade in the seas to the east of the Cape Good Hope (Stevens, 8). Peace negotiations with Spain gave the Crown pause. But on 31 December 1600, declaring that their efforts should serve "as well for the honor of this our realm of England, as for the increase of our navigation and advancement of trade of merchandise," Elizabeth consented. Her somewhat strained formula attached national honor not only to maritime expansion but also to commercial endeavors deemed ignoble in Aristotelian ethics and some elite circles.[5] The formula was strategic: to frame international traders, not as self-interested, shape-shifting entrepreneurs but as English patriots, reminded the merchants of the fealties attendant on the Crown's grant of exclusive privileges. She named them, "the Governor and Merchants of London trading into the East Indies, one body corporate and politic in deed and in name really and fully" (Birdwood, 167).[6] The signatories became "one body" possessed of rights and responsibilities within England and across the seas. The document acknowledged and integrated the powers of both the monarch and the designated coalition of her subjects. Merchants, mariners, and materiel performed the work of the Company; the queen's epistolary act, constituting them as a legal entity, summoned them to collective action.[7] Her charter antedated the initial voyage by some fourteen months.

Following a venerable tradition of classical, medieval, and early modern corporate theory, the queen endorsed a decisive precondition for the development of corporate power as we have come to know it today: she granted this potentially immortal joint-stock body the legal status of a person. In popular confirmation of the concept, common usage dubbed the corporation, when "he" ruled India, "John Company." Thus Sir William Foster elaborated the conceit: "As a young man just commencing business, he was content with a few rooms in Philpot Lane for his offices; . . . growing prosperous, he rented for a time one of the finest residences in the City (Crosby House)," and so forth (Foster, *John Company*, v). Twin legacies of enormous consequence took impetus from the 1600 charter: nation-based imperialism—"the honor of this our realm of England"—and the capital growth of multinational corporations possessed of the legal rights of persons.

Though the phrasing was venerable, the charter heralded a corporation unlike most others in Elizabethan England. Durable affiliation, not the pursuit of market shares and returns on capital, traditionally justified corporate recognition. The East India Company became a leading prototype of the multinational corporation dominant in our imaginations today: the private, for-profit, growth-oriented body of joint-stock investors. Yet, at their inception in Tudor

England, joint-stock consortia like the Russia Company, the East India Company, and Shakespeare's playing company represented something new. Protocapitalistic institutions informed by transoceanic appetites, they emerged amid an abundance of corporate structures, theorized since antiquity, that textured the social order. Thus Henry Turner describes the great variety of "corporations aggregate" in sixteenth-century England: "They were educational, ecclesiastical, charitable, political, and commercial, and they ranged in size from the universal church, extending across territories and indeed across time, to the angels in heaven . . . to the kingdom, or the community of the realm; to Parliament; to English corporate towns; to the two universities of Oxford and Cambridge; to the new joint-stock companies devoted to trade and exploration; and down to individual parish churches, chantries, and hospitals."[8] As Turner suggests, an informed critique of the joint-stock corporation must "defamiliarize" that institution, not suppose its current ascendancy to be a "teleological inevitability" (*Commonwealth*, 28).

The Joint-Stock Corporate Body

A compelling appeal of joint stock was its tolerance for catastrophe. Together, shareholders mounted expeditions beyond the reach of the solitary investor. East India Company profits derived from the return of sufficient cargoes, not particular ships or personnel. The Company's traffic fused risks incommensurate in existential gravity and potential reward. Each investor wagered an affordable sum on the prospect of high returns, each (noninvesting) mariner wagered his life on fixed wages; the latter was far likelier to lose his life than the former his or her investment. By insulating shareholders from financial ruin, joint stocks turned shipwreck into a cost of doing business. Further, incorporation lent the communal body longevity independent of the life spans of its members and employees.

Queen Elizabeth named the East India Company's 229 signatories "one body corporate and politic in deed and in name really and fully, for us, our heirs and successors" (Birdwood, 167). Her language—from the Latin *corpus politicum et corporatum, communitas perpetua*—as Philip J. Stern notes, derived from classical Rome. In Roman law, a "body corporate" is "a group . . . treated by the law as an individual or unity having rights or liabilities distinct from those of the persons . . . composing it" (*Webster's Third New*

International Dictionary, Unabridged, [1971]). As Stern explains, "All corporations shared a common purpose: to bind a multitude of people together into a legal singularity, an artificial person that could maintain common rights, police community standards and behavior, and administer over and on behalf of the collectivity" (Stern, *Company-State*, 7). An entity more durable (*perpetua*) than its constituents, the "body corporate and politic" announced in the queen's charter held the right to own property, defend its interests, discipline fractious personnel, and conduct business like any other person (Birdwood, 167). Elizabeth's language described the members as persons with individual rights before the law and collectively as an uber-person with the same, like others of "our liege people of England" (Birdwood, 168): subjects and agents of judicial process.

When applied to a joint-stock body, the fiction of artificial personhood becomes distinctively empowering. The designation equips the collective to exploit clear ontological differences between groups and actual persons so as to advantage both the corporation and its constituents. Pooled investments fund bold initiatives while insulating each shareholder from financial devastation. Legal personhood arguably shields members from personal accountability for corporate losses or malfeasance. Moreover, the corporation's answerability to ethical and legal standards geared to individuals remains itself negotiable. As Turner observes, Pope Innocent IV, for one, argued that, since the *universitas* or corporation was an abstraction, "it had neither mind nor soul; therefore it could not sin and could never be excommunicated. Nor could [it] be imprisoned or subject to capital punishment, since it had no body. These formulas, along with Innocent's declaration that 'it is impossible for a corporation to commit a crime' . . . have become infamous in the context of today's debates over corporate personhood" (*Commonwealth*, 19). We will address the ethical burdens of the nascent East India Company, a concern implicit to this study, head-on in the closing chapter.

The doctrine of "one body corporate and politic" recalls the medieval concept of the king's two bodies: the body natural, which grows old and dies, and the body politic, an abstraction of state that endures. The present occupant of a perpetual seat, "the monarch herself," notes Stern, was "a form of corporation"—or, as Turner puts it, "a corporation with only one member."[9] A royally announced legal fiction, the corporation was potentially immortal—until, that is, the charter lapsed, as the queen's was set to do in 1615. On 31 May 1609, endorsing the endeavors of a consortium then constructing a great new flagship, King James I extended it indefinitely, naming the East India Company "a body, politic and corporate, forever, with perpetual succession."[10]

The king's charter recognized a company that had weathered major setbacks over the nine years since its inception. Directors and shareholders in London welcomed their renewed privileges in a spirit of heightened resolve. Having learned of numerous lucrative commodities and regions of access, yet troubled by reports of breakdowns of discipline at sea and in factories abroad, and vexed by the private trade of supposedly loyal corporate agents, they now understood their endeavor in the transoceanic trade to be political as well as financial and logistical: maximal profits required optimal governance of personnel. How best to manage the conduct of fleets and the commerce of factories remained enigmatic challenges. Much of that government, they recognized, depended on writing: corporate oversight and retention of discourse. The East India Company articulated its collective, regionally dispersed power through material networks of epistolary exchange. The paperwork of the nascent East India Company—royal charters and commissions, executive commissions, minutes of shareholder meetings, bonds of good faith, letters to and from agents abroad, voyage journals, cargo manifests, letters and grants from foreign rulers, books of account, and so forth—was integral to its identity and conduct as a corporation. The Company came to know itself on paper. The surviving manuscripts of its internal discourse, and the texts from the corporate archive that found their way into print, articulated ideological commitments that compel our critical attention.

The Founders

An informing premise of this book is that the Sixth Voyage and its attendant discourses constitute an especially rewarding focus for generation-based study. The venture epitomized the work of the East India Company's founders. The Company's governor throughout the opening two decades was the prolific Sir Thomas Smythe (1558–1625), a merchant magnate whose contacts, commitments, and organizational skills markedly advanced London's global traffic (fig. 1). Succeeding his well-connected father in Parliament and as customer of London, under Elizabeth, Smythe also served as auditor, alderman, and sheriff of the city. A freeman of the Skinners' Company and Haberdashers' Company, he joined the Merchant Adventurers Company by 1600

FIGURE 1. Sir Thomas Smythe, by Simon de Passe (1616), pub. John Woodall.
Courtesy of the National Portrait Gallery, London.

and took leading roles in several of London's trading companies. He governed the Muscovy, Levant, and Northwest Passage Companies; was instrumental in the founding of the Virginia Company (1606), serving as its treasurer until 1619; and he also governed its offshoot, the Somers Island Company (1615–21, 1623–25). Elected the first governor of the East India Company, he persisted in that office until 1621, with two hiatuses: 1601–3 and 1605–7. The first was occasioned by his suspected involvement in the Earl of Essex's failed coup. Although cleared of the charge, he remained in disgrace in the Tower of London for the balance of Elizabeth's reign. King James by contrast admired Smythe, knighted him in 1603, and in 1605 made him England's ambassador to Russia: the second gap in his East India Company governorship. Basil Morgan describes Smythe as a "merchant-prince" who provided the vital link between the Jacobean government and the mercantile community. "For thirty years he was overseer of virtually all the trade that passed through the port of London."[11]

Throughout his governorship, Smythe's home on Philpot Lane below Fenchurch Street, four blocks west of Tower Hill, was the London headquarters of the East India Company.[12] It was a busy establishment. Mariners and merchants crowded the halls to seek employment or back pay—and, with husbands at sea, wives and widows their long-postponed compensation. Meetings of the General Court, the full body of investors, took place in Smythe's great hall, where an Inuit canoe hung, a reminder of the governor's global interests and the Company's perpetual hope of a northwest passage to Asia. The Company's twenty-four "committees" (shareholder-directors) and other officers convened there. In 1607, by Foster's reckoning, there were just three regular officers, all overworked: a secretary, a bookkeeper, and a beadle. By 1608, there was also a solicitor, a cashier, and a husband or steward.[13] The *Court Book* minutes also note a treasurer, the charter member Thomas Farrington, as of 1607.[14] There was a strong room for valuables. The Company's archive, where papers accumulated relentlessly, was at Smythe's house as well.

Salient among the persons named in the original charter were the magnates of two interlinked initiatives: the Levant trade and anti-Spanish privateering. To protect and expand their interests in the import of goods from Asia, London's Levant Company merchants recruited subscribers into the larger East India Company. Edward Osborne and Richard Staper, the Turkey Company's founders and first two governors, involved themselves in the new corporation, as did Smythe, then governor of the Levant Company.[15] Much of the capital behind the new organization came from an attendant industry of great tactical and geographic flexibility: privateering, or state-sanctioned piracy. In principle, the Levant Company favored a peaceful Mediterranean trade, yet its members regularly committed their vessels to voyages of plunder elsewhere, and other Englishmen pillaged traffic in the Mediterranean in any case. Their predations increased late in Elizabeth's reign.[16] Both economies were fueled by the war against Spain, which drove England's former traders there to seek markets in the Mediterranean and reparations in the Atlantic and beyond, where they seized the rich cargoes denied them in Spain and the New World. Private initiative, operating with the Crown's connivance and sometimes investment, complemented Queen Elizabeth's relatively feeble navy.

The heady fusion of patriotism, Protestantism, and profit invigorated England's maritime industry and enriched many founders of the East India Company. Alderman John Watts, a Levant Company member and, writes Kenneth Andrews, "perhaps the greatest privateering promoter of his time," became the governor of the East India Company in 1601, when Smythe was in the Tower (Andrews, *Privateering*, 104, 108, 217; Stevens, 166). The distinguished Middleton family applied capital and skills earned in privateering to the Company: Sir Thomas Middleton, an original subscriber, was a prominent grocer, privateer, and subsequent lord mayor; his brother Robert became a governing member of the new company; and their cousins John, Henry, and David took commands on several voyages.[17] Other charter members included the great privateer George Clifford, the Earl of Cumberland, and several of his merchant backers: Sir John Hart, Alderman Paul Banning, Thomas Cordell, Alderman Leonard Holliday, and William Garraway, whose privateer the *Ascension* entered the Company's service (Andrews, 76–97; Stevens, 10–14). One of Cumberland's trusted captains, wounded in the capture of a Portuguese carrack in 1593, was Nicholas Downton. The Company's first flagship, renamed the *Red Dragon* when purchased from him, was Cumberland's greatest privateer, originally christened the *Malice Scourge* by Queen Elizabeth in 1595 at Deptford (Spence, 177).

In its sources of capital, joint-stock organization, and tactics at sea, under Elizabeth the Company openly perpetuated the aggressive tactics of the post-Armada years.[18] Privateering expeditions, while often departing in fleets, were typically ad hoc ventures that preyed on shipping and coastal towns by opportunity. Owners, mariners, and other parties at risk negotiated percentages of the take, sometimes just before an engagement, like James Lancaster in 1594, securing Dutch and French collaboration in an assault on the Portuguese settlement of Pernambuco in Brazil—an expedition funded by Watts, Banning, and "others of worship in the city of London."[19] Each venture pursued near-term profits. The windfall opportunism of Elizabethan privateering is epitomized in Sir Francis Drake's circumnavigation, 1577–80: the voyage exploited the unrepeatable occasion to take Spanish ships along the west coast of South America by absolute surprise. Departing with a ballast of sand and rocks, the *Golden Hinde* returned with precious metals in that service.[20] The fantastic profits, shared by the Crown, inspired and funded a marked expansion of the business model. Privateering became a major, if often ill-directed, component of Elizabeth's strategy of low-budget war against Spain; and Drake's circumnavigation made bold strategic claims for England. But, for the mariners and their backers, each expedition was a more tactical challenge: one dangerous, with luck lucrative, voyage at a time.

These naval and financial reflexes created both opportunities and dilemmas for the nascent East India Company. The London merchants met prolific frustrations in Indian Ocean markets. Many major ports were already occupied by Portuguese or Dutch forces; the English required well-armed ships and some truculence to proceed. English broadcloths and woolens sold poorly in the tropics. The Company's mariners soon learned that to conduct a peaceful trade, their ostensible aim, they needed bullion: they had to carry precious metals out of England to make purchases in the East, and then earn profits by conveying Asian goods to other regional markets, home to England, and back into Europe and the Levant. Theorized and defended in the 1620s by Thomas Mun, such a balance of trade required a long view of capital accumulation and a complex system of coordinated voyages that took decades to construct.[21] But each of the first twelve voyages, 1601–12, was financed separately—like a privateering venture with a spectacularly long list of backers—and investors grew impatient. Mun's thesis, moreover, countered powerful commercial interests—a "multitude, who bitterly exclaim when they see any monies carried out of the realm" (Mun, *Treasure*, 34)—who measured the nation's prosperity in its domestic bullion and faulted the Company for departing with treasure and returning with perishable frivolities. As Edward Misselden protested, "the money that is traded out of *Christendom* into" Turkey, Persia, and the East Indies "never returneth again."[22] Given the Company's abundant difficulties at home and abroad, the recourse to immediate, forceful enrichment at sea often proved to be irresistible.

FIGURE 2. Somerset House Conference, 1604. Courtesy of the National Portrait
Gallery, London. Cecil is seated at lower right.

But one-off, improvised, predatory ventures antagonized potential trading partners and, like the system of single-voyage-based investment that recommended such tactics, confounded the implementation of long-range
strategies vital to corporate growth. East India Company members differed
over the capture of prizes, as they did over much else: wrangling marked their
meetings at home and abroad. Some maintained that only manifest strength
at sea compelled the respect vital to the penetration of new markets; others
believed it counterproductive to offend potential benefactors and clients by
thuggish conduct that confirmed England's notoriety as a nation of thieves
and pirates. King James's 1604 treaty with Spain (fig. 2) imposed major pressures for reform, yet the London merchants, by inclination and necessity,
remained more hawkish than the king. While operating with the blessing of
the Crown, the Company maintained an independent executive that

advanced its own economic and political ambitions in England and abroad. Many leading members were pious Protestants nostalgic for the days of frank hostility with Hapsburg Europe. The Dutch, a powerful lobby at the Jacobean court, sailed in formidable fleets and were ambivalent about, and eventually hostile toward, English interlopers in the Indian Ocean. Portuguese forces, notwithstanding the 1604 treaty, generally opposed both the English and the Dutch in eastern waters.[23]

The alliance of royal and mercantile ambitions that, under Elizabeth, quickened England's maritime endeavor and precipitated the East India Company yielded to a more anxious collusion of dynastic and commercial interests under King James. The biography of a magnificent ship lost on its initial voyage, this book investigates a critical juncture of that collaboration, as the London merchants sought to reconcile neo-Elizabethan predation with the Crown's commitment to peace. At the same time, troubled by quarrels between their separate voyages and the erosion of corporate profits to the private trade of employees, the directors moved to consolidate their authority and maximize shareholder earnings in London. Driven by the need to profit from joint-stock enterprises of prodigious cost, danger, and scope; unburdened by royally dictated territorial ambitions; and prepared to defend their interests by lethal force, the East India Company plied the oceans as vast anarchic zones of opportunity for the creation and management of wealth. The process required social and material logistics of daring comprehensiveness. A pivotal challenge was to harness the reckless improvisations of privateering—corporate raiding—to the strategic needs of corporate sustainability. The decisive financial innovation was to move beyond the separate funding of each voyage, a system that injected dangerous volatilities into the business, and inaugurate a capital base of ongoing joint stock. The crisis that precipitated this reform took place on the Sixth Voyage: the tragic journey of the *Trades Increase*.

CHAPTER I

The Construction and Launch of the *Trades Increase*, 1609

A decade after Queen Elizabeth I chartered the East India Company, the corporation mounted its most ambitious venture to date, the Sixth Voyage, set forth in the spring of 1610 with great expectations and capital investments of over £80,000. The costliest of the twelve separate voyages organized before the creation of an ongoing joint stock, the expedition distilled the ambitions of the Company's founding generation. The London merchants and their supporters in Whitehall Palace conceived the Sixth Voyage as a spectacular affirmation of England's growing presence in the eastern trade. Under the command of the veteran Sir Henry Middleton, who had earned a knighthood as the general of the Second Voyage (1604–6), the Sixth Voyage (1610–13) launched the Company's first two custom-built ships. Actively contemplated since 1607, the vessels were the *Peppercorn*, a modest 340 tons, and the massive *Trades Increase*, at nearly 1,300 tons the greatest merchant vessel built in Jacobean England.[1] Prince Henry christened the former, King James the latter, as they dined aboard the great ship at Deptford on the afternoon of the launch, 30 December 1609. The vessels and voyage were designed to prove England's fitness to rival Portugal and Holland in the practice of a militant European innovation: cannon-equipped commerce in the Indian Ocean. Sailing south by the Cape of Good Hope into seas trafficked since antiquity, the dominant ships were now platforms for heavy artillery—for smashing other hulls at a distance—not ramming machines or mobile castles for archers and harquebusiers.[2] Gums and aloes from Arabia, silks from Persia, spices from Java and the Moluccas, calicoes from India, satins and porcelains from

China, "orient" pearls and jewels, and other exotica fueled elite markets throughout Europe. To access these commodities directly by sea removed the expenses of overland transport into the Ottoman Levant and brought substantial profits to enterprising investors, then called "adventurers," in major port cities of western Europe.

A belated contender for such access, in the early years London's East India Company met daunting difficulties marginalized in most overviews of the corporation that later ruled India. Characterizing the achievements of the first generation as more "rewarding and exciting" than those of the leaner 1620s and 1630s, Philip Lawson, for instance, overstates the precocity of Sir Thomas Smythe's London office, which, he maintains, "soon mastered the fundamental business skills of trading-company capitalism." The governor and his fellow directors, Lawson maintains, established institutions that "permitted speedy executive decisions" and enabled "the executive . . . always [to] be in touch with the most mundane Company activity."[3] But decisions often failed to yield desired outcomes, and managerial surveillance was never comprehensive. As this chapter will demonstrate, the governance of the first generation, though determined and resourceful, was beset by myriad contingencies beyond its control. Its operations were often cumbersome and inconclusive, its functions more prolific than its capacities, and its command of circumstance fitful. Furthermore, the challenges of central governance metastasized with distance from London. While the more robust Portuguese and Dutch consortia pursued imperial projects on land, the East India Company's charter generation, staggered by low investments and slow returns, struggled to maintain an oceanic presence.

The London merchants met resistance from rivals abroad and critics at home, who objected to their monopoly and decried the export of bullion as a drain on the nation's treasure. From the start, the eastern trade engendered division and controversy—within the corporation, around the country, transnationally—that intensified with the Company's growth. Moreover, the Crown's support sometimes wavered. To be retained, monopoly privileges compelled the traders to generate substantial revenues in royal customs and provide generous loans at the Crown's need. A cash-hungry monarch might abrogate the charter or invite interlopers to proceed, as King James did for Sir Edward Michelborne in 1604 and a Scottish East India Company in 1618, undermining East India Company interests.[4]

For her part, Queen Elizabeth honored the terms of the December 1600 charter. Yet, ten months into the experiment, she chided the London merchants for their slackness, declaring through her Privy Council that she expected them to send out multiple ships annually: that is, to conduct them-selves more like the Dutch, who "prosecute their voyages with a more hon-ourable resolution."[5] To date, the East India Company had dispatched but one fleet of five ships (1601–3) and awaited its return before mounting another. Committed in principle to a separate levy of stock for each voyage, yet short of funds, in the early years they were twice compelled to apply investments from one venture to another: from the First to the Second, and the Third (1607–10) to the Fifth (1609–11). Between these, the Fourth Voyage (1608–11) failed catastrophically: the *Ascension* foundered in the Gulf of Cam-bay, and the undermanned *Union* wrecked on the coast of Brittany, its cargo pillaged. But the returns of the Third Voyage, whose first ship, the *Consent*, reached England in January 1609 and whose flagship, the *Dragon*, arrived in September, were substantial: the combined profit of the Third and Fifth Voyages reached 234 per cent.[6] For the time being, these heady earnings stabilized the business. King James renewed the charter in May 1609, con-firming the East India Company's "right . . . to be a body, politic and corpo-rate, forever, with perpetual succession" (Bruce, 1:156–57). From 1610, the pace of investment and voyaging quickened, with two expeditions in 1611, four in 1612, and the introduction of an ongoing joint stock in 1613—a capital consolidation that marked a decisive advance in corporate vitality. The East India Company, finds Theodore K. Rabb, grew rapidly between 1609 and 1615, and that quickening expressed a larger trend: this interval marked the highest percentage of total admissions to all English trading companies between 1575 and 1630, at 36.5 percent (Rabb, 90–91, 76).

Sixteen nine, that is, was an unprecedentedly big year for London's joint-stock companies. Chronically short of funds, the East India Company invited numerous new "brothers" into its fellowship to raise money for the Sixth Voyage. The decisive factor in overall admissions that year was recruitment into the Virginia Company (chartered in 1606): 812 investors. Shares were alluringly affordable: £12 10s entitled one, in theory, to one hundred acres of land in the New World (Rabb, 32). As news of the great hardships the initial colonists suffered dimmed London's hopes for quick profits in Virginia, the Company's directors orchestrated and quickly printed an extraordinary clus-ter of sermons in 1609–10 promoting Virginia as a western Canaan set aside for Protestantism and England: an unclaimed land whose natives might be saved for Christ, unlike their unfortunate counterparts in Mexico and Peru, enthralled to the devil or the Papal Antichrist.[7] Enrollment surged as the

Company renewed its charter in May 1609 and the fleet carrying an interim governor to precede Lord De La Warre to Jamestown, Sir Thomas Gates, prepared to sail (Rabb, 90, 82–84). He departed at the start of June in the *Sea Venture*, the story of whose ensuing wreck percolated into Shakespeare's *The Tempest*.[8] In the event, while the *Sea Venture*'s passengers and crew recuperated and factionalized in Bermuda, most who reached Jamestown perished miserably. The winter of 1609–10 devolved into the most horrible in that settlement's history, "the starving time," when the besieged population plummeted from perhaps three hundred to sixty, and some persons, archaeologists have confirmed, resorted to cannibalism to survive.[9] But in London that year, investment in Virginia—"a Territory . . . so rich, fertile, and fruitful," declared the preacher Richard Crakanthorpe at Paul's Cross on 24 March 1609 (Wright, *Religion*, 97)—looked to be a patriotic, pious, and in the long run, probably lucrative wager. East and west, the prospects seemed compelling. In Rabb's table of admissions to trading companies from 1575 to 1630, 1609 stands out spectacularly, with 1,294 enrollments, seconded by 1611, with 794 (Rabb, 84, 74–75). The terrible distance that year between enthusiasms in London and material conditions in Jamestown engendered tragic loss. Soon enough, a similar irony ensnared the Sixth Voyage.

The year 1609 was also marked by ambitious building projects in greater London and beyond. In the seventeenth-century's opening decade, as late Elizabethan factionalism played out and the Stuarts' arrival stimulated fresh jostling for precedence, "all the great court figures were building," Lawrence Stone has observed. Major families constructed mansions in London and, on their country estates, houses fit to receive the court on annual progress: "The Howard clan set the pace with Northampton House at Charing Cross, Greenwich House, and Audley End in Essex, while the Earl of Dorset was building at Knole. But Robert Cecil was not far behind with Chelsea House, Salisbury House, and the New Exchange in the Strand, Cranborne House in Dorset, and finally Hatfield House in Hertfordshire" (Stone, 63). Robert Cecil, the Earl of Salisbury, was born in Westminster, a district grown fashionable as the aristocracy took townhomes near Whitehall Palace. In this neighborhood, he built the New Exchange, a luxurious mall for chinoiserie and assorted fineries, to expand the retail opportunities for his friends in the eastern trade. The edifice rivaled Sir Thomas Gresham's Royal Exchange in the City of London. Claiming imperial functions for the new facility, and honoring King James's will to unify England, Scotland, and Wales in a greater Britain, Cecil named the building "Britain's Burse." The royal family

FIGURE 3. Phineas Pett and the Construction of the *Prince Royal*
(det.), c. 1612. Courtesy of the National Portrait Gallery.

attended the opening festivities on 19 April 1609, and the king performed the
rite of naming. The event took vivid expression in a rediscovered work by
Ben Jonson, *The Entertainment at Britain's Burse* (ed. Knowles).

In the spring of 1609, Sir Hugh Middleton, Sir Henry's cousin, oversaw
the commencement of the enormous New River project, completed in 1613:
a canal nearly forty miles long that brought fresh water to the metropolis
through Islington—the most important improvement in London's water-
works until the nineteenth century.[10] Below London Bridge along the
Thames, the two greatest ships of the Jacobean era were under construction.
While the East India Company's master shipwright William Burrell built the
Trades Increase at Deptford, his friend the royal shipbuilder Phineas Pett
constructed an equally grand and more ornate vessel at Woolwich for Prince
Henry: the *Prince Royal* (fig. 3). The two shipbuilding projects and Cecil's
sumptuous emporium brought together many of the same personnel—the
royal family, aristocratic and mercantile elites, groups of skilled and common
laborers—in projects expressing London's rites of public ostentation, cultures
of personal and corporate adventurism, lavish consumption, and maritime

power. Together these construction projects, culminant instances of the decade's building boom, expressed the nascent imperial zeitgeist that animated the launch of the *Trades Increase*: the emulous will to assert the dignity of England, a small nation environed by the sea, as a player of consequence in an increasingly globalized world whose remote oceans other European powers presumed to dominate. It was a time of anxious optimism, disruptive ambition, sophisticated showmanship, quickened production, and extremely hazardous investment.

New Ships, New Investors

Multiple concerns converged at meetings of the Court of Committees in Sir Thomas Smythe's house. Pressures peaked late in 1609 as the *Trades Increase* and *Peppercorn* neared completion at Deptford. The directors advanced oft-revisited plans, contended with outcomes of prior and ongoing initiatives, read reports and heard testimony from agents abroad and in London, reviewed debts, heard grievances, received and paid off returning mariners, hired new personnel, inducted new investors, negotiated with agents of the Crown over nautical supplies and sales of pepper, and monitored the construction projects. Two of the three ships of the Third Voyage returned in 1609: the *Consent* in January and the *Dragon* [aka *Red Dragon*] in September. The former carried a rich cargo of cloves and reports of great promise in the Moluccas; the latter lingered, damaged, with a weakened crew at Plymouth, where the security of its cargo provoked managerial anxieties and interventions. The sometimes-daily Courts of Committees and the less frequent General Courts met in distinct yet overlapping constellations of the several groups of investors created since the Company's inception: "adventurers" in the "old," Third, Fourth, and Fifth Voyages. The last were recast as Sixth Voyage adventurers after the Fifth Voyage departed in April as an offshoot of the Third; the Fourth Voyage was eventually written off as a total loss. A vestige of privateering, the system of single-voyage investment aggravated problems of financial and material record-keeping, complicated the sharing of information among East India Company members, multiplied occasions for error and confusion, and perplexed long-range strategies for corporate growth. Each voyage was a new—and as its departure neared, hastily consummated—invention.

The *Trades Increase* and *Peppercorn* were the initial two of six ships built by the East India Company between 1609 and 1612. They were followed by the *Clove* and the *Thomas* of the Eighth Voyage, the *James* of the Ninth, and the *Hosiander* of the Tenth (Birdwood, xiv). The East India Company's first flagship, the *Dragon*, was purchased in 1600 from a charter member of the yet-unlicensed company, George Clifford, the Earl of Cumberland. Clifford was a leading Elizabethan privateer, and the ship, christened the *Malice Scourge* by Queen Elizabeth at Deptford in 1595, was his most formidable: a redoubtable vessel, variously rated at six hundred to nine hundred tons, with thirty-eight guns. Richard T. Spence places it among the great ones of the age, "because no other ship straddles those twin peaks of Elizabethan success, the sea-war against Imperial Spain and the company's nascent Far Eastern trade."[11] It served the Company dependably as the flagship of the First, Second, Third, and Tenth Voyages, and, after the East India Company stopped numbering its voyages, of the 1615 fleet that carried England's first royal ambassador to India, Sir Thomas Roe—a service that should have fallen to the *Trades Increase*, had the latter survived. If the entries allegedly extracted from General William Keeling's lost Third Voyage journal are genuine, the *Dragon* was also the stage for shipboard productions of *Hamlet* and *Richard II* outbound off Africa.[12] Nevertheless, as a refitted privateer, it did not hold the purpose-built grandeur fit to embody the Company's ascendant ambitions.

Throughout the first three voyages (1601–7), the East India Company awaited the return of one fleet before dispatching another, reoutfitting the same core group of vessels. The *Dragon* and the *Hector* served on all three voyages; the *Susan* survived the First and disappeared on the Second; the *Ascension* served on the First, Second, and foundered on the Fourth Voyage (Birdwood, xiv). The initial fleets embodied the East India Company's descent from the Levant Company and the privateering industry. A durable vessel of eight hundred tons, in 1599 the *Hector* carried the master artificer Thomas Dallam to Constantinople with the mechanical organ he built for the Levant Company as a gift to the sultan. On the East India Company's Third Voyage, the *Hector* became the first English ship to reach India. Also a former Levant trader, the 240-ton *Susan* was purchased from Alderman Paul Banning, a charter East India Company member, for £1,600. The 260-ton *Ascension* was a former privateer purchased from another charter member, William Garraway, in 1600.[13] Yet, as the Third Voyage prepared to sail in 1607, the directors resolved to dispatch another voyage the following spring. That initiative obviously necessitated more ships.

Determining to raise money "for the setting forth of two ships" on the Fourth Voyage, a General Court of 27 February 1607 pondered whether to hire "or otherwise prepare" them: should they subcontract, buy, or build (*Court Book*, B/3, f22)? The ensuing resolution of 15 May 1607 that "certain ships and goods for the next year" be prepared by Christmas (f30v), left little time for construction, so in August 1607, the East India Company bought the *Union*, a 400-ton vessel, for £1,250 (Farrington, *Catalogue*, 667) to sail in company with the *Ascension*, purchased from the shareholders of the Second Voyage for £485 (f43v, 29 July 1607). In the *Court Book*'s first mention of the vessels of the eventual Sixth Voyage, the 15 May 1607 court also moved to prepare "things necessary for the provision of building of some greater ships for the year then following," 1608 (f30v). To equip the Fourth Voyage while also constructing "some greater ships" should require, the directors then estimated, some £50,000. Suspecting that the Third Voyage shareholders, lately squeezed of £53,500 (Chaudhuri, 209), might not produce that sum, they called for a new subscription book in which "every of the adventurers of the former voyage" could pledge contributions. If by 20 June these had not met the mark, then the governor and committees would invite "all others his majesty's subjects" into the pool, with a minimal stake of £100, "until the said £50,000 be so fully set down" (f30v–f31). If they failed to deliver, subscribers would confront fines calibrated to the amounts promised. Notwithstanding these measures, investments did not accrue as hoped. Even throughout 1609, the committees found themselves postponing their severity, extending due dates. With the new ships finally afloat, a General Court of 19 January 1610—the last surviving minutes in the relevant *Court Book*—estimated that they would need perhaps £80,000 to conduct the Sixth Voyage. But to date, the pledges had amounted to £52,000, and the funds in hand, £40,000: just half of the requisite capital (f123v, f171).

An exclusive club, the East India Company was queasy about widening its fellowship but recurrently found itself compelled to do so. While first contemplating a Sixth Voyage, the shareholders proposed a familiar monopolistic protocol. A month after the June 1607 deadline passed without sufficient pledges, a General Court of 22 July 1607 capped the number of "chief adventurers" at fifty magnates, each good for £550, who could underwrite others contributing £100 or more (*Court Book*, f40v). One recruit then welcomed to the inner circle was the renowned actor Edward Alleyn, who had played Tamburlaine, Doctor Faustus, and perhaps Barabas with the lord admiral's men in the 1590s (*ODNB*). On 28 July 1607, having ventured £550, he was "received into the number of the 50 adventurers and also admitted and sworn a free brother of the fellowship" (f42v). New contributors of the lesser sort, however, were to be held at a distance. Though named in the Book of Accounts under their respective patrons or proxies, they were "not to have any hand or meddling in the business, but to leave it wholly to the foresaid fifty adventurers, by whom as by the chief heads the stock . . . shall be so furnished" (f40v).

Officially divided between the elected "committees," the twenty-four who managed the business, and the "generality," the larger body of voting shareholders who met every few months,[14] the East India Company further hierarchized the latter by differentiating chief from "under" investors in a given voyage: smaller stakeholders whose money the principal shareholders would manage while ignoring their voices. This adaptive system allowed the committees to widen recruitment while authorizing major investors to retain their dominance. Convening under proxies, smaller contributors might, for a fee, perhaps join the Company in their own persons later. Ambiguities and arbitrary exclusions were integral to the system: to advance from an "under-adventurer" to a sworn brother of the fellowship did not precisely elevate one to the status of a principal investor. Concentrating authority in ways that point to the insider cultures of corporate boardrooms and brokerage houses to this day, the core group thus moved in July 1607 to consolidate its control over the forthcoming venture. But the mounting expenses of the Sixth Voyage demanded more promotional postures. A General Assembly of 21 August 1607 voted to allow "any Court of the former 50 adventurers, to admit into this company any under-adventurer who shall have truly adventured (*bona fide*) £100 at the least or upwards . . . and to give them their oath for their admittance, according to ancient order" (*Court Book*, f48).

The Company's financial predicament remained stressful: in January 1609, they had to borrow £1,000 simply to pay off the crew of the *Consent*, a small vessel (f105v). As the costs of construction and outfitting climbed that year, the merchants moved to enhance their social and economic power by upgrading the class profile of their membership, which had hitherto included few gentry. The most influential of those invited into the brotherhood was Sir Robert Cecil, Lord Salisbury, a friend of the East India Company from the start: several months before the queen's 1600 charter, the treasurer of the navy, Fulke Greville, wrote to him about places where the English might trade in the East.[15] Since the 1590s, Cecil had owned the customs farm in silks and satins; as the lord treasurer since 1608, he oversaw imports and exports comprehensively. Perhaps the most controversial of these exports was the bullion indispensable to European trade in Asia, where gold and silver, not English woolens, enjoyed strong demand. As the secretary of state, Cecil was also the dignitary to whom East India Company directors appealed for help in matters of state abroad. In 1608, for instance, they asked him to solicit a letter of protection from Sultan Achmed I to trade in Ottoman-ruled Yemen; in August 1609, to procure the release of two factors imprisoned in Lisbon.[16] Their most powerful ally on the Privy Council, Cecil was intimately and comprehensively involved in the privileges, oversight, and profits of the East India Company, domestically and internationally. His personal interests in the business disposed him to represent them favorably to the monarch who relied on him.

On 11 May 1609, the East India Company won a grant of reincorporation by Cecil's order (Sainsbury, 184 [#440]), and on 30 May—one day before King James renewed their charter—a meeting of the East India Company's General Court welcomed him, together with a few other members of the highest aristocracy, into their ranks. The shareholders gave Governor Thomas Smythe the authority to make "the Lord Treasurer [Robert Cecil], the Lord Admiral [Charles Howard], the Lord of Worcester [Edward Somerset], & the Lord of Southampton [Henry Wriothlesley] with some other lords, knights, & gentlemen . . . free of the East India Company . . . whether any of them shall be an adventurer [investor] or no. . . . And further from time to time to admit such and so many other lords, knights and gentlemen favorers of the company & no mere merchants, as he in his discretion shall think meet."[17] Privy councilors, "no mere merchants," the new affiliates did not need to invest; unlike the affordable Virginia Company, the East India Company demanded at least £100 of common shareholders.[18] Shakespeare's patron Southampton nevertheless graciously offered to adventure £500, and at his swearing in on 13 October, promised "a brace of bucks annually" (Sainsbury, 195 [#463]). Two weeks later, Lord Monteagle, William Parker (discoverer of the Gunpowder Plot), who like Southampton joined the Virginia Company's governing council in 1609, likewise requested admission to the East India Company, matching Southampton's offer: an adventure of £500 and an annual brace of bucks (*ODNB*; Sainsbury, 196 [#463]). The infusion of aristocratic blood in 1609 set a trend: between then and 1619, nearly one hundred gentry joined the Company (Rabb, 32).

The recruitment of such luminaries was all the more welcome because it coincided with a loosening of criteria for overall membership. The financial pressures of 1609 compelled the shareholders to invite even youths and apprentices into their ranks. On 28 July, they moved to admit, for a fee of 40s, any "under-adventurers" who had contributed £110 or more to the Fourth Voyage, and to invite "sons, servants, and all other that shall be found capable thereof," including "children under age" (f130v). One of these was Richard Burrell, the shipwright's son, three months shy of twenty-one (f130–130v). On 14 August, they invited any subinvestor of £100 in the First, Second, or Third Voyages, upon payment of £10, "to be sworn a free Brother of this Society." Lowering the bar further, the committees moved to admit, for the sum of £20, "any person or persons his Majesty's subjects being a mere merchant," and for £40, any "shopkeeper, warehouseman, retailer, or tradesman." Queasy about such inclusiveness, the committees limited "mere merchant" inductees to ten and the latter group to five. They invited former apprentices of any long-standing brother of the Company to join for a mere 10s (f132v–133). On 12 September, the committees opted to let "any man . . . sell his adventure with the company" to "others not free of the company" who might then, for a fee, gain admission (f137v). Though framed with limits and conditions, these were extraordinary measures. To mount the Sixth Voyage compelled the members, albeit reluctantly, to widen their fellowship. Sharpening debates between the plutocratic core and the full assembly of shareholders, the campaign to embody the Company's quickened aspirations in a single great flagship both expressed and undermined the monopolistic economy of the business.

Plotting the Great Ship

At its launch, the full enormity of the *Trades Increase* should have surprised the vessel's initial planners. Early deliberations had called for one or two "great ships" well below the almost 1,300 tons of the new flagship (Farrington, *Catalogue*, 657). As noted earlier, the shipbuilding proposal was first introduced at a Court of Committees on 15 May 1607, two months after the Third Voyage had departed. While plotting a Fourth Voyage for 1608, the committees also considered the "building of some greater ships" for another fleet to sail in 1609 (*Court Book*, f30v). Resuming the matter on 22 July, a General Court discussed "timber for the preparing of two great ships" and proposed a stock of £25,000 toward the same (f40v; cf. f42v). By August, however, uncertain of their prospects, the investors had scaled back these plans. Anxious lest two large vessels on a single voyage glut the market on return, the committees concurred "that only one great ship of 700 or 800 tons be built and prepared against Christmas 1608" (f48, 28 August 1607). They intended it for the Fifth Voyage.

Yet the need to conduct fresh voyages outpaced the construction project. On 18 March 1608, four days after the Fourth Voyage left Woolwich, the investors voted to dispatch another expedition "with all convenient speed"— that is, before a new ship could be completed—and resolved "to make inquiry for men and ships fit for the same Fifth Voyage" (Foster, *Jourdain*, xix; *Court Book*, f86). On 22 April, the East India Company's master shipwright William Burrell recommended "one ship of 430 tons and a pinnace of 110 tons" for the venture (*Court Book*, f91). Whatever their urgency that spring, it was nevertheless a full year before the Fifth Voyage, reconceived in the light of fresh information from Third Voyage mariners, departed as a fleet of one: the 320-ton, recently purchased *Expedition* (Farrington, 239), commanded by David Middleton. The brother of Sir Henry, he had captained the *Consent* and returned in January 1609 with news of opportunities that the Company, at last, moved quickly to exploit: a General Court of 9 February 1609 voted that one or two ships be "sent away with as much speed as may be possible" (f107).[19] Their haste was likely sharpened by the memory of a kindred yet unconsummated resolution of eleven months before. The shifting calculations that eventually, and in the end hurriedly, produced the Fifth Voyage demonstrate the staggered rhythms and relative unpredictability of the East India Company in its opening years. Recurrently, urgent initiatives stalled or unraveled as the committees revisited plans in view of fresh reports and unforeseen impediments. Perpetually self-corrective, the management of the business was reactive and improvisational. The committees often found themselves crowded by dizzying contingencies—somewhat like Jonson's great comic schemers Dol, Face, and Subtle in *The Alchemist*, whose converging clients press the "venture tripartite" (1.1.135) to advance multiple plots concurrently.

While the Fifth Voyage coalesced and quickened, the construction project advanced slowly. In June 1608, the committees allocated funds "for the preparing of a dock" for the shipbuilding; late in October, the better to secure "the timber now brought thither" (f101), they purchased the Deptford dock leased since 1607. In mid-December 1608, they hired one John Waldowe "to be employed about the dock" and keep "account of the *preparations* . . . for the new building of the ship" (*Court Book*, f101, f103; emphasis added). The phrasing indicates that, at the end of 1608, the construction had not yet properly begun. The delay proved consequential, for the *Trades Increase* was built, not in 1608 as initially proposed, but during a much headier year: as enrollment surged in the Virginia Company and testimonies and returns from the Third Voyage heartened investors hesitant the year before. On 5 July 1609, the Court of Committees declared themselves, "upon diverse and sundry good grounds," confident "that the parts of the Moluccas and thereabouts will afford an ample and more beneficial trade than hitherto we have found" (f126). Embodying the quickened expectations of the new season, the great ship, completed swiftly once begun, materialized an enlarged and hopeful vision.

England's maritime community divided over the optimal size of the "great ship." Prince Henry no doubt found the size and splendor of the *Prince Royal*, then under construction, both appropriate and necessary, and many veterans of the sea war against Spain would have agreed. Sir Richard Hawkins maintained that "the Prince's ships, and such as are employed continually in the wars," should, for considerations both theatrical and tactical, "be built lofty": "First, for majesty and terror of the enemy; secondly, for harbouring of many men; thirdly, for accommodating more men to fight; fourthly, for placing and using more artillery; fifthly, for better strengthening and securing of the ship; sixthly, for overtopping and subjecting the enemy; seventhly, for greater safeguard and defense of the ship and company" (Williamson, 137). Hawkins's overlapping criteria express the residual and emergent technologies of the day: the warship as a towered garrison whose soldiers take other ships by boarding them, or as a mobile battery whose artillery sinks them. Accommodating both concepts, the shipwright Phineas Pett's design for the *Prince Royal*, the first three-decker in the English navy (Strong, 57), likewise grandly fulfilled the criterion of "majesty": the need to project power and inspire awe. "For it is plain," Hawkins continues, "that the ship with three decks, or with two and a half, shows more pomp than another of her burthen with a deck and half, or two decks, and breedeth greater terror to the enemy" (137). Fittingly, the Naval Commission of 1618, overseen by the new lord high admiral, James's favorite, the Duke of Buckingham, created a category apart for "Royal Ships": those over eight hundred tons (Lavery, 14).

Many naval veterans, however—including Prince Henry's great mentor, Sir Walter Raleigh—faulted the outsized ship. Addressed to the "most excellent Prince," Raleigh's *Excellent Observations and Notes, concerning the Royall Navy and Sea-service* maintained that well-armed ships of modest tonnage constitute a more versatile and affordable force at sea. He observed that "the greatest ships are the least serviceable, go very deep to water, and of marvelous charge and fearful cumber, our channels decaying every year. Besides, they are less nimble, less maineable, and very seldom employed."[20] For Raleigh, massiveness impedes the strength it advertises. The enormous ship runs aground in shoal waters smaller vessels cross; its more numerous cannon are compromised by the vessel's inertia. A "ship of 600 tons," writes Raleigh, "will carry as good ordnance as a ship of 1200 tons, and though the greater have double her number, the lesser will turn her broad sides twice, before the greater can wend once, and so no advantage in the overplus of Ordnance" (9). As the process of reloading took several minutes, a warship did better, Captain Nathaniel Butler explained in 1634, to turn and bring fresh cannon to bear on the target while those just discharged reloaded, than to rely on repeated broadsides.[21] Safety, maneuverability, and focused firepower were Raleigh's key concerns. He invoked the *Mary Rose*, its lower gun deck fatally near the waterline, "(a goodly vessel) which in the days of *Hen. 8* being before the Isle of *Wight* with the rest of the Royal Navy, to encounter the French fleet, with a sudden puff of wind stooped her side, and took in water at her ports in such abundance, as that she instantly sunk downright and many gallant men in her" (11–12). Built in emulation of the unusually full-hulled *Tre Kroner*, the Danish flagship that carried King Christian IV to London in 1606,[22] Pett's design tolerated the "overplus of ordnance" that had doomed the *Mary Rose*, yet its proportions stirred controversy. In implicit agreement with Raleigh, the 1618 commission recommended no more "Royal Ships," but ten smaller vessels, six of them "Great Ships" of six hundred to eight hundred tons, which "are held as forceable, and more yare, and useful than those of greater burden, and are built, furnished, and kept with a great deal less charge" (Lavery, 14). The fate of the *Trades Increase*, a ship eventually crippled by its enormity, confirmed the rationale of this decision.

Debates about size, of course, applied to ships of trade as well as those of war. Hawkins prefaces his remarks on the "Prince's ships" with "a point much canvassed amongst carpenters and sea captains, diversely maintained, but yet undetermined: that is, whether the race or lofty built ship be best for the merchant" (Williamson, 137). While offering that the sleek or "race ship is most convenient," other criteria complicate the question: "every perfect ship ought to have two decks, for the better strengthening of her; the better succouring of her people; the better preserving of her merchandize and victual, and for her greater safety from sea and storms" (137). Concerns of seaworthiness, durability, and firepower were paramount for East India Company vessels, required to cross several oceans, stifle hostilities from pirates or rivals, and capture other ships at need throughout two to four years on a given voyage. Substantial size and visible strength were vital assets. Further, as an icon of the wealth and power of the corporation whose flag it flew, the great ship outperformed its cost equivalent, two or three modest vessels, decisively. Finally, the need to amass precious cargoes gave East India Company ships a commercial incentive for grandeur: efficiency of scale. In receptive markets, to enlarge the yield of any given act of transport increased profits.

The Works at Deptford

William Burrell directed the construction of the *Trades Increase* and *Peppercorn*. A commercial shipwright with a yard at Ratcliffe, Burrell had built the well-traveled *Hector* and continued to maintain it, coming aboard, for instance, to inspect a leak as the departing Third Voyage tarried in the English Channel. A charter member who bridged labor and management, he was elected to the Court of Committees in 1609 (*Court Book*, f125) and remained active in the Company for some twenty-five years.[23] In 1618, he served on the above-noted Commission of Inquiry into the navy. Over the course of his career, he is known to have built at least fourteen ships, including ten for the Royal Navy (1619–23) that enjoyed long lives, and one, with four attendant galleys, for the Shah of Persia (McGowan, 97–99) (fig. 4). Throughout the founding generation, Burrell was the East India Company's authority on matters of naval engineering. With the *Ascension* under repair for the Fourth Voyage, for example, a meeting of that venture's fifty chief investors on 1 August 1607 "ordered that nothing be done unto the said ship without the advice and counsel of Mr. Burrell" (*Court Book*, f44v). When a larger assembly on 28 August 1607 resolved to build in London "one great ship" (f48v) of "about some 800 tons" by "Christmas come a twelve month . . . Mr. Burrell now showed a plot how the same was to be made, neither too flat nor too sharp." He evidently planned a well-proportioned galleon—a design, to invoke Hawkins, that balanced the "race" and the "lofty." Elizabeth's great shipwright Matthew Baker (1529/30–1613) had introduced technical drawings with proportional formulae in ship design (*ODNB*), and Burrell emulated the practice, which widened in the seventeenth century (Woodman, 67) (fig. 5). Awarding him an annual salary of £200, the Company named Burrell the "principal director for the building of

FIGURE 4. Hendrik Cornelisz Vroom, "Return of Prince Charles from Spain,
5 Oct 1623." Courtesy of the National Maritime Museum, Greenwich. The lead ship
is the *Prince Royal*, built by Phineas Pett. Following it on the same tack are three
built by William Burrell: the *St. Andrew*, *Defiance*, and *Swiftsure* (McGowan, 96).

her [the great ship], in as good manner, for the good of the company, as if she
were his own" (f49; McGowan, 92).

At Burrell's initiative, the Company leased the above-noted dock and
yard at Deptford for £30 a year and appointed the charter members Robert
Bell and John Busbridge to help him find "fit timber and plank" for the
project (Birdwood, 165). To consummate that quest was a serious challenge.
Stands of old-growth forest near London were depleted by 1609. Both the
Crown and Parliament weighed in on the problem. Lamenting the "great
spoils and devastations . . . within our forests, chases, parks, and wastes," on
14 February 1609 King James issued a proclamation for the "preservation of
woods."[24] The edict called for self-restraint in wood-gathering, the protection
of all promising saplings (208), invoked "the especial wants of our navy," and
prohibited the cutting of "any trees appointed and marked by our said officers" (209). In Parliament a year later, Sir Robert Johnson, likewise lamenting
"the great decay of timber within England," introduced "An Act for the
better Breeding, Increasing, and Preserving of Timber and Underwoods."
The House of Lords had addressed such an initiative in 1607 and revisited it
in 1610.[25] Given the regional scarcities, Burrell expected to look to Shoreham
in Kent (c. twenty miles from Deptford), Odiham in Hampshire (c. fifty-five
miles), "or elsewhere" for timber (*Court Book*, f49; cf. f52v).

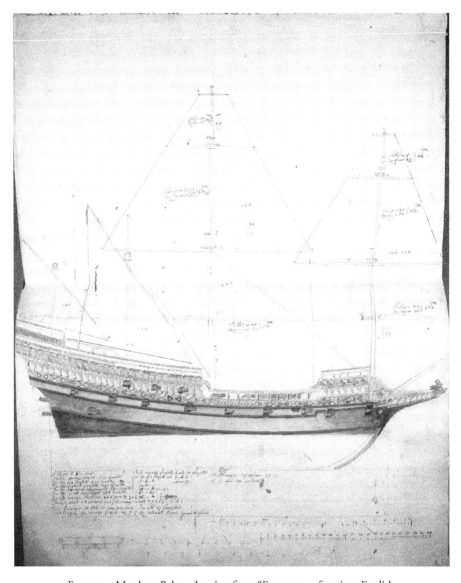

FIGURE 5. Matthew Baker, drawing from "Fragments of ancient English shipwrightry." Courtesy of Pepys Library, Magdalene College, Cambridge (PL 2820, p115). The image measures yardages of canvas for each sail and derives a formula for "a ship of 700 ton. . . . To know what is contained in all the sails, multiply the mainsail by 3. The cotient [quotient] shows your desire."

The search was the more urgent because King James was protective of his navy's ship timber, and the East India Company's recourse to the royal stores at Deptford had already made for misunderstandings with agents of the Crown. On 9 September 1607, the committees pondered how to satisfy "the king's officers" who made "demand for more timber wanting at Deptford." Evidently Burrell's team, on a yet unconsummated promise of restoration, had appropriated some of the navy's supply, "together with a long boat . . . returned . . . again." Thomas Cordell—another charter member, a former privateer affiliated with the Earl of Cumberland (Birdwood, 164; Andrews, *Privateering*, 76–77)—offered to pay the officers £27 of the East India Company's cash in his possession if "the company would save him harmless from his Majesty's officers" for further charges he claimed to have incurred on the shareholders' behalf, "to the sum of £20 and a hawser" (f53). The puzzled committees turned to "Mr. Burrell to know the particulars thereof" (f53). Two months later, the matter remained unresolved: on 2 November 1607, the committees read a complaint from "officers of His Majesty's Navy for restitution . . . for certain provisions of plank, masts, stores, etc. . . . out of his highness' store" (f57v). The dispute persisted on 4 April 1608, Cordell still holding the £27 despite having long since "engaged his word for the company to see them [the officers] contented for their things" (f88). The adjacency of the East India Company's two shipbuilding projects and the royal stores at Deptford interpenetrated royal and commercial accounts.

Once the construction of the *Trades Increase* began in earnest, deliveries of wood from the countryside—freighted by inland waterways in timber hoys, hauled on poor roads in long wagons with large teams of oxen or horses (Goodwin, 3)—posed regular logistical and financial challenges. At a Court of Committees on 30 June 1609, Burrell, who "usually cometh very suddenly for his moneys for timber," requested the release of funds without the usual four committee signatures, because "the parties to whom he is to pay the same [are] dwellers in the country" (f122v), and they needed quick payment in London. Though hesitant, the committees made Smythe's solitary signature sufficient. At the same meeting, Burrell explained that his timber acquisitions had ensnared them in a legal dispute: "Mr. Burrell declared that he had some trouble with a Promoter about the timber brought out of the country for the service of the company, in that the same was felled out of the due time limited in that respect, notwithstanding it is allowed by the statute to fell timber at any time for mills and shipping" (*Court Book*, f122). Quasi-freelance agents of the Crown, promoters, something like bounty hunters, were prosecutors or informants who earned a portion of fines assessed in a conviction. The Company now found itself in alleged violation of a law corollary to the February 1609 decree for the "Preservation of Woods."[26] Confident that "at length the statute would defend him," Burrell asked the Company to cover his expenses in "this suit" (f122).

The request is illuminating. Lacking a modern bank account, the Company, as with Cordell above, often made payments through members who fronted their own money or credit. The practice blurred distinctions between personal and corporate accounts and generated delays, contending claims, and confusion. Another inference from the 30 June 1609 minutes is that the wood was recently cut. Built within a year, the new ships clearly held a high percentage of green timber; and uncured wood made for problems at sea, particularly in tropical zones. Thus John Saris lamented the condition of the *Thomas*, lately built in Ireland and plagued by leakage on the Eighth Voyage, "her plank being so green, which in this extreme heat makes the seams open as fast as they calk them."[27] The problem impacted both seaworthiness and storage.

On the question of "what sorts of masts would be fittest" for the new ships, Burrell looked far indeed: to Latvia. An investors' meeting of 27 January 1609 entreated Sir William Cokayne, "with all expedition to give order to such of his friends or servants in the East parts for the provision and sending home of some fourteen Lettowes [Latvian] masts for this use, by the first means they may" (*Court Book*, f106v). Cokayne, a leading member of the Eastland Company, which traded in the Baltic Sea, joined the East India Company in 1606 and served on the Court of Committees after 1 July 1607 (Rabb, 267; *Court Book*, f36v; *ODNB*). The Baltic provided a range of naval materials: "hemp, pitch . . . masts for ships, boards and timber," as Fynes Moryson reported of Poland in his *Itinerary* (1617). The Eastland merchants' 1620 Petition to King James likewise noted "poldavis [sail canvas], coarse linen, masts, deals, spars, wood of diverse sorts" among their chief imports.[28] Burrell was thinking large. He wanted "four of them [masts] to be of the biggest of the most, best grown upwards, and of the longest that may be had, and the residue to be of sixteen and seventeen hand [circumference], of the longest sizes containing 30, 31, and 33 yards long per piece" (f106v). No subsequent entry, however, confirms that this massive Latvian timber ever arrived. Indeed, other evidence suggests that it did not.

Resolving to make new cables locally that summer, a Court of Committees on 23 May 1609 also addressed "masts and yards for the new shipping" (f119v). Minutes in the *Court Book* typically supply marginal notation of prior resolutions pertinent to the day's discussion, but those of 23 May offer no such link to 27 January. The committees simply chose "to confer with Mr. Burrell for the sizes thereof." Evidently uninformed about the materials in question, the 23 May decision makes more sense if the Eastland connection failed than if the shipment were in transit to or resting at Deptford. Cokayne, who in 1609 became the sheriff of London and withdrew from the East India Company Court of Committees (*ODNB*; *Court Book*, f125, 4 July 1609), probably did not consummate the timber deal.[29] A striking item on 7 December 1609 lends credence to this inference. The committees wondered if the *Dragon*, lately returned from the Third Voyage, "conveniently . . . may be brought to Deptford for the better placing of the masts in the new ship and displacing of her own" (f158v). Burrell evidently desired to work on both ships together. Did he intend, perhaps, to use the *Dragon* for leverage in mounting the new vessel's masts, or instead to redeploy the *Dragon*'s masts on the *Trades Increase*—a vessel of at least one-third greater burden?

The masts were fixed postlaunch. Minutes of 11 January 1610 put the *Dragon* en route to the Deptford dock, "where she is to be viewed how far she may be serviceable for the Company" (f168v). Nicholas Downton, who helped set the masts on the new flagship, notes of 12 and 13 January that a storm "brought her and the *Dragon* together aground, and on Saturday they were moored again" (Downton, "Diary," f35). It would seem that the ships were adjacent on 12 and 13 January. The *Dragon*'s masts could indeed have been replanted on the *Trades Increase*. Whatever the case, the latter's extraordinary tonnage called for timber of tremendous girth, height, and strength, and the masts installed proved almost immediately insufficient. On both it and the *Peppercorn*, shortly after the fleet left England, masts fractured in a storm. The mainmast irreparable, the flagship's carpenters fashioned a new one from trees felled at Cape Verde. In the end, as noted in the Introduction, that mainmast failed too, fatally. Perhaps the desired Latvian timber might have saved the great ship. The East India Company, in any case, had built itself in 1609 a flagship too massive for available stands of English mast timber to sustain. The compromised mainmast makes an apt symbol for the action chronicled in the following chapters: the bewildering distance between the Company's ambitions and capacities—the expansive designs, irresistible earnings, and technological limits of transoceanic corporate trade—engendered tragedy.

Negotiations, Returns, Payments, Preparations

Despite sporadic confusion over reimbursements, the East India Company maintained amiable relations with the Crown in 1609. The year's construction projects included twenty-four pieces of ordnance forged with the Company's coat of arms (*Court Book*, f135). At their completion in September, the committees asked the navy treasurer Sir Robert Mansell "for leave to lay the iron ordnance on the king's wharf at Deptford" (f139), as the Company "have not as yet any convenient place for the stowage thereof" (Birdwood, 307). The request was presumably granted: on 6 October, Mansell was welcomed into the Company's fellowship without the usual fee (f125, f139, f142v; Rabb, 338). On 10 November, the committees asked Mansell to relieve a navy purser, Richard Middleton, of his regular duties so that the officer could assist the Company in "setting up and placing of the masts in the great ship and . . . fitting of her tackling and rigging," for a stipend of £4 a month (f149).

Yet the collusion of royal prerogatives and commercial interests sometimes faltered. After word arrived on 25 September that the *Dragon* had reached Plymouth but was unfit to make for London, King James made an alarming declaration. The merchants had dispatched several committees and a carpenter to Plymouth (f138v) and ordered that "the cellars under the Exchange and the warehouses at Mr. Governor's" be made ready to receive goods from the *Dragon* (f139),[30] when King James informed them that he wished "to buy all the pepper now brought home, at such rate and price as any other would give for the same" (f139v, 27 September 1609). The proposal touched a nerve. In 1603, the king's large purchase of pepper from the First Voyage had perplexed a suddenly glutted market. Threatening to block the Company's sales until the Crown had liquidated its supply, the then lord treasurer Thomas Sackville had proposed that the merchants buy back the king's pepper or market it on his behalf in tandem with their own. They respectfully declined (Birdwood, 42–45). The 1609 proposal similarly vexed the shareholders, who maintained that "the merchant that beareth the dangers of the sea and land should have the gain happening by a rising market" (f139v). They meant to orchestrate the commerce themselves. The king's intervention, while expressing animated interest in their business, was unseemly.

Reluctantly, a General Court voted the next day to accept the king's offer. Yet they also moved to "appoint some fit man to make the Lord

Treasurer [Salisbury] acquainted" with the Company's quandary (f140v). This tactful emissary would explain to Cecil "the inconveniences that may happen both to his Majesty and the Company by setting a price . . . before the [pepper] be first seen and known" (f141). Six dignitaries were selected to finesse the errand, including Governor Smythe and Deputy Greenwell. Cecil lent them a sympathetic ear. At a large committee meeting on 6 October, Smythe reported that the lord treasurer intended "to use all possible means for encouragement of the company in this their trade both honorable and profitable for this kingdom" (f142). Happy news of the latter's success arrived on 18 October when "a very honorable and kind letter from the Lord Treasurer" was read to the General Court: "his Majesty was not now inclined to deal with the pepper or any part thereof, for that he was altogether unwilling to do that which might be distasteful unto them, freely leaving the same to be disposed of by the company as they shall think good" (f144v–145). With Salisbury's help, the merchants retrieved from a cash-hungry monarch their due commercial prerogative. In November, seeking the manner of royal intervention they preferred, they petitioned the Crown to restrain the sale of Dutch-imported pepper, and the king obliged them with a proclamation (Birdwood, 210; Sainsbury, 199 [#468]). As their great ship neared completion, East India Company magnates enjoyed considerable favor at Whitehall.

As for labor relations during the shipbuilding, some of the carpenters grew restive. When two absconded, the court resolved on 25 September to write "to the Justices at Crayford to deal with the two carpenters . . . according to the statute in that case" (f139). Smythe's letter of that date to Sir Thomas Walsingham and the Crayford justices describes the absence of these "shipwrights" as a "great hindrance" and an "evil example unto others" that demanded punishment (Birdwood, 307). At home and abroad, the East India Company's employment contracts were binding, and state authorities supported the policy domestically. On 21 November, the court compensated "Justice Keys of the Tower" with several pounds of pepper, cloves, and nutmeg for his intervention "in the difference with those carpenters who abused themselves in the company's work at Deptford" (f153v). This sounds like a different incident in which the Crown again supported the Company. To balance the needs of workers against the earnings of shareholders was a dilemma: the Company's magnates believed themselves charitable, yet labor was abundant in London and profits slow to accrue. The Sixth Voyage's first fatality, a construction accident, focused these concerns. On 18 August, the Court of Committees voted to compensate Sara Maste for the death of her husband Richard, "lately slain in the Company's work about the ships at Deptford by some mischance happening by an axe" (f134v). In consideration "of her poverty and charge of children," they gave the widow £5—a helpful, yet not a sustaining, sum—granted on condition that she never demand further payment.

The divisions of risk and reward in the Company were split along contractual lines that protected the class of investors. The Court of Committees was vigilant to cap wages, limit compensation, and maximize profits. Paying off Third Voyage crews, the Company distributed to widows the wages due their late husbands. With the *Dragon* in Woolwich on 19 December, the court ordered the cashier Richard Atkinson to "pay the deceased mariners' wages to their wives, so far as the same shall appear due unto them" (f161). Unusual or interim pleas for relief, by contrast, were reviewed case by case. Widows of principal mariners won larger compensation than those of common seamen, yet all petitions advanced slowly. Sara Brum (Brund), the widow of the *Ascension*'s Captain William Brund, tragically slain by a cannon salute during obsequies on the First Voyage late in 1601, was awarded £10 "by way of charitable gratification"—in 1608, five years after the voyage concluded![31] On 30 August 1609, "in regard of her great necessity," the committees granted the wife of a sailor on the *Expedition*, which had departed that April, two months of her husband's wages, forty-four shillings, to be deducted from his pay at his return.[32] But "if her husband happen to die before the said sum shall grow due unto him, they will see the sum repaid again to the Company" (f135). Seeing her in multiple, loathe to set a costly precedent, the Court of Committees was prepared to demand repayment from a desperate widow. Their rigor about such appeals persisted. In 1614, the widow of Giles Thornton, the master of the *Trades Increase*, petitioned for "some relief from the company in regard of the loss of her husband, son, and two servants, who all died in the said voyage." Finding that "all is paid unto her that was due upon those accounts, which was a matter of 400 and odd pounds, . . . they conceived this a too dangerous precedent to begin," and denied the request (*Court Book*, B/5, f202, 19 August 1614).[33]

Late 1609 was a surpassingly busy season for these dignitaries, who met twenty-five times between 10 November and 23 December. They convened to hire personnel, review finances, induct investors, monitor the *Dragon*'s approach and disposal of its cargo, recalibrate plans in light of new letters from abroad, plot negotiations with the Crown, oversee the completion of the new ships, and make preparations for the launch. Advising a General Court on 27

October that the sums currently pledged amounted to just £43,000 of the £60,000 he expected the venture to cost, Governor Smythe reported that "his Majesty had an inclination to be at the launching of the great ship, and to give her her name," and, the launch imminent, he duly exhorted each investor "to set down one third more than what he hath already set down in adventure for . . . this voyage" (*Court Book*, B/3, f148). On 10 November, with an eye to naval spectacle, the committees ordered a silk ensign or banner "for the great ship with the company's arms in silk or metal" (f149). Three days later, however, their preparations yielded to alarm over their goods in transit: Captain Gabriel Towerson was anxious about the condition of the flagship at Plymouth. Invoking "the danger that may happen unto the company by bringing the *Dragon* about this winter season," he requested "that some shipping be sent to unlade her there." Envisioning their goods offloaded promiscuously by unsupervised carriers, the committees directed Towerson to bring the ship home at once, "with the first good wind that God shall send" (f150–150v). They resolved on 15 November "that some of the company be sent aboard . . . for prevention of embezzlement, etc." (f150v). They drafted a commission for one Mr. Barber, "to repair aboard . . . the *Dragon*" to see that "no goods . . . be conveyed or carried out of the said ship without the warrant of the Governor . . . in writing" (Birdwood, 308). As the Fourth Voyage had prepared to sail, they had likewise dispatched rotating pairs of trusted men—a principal shareholder and an outgoing factor—to watch over the ships during the final weeks (*Court Book*, f79–79v, 19 February 1608). They now resolved to supervise the homeward progress of the *Dragon* in similar fashion.

On 27 November, the committees sent two of their own, Robert Offley and Thomas Stiles, "to Gravesend, Tilbury Hope, Lee or where they may first meet with the *Dragon*, and to remain in her for better prevention of diverse inconveniences until her arrival . . . near London" (f155). Representative "inconveniences" surfaced in an 8 December conversation with the generally reliable Mr. Poynett, the *Dragon*'s pilot from Plymouth to the Thames, who had guided the ship outbound and would perform the same office, outbound and inbound, for the Eighth and several other voyages.[34] Poynett advised the committees that his ketch had carried pepper and cloves ashore for the ship's carpenter and that "one Cuttingham's bark of Dover likewise carried away certain goods out of the *Dragon*" (f158). Several such reports accumulated. Anxious about Third Voyage investments, the committees stepped up simultaneously their surveillance on the *Dragon* and their provisions for the launch. Remedial and preparatory delegations multiplied as 1609 drew to a close.

Once the *Dragon* reached Woolwich, the court sent committees aboard regularly. On 11 December, considering the motion to establish "a day for launching of the great ship" and perhaps "to give his majesty a banquet," they tabled the matter for more urgent business: violated storerooms on the *Dragon.* They heard testimony from a steward's mate who confessed to selling "three small barrels of pepper at Plymouth" (f159), yet who could not account for "the want of pepper . . . [in] the forepart of the ship. . . . He declared that diverse chests were sent on shore out of the *Dragon.* . . . It is also said that the gunner, steward, and others have had greater quantities of goods now brought home, and that since the *Dragon's* coming into Woolwich there is entrance made through the bread room into the other parts of the ship, insomuch as some embezzlement of the company's pepper is doubted [suspected] to have been made that way" (f159). The court sent Offley and Stiles back to Woolwich that afternoon. Hugh Hammersley agreed to go on the twelfth, Humfrey Robinson on the thirteenth. On 22 December, two newly hired Sixth Voyage boatswain's mates, ordered "to lie aboard the *Dragon* and to take vigilant care of the ship and things in her, and that nothing be wanting" (f161v), put muscle to the surveillance. A formal inquest of *Dragon* mariners on the twenty-third disclosed a range of abuses: quartermasters colluding in the theft of pepper, a boatswain selling in Plymouth four hundred pounds of pepper "which he bought aboard the ship for China dishes," a steward's mate selling in Plymouth three times the pepper he purchased at Priaman, barrels of gunpowder carried ashore at Bantam, and negligent supervision of the "gunner's stores" in general. Unable to say how "the want of pepper cometh," the witnesses agreed "that it must be with the consent of the quartermasters, stewards, and such other officers that had the charge of the hold" (f162v–163). Resolving to pay only the mariners named on Hammersley's list, the committees referred all the rest "to further consideration," detaining their wages. To estimate and deduct private earnings from Company payouts was a contentious process that would take some time.

The Launch of the *Trades Increase*

When the committees next met on the morning of 29 December, the launch was upon them. Having awaited the king's confirmation of a date, they learned of his decision:

At this court Mr. Governor declared that in conference yesterday with the Lord Treasurer and the Lord Admiral, he understood that his Majesty was pleased to be at the launching of the great ship at Deptford *tomorrow* about one of the clock in the afternoon. Whereupon it was ordered and agreed that the Company do entertain his Highness with a banquet aboard the ship in China dishes, and Mr. [Robert] Johnson is entreated to provide the same; and such Tapestry and Chairs as shall be needful. And Mr. [Robert] Bell is required to provide wine of such sorts and quantity as shall be fitting. The which banqueting stuff and wines are this afternoon to be brought to Mr. Governor's to be sent with some other things early on Saturday morning to Deptford. And Mr. [Richard] Mountney is to provide barges for carrying thereof and of the committees who are to dispose of all things at their coming thither as shall be by them thought fit.[35] And further, it is ordered to give his Majesty the better content, that certain chambers be provided to be shot off with the other pieces at his Highness' coming thither. (f163–163v; emphasis added)

Anxious to receive the monarch who had graciously withdrawn his bid to engross their pepper and who now desired to name the ship as he had the New Exchange in April, the directors hastened to produce their rumored "great banquet" for the royal family (MacClure, 1:292). Like Jonson's *Entertainment*, "written rapidly" for the opening of Cecil's swiftly built emporium (Knowles, 3:354), the feast on the great ship built within a year was quickly set. Assigning each man to discharge his appointed role as he "thought fit," the Court of Committees improvised imperial stagecraft: they decorated the vessel with portable properties and sumptuous tapestries as if it were the Globe or the Whitehall banqueting house. Unlike those landed venues, of course, this floating theater was movable and ringed with ordnance. An epitome of the fortified island of its origin, the *Trades Increase* would project the nation's commercial power and dignity into remote seas.

The furnishings of the feast articulated the imperial claims the ship embodied. The porcelain, tapestries, elegant chairs, and fine wines evoked distant worlds, regal dignity, and luxurious consumption. The wines spoke to Britain's ancient reliance on vintners overseas for elite alternatives to ale and cider. The wine trade instituted the primary unit of vehicular volume: a ship's "tonnage" originally numbered the tuns—the casks of wine—it freighted home from Bordeaux or Lisbon. Chinese porcelain, while widely available in the East Indies—as just noted, a boatswain on the *Dragon* bartered some for bags of pepper—was a rarity in early seventeenth-century England. By 1609, "highly prized as a luxury status symbol," James Knowles explains, it was "appearing in more middling households; it was an ideal aspirational object" (Knowles, *Entertainment*, 3:355). Cecil, with sixty-five pieces listed in the 1612 Salisbury House inventory, was "among the first great collectors of Chinoiserie" (Knowles, "Shopping Center," 15). Evidently, the East India Company's Robert Johnson was another.

Spectacles of princely magnificence, the tapestries were likewise aspirational. Hung at palaces when the monarch was in attendance, sometimes produced at royal processions, tapestries took prodigious time and labor not only to fabricate but also to take down, transport, clean, rehang, and maintain. In the early sixteenth century, Lisa Jardine and Jerry Brotton maintain, "the large-scale tapestry series became a symbolically over-determined artefact upon which the political hopes and aspirations of the imperial courts of the period were repeatedly projected. . . . Imperial authority was increasingly measured through the conspicuous purchasing power required to commission, transport and repeatedly display massive, visually overpowering tapestry cycles."[36] As Thomas P. Campbell explains, the great Tudor collection "continued to play a major part in [Stuart] court ceremony," and tapestry remained "the principle medium of courtly magnificence" (Campbell, 353). Like porcelain, tapestries were currently finding their way into households of the mercantile elite. By investing their new flagship with such icons of dynastic power, the merchants implicitly endorsed King James's vision of a unified Britain, claimed imperial synergy for the regal-commercial alliance solemnized at the launch, and promised to project it globally. The feast was the foundational celebration of the great ship as a theater of British dignity, consumption, and power: the ur-performance of the patriotic hospitality to be extended to magnates who came aboard in eastern seas.

On the day of the launch, the court gossip John Chamberlain reported, "The King, Queen, and Prince went this morning to the launching of the great East Indian ship newly built, where they were to have a great banquet, and Sir Thomas Smythe to be graced with a great chain of gold and a medal to be put about his neck by the King's own hands" (MacClure, 1:292). On 13 January 1610, Chamberlain elaborated: "Our East Indian merchants have lately built a goodly ship of above 1,200 tunne, to the launching whereof the King and Prince were invited and had a bountiful banquet: the King graced

Sir Thomas Smith the Governor with a chain in manner of a collar better than £200, with his picture hanging at it, and put it about his neck with his own hands, naming the great ship *Trades Increase*, and the Prince a pinnace of 250 tunne (built to wait upon her), *Peppercorn*" (MacClure, 1:294). While the latter name invoked the East India Company's principal import to date, the king's speech act was more forward-looking. The monarch's coinage evoked the aura of promise projected in the magnificent ship: the massive capital growth achievable through deep-ocean commerce, the global reach of England's corporate enterprise. The name announced the East India Company's defining commitment to growth. King James's gift to Governor Smythe was appropriately stunning. Around the neck of the man who embodied the East India Company's corporate person, he placed a heavy chain of gold, worth even more than the Company had paid its master ship-builder that year. On the pendant, the royal portrait, likely a miniature by Nicholas Hilliard, hung (fig. 6). The ceremony reconfirmed the 1609 renewal of the Company's charter, honored the corporation as a collective subject fit to represent the king's person, and admonished all delegated to do so to conduct themselves with dignity and good faith.

Among those in attendance was Phineas Pett, mindful of his own reception and probably of protocols for the forthcoming launch of the *Prince Royal*. Differing slightly from Chamberlain's, his account concludes unhappily:

> His Majesty with the Prince and divers lords were present, and feas-
> ted with a banquet of sweetmeats on board the great ship in the
> dock, which was called the *Trades Increase*; the other was called the
> *Peppercorn*, the names being given by his Majesty. I did there attend,
> and received gracious public usage from his Majesty, the Prince, and
> the Lords. But the tide was so bad that the great ship could not be
> launched out of the dock, and the smaller, which was built upon
> the wharf, was so ill stroken upon the launching ways that she could
> by no means be put off, which did somewhat discontent his Majesty.
> (Perrin, *Pett*, 75–76)

The climax of the feast, the launch itself, was a fiasco. In explanation, Pett invoked both misfortune—an insufficient tide, his rationale for the subsequent failed launch of the *Prince Royal* (Perrin, *Pett*, 81–82)—and technical ineptitude, the *Peppercorn*'s flawed release onto the launching ways. In a

FIGURE 6. King James I, Nicholas Hilliard (c. 1610). Courtesy of the Victoria and
Albert Museum.

darker vein, Downton expressed unalloyed frustration in the first entry of his
launch diary: "On Saturday the 30th of December, great labor was taken in
sight of the king of launching of the two East India ships, wherein all things
failed and nothing was effected" ("Diary," f35).

The king departed in disappointment. Deep embarrassment for the
Company's directors, builders, and mariners persisted. Two days later, the
Peppercorn floated free on a higher tide while the flagship remained, reports
Downton, "a little removed, but not launched." Workers struggled until 3

January to release the *Trades Increase*. One problem was fundamental. With "half her length removed" on 2 January, they discovered that "the dock head was too narrow for the passage" of the ship (Downton, "Diary"). The impasse looks, from one angle, like an astonishing lapse in planning: the ship was built too broad of beam to exit from the drydock flooded, like a lock, for the launch. In their urgency to complete the vessel, suppress intracorporate pillage on the *Dragon*, and entertain the royal family, evidently no one thought to measure the span of the dockhead against the maximal breadth of the immersed hull where it should meet the pilings.

Yet the predicament also marked a defining condition of the construction project and the voyage it initiated: incalculability. Burrell possessed sufficient knowledge to build an enormous ship but perhaps not to predict its initial waterline nor the tide's height on the afternoon the king chose to appear. Pett had the same problem on 24 September 1610. The two shipwrights were leaders of their craft and adepts at naval ostentation, but the material outcomes of their efforts were approximate and exploratory, not predictable. For example—Sir Isaac Newton not yet having invented calculus—the exact tonnage of a ship, the hull's capacity, came clear only in the process of lading it. With the flagship stuck on 1 January, Downton estimated it to be "of some 1,000 tons" ("Diary"), and on 13 January, as just noted, Chamberlain rumored it to be "above 1,200." But the directors, either uninformed or more likely requiring exactitude, evidently awaited material proof before declaring a figure to port authorities. With both vessels afloat, the Court of Committees moved on 11 January 1610 to "enter" them at the Customs House without "mention of their several burdens, as yet unknown" (*Court Book*, f168). In 1615, in *The Defence of Trade*—a treatise we will examine at length in the closing chapter—when Sir Dudley Digges cited the late *Trades Increase* in a catalog of East India Company ships, he put the tonnage at 1,293 (Digges, 20).

Smaller breakdowns at the launch intimated that the great ship's burden overstressed the materials devised to manage it. Somehow a pulley caught fire, and a hawser snapped. Were the cables adequate? A subsequent Court of Committees on 10 January, with Burrell and a few key mariners in attendance, found the cordage, "as good as can be made, and better than otherwise can be now had." Having attributed the problem to "some casual accident of fire in the pulley, and by overstraining the same more than was usual for a hawser to endure," they ordered Boatswain Middleton, "to have especial care not to take any cordage but such as shall be sufficient for this service" (*Court*

Book, f167)—not to mention stout, well-lubricated pulleys. These launch-related problems, large and small, raised ominous concerns not only about the adequacy of the ship's materials and machinery but also about the informed capacities of the personnel entrusted with its conduct and repair. Like the shipbuilders, who could prepare but might not consummate a roy-ally attended launch, the East India Company and its mariners knew enough to initiate, but perhaps not to complete, any given voyage to the East Indies. The voyage itself became the test of that. Hazard and uncertainty were inte-gral to the business. While the shareholders regrouped to raise money for another venture, the ships and their crews navigated, at entire personal and communal risk, predicaments surmised and unforeseen. Much rode on the outcome. The day the new flagship finally floated, Downton, noting the relative neglect of his own charge, the *Peppercorn*, wrote of the former, "On this ship was all the company's pride set. She was altogether regarded, tended, and followed" ("Diary," 3 January 1610, f35). As the new century's second decade dawned, the East India Company identified its future with the prom-ise of the *Trades Increase*.

CHAPTER 2

From England to Arabia Felix

The first major crisis to befall the Sixth Voyage took place in Ottoman-ruled Arabia Felix—"Happy Arabia," Yemen—and it arose from managerial negligence, not mechanical failure. The directors failed to equip Sir Henry Middleton with Sultan Achmed I's indispensable letter of protection for the Red Sea region. The letter was formally received by the Court of Committees in London in October 1608, a full eighteen months before the voyage left England. But as overworked clerks processed papers at Governor Smythe's house, and executives busied with the *Dragon*'s return hastened to equip the new voyage, this critical manuscript was either misplaced or forgotten. The result, though it surprised the voyagers, was predictable. Initially welcomed into Aden and Mocha in November and December 1610, for lack of the pass the mariners were arrested as infidel intruders, several slain, and scores imprisoned before they managed, six months later, to break free and sail to India.

After their expulsion from India, a second crisis befell them upon their return to the Red Sea. This time, the trouble arose from structural problems in the Company's business model. They had shut down the Surat factory, England's first on the subcontinent, and returned to the Straits of Bab-el-Mandeb to even their scores forcefully. While Middleton's negotiations were unraveling in India, however, Captain John Saris and the Eighth Voyage reached the Red Sea. Possessed of the sultan's pass, Saris had initiated promising negotiations for trade and a factory in Mocha when Middleton arrived to enforce his blockade, extort from Gujarati ships the goods denied him in India, and demand reparations from his late Ottoman captors. The voyages found themselves at cross-purposes.

The East India Company had no protocols to resolve disputes between the generals of separate fleets. Each venture, moreover, advanced its own portfolio of investments. Plagued by cash shortages, the Company had not yet developed an ongoing joint-stock system. Keen about his prospects, Saris was stunned and indignant at being compelled to blockade Mocha, a thriving, ancient port where he believed himself to be making historic progress for England. But Sir Henry, who outranked him both socially and as his late general on the Second Voyage, believed himself to speak for the Company's wider interests. He identified these with the interests of his own voyage. The division between "these two ill met captains," as Middleton's lieutenant general Nicholas Downton termed them, confused and demoralized both fleets (*LR*, 1:168). With Middleton obdurate, Downton and Gabriel Towerson, Saris's second-in-command, mediated an agreement by which Saris grudgingly consented to join the blockade for a third of the take. But he and Middleton clashed repeatedly over negotiations with Ottoman authorities, procedures with the detained Indian ships, and commodities seized from the latter. Resentments festered. With each general fixated on his own voyage's profit, the spring and summer of 1612 devolved into a dark, bewildering interval for both fleets, the irascible Middleton threatening more than once to sink Saris's ships unless satisfied.[1] To the detriment of both voyages and the Company's interests, their quarrels resumed in Bantam.

Their trials in Arabia Felix foregrounded critical lapses in the Company's provision for its mariners and integration of strategies across multiple voyages. Though ultimately answerable to London, each venture served its own stock. The division between Saris and Middleton demonstrated with unmistakable clarity that the practice of voyage-based investment, a legacy of privateering, made antagonists of nominal collaborators. The funding system compromised the corporation's pursuit of sustainable capital growth. Another residual reflex of privateering evident in the Red Sea crises proved perhaps more amenable to such aims: extortion at sea when thwarted ashore. Yet that course was dangerously volatile.

The Shareholders Assert Their Authority

The interrogation of *Dragon* mariners late in 1609 quickened shareholder anxieties over the security of cargoes and invigorated their oversight of subsequent voyages. The directors grasped in fresh scope and detail a host of problems—managerial, logistical, financial, archival—inherent to their commerce. Lengthy, high-risk missions exacerbated challenges integral to deputation: How can owners maximize the likelihood that their agents overseas prioritize corporate over anarchic personal interests? The Sixth Voyage investors sought answers, not by offering extraordinarily generous salaries, but by widening the scope of metropolitan control. In a striking move, their commission asserted London's authority over earnings and bonuses left to parties in the field before. Crewmen on the First Voyage made winnings beyond their wages, and the voyage itself became profitable, by the capture of a Portuguese carrack in the Straits of Malacca. Following King James's 1604 treaty with Spain, however, the owners discouraged such unprovoked predation. By 1610, they were further convinced that marginal trafficking by mariners—a normative means for sailors to enhance their earnings—eroded shareholder interests.[2] Moving forcefully to internalize their monopoly of the eastern trade, they curbed the entrepreneurial initiative of seamen, the private trade of merchants, and the executive reach of principal mariners and factors. Wherever it sailed, the *Trades Increase* would cut a larger figure for the London Company, and the voyage's commission duly promulgated the executive resolve to make their servants in the east answerable directly to London. The quest for ongoing capital growth thereby motivated the founders of the East India Company, a protoglobal corporation, to reconfigure labor relations within the English maritime industry.

The letters carried home in the *Dragon* included one by John Saris, written on 4 December 1608 at his appointment to chief factor in Bantam, when his predecessor Gabriel Towerson departed in command of the same vessel. Beyond poor sales of English cloths, Saris noted the problem of seamen underselling the Company.[3] Crewmen, he reported, would sell for ten rials apiece "fabrics [that] were ordinarily sold for 20." Such marginal commerce elaborated an inconvenience inherent to the factory, where different voyages converged. The arrival of a ship laden with cloth cheapened fabrics in the warehouses; attendant salesmanship by sailors undercut the corporate fixing of prices. Saris's testimony complemented the inquest's finding that many sailors "in the *Dragon* brought home store of pepper, which causeth us to think that the same was stolen from us and occasioned the want we found of our pepper in the said ship" (Birdwood, 314). At home and abroad, common sailors, "long accustomed to looking out for themselves" (Fury, 85), behaved like freelance embodiments of the commercial opportunism animating the East India Company's corporate body. They pursued their own advantage with materials at hand.

Finding that mariners of various stations were colluding in the process, the alarmed committees drafted stern letters for the Sixth Voyage to deliver to personnel abroad, and they stiffened their directives to the outgoing mariners. Their March 1610 missive to the Fourth Voyage factors announced a new policy against private trade: all personal investments would henceforth be folded into the general fund.[4] In similar terms, they chastened the factors in Bantam and Surat: "We find," they admonished the former, "that those who have had the managing of our business have had more care to enrich themselves than to seek our profit" (Birdwood, 313; cf. 317). Observing that the "very leaky" *Dragon* "came weakly home" (Birdwood, 312) under Towerson's command, they decried the ship's "want of government," with "every man doing what he listed" on a vessel "pestered . . . with at least one hundred tons of mariners' goods more than her burthen" (Birdwood, 317). The welter of private cargoes and random "luggage," the committees concluded, "had well near been the loss of the *Dragon*" (Birdwood, 317). Such flagrant abuse of their tolerance of marginal trafficking by seamen inflamed their urgency to curb it. The Sixth Voyage commission duly instructed the officers and purser to prevent any "dealing by exchange betwixt party and party, neither money for money, commodity for money, or commodity for commodity." No man should bring aboard goods beyond those that "their chest appointed them will contain" (Birdwood, 332). The chest containing each sailor's personal effects—"his proportioned chest of allowance for this voyage" (Birdwood, 344)—was henceforth to be the sole container allowed him.

Other Sixth Voyage innovations went further. The principal mariners and merchants were to be expensively bonded as usual, and "their sureties" extended further than before: "not only to forbear all private trade directly or indirectly for themselves, but also to forbid and hinder all others from the like" (Birdwood, 317). Resolved to limit expenses, the directors also denied commanders the authority to grant bonuses or elevate wages. Until a reckoning could be made in London, factors were to expect nothing beyond their assigned wages except a few pounds for respectable clothing—and, furthermore, to expect these wages only upon their return to London.[5] The directors further stipulated that, in the not unlikely event of a promotion, the new appointee must remain content with his old salary until adjustments might be made in London.[6] Such rigor about raises likely motivated some personnel to seek for themselves the compensation they felt they deserved and knew they might not live to receive back home.

Indeed, as General Keeling documented in his 1615 journal, the policy held dysfunctional consequences. Complaining that "the company have taken from me all means to reward the well meriting in whatsoever kind," he noted that the confinement of such powers to London compromised a key item in their commissions: that voyage journals be composed collectively.[7] Each writer now maintained his own account. For "the mariner endureth not to publish his strength to enable others, or his weakness to disable himself, and the better of them" strive to make their peculiar merits known to readers in London "in hope of gratuity" there (Strachan and Penrose, 65). The breakdown of corporate writing protocols was a rational response by employees to the denial of raises in the field, where commanders witnessed merit directly. Categorically dividing the communities abroad from the executive body in London, the new policy perplexed corporate loyalties and morale—and thus, ironically, incentivized the personal enrichment that the shareholders sought to minimize by widening their oversight of the business.

An emergent transnational institution with growing concentrations of capital and labor, Smythe's East India Company was a body of contradiction. In their plans for the Sixth Voyage, the Company's founders plotted to project their will to the far side of the world. They sought to impose diligent, top-down management on members of a maritime community long accustomed to looser aggregations of interest that relied on, and rewarded, considerable self-determination by mariners. Reinforced by the immense distances between England and the East Indies, that tradition resisted London-centric governance. The very scope of their traffic, not to mention their different regimes of risk and reward, divided the mariners and the shareholders whose collaboration sustained the corporate body. Earnings in London were substantial yet slow to accrue, and investors were understandably vexed at the erosion of their profits to the personal initiative of factors and sailors. Yet, given that the success of a voyage required the willing labor of personnel whose hazards were mortal, salaries fixed, and opportunities at eastern ports of call prolific, no directive from London would terminate their self-interested improvisations. As Governor Smythe later conceded, it was impossible to eliminate personal enrichment altogether: "Private trade," he declared to the committees in 1614, "cannot be avoided."[8] Its persistence, in any case, justified the modest salaries that attended the efforts of Smythe and his colleagues to contain it.

The Company's Commission for the Sixth Voyage

A notable index of the committees' rigor to augment London's authority appears late in the Sixth Voyage commission. Those for the first five voyages named relays of command in the event of a superior officer's death.[9] The Fifth Voyage's commission also delegated crucial decisions to the persons on the scene, leaving it to the factors in Bantam to elect the successor to Captain David Middleton, should he die there (Birdwood, 302–3). The Sixth, by contrast, introduced a far more secretive process. Downton was to succeed Middleton. Yet if Downton too perished, then the principal survivors, agreeing to "submit themselves" to the result, were to break open a lockbox "sealed with hard wax" that held "a writing subscribed by the Governor and sealed with the seal of our Company." The box was entrusted to Middleton to preserve unopened so long as he or Downton lived (Birdwood, 345). These protocols were unusual. As papers of quasimystical power, royal and corporate commissions were openly displayed, consulted repeatedly, sometimes read aloud to seamen or brandished in a crisis of command. The hidden directive constituted a different, distinctly Jacobean order of authority.[10] The sealed box of mortal secrets was an icon of the committees' will to hold a more absolute and mystified command over the persons who sailed their ships and conducted their business.

The commission articulated in comprehensive detail the directors' designs for the voyage. A pivotal reform of the 1610 document was to promote and regulate its own medium: paperwork. The committees required as usual that principal mariners on each ship draft journals "with a true relation of every material thing that passeth . . . so as a perfect discourse may be set down to be presented to the Governor and Company when God shall grant them a safe return, to be kept for the better direction of posterity" (Birdwood, 331). "Perfect"—that is, complete—"discourse," they maintained, must be composed collectively so as to voice the knowledge and experience of the group person. Their own directives, like those to "our loving friend Sir Henry Middleton" (Birdwood, 328), assumed a voice in which, as Henry Turner puts it, "'I' and 'we' become interchangeable," and the "corporation has stolen the collective first person from the monarch" (*Commonwealth*, 101). Yet, while normative for the Court of Committees in London, the mariners, as Keeling would observe, often preferred to speak for themselves. Overall, the epistolary negligence of their agents in the field vexed the directors. As they drafted the commission, they had received no letters from the *Union* or

Ascension, which had left Woolwich a full year before. Rumor—"some uncertain reports from Cairo" (Birdwood, 308)—had supplied their sole news of the fleet's progress.

Their concomitant letter to Bantam, troubled by the muddled documentation of goods both private and corporate on the *Dragon*, requested that henceforth "your journal or book couchant may continually lay open" for all factors to survey and document all transactions (Birdwood, 312).[11] The lack of such a book compromised records in both London and Bantam. The factory's account book—its financial memory—should abide in place, with copies dispatched periodically to London. But both Towerson and his predecessor Edmund Scott, who kept the accounts, brought their books home and left no copies (Birdwood, 312). A key item for each factory visited by the Sixth Voyage was, therefore, "a large book to be a continual couchant, . . . public and common to all" the factors (Birdwood, 313, 342). In future, whenever a chief factor returned to London, he would bring a copy, not the urtext, signed by his successor and two others, and "sealed up" to forestall any emendations in transit (Birdwood, 342). These proposals expressed documentary aspirations for the Sixth Voyage as grand as its flagship: a comprehensive regime to maintain and share accounts of the Company's myriad transactions across the East Indies. It did not happen.

The Sixth Voyage comprised three ships: the *Trades Increase* (1,293 tons), *Peppercorn* (340 tons), and *Darling* (90 tons), commanded respectively by Middleton, Downton, and William Pemberton. The "pilot major" of the voyage was Matthew Molyneux (Birdwood, 329), who had lately navigated the *Hector* safely to Surat and Bantam and the *Dragon* home to England.[12] Their primary destination, "the main and principal scope of this our voyage" (Birdwood, 333), was Surat, in Gujarat on India's northwest coast at the Gulf of Cambay. The first to reach India, the Third Voyage deposited the tenants of a hopeful factory there, including William Hawkins, the *Hector*'s captain, now England's ersatz ambassador to India.[13] The region was ruled by the Mughal Empire, friendly to the Portuguese, whose colonial capital was further south at Goa. The Portuguese held favor at the court of Emperor Jahāngīr in Agra and made considerable trouble for the English there and in Surat. Although the terms concluded between King James I and Philip III in 1604 guaranteed freedom of passage to and from "all the said Ports, Kingdoms and Dominions" where their subjects trafficked, the Portuguese in Surat, unlike the first party of Englishmen there, behaved otherwise.[14] In September 1608, some three weeks after the *Hector*'s factors opened negotiations, the Portuguese seized an unarmed, richly laden pinnace on its return to the ship and imprisoned the mariners.[15] The Company's 15 March 1610 letter to Surat's factors, carried by the Sixth Voyage, expressed alarm at this "unhappy surprise of your men and goods" and reproved the merchants for their hapless conduct.[16] The incident sparked ongoing skirmishes between the English and the Portuguese in the Gulf of Cambay.

The committees envisioned a sweeping roster of achievements for the Sixth Voyage. The expedition's geostrategic aims extended to Java, where James Lancaster founded the East India Company's first factory in 1602, and the Moluccas, where Middleton took the *Dragon* on the Second Voyage. Outward bound, they were to stop at South Africa or Madagascar for refreshment, then sail north to Socotra, an Arab island taken in 1507 and abandoned in 1511 by the Portuguese and free of the Ottoman dominion on the Yemeni mainland. The Third Voyage had established amiable relations in Socotra and built a pinnace there, the *Hopewell*, which accompanied the *Hector* to India.[17] If the monsoon prevented timely progress to Surat, they were to try for the Red Sea and the markets at Aden and Mocha, "at which port . . . we have heard the ships of the fourth voyage have traded." Having cultivated these opportunities, and taken "especial care that your men give no offence to the people there, still keeping good watch and standing upon your guard, and that out of any danger of any castle, fort, or galleys" (Birdwood, 334), with the monsoon in late August, they were to cross the Arabian Sea to Surat. Here, while investigating the fortunes of Hawkins and the factory, and appraising the strength of the Portuguese, they were to purchase goods for England and subsequent markets in Sumatra, Java, Banda, and the Moluccas, where English woolens were in disconcertingly small demand.

Lawrence Femell, "our principal agent," was to take charge of the factory and coordinate efforts in Surat and Agra to persuade Mughal powers to view England as a worthy trading partner. Recognizing the need for dignified self-presentation in this endeavor, the Company provided the *Trades Increase* with "velvets of diverse colors" (Birdwood, 335) and "guilt plate" to distribute as gifts.[18] As the more richly equipped Ambassador Sir Thomas Roe would later testify, however, the Company's modest presents were an embarrassment at theaters of imperial reception in India.[19] Nine of the fleet's merchants were to remain with Femell in Surat, residing in a substantial house, "such a one as may be strong" and defensible (Birdwood, 336). Here, while lading the *Peppercorn* and/or the *Darling* for England, they would provide the *Trades Increase* with Indian goods for regional trade, "calicoes and other commodities as may be fitting for Priaman, Bantam, Banda, and the Mollucas" (338), together with iron, lead, English cloth, and the remainder of the ship's 50,000 rials of eight. The directors did not yet know that the Company's hopes had been dashed in the Banda Islands. Expelled by the Dutch, Keeling did not reach England until May 1610, a month after Middleton had sailed. Having left "a convenient number of factors and stock" at Banda (339), they would proceed to the Moluccas for the nutmeg, mace, and cloves whose value far surpassed that of the pepper available in Bantam, which they would also thereafter visit. Having inaugurated responsible regimes of bookkeeping at that factory and others, they would return to England with signed copies of the latest accounts.

The committees recognized, of course, that these scenarios might prove wishful, and they appended a contingency of major consequence. If the initiative failed at Surat, the fleet should repair to the Gulf of Aden to see "what might be done for the vent of our commodities" (340), thereby advancing London's quixotic quest to market domestic goods in the East. Middleton's fleet duly visited Aden and Mocha on the way to India, with disastrous results. Subsequently expelled from Surat, they abandoned the Company's foothold there. The Red Sea, however, as the commission advised, held compensatory possibilities. Though perhaps ignorant of its antiquity, the committees understood that the seasonal traffic across the Arabian Sea was vigorous.[20] Divided by an island, the Straits of Bab-el Mandeb off the Horn of Africa are narrow (the east channel two miles, the west some sixteen). Inside them, the thriving port of Mocha received ships from Gujarat replete with goods which Middleton's factors, with better luck, might have purchased in India. "You may be fitted by the Junks arriving there from diverse ports out of the Indies, with merchandise fitting for England," the directors speculated.

Before sailing for Sumatra and Java, the Sixth Voyage followed this counsel. Their royal commission granted them leave, notwithstanding King James's professed amity with all Christian princes, to seek "recompense" for any "disturbance or hindrance whatsoever your quiet course of trade." At sea, they were free to "attempt, surprise, and take the persons, ships, and goods of any prince or state by whose subjects you shall sustain any wrong or loss" (Birdwood, 358). They returned to the Red Sea to seek opportune compensation. Privateering had enriched key founders of the East India Company, and extortion at sea remained an option for the "honorable company" when denied access to markets of desire. In the event, however, Middleton's course nearly sundered the corporation.

Principal Texts and Personnel of the Voyage

The key primary sources on the full progress of the voyage are the journals and letters of its general, Sir Henry Middleton, and lieutenant general, Captain Nicholas Downton. The journal of the merchant Benjamin Greene, a factor assigned to the *Darling* who also sailed on the flagship, offers valuable, sometimes unique, testimony. The chief merchant of the Fourth Voyage, John Jourdain, joined the Sixth in its departure from India and became Middleton's most trusted adviser in the Red Sea and near the end in Bantam, where he became chief factor in 1613. His journal and letters offer detailed, incisive witness to the latter half of the voyage and the demise of the *Trades Increase*. Another indispensable source is the unpublished opening half of the journal of John Saris, the commander of the Eighth Voyage, which met the Sixth in the Red Sea and Java.[21] A substantial body of Sixth Voyage correspondence also survives, transcribed and published in 1896. Samuel Purchas published the Middleton and Downton journals in 1625, and while the former's manuscript has vanished, a few by Downton exist and include lengthy passages absent from the printed redaction.[22] Greene's journal, which opens several months into the voyage and terminates in Bantam, where he died, remains unpublished. Middleton's account breaks off before the passage to Bantam. Downton's extends through his homeward journey in the *Peppercorn*, the fleet's sole ship to return.

Sir Henry Middleton was one of several sons of a commercial family with strong connections in the government of London and the East India Company. His cousins included Sir Thomas Middleton, a prominent grocer, privateer, and original subscriber of the Company who became lord mayor (1613–14) and represented the city in Parliament (1624–26). Sir Thomas's brother was the goldsmith and projector Sir Hugh Middleton, who spearheaded the New River Company that brought fresh water from springs in Hertfordshire through Islington to London, a major public works project. The playwright Thomas Middleton wrote pageants for them both: the canal's grand opening on Michaelmas Day 1613 featured a troop of some sixty laborers praising the "one man's industry, cost, and care"—Sir Hugh's—that brought the "great work" to "perfection"; a month later, *The Triumphs of Truth* celebrated the installation of Sir Thomas as lord mayor.[23] Henry's brothers John and David took commands on various East India Company voyages. On the First (1601–3), which established a factory in Bantam, made sound profits, and earned General Lancaster a knighthood (fig. 7), Henry

Figure 7. Sir James Lancaster. Courtesy of the National Maritime Museum, Greenwich. Poised over the open sea of a sphere marked with tropics and lines of latitude, Lancaster's right hand pledges his, and England's, mastery of the global ocean.

served as a factor. He had been recommended to the Company by his elder brother John, Lancaster's lieutenant general, and oversaw the refitting of the *Malice Scourge* into the *Dragon* at Woolwich before joining the voyage. Henry became the captain of the *Susan* at the death of its commander, John Hayward.[24]

His brother John died in Bantam on the First Voyage. Henry was named general of the Second (1604–6), accompanied unofficially on the flagship by his brother David. Upon his return, despite the expedition's mixed success, like Lancaster, he received a knighthood. The voyage targeted Bantam and the Moluccas, where the merchants hoped to secure cloves and other spices. As reported by the anonymous writer of *The Last East-Indian Voyage* (1606), the ships departed on 1 April, shortly before the commencement of peace negotiations with Spain.[25] The East India Company expected Portuguese "malice" and "annoyance" in the Moluccas (Birdwood, 62), but 1604 was not the season to make prizes of Portuguese carracks. The fleet repopulated the factory in Bantam, which had lost twelve of the twenty-four men Lancaster had left there (Foster, *Middleton*, 60).[26] In the Moluccas, the solitary, under-manned *Dragon* sailed into a colonialist war between the Portuguese on Tidore and the Dutch on Ternate. The former, discerning a potential ally, welcomed the English (33). After the Portuguese garrison fell, Middleton negotiated the departure of the prisoners for the Philippines. But his tense diplomacy secured no profits for the Company. Initially friendly, the Dutch now controlled Moluccan commerce and were convinced, perhaps rightly, that Middleton had sold arms to the Portuguese. They forbade the islanders to trade with the English. The *Dragon* departed with little more than a letter and a gift of cloves from the king of Ternate to King James (58–59). It was the first of multiple English failures in the Spice Islands. In a wishful vein, the journalist reports that they had, at least, amended England's piratical reputation: "Both [the king] and all his people were very sorry for his [Middleton's] departure, finding we were good people and not such as the Hollanders did report us to be, which lived only by robbing and stealing" (59).

His health suffered during the voyage, and the newly knighted Sir Henry, speculates William Foster, "probably felt the need of a good rest" (Foster, *Middleton*, xxxi). He sat out the Third Voyage and, when offered command of the Fourth in November 1607, declined. But the prospect of taking charge of the greatest English merchant ship of the age lured him back to sea in 1610. A proud, determined man, Sir Henry possessed the gravitas, expertise, and firm resolve the Company desired in the conduct of this pivotal expedition. He was a resourceful practitioner of sea power as a tool of diplomacy. The Company's commission praised his "integrity, wisdom, and resolution" and anticipated his "diligence . . . [to] prosecute our designs and . . . bring this costly voyage to a happy end" (Birdwood, 329). His employers could not have foreseen that protracted captivity and pervasive frustration would strain Middleton's proud temperament in mission-damaging ways.

Less is known of the Downtons than the Middletons. Baptized in 1561 in Bushley, a village near Tewkesbury, Nicholas Downton, aged forty-nine years when the voyage began, was probably Middleton's elder. Noting local bequests to the poor in the will, Sir William Foster speculates that, having early begun a career at sea, Downton lived, married, and started a family in Gosport, near Portsmouth, before moving to the parish of St. Mary Woolnoth in London. His only son, George, accompanied him on both of his East India Company voyages, probably as a personal attendant.[27] Downton saw hard service as a privateer. In 1593, as the captain of the *Samson*, he sailed to the Azores with the Earl of Cumberland and was severely wounded in a fight with the Portuguese carrack, *Las Cinque Llagas* (The Five Wounds). Describing him as a "discreet and valiant captain," Richard Hakluyt included Downton's narrative of the incident in the second edition of *The Principal Navigations* (1598–1600). In 1605, he commanded the *Pilgrim* on a trading voyage to the Caribbean Sea in which Cumberland was the other principal investor (Foster, *Downton*, xiv).

Downton's 1610 launch diary describes the shipbuilder William Burrell as "my good friend" and indicates that Burrell first recommended him to Smythe and the committees and thereafter urged him to accept their offer to make him the lieutenant general and captain of the *Peppercorn*.[28] Downton named Burrell an overseer of his will. The other overseer was Edward Wright, a mathematician and hydrographer of Caius College, Cambridge, whom he may have met through the Earl of Cumberland; in March 1614, Downton recommended Wright, then delivering lectures at Governor Smythe's house, to the Court of Committees to work with returning mariners to refine the charts of voyages.[29] Though greatly weakened, Downton survived the Sixth Voyage and, scarcely recovered from the rigors of the journey home, was named general of the 1614 voyage, his last, the inaugural East India Company venture financed by ongoing joint stock. Like Thomas Best's before it, the expedition consolidated English access to India by defeating a Portuguese fleet off Surat. Foster published the papers of these celebrated voyages but left Downton's lengthy journal of the Sixth Voyage to the archive and the editorial mercies of Samuel Purchas. Like Middleton two years before, Downton died in Bantam in 1615. So did his son (J, 301–2; Foster, *Downton*, xxxi, 25).

The lead cohort of East India Company shareholders consisted of openly pious men who believed that God rewards those who pray in earnest.[30] Their commissions called for twice-daily prayer services at sea, "the whole company called thereunto, with diligent eyes that none be wanting" (Birdwood, 329). A hardworking seaman, Downton was cut from less pious cloth. Practical, often inward, he bristled at the committees' indefatigable regime of prayer. On the 1614 voyage, the Reverend Peter Rogers, destined to disembark in Surat, earned less respect from Downton than he believed was his due and complained: "He is not the man you take him to be touching religion, but a contemner of the word and sacraments both." Rogers reported that Downton faulted the directors for practicing an ostentatious piety, "accusing you that though you professed religion, many of you, he always found those that made not so great a show to be more generous" (*LR*, 3:76). Evidently Downton cared more for the substance than the show of virtue and likely felt that East India Company mariners deserved better compensation for their long suffering at sea.

Courageous yet tentative, prone to self-doubts explored compulsively in his journals and memoranda—"He thought best with his pen in his hand," remarks Foster—Downton was a searching secular witness to the terrible difficulties that beset the Sixth Voyage. Foster evidently preferred in his early modern mariners the decisiveness he believed to augur imperial achievement, and the archivist, noting the merchant-emissary William Edwards's scoff at Downton's "plenteous formality of words," insinuates that the veteran mariner's cautious temperament and "labyrinthine" sentences flawed an else-commendable character.[31] But to a postcolonial eye disabused of fantasies of empire, Downton's testimony is invaluable. At the onset of global capitalism, his writing details the fatal distances between initiatives and outcomes in the London East India Company: between the domestic growth of the corporate body and its operating costs in ships and personnel abroad. His distinctive voice is candid, penetrating, anxiously reflective, often skeptical, brooding, recurrently despondent. An exacting diagnostician of the dysfunctions, perplexities, breakdowns, and sorrows of a tragic expedition, he expounds the contradictions between the grand designs and recurrent failures of a mission that he variously invokes as "our journey begun with glory (which drew great expectation in all estates), set out with great charges" and "our every way thwarted journey."[32]

The Voyage South

The fleet sailed from the Downs on 4 April 1610 in company with a supply vessel and a Dutch ship as far as the Cape Verde Islands off West Africa. The victualler, one Mr. Tucker in the *Samuel*, had contracted with both the English and Dutch ships and departed with the latter when the fleet resumed the southward voyage. The Dutch presence at the outset marked a regional collaboration that did not endure the global rivalries of capitalist expansion. The "Hollanders," a strong mercantile faction at the Jacobean court, generally behaved in European seas as allies or colleagues of the English, whose armies had assisted the Low Countries in the late struggle against Spain. Dutch investors constituted the largest group of foreign subscribers to the London East India Company, whose Seventh Voyage, then in preparation, was proposed and directed by the Dutch merchants Peter Floris and Lucas Antheunis. In 1610, there was talk of uniting the London Company with the Dutch East India Company (VOC). Initially resisted in London, this initiative—whose negotiations inflected arguments over the eastern trade treated in the closing chapter—eventually produced the "Anglo-Dutch Accord" of 1618. The agreement was both motivated and undone by the rivalries between the two joint-stock bodies in Java and the Moluccas, where formidable Dutch fleets, having expelled the Portuguese, variously tolerated and repelled the English.[33] Now in command of "a ship of wonderful importance" (*LR*, 1:43), Middleton, a veteran of these quarrels, must have welcomed Dutch witness to his Company's enlarged capabilities at sea.

However bright Middleton's prospects in the spring of 1610, the voyage relentlessly dismantled them and him. The breakdowns began early. The opening stretch is thinly documented. Purchas's redactions of Middleton's and Downton's journals begin, respectively, on 1 May in Cape Verde and 22 July at the Cape of Good Hope.[34] The surviving testimony indicates that, very early, the fleet hit heavy weather that seriously damaged at least two masts, one of these the flagship's mainmast. They sought sanctuary at "Saffee in Barbery," probably Salé in Morocco (Markham, *Lancaster*, 145n, 147). There, the carpenters reinforced the *Trade*'s mainmast with "fishes," timbers grafted into the weak spots, a temporary fix. Downton's opening lines, a fragment probably from 18 April, note in Salé that "the general determined to hasten to Cape Verde, both for the care of our masts and taking in of our provisions" (D, f1). They departed on 21 April, passed the bar between Barbary and Guinea on the twenty-ninth, and reached Cape Verde's inner island, where a ship from Dieppe was anchored, on 21 May (D, f1; Markham, *Lancaster*, 152). The next day, Middleton reports, "we found the mast exceeding bad, and above the upper deck some three foot wrung more than half asunder: had we met with any foul weather, it must needs have gone by the board." A new mast was imperative. Middleton sent a carpenter ashore "to search for trees, who returned that night and brought me word that he had seen some which would serve our turn" (M in P, 3:115–16). Middleton invited the Alcayda—the governor of the island's Iberian fort—to dine aboard the flagship, gave him some Rouen cloth purchased from the French vessel, and won his blessing to fell trees. England's peace with Spain and Portugal enjoyed happier effect in the North Atlantic than the Indian Ocean.

So they rebuilt the mainmast with fresh-cut timber—a compromise that demonstrated the improvisational skills indispensable to voyaging in the seventeenth century yet perpetuated a critical weakness. As noted in the opening chapter, Burrell's efforts to secure superior mast timber from Latvia probably gave way to the installation of the *Dragon*'s well-traveled masts, to which the tonnage of the new flagship applied unsustainable stress. Nor were the new masts sufficient. Breakage persisted on the voyage. At sea on 30 May, reports Downton, "our admiral broke her top mast" (D, f2); on 17 June, Downton sent his carpenters to the *Darling* and the *Trades Increase* to repair their respective main and fore yards; on 2 July, he reports again, "our admiral spent her main topmast" (D, f2v). Finally, at Pulo Panjang off Bantam three years later, the oft-rebuilt mainmast broke again, fatally.

Pleased by this sanctuary that lay directly in their southbound course, Middleton praised Cape Verde as "the best place I know for our outward bound ships: for that the road is excellent good, fit for dispatch of any business, and fresh fish to be had in great plenty" (M in P, 3:116). They made repairs, took in fresh water, and caught "great store of fish" (D, f1v) through the first half of May. Back at sea on the sixteenth, Downton, having conversed with customs officers about the island's inhabitants, wrote of them half-admiringly:

> If they had the true knowledge of God and care to serve him as they
> do the sun at his rising (and what more I know not), I should
> account them happy people, being rich in content with what they
> have. They eat what the earth and sea yieldeth them without any
> great pains; and for their apparel, it is easily provided, they going in
> a manner all naked. . . . These people in general will beg earnestly

... some of them will steal from white men, whom they call 'blanks,' but I never heard or knew of any cruel deed done by them, as to murder any man for that he had. (D, f1v; Markham, *Lancaster*, 153)

While dutifully providing information for future voyagers, Downton's remarks go beyond Middleton's. With a mixture of amused condescension, respect, and—he being a hardworking seaman—a trace of envy, Downton contrasts the islanders to Christian Europeans. Some of their practices evoke the golden age, yet their diction holds traces of Spanish (*blanco*). Perceiving them as human subjects with voices and agency, not as potential slaves, he takes interest in their customs and worldview and, if dismissively ("what more I know not"), concedes how little he knows of their beliefs. The passage exemplifies Downton's surplus investment in the task of journaling. Repeatedly, he takes the obligation to record his ship's passage as a spur to reflection, in this case ethnographic. Often more detailed, inquisitive, and reflective than Middleton's, his writings—intensely personal, collectively responsible—resist, fulfill, and transcend the exigencies of corporate discourse and hold literary interest.

The optimal route from Cape Verde to the Cape of Good Hope was a matter of dispute among European mariners, who often neared Brazil before turning southeast. Resolved to avoid "the Bay of Ethiopia" (the Gulf of Guinea and below along West Africa), "which place is thought very dangerous if we should run far into it," the Third Voyage instead found itself dangerously idled off Brazil for several weeks before sailing due east to Sierra Leone for sanctuary.[35] To the ambassador's vexation, the fleet that carried Roe to India in 1615 likewise moved far away from Africa, sailing south to the latitude of the cape before heading east.[36] The inability to measure longitude with any precision, and the acute risks of falling onto a lee shore, recommended such methods. At a meeting with Downton and the ships' masters on 15 May, Middleton resolved on a sensible trajectory: to sail south-southwest for sixty leagues, then south-southeast to the equator, "then to hale over easterly" (M in P, 3:116). Downton's log of the passage to South Africa, 16 May to 22 July (D, ff2–3) charts their actual, less deliberate course, which roughly approximated Roe's. They carried south-southwest with prevailing winds to 24 degrees south latitude before managing to turn east-southeast, and finally, at 33 degrees south, hard east for "Saldania," Table Bay at the Cape of Good Hope.

Narrative testimony of the events of this passage is sparse—Purchas cuts directly from 15 May to 24 July with Middleton and opens Downton's account as they sight South Africa (P, 3:116, 194)—but, beyond the mishaps just noted, are entries in Downton's journal that illuminate his temperament, relations between him and Middleton, and an intriguing incident of shipboard entertainment. Having fallen ill, Downton logged only positional data (leagues, latitude, course, winds) from 30 May to 16 June 1610, at which time Middleton looked in on him: "My general came aboard the *Peppercorn* to visit me being sick, whose presence somewhat revived me," he wrote (D, f2v). Other East India Company writers typically name a fleet's commander "*our* general"; Downton's "*my* general" evokes an affective bond reflective of their proximate stations and mutual dependencies. For meetings at sea, Middleton typically received other mariners aboard his flagship. His visit to the *Peppercorn* expressed solicitude that, while speaking to Downton's weak condition, revitalized the lieutenant general. Downton noted his return to business the next day, sending carpenters to the other ships as mentioned earlier. The day after, he visited the flagship: "The 18th day my general invited me to dinner and to play, and had Thomas Love, one of my master's mates, out of the *Peppercorn* unto the *Trades Increase*" (D, f2v). Love's entry confirms Downton's reference to festivities on 18 June. Noting his transfer to the *Trades Increase*, the master's mate indicates, "We had a great feast and a play played" (Markham, *Lancaster*, 147). These 18 June 1610 entries may document a continuity of theatrical sports between the Third and Sixth Voyages, whose flagship crews overlapped; alleged extracts from Keeling's lost journal note performances of *Hamlet* and *Richard II* outbound off Africa.[37] Whatever did or did not happen on the *Dragon* in 1607–8, as a rite of passage, the feast and play that Love and Downton document celebrated the latter's return to health and fellowship.

In the stormy latitudes further south, however, Downton's difficulties resumed. An incomplete entry on 5 July declares, "There befell us two great mischances: first we sprang a very great leak in our powder room" (D, f2v). On the night of 10 July, "a great fret of water began which continued, very vehemently, 16 hours" (D, f3).[38] As the skies cleared three days later, Downton was again indisposed: "The 13th day began very gentle weather. My general sent his master and others to visit me not be[ing] well, suspecting my grief proceeded from my late misfortunes" (D, f3). The next narrative entry, 21 July, is somber: "Peter Pridies, the boatswain's boy, was drowned" (D, f3). Downton's sickness and its etiology, both mysterious, are at once mental and physical—not being "well" here means "grief," not dysentery—and would seem to have been brought on by "great mischances" at sea. His journals and letters suggest that, beyond the inevitable somatic insults of voyaging, depression sometimes afflicted Downton—especially whenever he and Middleton were at odds.

Refreshment and Reflection in South Africa

Although the First Voyage stopped in South Africa ("Saldania"), Sir James Lancaster advised his successors to bypass Table Bay for refreshment at "St. Augustine" in Madagascar ("St. Lawrence"). This durable recommendation proved ill advised. Pursuing that plan, Generals Middleton and Keeling on the Second and Third Voyages both found themselves compelled by the protests of sick and starving crewmen to put in at Saldania. Otherwise, as eighty mariners—some 40 percent of his crew—petitioned Middleton, "they were but dead men. The general, perusing their pitiful complaint, and looking out of his cabin door, where did attend a swarm of lame and weak, diseased cripples . . . extended his compassion towards them and granted their requests."[39] A written plea and direct action by common mariners countermanded London's counsel. It took several years for the Company's directors, busy men remote from the traffic they organized, to absorb the accumulated wisdom of their voyagers. General Alexander Sharpeigh's commission for the Fourth Voyage (1608) again recommended "the port of St. Augustine in the island of St. Lawrence" as "the fittest place of refreshing" (Birdwood, 244); Sharpeigh too relented to the pleas of the *Union's* principal mariners and stopped at Saldania. Once there, they unloaded materials, built a pinnace (the *Good Hope*), and stayed for more than two months.[40] Finally flexible, David Middleton's Fifth Voyage (1609) commission recommended "Saldania or elsewhere therabouts, where you shall think most convenient and good for harbor" (Birdwood, 298). Sir Henry's instructions in 1610 likewise referred the choice between St. Lawrence and Saldania, "to your discretion" (Birdwood, 333).

As an aid to fleet cohesion and subsequent voyages, Middleton's Second Voyage commission recommended "leaving some apparent mark behind you" at watering places "by raising some heap of stones together, setting up of a stake or mark and leaving there some letter in or near the place" (Birdwood, 54). As a regular stop for English and Dutch ships, Table Bay (fig. 8) became

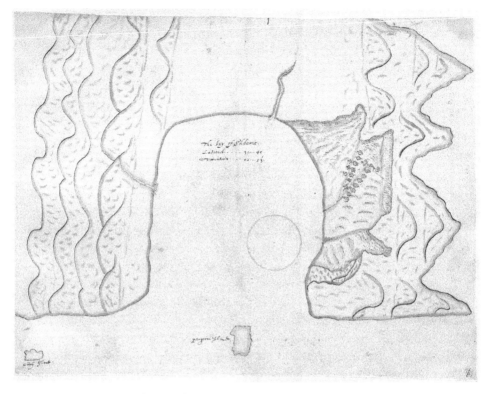

FIGURE 8. The Bay of Saldania. Courtesy of the British Library Board.
Drawing in John Saris, "Journal," f24.

an important communication post. On stones near the source—"the ledge of rocks . . . near the shore . . . laid (as it were) in the swamp between the high mountains, called the Table and Sugar Loaf" (D in P, 3:194)—early East India Company mariners chiseled notes of their passage and deposited letters in cairns. Having lost track of the *Consent* early in the voyage, officers of the Third Voyage's other two vessels, wrote Anthony Marlowe, found "upon a rock engraven with a chisel, Captain David Middleton the 24 July in the *Consent*. At which inscription, as our general was glad to hear well of her, and of her good passage, so it seemed that he was grieved that the winds had not favored us to have had the like, having been here almost five months before us. Then the general went to an oven, which in times past our people had made to bake in, and there caused search to be made for letters, but we found none" (Barbour, *Journals*, 100; cf. 190).

In mingled relief and vexation, gripped by the presence and the absence of texts, Keeling's party duly etched advertisement of its passage there. On 15 July 1608, members of the Fourth Voyage found the names and dates of Keeling and Hawkins near David Middleton's (J, 13)—a symbolic reunion of the Third Voyage, its diachronic separation indexed on adjacent stones. Notice of David Middleton's subsequent passage in the *Expedition*, and of Keeling's return in January 1609, were discovered by Sir Henry when he arrived in the *Trades Increase*, 24 July 1610. Like Keeling, he too searched for "a letter buried under ground according to agreement made between him [David] and me in England." Finding it, he was bitterly disappointed: "It was so consumed with the damp of the air that I could not read any part thereof" (M in P, 3:116).

These messages chiseled on rocks, "postal stones," make up a distinctive subgenre of voyage-generated texts.[41] Paper documents, like bales of cloth and sacks of pepper, travel well. Being duplicable and shareable, they allow managers in London and agents in the Indies to cultivate global networks of communication. By contrast, etchings on shoreline terrain—liminal, highly charged space—are site-specific. They do not travel. The engravings lend the stones a numinous presence-within-absence, evoking the particular persons who marked them. Their primary readers constitute an exclusive coterie of wanderers whose prerogatives derive from literate seamanship, not metropolitan authority. Contemporary European readers of these engravings will have submitted themselves to the same risks the writers endured.

Unlike Plymouth Rock in Massachusetts, the rocks chiseled at Table Bay by the first generation of East India Company mariners testify to transit, not possession: the texts make exploratory, not colonial, claims. Across enormous spans of time and distance, the rocks affirm a renewable fellowship of interim survivors who stand at the southern extremity of their passage. The East India Company inscriptions express, along with the corporate duty to give notice of one's progress, impulses more existential: the personal and collective will to leave traces of one's passage across engulfing vastnesses of ocean. In mid-January 1608, two weeks after the Third Voyage left Saldania, the *Hector* and *Dragon* nearly collided head-on in high winds, to "the utter ruin and overthrow of us all," wrote Marlowe. "Oh what a miserable and lamentable thing had it been," he expostulated, in the sole vocative moment in his journal, "if these two goodly ships should now and in such a manner the one have struck the other, not a man left alive to lament our misery, nor to report what had become of us!" (Barbour, *Journals*, 105). Beyond the tactical exigencies of voyaging, Marlowe's horror at the thought of their vessels slipping unnoticed into the deep informs the mariners' practice of leaving inscriptions on remote terrain.

Three Dutch ships rode at Table Bay when the Sixth Voyage arrived. Downton suspected that "the Dutchmen we here found, who use to spoil all places where they come (only respecting their own present occasions)," had created shortages and inflated the costs of sheep and cattle. The inhabitants now demanded pieces of copper, not mere strips of iron, in trade. "We could procure nothing . . . for our sick men's relief but four cows . . . so old and lean that there was but little goodness in the flesh." This scarcity in a place formerly "comfortable to all our nation traveling this way" (D in P, 3:195), and Downton's foundational concern for more than "present occasions," shaped his vivid meditation on the will to leave traces of one's transit:

> At this time was their spring, both trees and herbs blowing over the earth. It much repenteth me that I came unprovided of all sorts of garden-seeds, which might be helpful or necessary for relief of any Christians which hereafter might come hither, which . . . every Christian captain would seek to augment, and re-edify the same. Also acorns, which in time may do good to posterity, for trees are not here so long in growing, as in our cold countries. I will not contradict all such as will esteem it more idleness in me, to wish to sow where it is many to one I shall never reap; yet for myself I esteem it more idleness in me that I had not been so provident as to have sought means in England to have performed the same. And I would to God I could or had means to leave a profitable remembrance for Christian travelers unto the end of the world, in any place where I shall come. (D in P, 3:199)

Unknowingly, his reflections recalled those of the merchant John Jourdain two years before. Observing of Table Bay, "If it were manured, I am of opinion that it would bear anything that should be sown or planted in it," Jourdain elaborated: "If this country were inhabited by a civil nation, having a castle or fort for defense against the outrage of those heathenish people and to withstand any foreign force, . . . it might be . . . able of itself to furnish all ships refreshing" (J, 18). Jourdain's vision is markedly colonial, Downton's more personal: the latter imagines, not a fortress with well-managed gardens, but wild orchards to provide for his successors and commemorate his passage. Yet neither Jourdain nor Downton was equipped to materialize the fantasy.

Had they sailed for Virginia with Sir Thomas Gates, like John's brother Sylvester, they would have carried "muskmelons, peas, onions, radish, lettuce, and many English seeds and kitchen herbs" to plant (Strachey, 23). But early East India Company voyagers pursued trade, not plantation. Downton's and Jourdain's visions inject variant protocolonialist impulses into a migratory mentality alert to regional constraints and opportunities. Unlike Jamestown, whose inhabitants meant to harvest where they sowed, South Africa represents for them a place of refreshment and provision for future voyages. Jourdain's hypothetical settlement is littoral and maritime: it looks to the sea, not to continental expansion into Africa. Thinking similarly, Spanish mariners presumably stocked the unpopulated Bermudas with hogs—a godsend for the Jamestown colonists who wrecked there in 1609.[42] A maritime, protoglobal, wishful Johnny Appleseed, Downton envisions not a fortified compound at Table Bay but stands of self-sustaining English growth in wild terrain. Yet both he and Jourdain lacked the seeds and cuttings. In its rhetorical plenitude, Downton's entry voices the ache of emptiness amid potential abundance: an absence framed in writing, like the report of letters missing and illegible that Keeling and Middleton sought at the watering place. The manuscript that documents Downton's frustrations also holds compensatory promise: should the journal endure, its leaves, if not those of trees at Table Bay, would articulate his foundational vision and yield "profitable remembrance" of his transit.

When Middleton stopped there in 1604, his men negotiated ineptly with the cautious inhabitants, the pastoral Khoi (or Khoikhoi) people, whose personal habits disgusted the English—a reflex ripe with irony, given the poor hygiene and foul conditions on the latter's ships. The native people smeared a "filthy substance" on their skins and wore "guts of cattle about their necks, which makes them smell like a butcher's slaughterhouse," Downton observed in 1610, while still admiring their straight stature, nimbleness of foot, and weaponry (D in P, 3:196). The anonymous 1604 journalist reports that, when "they saw us begin to set up our tents," immediately "they pulled down their houses and made them fast upon their beasts' backs and did drive away." Before long Middleton's men, deprived of trade, dispersed into groups raiding and skirmishing for cattle, thereby ignoring the commission's injunction that shore parties should "keep good order and discipline, by warlike guard for the safety of your company." One crewman was wounded by several arrows (Birdwood, 54; Foster, *Middleton*, 9–10, 13–14).

The general no doubt remembered these broils. Yet he evidently took no special precautions upon landing there in 1610. Downton had proposed a limited wood-cutting expedition with Middleton and thirteen others, including four "small shot" (D in P, 3:197). Three miles in, however, after the cutting, the general extended the hike into a rambling, fruitless search along Table Mountain for cattle. They lost their way, struggled along and down cliffs, across swamps, traversed near-impassable terrain—"a most vile, tiresome travel" Downton observes—and finally built a fire and rested part of the night. Returning to the tents near daybreak, they found their shipmates, "disturbedly in arms" (D in P, 3:198), dividing into two parties to search for them. The reunion was happy. But Middleton had put the primary leadership of the voyage at risk on an ill-conceived foray. As they soon learned in Madagascar, his shore party was far luckier than the *Union*'s.

To Madagascar and Socotra

The Sixth Voyage departed from Table Bay on 13 August 1610 and made a relatively easy passage to Madagascar, arriving on 6 September. Two manuscript entries of the interim, however, absent from Purchas, indicate social tensions within the fleet: testy relations between the *Peppercorn*'s factors and principal mariners, and a gratuitous rebuke of Downton by Middleton. On 22 August, Downton obtained the general's leave to open a butt of wine from which he drew five quarts for himself and Abraham Lawes, the ship's master (Birdwood, 329). The rest, five and a half gallons, went to "the factors and minister," the latter probably commissioned to the factory in Surat. These worthies begrudged Lawes and Downton their five quarts. They "would have a full butt for themselves," they insisted, claiming that "Mr. Stiles"—Thomas Stiles, a committee member busied with the wrap-up of the Third Voyage and preparation of the Sixth—had advised them that "there was a butt of wine put in for them, whereof they would drink what they list, and carry the rest on land" for the factory (D, f6v). Given the tenor of the complaint, one doubts whether the cask would have lasted for the land service.

On the twenty-eighth, Middleton summoned Downton and Lawes to the *Trades Increase* and rebuked them "for bearing too slack a sail one night." Downton had already addressed the problem and replaced the master's mate responsible. But Sir Henry saw fit to shame him and assert his dominance anyway. The general had also looked into the factors' claim that Stiles had set aside for them a full butt of wine. He now thought better of his earlier directive to share the cask: "I should let the factors," Downton reported, "have none of the ship's wines, for he was abused, and finds none put in for them" (D, f6v). The ship's wines were intended for maritime officers exclusively. The factors should have provided for themselves. This unseemly squabble over wine allotments discloses not simply the stresses of coexistence on a crowded vessel but, particularly for the factors, the tedium of voyaging with few duties beyond the occasional reshuffling of cargo. Of course they wanted more wine. The rancor over the *Peppercorn*'s wine stores evidently persisted. Months later in the Red Sea, among the reasons Downton cited for hesitating to take command of the flagship during Middleton's captivity, he noted that even brief absence from the *Peppercorn* "would have turned me to more disturbance by waste [consumption] of my best drink, or else the abuse of the steward's" (D, f40v, 11 May 1611). He could not trust the ship's merchants not to raid his and others' caches of wine and spirits.

At St. Augustine's Bay in Madagascar, the fleet came upon the *Union* of the Fourth Voyage—an expedition begun, wrote its General Sharpeigh, "in an unfortunate hour" (P, 3:61). The day after they left South Africa, the *Union* and *Ascension* separated in "much wind with an overgrown sea," wrote Jourdain on 20 September 1608 (J, 20). In the Gulf of Cambay late in 1609, the *Ascension* ran aground, and the pinnace, the *Good Hope*, was abandoned ashore (P, 3:16, 61, 68). The crews survived and dispersed with the remains of the owners' capital. Upon separation from the flagship, the *Union* awaited the former for three weeks at St. Augustine, then sought them at Portuguese-controlled Zanzibar. There, an initial kindly reception gave way to an ambush in which two men were slain and one captured (Bradshaw, 74–75). In a subsequent search for water, they put in at a bay on the northeast point of Madagascar, catastrophically. The local ruler promised a small shore party ambergris—a commodity itemized in their commission, "to take notice, and buy thereof" (Birdwood, 246)—whereupon Richard Reve, the cape merchant, persuaded Captain Richard Rowles and five others to go ashore, where they were seized and evidently slain. Then, reported Downton, "there sallied out of the woods a great number of people" to attack the longboat, which escaped under the cover of shot from the ship. Several days later, as the *Union* lingered in hopes of news of the men ashore, a fleet of one hundred canoes, "which came in order and form of an half moon" (D in P, 3:200–201), neared the vessel and were driven off by ordnance. Under compulsion, the *Union* resumed its voyage without a captain.

They tried and failed to reach Socotra, missed the monsoon for Surat, and made for Sumatra, where they traded successfully and decided to return to England. When the Sixth Voyage came upon them in Madagascar early in September 1610, the ship, "in great distress for want of victuals," had been anchored there for six weeks, reports the *Peppercorn*'s anonymous journalist ("Journal kept on the *Peppercorn*," 6 September 1610; cf. D in P, 3:200). Reduced from an initial sixty-five (by one report, seventy-five) to thirty-six, the mariners had divided rancorously. Driven by hunger, "disordered fellows" purchased their victuals independently, not through the ship's purser, driving up prices (D in P, 3:202). In nominal command since Rowles's disappearance, the factor "Samuel Bradshaw, for his sober, discreet, and provident carriage in the company's business [was] much envied by their factious master and his adherents," Downton reported (Farrington, *Catalogue*, 667; P, 3:81, 82, 201). Middleton supplied them with victuals and, Downton chose to believe, "united them in love one unto another" (D in P, 3:201). Soon enough, however, the *Union*'s entropy resumed. The next testimony to the ship's progress was penned five months later on the coast of Brittany, where it was learned that, in the South Atlantic, they had failed to find critical resupplies at Saint Helena. Most of the survivors perished between Cape Verde and Europe (P, 3:81). As the vessel neared the English Channel in February 1611, carrying just four men too weak to manage the sails or even cast dead bodies overboard, "scarce able to speak" (P, 3:79), it wrecked on the rocks of Audierne. Some pepper, the ordnance, and the anchors were salvaged. But most of the cargo, well before any brokers for the East India Company arrived, was pillaged (P, 3:82; J, xxi). The Company wrote off the Fourth Voyage as a total loss.

Middleton's fleet left the *Union* in St. Augustine on 9 September 1610. Striving northward against contrary currents, beset by calms near the equator, then assisted by northbound and eastbound currents, on 18 October in the Arabian Sea near the Horn of Africa, they reached Socotra. The island's inhabitants confirmed a suspicion "which to our grief would prolong our voyage: . . . that the Easterly monsoon was already come, and all our hopes of getting to Cambay were frustrate for this nine months" (D in P, 3:205). On the north coast three days later, they anchored in the bay of Tamrida or Tamerin (today's Hadibu), the capital. The island's ruler, Mulli Hamour Bensaid—whose father ruled a mainland coastal province, Fartaque, independent of the Turks (D in P, 3:208)—had generously received his first English visitors, General Keeling and his crews in 1608. He welcomed those of the

Ascension and the *Good Hope* separately in 1609, and Anglo-Socotran relations were guardedly cordial (Barbour, *Journals*, 17, 133–38, 225–28; J, 108–12).

Heralded by rounds of ordnance from the ships, the principal factor Lawrence Femell, seated beneath a handsome red pavilion in the pinnace, landed with gifts. The next day, Bensaid received Middleton and his entourage, which included "a good guard of armed men," at his mansion (M in P, 3:120). Inquiring about opportunities for trade in the Red Sea, Middleton was pleased to hear that "the people of Aden and Moha were good people and would be glad of trade with us; and that the *Ascension* had sold all her goods there at good rates, and came so lightly to this place, that they took in good store of ballast" (M in P, 3:121). Presumably, Middleton did not pick up the hinted distinction between "the people" and their Ottoman overlords—a difference that Middleton's Arab greeters off Aden, even while confirming Sharpeigh's success, made explicit: while the current Basha of Sana'a was "a little better" than his predecessor, "all the Turks in general [were] stark naught" (M in P, 3:122). Bensaid then delivered the dispiriting news that the *Ascension* and its pinnace had been lost off Surat. Preparing for what proved to be the final leg of its journey, the *Ascension* had indeed taken in "two or three boats of stones for ballast," Sharpeigh's narrative confirms. Yet it was not, as Bensaid supposed, the sale of "all her goods" that had recommended the ballast, but the loss of two anchors in the Red Sea ("through the head-strongness of our master"), and two more to strong winds at Tamrida (P, 3:67). Their efforts to conduct trade in Aden and Mocha had failed pathetically. Middleton asked "if they had left any writing behind them" for subsequent voyagers, and Bensaid replied, "He had one, but his servant lost it" (M in P, 3:121). Nor, on the assumption that other ships would "dare not come into this place while we are here" (D in P, 3:207), did he wish the English to linger to build a pinnace, as the Third Voyage had done. Thus, having filled their water casks, the fleet sailed on 28 October 1610 for the Gulf of Aden. Their expectations were elevated by misleading, and perhaps misinterpreted, oral report, and they lacked two indispensable documents: Sharpeigh's cautionary letter and, like that general, the sultan's letter of protection.

Arabia Felix and Jacobean England

Like many other parts of the Muslim world, occupying terrain from which defining European religions and mythologies derived, Arabia Felix, the relatively fertile Southland of the Arabian Peninsula, was a place of cognitive dissonance for early modern England. Imperial Rome distinguished the region so named from Arabia Petraea ("stony" Arabia to the northwest) and Arabia Deserta (the peninsula's arid interior). As the fabled origin of the phoenix, which both Queen Elizabeth and King James took as an icon of their rule, Arabia Felix symbolized mythic renewal for Britain. The series of triumphal arches at King James's 1604 royal entry to London included "*Nova fœlix Arabia*, the New Arabia fœlix, . . . under which title the whole Island of *Britannia* was figured" (fig. 9). With an elaborate allegory of the five senses, deadened by Elizabeth's death until awakened by King James's arrival, the arch elaborated the classicism of the ceremony, which figured King James as the heir of Trojan Brut and envisioned London as the new, now pacifistic, Rome. Like the city's annual lord mayors' pageants, the entry appropriated Roman rites to British purposes.[43] Conceiving it as the imperial center of a symbolically united Britain, the ceremony praised London as the rejuvenate nexus of both "Eastern" and "New World" mysteries. Following "*Hortus Euporiae*, Garden of Plentie," at the Fleet Street conduit the king next passed through "*Cozmoz Neoz*, New World," where Fame described the arch prior to the Garden as "*A new* Arabia, *in whose spiced* Nest, / *A* Phoenix *liv'd, and died in the Sun's breast*," in the lands of sunrise. Euphrosine praised the unique bird's resurrection in King James:

> *Thou being that sacred* Phoenix, *that doth rise,*
> *From th'ashes of the first; Beams from thine eyes*
> *So virtually shining, that they bring*
> *To* England's *new* Arabia, *a new spring.*[44]

The image celebrated Britain's new regime, exceptionalist mythos, classical heritage, and imperial promise. But, however convincingly London honored Stuart authority on 15 March 1604, the figure of the Orient as a "spiced nest" of renewal and abundance destined for England effaced the formidable challenges of such translation. As London's mercantile elite strove to materialize the conceit through direct maritime contact with the fabled East, their agents entered worlds whose realities chastened English assumptions.

The wretchedness of contemporary Yemen—lately viewed by Western powers as a staging ground for terrorism, currently devastated by civil war, weaponized famine, and regional conflict between Iran and Saudi Arabia—puts mordant irony to the classical designation "Happy Arabia." So did conditions in the sixteenth and seventeenth centuries. The peninsula's southern

FIGURE 9. Nova Felix Arabia Arch from King James's royal entry, 1604.
Stephen Harrison, *Archs of Triumph* (1604), plate F.
Courtesy of the Huntington Library.

stretches enticed and frustrated imperial powers for millennia. Linking Asia
and Africa to the Mediterranean, the region was from ancient times a vital
nexus of world trade. Pharaohs brought spices and exotic animals into Egypt
through the Red Sea; the Ptolemies consolidated the route by importing
African elephants to strengthen their armies. Under Caesar Augustus, the
Romans conquered much of the peninsula, but not Arabia Felix. In the early
modern period, merchants from Egypt, Persia, and India met regularly in
Mocha. The country was destabilized by imperial projects in the early sixteenth century: Portuguese attempts to dominate the Gulf of Aden provoked
a Mameluke invasion that yielded to Ottoman expansion under Suleiman
the Magnificent, who, following campaigns in Persia (1534–36), took coastal
towns in southern Arabia (1538–39). Ottoman rule persisted in Yemen until
1635, spreading upland but never fully subduing the mountainous interior.[45]
Robert Stookey describes the late sixteenth century in Yemen as "a tangled
and dolorous [story] of Turkish oppression and localized revolt" (137). When
the English arrived in 1609, the seat of government was inland at Sana'a,
captured by the Ottomans in 1548, where Ja'far Basha, the sultan's deputy,
had ruled since 1607 (Stookey, 145). Achmed I (1603–17) presided in Istanbul,
where the talented, controversial Sir Thomas Glover served as England's
ambassador (1606–11).

The London merchants supposed themselves to be welcome in Yemen
because the Portuguese held no claims to the territory, and the 1580 capitulations that Sultan Murad III (1574–95) granted the subjects of Queen Elizabeth through Glover's predecessor William Harborne (1582–88), periodically
renewed, ceded them freedom of movement throughout Ottoman
dominions:

> Their galleons and other ships shall at all times come to and go
> (from) the ports and harbours and the rest of our well-protected
> dominions in peace and security. . . . Let those who happen to be
> present . . . give assistance when storms at sea distress such people
> as these, and in their other moments of need; and let no one prevent
> and inconvenience (them) in the obtaining of their supplies. . . .
> And if the sea should fling their ships on to the land let the begs and
> cadis and others give assistance; the goods and properties which are
> rescued shall be given back to them, let no harm be done. Let no
> one hinder the Ingilereliler (English) who are travelling either by

sea or by land, minding their own business; they shall not trouble
and molest (them). (Skilliter, 87)

Such protection was vital for Christian travelers, as S. A. Skilliter explains:
"*Harbis*, or 'forestiers', are, according to orthodox Muslim theory, those . . .
non-Muslims not protected by treaty who inhabit the *Daru'l-harb*, that is,
any part of the world which has not yet accepted Islam. . . . The life and
property of a *harbi* venturing into Muslim lands are completely unprotected
by law unless he is given a temporary safe-conduct, *aman*" (Skilliter, 1–2). By
1600, when many of its members joined the East India Company, the Levant
Company was long accustomed to the capitulations renegotiated with
Mohammed III (1595–1603) and Achmed I by England's ambassadors in
Istanbul, Edward Barton (1588–97) and Henry Lello (1597–1607) (A. Wood,
251). The London merchants, however, did not anticipate the severity of two
impediments in the Gulf of Aden and the Red Sea: England's reputation as
a nation of pirates and the specific problem of entering the Muslim holy
land without the sultan's pass. A breakdown in the protocols of textual self-
presentation was the crux of their problem in Arabia Felix.

The East India Company Reaches the Red Sea

Arabia Felix was a multicultural contact zone of distinctive interest for its
proximity to Mecca and remoteness from both Istanbul and London. The
powers of these capitals were attenuated there, London's acutely. Located
inside the Straits of Bab-el-Mandeb, the port city of Mocha had been an
important hub of Euro-Asian trade since antiquity, attracting both maritime
and overland traffic. Seasonal monsoons enabled round-trip voyages across
the Arabian Sea; the Red Sea offered access to Egypt; and the Arabian Peninsula extended northward to the Levant and eastward to the Persian Gulf.[46]
When the English arrived, the effects of ongoing struggles between Arab
communities and their Ottoman overlords were evident. Of the fortress town
of Aden, for instance, Jourdain wrote in 1609, "Aden hath in former time
been a famous and strong place, but at present is ruinated and destroyed by
the Turk." Inside its "stone wall, very strong," were "very fair buildings . . .
falling to the ground for want of repairing" (J, 74–75). A year later, Downton
wrote similarly, "This city in times past hath been great and populous, but
at this time, the houses both great and small are greatly ruinated and sunk in

every part of the town, shops of merchandise there are none of any account, merchants none to be discerned worthy of that calling" (D in P, 3:216–17). Downton equates civic with commercial vitality and sees neither in Aden. In the spirit of the adage Richard Knolles cites in *The Generall Historie of the Turkes*, "that wheresoever the Grand Signior his horse setteth his foot, the grass will there no more grow," the English mariners blamed the Ottoman overlords for the decay and expressed sympathy for the Arabs (Knolles, Fffff2v, 1156).

In plotting a course for the Red Sea, the London merchants did not foresee the promise of coffee, eventually their most important commodity in Arabia Felix.[47] They were simply pushing the envelope of trade and inferred that the area held rich possibilities. With the Third Voyage in progress, the Company petitioned Lord Salisbury to write Glover to solicit a letter of protection from Achmed I for the region (Birdwood, 217–18). The petition succeeded. The pass was duly produced at a meeting of the Company's General Court on 5 October 1608 (*Court Book*, B/3, f100). In the Company's translation of a second such letter in February 1611, Achmed commands his subjects in Yemen, Aden, Mocha and beyond to "kindly and lovingly entertain and receive the said merchants, subjects of *England*," threatening his "high displeasure" if "you do offer them the least wrong."[48] But the Fourth Voyage, England's first to attain the Red Sea, departed in March 1608: six months before the sultan's initial letter reached London.

Long separated from the *Union*, the *Ascension* reached the Yemeni coast in April 1609 in the company of a Gujarati ship that had loaned them a pilot for the passage from Socotra (J, 57–58). Aden's governor in 1609 was Regib Aga, a Greek-born "renegade" or convert to Islam, as were "the chiefest of all the Turks of this place," who answered directly to Ja'far Basha in Sana'a, Jourdain learned (J, 77). Having saluted Aden's castle with five rounds of ordnance, the *Ascension* was visited by the Regib Aga's "caya" (factotum), carried to the English vessel in the Gujarati ship's boat. This official assured them "great matters for the sale of our commodities," "good entertainment," reasonable customs of 5 percent, "with many other fair promises." A small party from the *Ascension* then disembarked to a dignified reception: "At our coming aland, we had horses provided by the water's side to carry us to the governor's house. When we came near his house, we were entertained with tabor and pipe and other heathen music, and presently carried to the presence of the governor, who saluted us and confirmed by a writing under his hand all that the caya had promised us, with many more complements; and with the same gave us vests of cloth of gold, and set us again on horse back, to carry us to a faire house which he had provided for us, with our former music" (J, 59). "Our house, alias prison" (64), Jourdain soon renamed it: Regib Aga had written to the basha of their arrival, and "before he had his answer, he durst not suffer" the general to return to the ship (61). Several weeks of negotiation ensued, the governor urging Sharpeigh to land his goods lest "the country people" conclude "that we were men of war and not merchants," Sharpeigh delaying with small deliveries of tin and iron while they awaited word from the basha (61–62). The arrival of his letter quickened their traffic, yet Sharpeigh remained a prisoner. Jourdain thereupon invited a few dignitaries aboard the *Ascension* to inspect cloth and took them hostage to secure the general's release. Suddenly cooperative, the governor then loaned them a boat for an exploratory party to Mocha. Yet, when Sharpeigh thereby learned that Mocha's market far surpassed Aden's and resolved to depart at once, Regib Aga demanded suddenly inflated customs, "which if the general denied to" pay, wrote Jourdain, "he would send Phillip Glascock and my self prisoners to the Basha" in Sana'a (70) to resolve the matter.

Thus, as the *Ascension* sailed from Aden on 26 May 1609, with money in hand Jourdain and Glascock traveled inland in the custody of "two renegados, our drogomon [translator], one Italian, and another a Frenchman, with the governor's secretary, who had the charge of us to deliver us to the Basha" (81). The first Englishmen to enter the region, they did so under compulsion, fearful and confused. Delayed in "Hatch" (Al-Hauta) their second day out, Jourdain suspected the worst: "seeing our ship was gone, that he [the governor] would secretly have put us to death and so keep the money to himself, as our drogaman did much fear of it too" (82). This fear proved paranoid: more careful about documentary protocols than the English, Regib Aga simply wanted their signatures to verify that he owed the English nothing for the gifts they had given him. In the company of "eight soldiers to conduct us for fear of thieves, being a wilderness where many are robbed" (82), they reached Sana'a on 11 June. Ja'far Basha, whose vest they kissed while held fast by both arms in the manner of imperial reception in Istanbul (89),[49] denied them permission for an English factory "without express order from the Great Turk his master" (89), because, he explained, "it was near their holy house of Mecca." Recognizing nevertheless that they "were friends to . . . his master," he gave them leave to trade and depart and forgave them Regib Aga's surcharge. But he refused to answer King James's letter "without acquainting the Great Turk his master; . . . otherwise it would cost him his head" (93).[50]

Finally, he admonished them, "to come no more without order from the Great Turk" (90). Afterward, informed by his dragoman that the Basha "expected great presents from me" (91), Jourdain sent the ruler assorted cloths, gunpowder, vests, and "two faire pieces, . . . but he seemed not satisfied with the present" (92).

That the English lacked not only the license but also the wealth, goods, prudence, and intercultural finesse to thrive there, became vexingly clear to Jourdain when he and Glascock rejoined their countrymen in Mocha at the end of June. In Aden, General Sharpeigh had angered Jourdain by refusing a gift horse from the governor, "a faire jennet" (73), on the pretense that it was "too much charge to keep a horse for so little time; . . . which he [Regib Aga] took very discontenteous." Jourdain objected, "There had been great hope of trade; but wee were so sparing that [it] lost us twice as much, besides contemned of the Turks for our miserableness" (74). Now in Mocha, to haul up the pinnace for repair, the English had landed "most of our men" (98), thus putting both the *Ascension* and its crew at great risk. "I hold [this] to be very carelessly done," wrote Jourdain, "and without discretion, . . . seeing how we had been dealt withal at Aden . . . and my self at Senan sent prisoner, not as yet knowing how matters would pass with us there." Their incaution ashore prompted an acerbic observation on the gullibility of his countrymen: "But it is a general rule with the English, that if they have but a parcel of fair words given, that there need no more fear; which the Turks themselves say: If thou wilt have any thing of an Englishman, give him good words and thou shalt be sure to win him" (99). As they entered the Red Sea, the mariners of the Sixth Voyage were ignorant of Sharpeigh's and Jourdain's reception in Arabia Felix, and the force of the latter's complaint would be proven on their persons.

When the merchant William Revett reached Mocha in the governor's borrowed boat in May, the abundance and diversity of its traffic impressed him immediately. He noted "many ships riding, some of Dabul, some of Diu, some of Chaul, of Surat, Cochin, and Ormus. . . . Here are also two galleys of the Grand Signior's" (J, 352–53).[51] Revett described a great "resort of merchants, . . . Turks, Moors, Armenians and others, which came from Constantinople, Aleppo, Damascus and Tripoli and other parts unto Suez and Zidda [Jedda] with the caravan, and brought with them cloth, kerseys, tin, coral and all sorts of silk stuffs, but principally ready monies; which they invest in this city to merchants which commeth from Ethiopia and all parts of India" (J, 354–55).[52] Ill equipped for this cosmopolitan market, requiring more "ready monies" and flexible pricing of their own goods, the Fourth Voyage merchants were also at odds with each other and with the prior East India Company voyage. When, at a price Jourdain and Revett found acceptable, they were closing a sale of iron to the Banian (Cambayan) consul, an indispensable man—"none can buy nor sell without his order, nor show any commodities" (J, 104)—"the general burst out in anger, saying that they mocked him to offer him so little" (J, 99). Probably the broker named Shermall in Sixth Voyage documents, the offended magnate terminated the meeting and refused to deal with them further. Ironically, their iron had been devalued by the arrival of thirty tons purchased from the Third Voyage in Surat. "I could sell nothing but a few sword blades," Sharpeigh complained (J, 358). The governor asked them, pointedly, "To what end . . . came ye thither, if you are not minded to buy or sell?" (J, 100). Suspecting that they might resort to pillage, he detained them for a few days at the ostensible request of Indian mariners who wanted to depart unmolested.

In this vital marketplace of Mediterranean, African, and Indian Ocean traffic, the Fourth Voyage merchants simply could not compete. Their lack of the sultan's pass was the primary, yet not the sole, impediment. Their domestic cargoes were of small interest, their funds limited, and their transportation costs higher than those of other merchants on the scene. Jourdain described the "many merchants from Grand Cairo, who bring rials of eight and chequeens of gold in great abundance to buy these commodities and transport them by sea and land. . . . All kinds of commodities are there so dear that there is no dealing for us to buy them for England at the rates which they sell them to the merchants which comes from Grand Cairo. The Guzeratts and other merchants of India doe make profit by their commodities, being but a voyage of 20 days sailing from the Indias with the wind in poop" (J, 104). England and its belated merchants looked puny in a mart where "rials of eight and chequeens of gold in great abundance" fueled regional and global economies of great longevity. Jourdain's sense of England's remoteness from the opulent circulations he witnessed there probably helps explain the East India Company's impulse to build a massive flagship: a vessel fit to carry larger cargoes and, above all, to compel respect in Asiatic markets of daunting richness and intercultural complexity. Jourdain was making critical discoveries: if the Company were to thrive, it would have to carry ample bullion and ply the "country trade," offsetting transportation costs with earnings from regional traffic, as well as freight exotic goods home to London. It had to consolidate the interests and coordinate the tactics of various voyages. But at this juncture, as we have observed, each voyage was funded separately. Both the planners in London and their personnel at sea were improvising. Moreover, they were often, like the Sixth Voyage as it entered the Red Sea, ill-informed and unprepared.

CHAPTER 3

Captivity in Yemen

Anchoring before Aden near sunset on 7 November 1610, Middleton admired the view: "The town standeth at the foot of a mountain in a vale, and maketh a fair show: it is environed with a stone wall, and forts and bulwarks in many places" (M in P, 3:121). Pleased at this prospect, ignorant of Ja'far Basha's stern directive to the English to "come no more without order from the Great Turk" (J, 90), and flattered by the Socotran report of the *Ascension*'s success there, he found the happy rumors confirmed the next morning by three Arabs sent to the *Trades Increase* by Aden's lieutenant governor: "If we were Englishmen, we were heartily welcome." They declared that, "the year before, Captain Sharpeigh had been there, and from thence went to Mocha, where he made sale of all his goods." When Middleton asked them "if Mocha were a good place of trade," he heard of commerce on the scale of Marlowe's Jew of Malta: "There was one man in Mocha, that would buy all our goods" (M in P, 3:122). Perhaps they were referring to the indispensable Shermall, the Banian consul. Middleton resolved to sail there as soon as Aden could produce a pilot for the passage.

Downton's initial survey of the coast, by contrast, ironized the epithet "Happy Arabia." The terrain struck him as inhospitable: "mountains within the land all high, very rough, without show of grass, wood, or any other fruitfulness." He admired fertile zones like Table Bay, not this. Nor was he drawn to the city of Aden, poised "under the foot of an unfruitful mountain, a place where I should scarce have looked for a town." Its utility, he surmised, was military, not civic: "It is set there for strength, where it is very defensible" (D in P, 3:210, 211). Recounting their arrival, both writers possibly framed the moment with an eye to the disastrous sequel: Middleton to underscore his benign intent and Turkish perfidy, Downton, the wisdom of his unease.

Their narratives, in any case, demonized the Turks and elided their own and the Company's blunders in Arabia Felix.

Weighing anchor was a laborious, protracted process. Early on 9 November, as the ships prepared to depart, Middleton dispatched a boat to hire a pilot from the town. The fleet was under sail when the boat returned—with word that they might obtain a pilot only by the exchange of "two or three of our chief merchants for pledges," and the request "not to depart with all our ships, but to leave one for that port," where "they would buy all the goods in her" (M in P, 3:122). Middleton decided to keep the fleet together while pondering these contingencies. Skeptical of the market in Aden, Downton mistrusted the "glozing shows of indigo, ollibanum [frankincense], myrrh, and diverse other things" produced to entice them (D in P, 3:213). Over the next three days, his suspicions sharpened as the promised pilot failed to appear. Regib Aga had been promoted to governor of Mocha since the Fourth Voyage departed; Aden's new governor, Abdraman Aga, attributed the town's evident lapse of trade to his predecessor's "ill usage of strangers" and insisted that he hoped "by us to make a beginning."[1] He declared that the basha desired commerce here and would fault him if they all sailed off.

Persuaded by Abdraman Aga's appeal, Middleton determined to divide the fleet and keep the *Peppercorn* in Aden. But by 12 November, when the *Trades Increase* and the *Darling* departed for Mocha, still without a pilot, both he and Downton had grown cautious. They canceled their initial plans to carry perhaps a quarter of the *Peppercorn*'s goods ashore. If Aden's merchants "had any need of our commodities, as they pretended to have, they should buy and pay for it aboard the ship." The groups might exchange "pledges"—temporary hostages of corresponding rank—to establish trust (D in P, 3:214). But when a small party went ashore to propose this arrangement, the displeased governor detained them to prevent the *Peppercorn*'s departure and demanded a hefty anchorage fee: "fifteen hundred Venetianos of gold, every one [valued] at one rial and a half of eight." Thus began, Downton recounted, "before this town of Aden, . . . my unprofitable abode until the sixteenth of December" (D in P, 3:215).

Middleton's Arrival in Mocha

The coastal passage from Aden to Mocha was fraught with shoals, and the English recognized the need for a pilot to guide the deep-drafted *Trades*

Increase. After it and the *Darling* passed the western strait of Bab-el-Mandeb on 13 November, Middleton sent a pinnace to a village on the north shore to find one. The boat soon "returned with a couple of Arabs, who took upon them to be very skilful" (M in P, 3:123). The general put his trust in them. They continued not far offshore at depths of eight to twenty fathoms toward Mocha, which came into view late that afternoon. Then the weather changed. Turning closer into a stiffening wind, "we split our main topsail, and putting abroad our mizzen, it split likewise." Then crisis struck: "Our pilots brought our ship aground upon a bank of sand, the wind blowing hard, and the sea somewhat high, which made us all doubt her coming off" (M in P, 3:123–24). Wind and waves stressed the stranded vessel. The predicament was suddenly urgent.

Their grounding was witnessed ashore. A boat arrived from Mocha that evening "with a Turk in her, a proper man, sent by the governor of the town, to know what we were." At word that they were English merchants, "he answered, if we were Englishmen we were heartily welcome." He assured them that "it was ordinary for great ships of India to come a-ground, and yet [he] never heard that any of them sustained any harm thereby" (M in P, 3:124). Thus, Middleton's contact with Mocha's authorities began in consternation and embarrassment. Striving to refloat the ship, the crew staved water casks and hastily off-loaded "anything that came to hand" into lighters provided by the Turks for carriage ashore; they took care to send valuables, "all our money, elephants' teeth [ivory], and all our shot, aboard the *Darling*." Fearing the worst, Lawrence Femell departed in one of the lighters, Middleton reported, "before I was aware thereof, carrying all he had in the ship with him" (3:124). This scene of damage-control was assuredly not the grand arrival Middleton had hoped to perform. The *Trades Increase* was immobilized for six days before it floated free.

The general's frustration must have been profound. More than an outsized container for cargo, the *Trades Increase*, as proven at its launch, was also a theater of state: a large, impressive, ordnance-ringed space for the performance of English culture, diplomacy, and power. Middleton, its highest officer—successor to Sir Thomas Smythe, honored on this deck by the king at Deptford—was the pivotal actor on its stage. A proud, patriotic man, Sir Henry understood his personal carriage to embody the dignity and power of the "worshipful company" and monarch who had vested him with authority. His self-presentation achieved critical traction during moments of cross-cultural encounter. Yet, as the first full dignitary from the Ottoman Empire climbed aboard, the stage space was destabilized, confused, imperiled: unfit for a rite of reception. It was the "Lord of the Sea," as the general soon learned to term him, not Middleton, who held the authority to declare the predicament not extraordinary, the ship unlikely to be lost. In this nautical emergency, as in subsequent landed attempts to perform English dignity in Yemen, Middleton did not control the circumstances of his self-presentation. By various means before various audiences, theatrically and on the page, by gestures alternately willful and compulsory, the general struggled to wrest personal, corporate, and national dignity from scenes of humiliation and abjection. The meeting on the compromised flagship was the opening act in a drama of deconstruction that devolved into six months of captivity.

Throughout most of his confinement, Middleton retained substantial freedom of expression in the journal, whose composition was required by his office. The general was not an autonomous agent but a bonded servant of the Company: a scripted subject whose powers and obligations were announced in his royal and commercial commissions. To fulfill his epistolary duty—to write with an eye to corporate readers in London—stabilized his role as England's primary representative on the scene. Journaling focused the will to maintain one's assumed public identity under self-estranging stress. As Linda Colley observes, captivity abroad challenged the mental balance of officers who, like King Lear on the heath, stunned by his weaknesses, had assumed power and authority integral to their persons.[2] The shock of imprisonment often hit such men more severely than it did common seamen long subject to regimes of maritime discipline.

As his experiences in Yemen strained Middleton fundamentally, his writing, a task at once corporate and personal, helped recenter him. Framing the Turks as treacherous and rapacious, and thereby minimizing his own and the East India Company's complicity in their capture, he and his fellows constructed a narrative in which the English were set up and betrayed. He depicted himself behaving boldly under duress. To defend against the abjection he also recounted, he cultivated masochistic and proto-orientalist tropes of Turkish cruelty. In approaching the journal, one should allow for its self-affirming utility to the writer, his concern for his reputation and the ideological assumptions of his corporate readers, and the imperial enthusiasms of its editor-publisher, Samuel Purchas. To read against the grain of the text at times, and triangulate Middleton's account with others, are necessary critical moves.

Explaining their disembarkation into captivity, "we not suspecting the least villainy or treachery," Benjamin Greene invoked the duplicitous insistence of the "traitor Regib Aga," who, "as soon as the ship was afloat, . . . desired with great importunacy . . . the general [to] come ashore in token of friendship."[3] In accordance with his commission, Greene notes (fi), Middleton initially resisted. But after several days of entreaty, convinced that "I must come a-land . . . otherwise they would not be persuaded but that we were men of war" (M in P, 3:125), on 20 November 1610, like Sharpeigh before him, he was welcomed with pomp ashore:

> I was received at the water side by diverse chief men, and with music brought to the Aga's house, where were assembled all the chief men of the town. My entertainment by the Aga and the rest was with extraordinary great kindness. I was seated close to the Aga, all men else standing, where he held me with complements, many times bidding me welcome, offering himself and the country to be at my service. I delivered his Majesty's letter with a present to the Basha.
> . . . Likewise I gave the Aga a present, which he took very kindly, telling me, I and my people should have as good and peaceable trade, as any of our nation had in any parts of the Turk's dominions.
> . . . He caused me to stand up, and one of his chief men put upon my back a vest of crimson silk and silver, saying, I needed not to doubt of any evil; for that was the Grand Senior's protection.
> (3:125–26)

Middleton took pride in these rites of reception. His concern to make a compelling impression is evident in his postcaptivity letter to Lawrence Femell requesting the return of the livery cloaks for his attendants, "for I cannot go ashore anywhere *with credit* without them" (LR, 1:101; emphasis added). In Mocha, he continues, "I was mounted upon a gallant horse with rich furniture, a great man leading my horse" (M in P, 3:126). (Downton heard that "the Governor [held] the horse while the General gat up" [D in P, 3:226]; Greene describes the animal as the aga's "own horse" [G, fi].) The vest nevertheless denoted Middleton's elevated submission to Ottoman authority, which soon stiffened.

A week passed amiably. Awaiting Ja'far Basha's response to the news of their arrival, Regib Aga sent Middleton presents and commendations each day and proposed, once Ramadan had passed, "to have me ride abroad with him to his gardens, and other places of pleasure to make merry" (3:126). Unknowingly recapitulating the complacency that Jourdain critiqued in Sharpeigh, Middleton obtained permission from the aga to build a pinnace for the passage to India, and he brought many men ashore to that end (G, f1, 23 November 1610). Then, after sunset on 28 November, as he, Femell, and Pemberton relaxed in front of the house, and learned from a janissary that the aga "had received good news from the Basha" (3:127), suddenly their building was assaulted from behind. Eight crewmen were slain, fourteen wounded (3:128), and Middleton, rushing in to rally his men, knocked unconscious. Awakening to the "extreme pain" (3:127) of his hands bound behind him, the general was stripped of his money and tokens of authority—"three gold rings, whereof one was my seal, the other had seven diamonds which were of good worth, and the third a gimmal ring" (3:128)—and clamped by the neck in irons with seven others, "so that one could not go aside to ease himself," Downton elaborated, "but the rest in a row must go with him, to their great annoyance" (3:228–29). Greene described their plight, "all bound with cords, hands behind us, and carried to the governor's house, where we were all fast pinioned with irons about our necks and gyves upon our legs and manacles upon our hands" (G, f1, 28 November 1610).

The Sixth Voyage mariners had violated Ja'far Basha's directive to Jourdain that the English must stay out of Yemen until licensed by Istanbul to traffic there. Moreover, as Middleton would soon learn, since issuing that warning, the basha had received letters from the sultan commanding him to capture or kill Christians who entered the region. He obeyed. Mischance, blunder, and overconfidence produced the crisis. Had the letter Sharpeigh left in Socotra not been lost, they would have gone elsewhere, as Downton declares: "We trusted them as men of humane feeling, being ignorant of what was against us, for if we had known but only the danger of coming hither at this time, we should have been unwilling to put ourselves and our ships into such a place."[4] The basha evidently mistrusted them: later in Sana'a, reported Greene, Middleton learned from Aden's Governor Abdraman Aga "that *Regib Aga* was the cause of our hard entertainment, for by his letters he always persuaded the Basha that we were men of war, and that we were come to take the country, and not as merchants. Whereupon was the Basha's command to apprehend us and use us in manner as we were" (G, f2v, 11 January 1610/11). Had they possessed it, the sultan's letter of protection, identifying them as merchants, should have won them friendlier entertainment. At the very least, it would have required Ja'far Basha to reconcile competing directives from Achmed I, and it would have justified clemency.

The same day, an assault force—"three great boats with one hundred and fifty soldiers," turbans removed in disguise (M in P, 3:128)—boarded the *Darling* and quickly slew three men. But when many assailants reportedly misunderstood a command to cut the hawsers and left in the boats instead, the crew rallied, tossed a keg of powder into a sword-clattering crowd in the waist of the ship, lit a firebrand, and burned a number of them. Under musket fire, the Turks fled to the half deck and poop, where, "entertained with another train of powder," many leapt into the sea and drowned. Those "hanging by the ship's side, desiring mercy," received none. Only one, who hid during the tumult, survived. Proud to share this report of English valor, Middleton inflects the account with sadistic irony ("entertained") while savoring an action that answered the story of his capture with a vision of revenge. He concludes the episode in a pious vein: "Thus God of his goodness and mercy delivered our ship and men out of the hands of our enemies, for which his holy name be blessed and praised evermore. Amen" (3:129).

But Middleton's revenge, far less decisive than the *Darling's* repulse of its attackers, was a long time coming. His second audience with Regib Aga cast him not in singular dignity but as one of eight in chains. "He with a frowning . . . countenance, asked me how I durst be so bold as to come into this their Port of Mocha, so near their holy city of Mecca." Middleton's answer, "I came not a-land but by his earnest entreaty with many promises of good and kind usage," provoked the admonition that he should have known better: "the Basha had express order from the great Turk, to captivate all Christians that should come into those seas, although they had his own pass" (3:130). Offering then to "let us have the small ship to carry us home," he told Middleton to write to the crew at sea and command them to surrender the great ship. The general refused: "I said it was a folly to write any such thing: for they that were aboard and had their liberty were no such fools, as upon my letter to forsake the ships and goods, and come a-land and be slaves. He said, he knew if I did write a letter to that effect, they durst not disobey me. . . . He urged me again to write . . . or he would cut off my head. I bade him do so: for therein he should doe me a great pleasure, for I was weary of my life, but write to that effect I never would" (3:130–31). Middleton's act of public defiance is at once theatrical and epistolary. Cultivating the protoorientalist conceit of Turks as the slaves of despots—the aga cannot imagine a disobedient crew—and Englishmen as lovers of liberty, he salvages his self-respect by refusing to write the commanded letter and performing the corporate duty of writing in his journal instead. That night, however, the aga's lieutenant visited him privately and urged him to write another letter to the ships requesting news of the Ottomans killed or captured on the *Darling*. He was to omit his "hard usage" and the deaths of crewmen and to state only that "we were detained in the Aga's House (where we lacked not any thing) till further order came from the Basha. This letter," Middleton admits, "I did willingly write." In it, he warned the mariners "to look well to their ships and boat" (3:131) and not to come ashore. In the event, no Turk was willing to carry the letter aboard, so Middleton had to write a second one, "perused as was the former," to be delivered by someone willing, an Italian-speaking Tunisian. In their response, the mariners expressed great relief at hearing from Middleton, for the Turkish survivor of the attack on the *Darling*, "Russwan, a common soldier, . . . thought we were all slain" (3:132). They were allowed no further communication until 15 December.

Middleton's journal, then, details the misery his compelled letter elided: manacled and fettered, he was cast alone "in a dirty dogs' kennel under a pair of stairs." That evening, "at the entreaty of Shermall, consul of the Banians, I was taken out and placed in a better room. . . . My lodging was upon the hard ground, and my pillow a stone, my companions to keep me waking were grief of heart and multitude of rats: which if I chanced to sleep, would awake me with running over me" (3:131). He was still there, "fettered hands and feet in irons," when he was visited on 15 December by John Chambers, a quartermaster on the *Trades Increase* (D in P, 3:228) who, with a "flag of truce" and an Indian shipmate as translator to explain the errand, was escorted in "to my dark cell; who coming out of the light was a great while before he could see me" (M in P, 3:133). Chained in the dark, Middleton was the antithesis of the eye-catching figure on the "gallant horse" (3:126) some weeks before. If acts of theatrical self-presentation confirm identity and legitimate public authority, he was nothing now: a clutch of shadows.

The *Peppercorn* at Aden

While his generous reception made Middleton somewhat incautious in Mocha, the seizure of envoys from the *Peppercorn* as the other ships departed made Downton "very suspicious and wary in sending but few men" (D in P,

3:218) into Aden. Alternate scenarios and imponderable contingencies immobilized him. The ship's predicament, anchored in nine fathoms off a lee
shore, was precarious. Winter was coming. He feared they might be driven
shoreward by "tempestious" weather and "the violence of the mounting bil-
lows," thus falling "under command of their ordnance. From whence without
their leave, we could not have carried her out again" (3:218). He suspected
that the Turks wanted a ship to remain at Aden, not because they desired
trade, but because "it was more likely for them to work their wills on one
ship, than on three" (3:217). He surmised that the governor's generous treatment of the captive merchants was a charade: "He gulled us by pretended
friendship" (3:219) while requisitioning soldiers from inland towns to pose as
merchants visiting Aden to buy English goods. Meanwhile, the governor
allowed no one, "not so much as an Arab fisherman . . . to come near unto
me, lest they should tell me the truth, to his disadvantage" (3:216). Downton
found small hope of trade when an exploratory party reported houses "ruinated and sunk in every part of the town" and few shops or other signs of
commercial activity: "Money seemeth to be very scant amongst them. . . .
When our men offered to change a piece of eight for aspers," people passed
it "from hand to hand, gazing as at a strange thing." Downton found this
behavior—surprise at a common coin—"an ill sign in a place where a ship's
lading of merchandize is brought to sell" (3:216–17).[5]

The governor left town on 23 November and returned on 1 December,
doubtless informed of Ja'far Basha's policy toward the English and their capture in Mocha. Lacking news from that quarter, Downton hovered in perplexity. He desired to reunite the fleet yet was loathe to abandon his factors
ashore. He also feared that if he sailed for Mocha, the monsoon might prevent their return until May or June (3:219). He made repeated shows of
departure in futile hopes of reducing the anchorage fee. Desiring release,
more optimistic about their prospects than Downton, John Fowler and the
other merchants ashore grew impatient with his inaction. Dark forebodings
and self-doubts beset him, as he confessed in a passage omitted by Purchas:

> I would gladly have been gone, for by dreams by night, and disturb-
> ing motions by day, I was made doubtful all was not well with my
> friends at Mocha. Yet I having so narrow a path to walk in being
> here left to seek trade, . . . which we were in no way denied but
> promised so soon as our goods were brought on land, which if I
> through dreams, doubts, and suspicions, without apparent reasons,

should have abandoned the place, my factors that I should have left
behind me and others, to my reproach and scandal, might have said
I was mere afraid than hurt, and that the company's goods might
have been well sold, had not I been afraid of my own shadow. (D,
f19, 16 November 1610)

Upon his return, the governor promised to release the three hostages without
payment of an anchorage fee "so soon as we should begin to trade," reported
Fowler, whose letter urged Downton to write Middleton, "to know his pleasure . . . for landing of our goods." Observing that "I might have done it
myself, if I had seen any sign or likelihood of good dealing," Downton held
off (D in P, 3:219). To hesitate was wise. But as the lieutenant general notes
in his manuscript, such "restraint drew on me much secret envy and backbit-
ing rumors amongst my unbridled people, which by importunities had
almost tired me" (D, f21, 16 November 1610). He greatly desired word from
Middleton, "to know how they do, and what entertainment they there have
. . . and to be informed what dangers there are between these two towns, to
give knowledge of our men's imprisonment, and crave aid if need required
from hence by the general's means" (D, f21v, 1 December 1610). He dispatched a messenger to Mocha, not knowing that Middleton was already
imprisoned there.

    After eight days with no word from Mocha, the boatswain, reporting
that the ship lacked small cordage, asked if he and several crewmen could go
ashore to work on ropes near the town wall, where requisite space was available. Downton secured the blessing of the governor, who further offered "a
house at night to put up their things till the next day" (D in P, 3:220). While
the sailors labored, smiths inside the town were making shackles, an ominous
development to which a few people, probably Arabs, tried to alert the English
"by signs." The mariners, however, laughed off these gestures, taking "as a
merry jest" what "afterwards they found in earnest" (3:220). On the afternoon
of 12 December, writes Downton, "my men were all betrayed that went on
shore, bound shackled, and pinioned, and some put in the stocks: all tortured
and grievously abused, stript of their money and all else they had." The
pinnace and its crew, having left the boat unattended to help with the ropes,
were taken as well. In all, the *Peppercorn* lost twenty persons: "two merchants,
a purser, and one to attend on them, a gadding apothecary, my surgeon and
master caulker, . . . my boatswain and one of his mates, two quarter masters,

the cooper, carpenter, and gunner's mate, and my cockswain and five more of the cock's ging" (3:220).[6]

In a passage absent from Purchas, Downton describes his "cloud of bitter grief" at having failed to prevent a catastrophe he was "formerly suspicious and wary of. . . . With what compassionate sorrow I was now perplexed," he wrote, the men's "tortures and cruelties . . . being beyond my power to mitigate and ease" (D, f22v, 12 December 1610). Not understanding that their failure to produce the sultan's letter of protection had provoked this treatment, Downton feared the governor had seized the crewmen to compel him to land goods or pay the anchorage fee "or the next day in my view on the island, they should be all hanged. . . . Yet I desired better to know the reason, wherefore they should deal this injuriously with us, our kings being in league" (D, f22v). Hoping to ransom his men, he negotiated for the payment to be delivered offshore, from one boat to another, within reach of the ship's ordnance. An Arab in a canoe approached the waiting boat, viewed the bags of money, and returned to the town to discuss "what were best to be done in this business. And what came to their minds I know not" (D, f23). For reasons unclear to Downton, the Turks canceled the deal: "I cannot now have my people for my money." Amid increasing risks, hopeless of progress here, at the aga's report of a "falling out between our people and them of Mocha," with "some fourteen of our men killed and hurt" (D, f23, 12 December 1610), Downton resolved to sail there at once and lend assistance. With a lessened crew, the *Peppercorn* left Aden on 16 December and reached Mocha road on the twentieth—just two days before Middleton departed for Sana'a (M in P, 3:135).

A Forced Journey to the Capital

Fearing "every hour" (3:134) that a sentence of death or perpetual imprisonment would arrive from Sana'a, Middleton learned instead that he and many crewmen had been summoned there to justify themselves, an arduous journey of some 270 miles.[7] On the morning of 18 December, Regib Aga, the basha's emissary Ismael Aga, and another official came into his cell to deliver the news. The governor asked him again, "how I durst be so bold as to come in that country so near their holy city, without a pass from the Gran Senior." Middleton answered, "the King my master was in league and amity with the Grand Senior," whose "articles of peace . . . allowed us free trade in all his dominions, and this being a part of his dominions, there needed no pass." Regib Aga insisted otherwise: "This was the door of their holy city, and therefore not lawful for any Christian to come hither" (3:134). Interrupting this unequal standoff, Ismael Aga explained that he had come from the basha "to conduct me and all my people" to Sana'a. He advised Middleton to provide warm clothing from the ships "for that we should find it very cold in the mountain country" (3:135). The general ignored this counsel.

He and some thirty-four others from the *Trades Increase* and *Darling* would make the journey. The carpenters and smiths remained, in chains, to build the pinnace, now intended for the basha (P, 3:135, 229). A few magnates in Mocha tried to ease their hardship. One Hamet Aga sent Middleton "diverse presents and willed me to be of good comfort, for my cause was good," and he gave the crew bread for the journey; Shermall, the Banian consul, having brokered a better cell for Middleton, visited him daily with presents; and one Tookehar, who had provided the captives with bread, dates, and plantains, departed two days before them to argue their case in Sana'a (3:136). Before dawn on 22 December, the English mariners left Mocha. They traveled upland with Middleton and Femell mounted on horses, the crewmen, "with manacles of iron," on asses (G, f2; P, 3:135). After several miles, the *Darling*'s master William Pemberton, fearing for his life as they all did, slipped away, reached the seashore a few miles from the ships, found a canoe, improvised a sail with his shirt, and with great difficulty attained the *Trades Increase*.[8] The others were less fortunate. In a major index of his abjection, Middleton, likely deprived of paper, ink, and quills, stopped writing the journal. He had to reconstruct the interim later (3:137), probably after 9 March 1611 back in Mocha, when Pemberton by request sent him writing materials—"two quire of paper, one-half a dozen of knives"—and sundry other items (*LR*, 1:59). Through towns along the way, they were exhibited as slaves. In the first, Taiz, "Upon Christmas day . . . we were marshalled into the city two and two in a rank, as they do at Stambola [Istanbul] with captives taken in wars, our Aga riding in triumph as a great conqueror, being met a mile out of the town with the chief men of the city on horse-back, multitudes of people standing all the way gazing and a wondering at us: thus we were used in all cities and towns we passed through" (3:137). Between Taiz and Sana'a the chill turned bitter, "our lodging being the cold ground," most of the men "slenderly clothed." Middleton bought furred gowns for himself and the others; "Otherwise," he declares, "I think they would have starved [perished]." He found himself "wishing when it was too late, I had come better provided" (3:137)—an apt epigraph for the entire expedition in Yemen.

The humiliating pageantry of their progress climaxed with their entry to Sana'a, 5 January 1611. About a mile outside the city, Middleton reports:

> We were met by the Subbassie or Sherif, with at least two hundred shot, drums, and trumpets: we were caused to go one by one in order, a pretty distance one from the other, to make the better show; our men had their gowns taken from them, and were caused to march a-foot in their thin and ragged suits; the soldiers led the way, after came our men one by one; our trumpeters were placed before me, and commanded by the Aga to sound; but I forbad them: after the trumpets came M. Femel and myself on horse-back; and lastly came our Aga riding in triumph, with a spare horse richly furnished led before him. In this order we were led through the heart of the city . . . all the way being so full of people, we could hardly pass for them. (3:137–38)

The limit of Middleton's authority in this scene was to silence the fanfare announcing his preeminence in a parade of captives. Whether or not they recognized the irony, their humiliation vividly contradicted the claims of King James's royal entry in 1604, whose rites of imperial assertion, as noted in the prior chapter, adopted the language and forms of the Roman triumph. The London ceremony harnessed even Arabia Felix, a region Rome never conquered, to a spectacle of Stuart dominion. Now in that country, Middleton and his men learned on their bodies what Knolles had argued in *The Generall Historie of the Turkes* (1603): that the Ottoman genuinely resembled the Roman empire in extent and style (A5v), that Istanbul's claims to Rome's inheritance were not only, like London's, theatrical and self-congratulatory but also territorial and substantial.

Arriving at the castle, they passed through two heavily guarded gates. At the second, bracketed by "two great pieces of ordnance," the soldiers "discharged their shot" and joined others forming a lane for the captives across a "spacious yard, twice the length of the [Royal] Exchange in London," at the end of which two flights of stairs ascended to a "spacious gallery . . . covered all over with Turkey carpets." At the upper end sat the basha flanked by standing dignitaries while others lined the room on either side, "which made a good show" (3:138). Middleton and Femell mounted the twelve stairs. At the top, "two great men came and took me by the wrists, and held me very hard, and so led me to the Basha" (3:138).[9] This tense meeting recalled those with Regib Aga, of whose duplicity and harshness Middleton complained bitterly only to be admonished that "Regib Aga was but his slave, . . . and what was befallen to me and to my people, was by his order to Regib Aga; and that he himself likewise had such order from the Gran Senior, so to chastise all Christians that should come into those parts" (3:139). Denying Middleton's plea to depart, Ja'far Basha proposed they should both write to Istanbul, the general to his ambassador and he to Achmed I, to ascertain "what should become of us" (3:139). (It is not clear that they did so: Middleton notes no letter to Glover, and Ja'far Basha's subsequent decision invokes the sultan's response to the Fourth Voyage, not the Sixth.) Middleton was then dismissed. He concludes the episode with a sad anecdote: as he was brought before the basha, "one of our youths . . . thinking I was so led to have my head strook off, fell in a sound [swoon] with very fear, thinking his turn would not be long after; he fell sick upon it and shortly after died" (3:139–40).

Middleton was invited, with a few others, "such as I thought good," to lodge at the prison keeper's house, "and the rest [were] carried to the common prison, where for their welcome they were clapt in weighty irons" (3:139) and fed only brown bread and water. Fearing "they would all have died with hunger" (3:141), the general provided foodstuffs for them. On 17 January, captives from the *Peppercorn* arrived from Aden to a similar reception; three leaders were sent to lodge with Middleton, the others to the common prison. They all feared that in summoning them to the capital, the basha planned to execute the principal mariners and enslave the others (3:141). Desperate to leverage another outcome, Middleton warned the basha that he had advised his mariners to behave peacefully for twenty-five days, but that thereafter, lacking welcome news from him, he could not answer for the damages they might inflict on Mocha's shipping (3:141). Downton's 30 January 1611 reference to "the days expired, that by yourself was nominated that we might hear from you" (*LR*, 1:52), and a letter fragment of 20 December 1610 from Middleton and Femell to Giles Thornton, interim commander of the *Trades Increase*, support Middleton's claim, though the latter indicates that Middleton tried to prevent the strong-arm tactics he now threatened. Drafted two days before their departure for Sana'a, the letter expresses their alarm that John Chambers, who visited Middleton in his cell and evidently mistook something said there, had persuaded Thornton to order the *Darling* to prey on ships around Mocha—"to take all that they met withal." The letter admonishes Thornton that such a move would "be our utter undoing in this place" as well as Cambaya (*LR*, 1:49). Whatever Middleton's desires from the fleet, it is not clear that Ja'far Basha was moved by the threat of English retaliation at sea. The general did not pursue the theme with him further.

The English were fortunate that a number of powerful merchants, intrigued by the prospects of trade with the English, intervened on their behalf. As noted earlier, Yemen was an important nexus of international trade—"Hither is great resort of people from all parts," wrote Greene, "viz: Armenians, Greeks, Persians, Jews, and Indians" (G, f2v, 18 February 1610/11)—and magnates from various countries made vigorous appeals for clemency. From Mocha, Shermall and Hamet Aga had written to the caya, Abdela Chillarby, and made him "our friend" (M in P, 3:136, 140); throughout his six weeks in the capital, Middleton found sporadic encouragement in this potentate's company. On 7 January a Moor of Cairo arrived who, years before, had lent the basha "great sums of money at his coming from Stambola, when he was but poor." This unnamed magnifico, whose doings Hamet Aga and Shermall reported to Sir Henry, resided near the English in Mocha when they were taken captive, and he feared then that they would seize his India-bound ship in retaliation. But when "they let her quietly depart, contrary to his expectation, . . . he became our great friend." He wrote to Sana'a to protest the basha's harshness, "saying, he went about to destroy the country and trade, in taking such course with us" (3:140); then he traveled upland to make the plea in person, "willing him [the basha] to have a care, the trade of the Red Sea were not destroyed by his means" (3:140). Likewise, one "Hamet Waddy, an Arabian merchant, very rich dwelling at Zenan . . . stood my friend very much" (3:141) and spoke to Ja'far Basha. Shermall also made the journey, and his presence proved decisive. Middleton's reluctant promise to pay the caya 1,500 venetianos upon his release—the same sum demanded of Downton for anchorage in Aden—at last secured Chillarby's material assistance and largesse. Shermall negotiated and underwrote the bribe (3:142).

The interventions of this cosmopolitan group of elite traders proved critical. Middleton's new relationship with the caya brought friendlier access to the basha, who on 25 January received him and Femell in his garden and "bad me be of good cheer, for that shortly I and all my people should have their liberty" to return to Mocha. There, Middleton and some thirty others would remain in house arrest until ships arrived unimpeded from India.

Then, once the western monsoon began, the English would be allowed to depart (3:143). The basha referred their harsh treatment to the sultan, whose response to complaints that the *Ascension* had engrossed choice Indian goods in the region was to declare that "if any more Englishmen, or any other Christians did come into these parts," his deputies should "confiscate their ships and goods, or . . . kill or captivate all the men they could get" (3:144). Middleton wryly observes that, in explaining this policy, Ja'far Basha praised "his own mild nature" and declared them fortunate "to fall into his hands" (3:143).

The same day, Middleton and Femell wrote sternly to Downton, then in command of the fleet, "to forbear any dangerous action notwithstanding any former protestations." Shermall's messenger delivered the letter. Anxious not to disrupt the recent clemency of their captors, they were confident that "about five days hence we shall all set forth from hence to return for Mocha in the company of the Bannian Shabunder [Shermall], who hath been, and is, our great friend in our business" (*LR*, 1:51).[10] On 1 February Middleton and Femell were invited to watch, from "a place appointed us," a procession marking Ja'far Basha's investment as vizier, a post of great dignity. The latter met the sultan's emissary six miles outside town, where he doffed his old garments and took up "those sent by his master; and so in great pomp came riding through the city to his own house" (M in P, 3:144). At the caya's arrangement, Middleton's "trudgman" (aka "dragoman," broker-translator) took them to the house to offer congratulations and "to pray God give him joy: he gave me thanks, and bad me be merry: . . . he was very pleasant, and took this our coming kindly: and so, as a great favour, Master Femel and I were permitted to kiss his hand, and dismissed" (3:144–45).

The tone here is unstable, ambivalent. The sardonic light on the kiss (submission framed "as a great favour") is suffused with reluctant respect. Middleton recognizes that his invitation to witness the investiture and, however marginally, to augment the ceremony, *is* an honor. He had made progress in Sana'a. In the event, Ja'far Basha released the English with a warning reminiscent of the one he gave Jourdain the year before: "that neither we nor any other of our nation, would repair thither any more." Underscoring his lenity, he reported further that Achmed I, having heard complaints that the *Ascension*'s purchases had depressed imperial customs revenues, sent letters commanding him to capture or kill any Christians who "came into those parts" (3:143–44). The basha's more severe aspect, however, manifested the following day, when the general requested that he command Regib Aga not to "wrong me and my people." Ja'far Basha responded, by Middleton's report, with the cruel pomposity of a Turkish despot on the London stage: "Is not my only word sufficient to turn a whole city upside down? If Regib Aga wrong you, I will pull his skin over his ears and give you his head: is not he my slave?" (3:146).[11] The sudden sadism of the imagery is striking. Such orientalist tropes—vignettes of the boastful, raging, capriciously merciful or vengeful Turk—helped Middleton to arrest his admiration and recenter himself as an Englishman.

Their ordeals in Arabia Felix educated the English in the limits of their knowledge, power, and prestige. Sir Henry Middleton's humiliations—the commander stripped of his authority, chained by the neck to common mariners, restored to the relative dignity of a horse for more prominent humiliation as a captive—also challenged him personally and viscerally. Yet Middleton, "forced to endure with patience what I could not remedy till it pleased God to provide better" (3:152), proved resilient. His role as the preeminent captive probably helped sustain his sense of self-importance. Following the initial capture, the Ottomans recognized his authority. Moreover, the suffering that they all shared stirred his paternalistic sympathies for the common mariners in his charge, something as King Lear's exposures teach the aged monarch to pity the "looped and windowed raggedness" (3.4.33) of the poor. As noted earlier, in cold, rugged, mountainous terrain—in Sana'a, "we had ice a finger thick in one night" (3:137)—he bought warm gowns for his men; and he supplemented their rations in prison.

Like Jourdain before him, Middleton also expressed sympathy for the Arab population. If initially inclined to the emulous pattern Gerald MacLean finds in Englishmen abroad—who, even in captivity, "identified with the dominant Ottoman elite rather than the local peoples" with whom they shared postures of subordination—the writers of the Fourth and Sixth Voyages put aside that delusion in Arabia Felix (MacLean, 118). Jourdain found "the country people generally very good and honest; and [it] were a very pleasant place to bide in, were it not for the Turks' tyranny" (J, 105). Explaining that "diverse places in Arabia . . . are not under the command of the Turk," Jourdain noted that resistant Arabs, when captured, were "either put . . . to death" or "kept . . . perpetual prisoners" (94), "as pledges of peace of the cities and towns" they came from (93). Middleton detailed the confinements within the castle yard in Sana'a: "a great number of people, for the most part women and children, are kept prisoners or pledges, to keep their parents, husbands, and allies from rebellion. The boys while they be little go loose in the yard, but after they be come to bigness they are clapt in irons and carried to a strong tower, where there be many more kept in like case, there they remain during the Basha's pleasure" (M in P, 3:147). Greene theorizes the necessity of such measures: "rebellion . . . would soon take effect if the Arabs had any heads or leaders, for in this country they are ten Arabs to one Turk" (G, f2v, 18 February 1610/11). The shared experience of captivity having awakened their sympathies, the English identified with Arab resistance to Ottoman rule.

They departed for Mocha on 18 February 1611. En route, Middleton noted approvingly, "These craggy mountain countries are for the most part governed by the Arabians, for the people of these mountains cannot brook the proud and insolent government of the Turks" (3:148). While most indigenous groups in Yemen, Greene explained, "are not permitted to have or wear any weapon, . . . these people to the contrary never go empty handed of their weapons" (G, f3, 19 February 1610/11). Middleton savored the irony of Turks requiring passports in these regions. Reaching Mocha on the morning of 5 March 1611, the English performed their reentry in a spirit of masochistic solidarity with the Arab population. Middleton framed the ceremony as a successful appeal for subaltern sympathy: "At the town's ends, and all the way to the Aga's house, the people stood very thick, and as we passed by bad us welcome back, for it was nothing pleasing to the people of the country to hear how treacherously the Turks had used us" (3:151). The trope of Turkish treachery henceforth dominated his ruminations.

A Crisis of Command

The journals and letters exchanged among principal members of the Sixth Voyage during Middleton's captivity demonstrate that protracted separation, as distinct immediacies differentiated the concerns of groups at sea and ashore, put severe and damaging stresses to the voyage's structures of command. East India Company directors did not foresee such mission-critical challenges in the Red Sea, and their commission offered small counsel on the matter. The fleet's personnel had to improvise their own way forward. That process disclosed fundamental instabilities within the corporate body, embittered relations within the fleet, and fostered cynicism and mistrust of the Company in London.

When the *Peppercorn*, lacking a pilot, sounding carefully along the coast of Yemen, neared the *Trades Increase* off Mocha on 20 December 1610, the great ship, "as a signal of heavy news, . . . pulled down their flag," wrote Downton, "whereby I understood some misfortune was befallen my general" (D in P, 3:222). Master Thornton came aboard and, "after blasts of passion and grief," told them of the ship's grounding, Femell's "most fearful" exit with all his belongings, their subsequent enticement and betrayal ashore, and the repulsed assault on the *Darling*. Already saddened by the capture of *Peppercorn* crewmen, Downton took the news heavily. Their sorrows deepened when Middleton and company departed for Sana'a two days later. Their cheer at Pemberton's return sharpened their anxieties about the others. Weeks later, having at last heard again from the general, on 30 January 1611 Downton, Thornton, and the factor Hugh Frayne described to him their mood of irritable despondency: "The long time hearing nothing from you, and the variety of lies we ever receive from Mocha, hath bred variety of passionate thoughts, set a deep impression of sadness and discontent in such as have honest feeling of friends' miseries." They were angry with the Company in London for sending them into Yemen without the sultan's letter of safe passage. Downton assailed "the unchewed, giddy and rash directions given you by the company; which till our coming hither, I thought had (their means being so good in Turkey) better understood their own business" (*LR*, 1:52). Given the overlapping memberships of the Levant and East India Companies, Downton insinuates, the directors had conflated untested Red Sea with extant Mediterranean privileges—an Anglo-centric oversight with lethal consequences.

Middleton's concern upon their departure for Sana'a—that his mariners might try to extort his release by blockading Mocha, thus offending the powers he sought to conciliate—was well founded. Divided between terrestrial and nautical subject positions, the members of the Sixth Voyage saw their predicament, and the tactics it recommended, in contradictory ways. The general and his crew were either hostages to the fleet's good behavior or motives for its forceful intervention. The English were potent at sea, their concentrated firepower formidable. When first apprised of the *Peppercorn*'s arrival, Middleton, to prevent trouble with Regib Aga, directed Downton to return to Aden and await further word there, adding that he had sent the *Darling* their way in hopes of intercepting them with this message (D in P, 3:229). A prideful man entirely vulnerable in captivity, fearful of execution, Middleton came to believe that the voyage's prospects improved with his cultivation of persons and protocols in the capital; thus the large payment promised the caya upon his release, and his gracious attendance on the basha at the latter's promotion to vizier. For his part, Downton ignored the order to return to Aden. As the general left for Sana'a, Downton lusted to sail to Bab-el Mandeb immediately, "to stop the passage of all the Indian ships entering this sea, whereby to draw the Turks to release our general, people and goods" (P, 3:230). Altogether mistrustful of Ottoman gestures of good will—"for they, through custom of lying, cannot speak truth," he declared (D, f33v, 14 February 1611)—Downton feared that Middleton, blindsided and coerced ashore, might succumb to sirenlike appeals from Ottoman authorities: the commands of a captive general could compromise the interests of their voyage.

In the event, nothing came of Downton's resolve to blockade the Straits of Bab-el Mandeb. Foul weather and the need for sanctuary initially prevented it; later, Middleton's countermand. The passage thither was difficult, and the seas off Mocha, they found, afforded poor anchorage in winter. The winds dragged especially hard at the tall *Trades Increase*, which lost two anchors in a single day, and split the topsails of the ships underway, "they being sewed with rotten twine, as all our sails for the most part hath been," Downton complained (P, 3:231). The flagship's crew had staved casks when aground in November and urgently needed water now. Exploring in the shallow-drafted *Darling*, Pemberton found safe haven for the fleet on the opposite "Abaxin" (aka "Habesse") or Abyssinian coast, today's Eritrea, where water, goats, sheep, and cattle were readily available from inhabitants who proved friendly despite, Downton learned through an interpreter, the counsel of "the Turks, our friends, . . . to cut our throats" (LR, 1:55). The fleet departed for that coast on 18 January 1611 (D in P, 3:232). On the beach two days later, a landing party met a group of over a hundred "armed with lances," and one young man "of a bolder spirit than the rest" stepped forth to engage them, explaining that he "desired to go aboard with them." Named Allee, this "principal man's son . . . was very kind to us all the time we were in this bay: he this night did lie aboard the *Trades Increase*, where he was very kindly used to his great content" (D in P, 3:233, 236). The great ship performed timely service as a theater of English hospitality. Amicable exchanges ensued: receiving a goat from the father and brothers who were reunited with Allee the next day, Downton gave them "four of the *Trades* shirts put in by the merchants for the company [crew]." Curious about the inhabitants of this strategic region, the mariners reported later to Middleton in Mocha that "the people of the country be as black as the negroes of Guinea. They be all Mahometans alongst the seacoast: but up in the land they be Christians and subjects to Prester John," the mythical Christian ruler of Africa. Their king resided at Rahaita, "some forty miles to the southwards near the Bab" (M in P, 3:153–54).

Rewatered and refreshed, on 29 January the fleet sailed again under Downton's command for Bab-el Mandeb, determined "to make stay of all the Indian ships, that this year should enter this sea" (D in P, 3:234). But the winds slackened. As the tide pulled them toward "Crab Island," they anchored and went ashore to cut wood. That afternoon, they observed two jelbas approaching from Mocha,[12] one of which bore a (nonextant) letter of 15 January from Middleton, composed as his prospects improved in Sana'a— his first letter since their departure upland. Some of its content reappears in his missive of 25 January: "be careful to avoid any attempt . . . in revenge of our wrongs," he and Femell admonished; "forbear any dangerous action notwithstanding any former protestations" (LR, 1:51). Middleton feared that such action now "might prove prejudicial, not only to him and his company, but also to our nation trading in the Mediterranean sea" (D in P, 3:235). The fleet stood down. Dispatching an answer by the same messenger, Downton reported Pemberton's safety, sketched the hazards of Mocha road, noted his "present determination intercepted by his letter," commented on the "fair seeming, yet deluding promises" of the Turks, and described "our safe road and watering place on the Abaxin coast" (3:235), to which they duly returned.

There, in the above-quoted 30 January letter, he, Thornton, and Frayne forcefully articulated their motives for the more assertive course Middleton's letter interrupted. In it, Downton described an earlier "bragging or threatening letter" he had sent the general's way in the expectation that Regib Aga would intercept it,

> wherein I showed with what honest intent and purpose we were set
> out of our country; in what peaceable manner and sincerity, by the
> command of our king and directions of our governors, we are
> directed to carry ourselves to all people . . . ; yet now, in revenge of
> our friends betrayed, murdered and abused, we were all resolved
> (if the sooner we had not good assurance of the liberty, and return,
> of our friends injuriously withholden) to cast off all duty we owe to
> our king, who is a friend to Turks, and care for the business of our
> adventurers and merchants, our minds wholly transformed by the

disgrace and villainy received, for the right of ourselves and the reputation of our nation. In prejudice of the Turks we determined to
wear out our ships and to spend our lives, never thinking to return
out of these seas. (*LR*, 1:53)

Enjoying the freedom of the seas in formidably armed ships, Downton
threatened that unless their mates were released, the fleet would cast off all
alliances, avenge itself, and compel respect for England throughout Arabia.
If hyperbolical, the letter articulates a model of adventuring toward which
any given voyage of the East India Company, a body with privateering in its
blood, threatened to devolve: a predatory force targeting immediate needs
and opportunities.

Downton adds darkly, "Were it not for the prejudice of many others,
myself and many here could . . . put in execution what with reason is said"
(*LR*, 1:53). The remark suggests that Downton's course had met resistance
not only from Middleton and his counselors ashore but also within the fleet.
The letter's next item, questioning Middleton's stay of the blockade, was
more provocative: they mistrusted the general's judgment. "We could perceive little other but that you are wrought upon for the serving of their [the
Turks'] turns, and for the safe passage of the Indian ships, which is their own
especial good, and by which they may work us very much mischief. . . . I
suspect you are abused in this, and but made an instrument or, as it were,
one of us to bind another's hands, that the wolves may the easier devour us
all" (1:53–54). The suspicion that captivity has clouded Middleton's vision
directly challenges the general's authority. There were no clear East India
Company protocols to mediate the dilemma. For all its decisiveness on suc-
cessions of command, the Sixth Voyage commission did not address the contingency of a captive general.

As the captives reached Mocha on 5 March, the fleet awaited them on
the opposite coast, as Downton explained in a letter of 2 March: "The Aga is
unwilling we should come to Mocha road, pretending that the ships of India
dare not come where we are" (*LR*, 1:55). Welcoming Middleton and his men,
Regib Aga "prayed me to pardon him," reports the general, and professed
that henceforth "he would be my friend. . . . I soothed him up but believed
nothing he said." The English were initially shown to a large, pleasant house
near the sea but soon removed to quarters more secure: "a great strong house,
standing all alone in a spacious church-yard in the middle of the town,"
surrounded by soldiers (M in P, 3:151–52). Invited with Femell to share a feast

at the aga's garden house celebrating the arrival of "a great ship of Dabull," Middleton, doubtless recalling the evanescent pomp of his own reception, felt very much the looker-on: "The Dabullians were all mounted upon gallant horses with rich furniture, and we upon a couple of tired lame jades which we brought from Zenan" (3:153). Although many English sailors were freed on 8 March, those at sea remained dubious of Ottoman courtesies, suspecting that Middleton's and Femell's promised liberty was not forthcoming. Receiving the released mariners on the *Darling*, Pemberton wrote to Middleton and expressed the mood of the fleet: "When they [the Turks] have what they desire, that is, all the Indian ships in, and their ships and galleys from Mecca, then thinking himself strong, [the aga] will use you at his pleasure and like a Judas, . . . embrace you with a kiss and for the lucre of money, . . . betray you again" (*LR*, 1:58–59). The general had occasion to escape on 9 March, but he held off, he explains, for fear of leaving other men behind— particularly Femell, who would "by no means be drawn to" attempt it (P, 3:153, 239).

As the days passed, the mariners grew increasingly restless for Middleton to join them. Pemberton, the escape artist, recommended that the general impersonate a working sailor to slip away: "I think in disguising yourself in apparel, and to have your hair cut from your face, and besmutting yourself, and with a burden," it could be done. "I will be ready with my boat at the buoy of our anchor with shot to second you, and with my ordnance which will command half the way to the town, to rescue [you]," he promised (*LR*, 1:64). He closed another letter of 17 March, "desiring that God, who delivered the prophet David from the hands of wicked Saul many times, and Daniel from the jaws of the lions," will "deliver you out of the claws of those bloodthirsty lions, and grant you with speed your former liberty" (*LR*, 1:60). The next day—abstractly, to evade Turkish comprehension—Downton seconded the plan: "What passed from W. Pemberton to you was a thing among us ever thought, and what passed from you to him, . . . I well applaud, and therefore am come in the *Peppercorn* to observe and follow whatsoever you shall think good in your discretion to direct." Yet he recommended caution: "Put not yourself to a desperate point in your remove, while there is hope by other means" (*LR*, 1:61). Like Pemberton, he feared that, once the incoming ships had offloaded their goods in Mocha, Middleton would remain a prisoner, "to be ransomed at their pleasures, or sent back again to Zenan, and so to Stambola [Istanbul]" (D in P, 3:238).

The nature of those "other means" came clear in a second missive Downton penned to Middleton that day—a "bragging or threatening letter" like January's—framed for Regib Aga's eye. Downton explains in the journal that "if he should think good to show [the letter to] the Aga," it would prove "that so long as he was detained prisoner, his power extended not to command us that were free and at liberty" (P, 3:238). The argument replicated Middleton's initial protest to Regib Aga that he could not compel the mariners to "come a-land and be slaves" (P, 3:130–31), as well as the general's January warning to Ja'far Basha that if things went poorly for him in Sana'a, he could not restrain the fleet:

> There is no faithful performance to be expected from these truthless Turks. Wherefore, Sir, since you are in the tyrant's hands, I perceive you dare not do yourself right by any means which may offend the Aga; wherefore I pray you, with patience, give ear and consider that . . . now you are separated from us, and persuade for the Turks' content, I will no way obey you, but by the help of our great God, I purpose so to command and dispose of these ships as I shall think fittest, and if yourself, our people and provisions be not sooner restored and set at liberty, I trust by the help of God to make it as costly bringing of goods to the scale of Mocha as ever have been formerly known. (LR, 1:63–64)[13]

A postscript shamed their inaction as a failure of manhood: "Further, a report is brought with our people from Mocha, that the Turks have taxed us with conceit that we are not men, but women in men's apparel, else they say we would endeavor to make our own peace by force" (LR, 1:64).

It was one thing for Middleton to make such an argument, another for Downton. Either misconstruing or opposing the suggestion that the letter held tactical use if shown to Regib Aga, Middleton took deep umbrage at the message. He found it terribly timed. He responded with two stern letters of his own: one, which Downton copied into his journal on 19 March, desiring the *Peppercorn* to depart for the opposite coast the next day—"Captain Downton, your overmuch care may work your own harms, and do me and my company no good" (D in P, 3:238)—and another of 23 March (extant) to more forceful effect. Having duly left Mocha road on the twentieth, Downton received the latter on the twenty-fifth. Middleton expressed confidence that Regib Aga would obey the "Vizier Basha" and free them to sail off with the western monsoon—but only on condition that the English fleet avoid Mocha and its traffic in the meantime. The repeated "us" and "we" in the general's second letter, while variously referencing himself, others ashore, and the entire fleet, also echoed royal usage: it voiced the authority he wrote to reclaim. His "I" spoke at once for himself and the group person:

> I marvel what you can attempt, to give us full relief, or rather what
> can you do that will not more increase the flame. We have as much
> leisure and better means and experience to consider the depth of
> things touching that point, better than you or any other that have
> neither been actors nor spectators of what is passed and present,
> which afford us the preeminence to judge of that to come; neither
> think you we are insensible of the reputation of my country or
> myself, as time (by God's grace) shall hereafter manifest; neither that
> I fear or am obliged to the Turks, but could have been as safe aboard
> as yourself if I had not tendered the welfare of those that be here
> under my charge as becometh me in my place. (*LR*, 1:65)

"I" and "we" versus "you": in a superior vein, Middleton dismisses Downton's presumption that captivity has compromised the "preeminence" of the general's judgment and that a seaborne perspective should outweigh his landed observations. He and others ashore, not mariners sifting rumor and report, are the "actors" and "spectators" of the relevant Anglo-Ottoman drama. The tone is prideful, paternalistic, self-assured: We were there, you were not; I remain here to protect my people; you do not know what we know.

Noting that the aga desired the return of the man captured in the assault on the *Darling*, and fearing that this individual might create difficulties by reporting overheard plots for vengeance after Middleton returned to the ships, the general proposed that Thornton, "in the presence of the [Arabs], should set him free" aboard the *Trades Increase*, "and you [Downton] . . . come aboard and detain him" as a hostage for their release (*LR*, 1:66).[14] Thornton indicates that they performed this scenario (*LR*, 1:83). Resolved to stay in town for the time being, Middleton requested that Thornton "send me my two silk waistcoats, . . . my Grogran cloak and half the tobacco in my counter." Adding, "I have liberty to go where I will all day," he was evidently disposed to enjoy the season in Mocha (*LR*, 1:68).

Purchas's edition of Downton's journal cuts directly from 19 to 27 March. The manuscript, however, ventilates the lieutenant general's distress upon receipt of Middleton's letter, which he could not bring himself to copy. "Monday the 25th there came over from Mocha a jelba which brought part of our provisions formerly detained in Mocha, and in her John Williams bringing me a letter from my general, dated the 23rd of this present, being (by my supposition) a misconstruction of my former letters, by some malicious, fear blasted, caviling fellow to whom my general had showed my letters, his letter being very carping and most distasteful, which shall be needless to write" (D, f36v, 25 March 1611). Visiting the *Peppercorn* at this interval, Pemberton advised Middleton that he saw Downton "shed tears of grief that his good meaning should be ill taken." The *Darling*'s captain continued, "It grieveth me to see him in that sort, so grieved that hardly he could speak at my departure, but requested me to remember his duty to you, and wished evil to himself if ever he meant evil to Sir Henry Middleton, and truly I dare swear it" (*LR*, 1:84). Downton could not bear either the general's rebuke or the imputation that he had disrespected Middleton and his office. Displacing the censure, he converted his pain into rancor against the presumed "fear blasted, caviling fellow" who induced the general to misconstrue the letter. He surely suspected Femell, whose determination to stay in Mocha Middleton had noted (D in P, 3:239), and whose fearfulness Downton twice reports in the journal: when the cape merchant fled the grounded *Trades Increase*, and when, having returned to the ship in "some sudden apprehension of fear (as in faint-hearted people never wants)," he hesitated to disembark with Middleton into Mocha (D in P, 3:222, 226). Temperamental differences divided him from Femell—one a seasoned seaman and combat veteran, the other a corpulent merchant who enjoyed his creature comforts—and Downton resented Femell's intimacy with the general.[15] Their commission enjoined the principal mariners to "carry themselves with due respect one to another," so that "love and kindness may be continued on all sides" (Birdwood, 329); yet the fierce anxieties of captivity in Yemen, superadded to the baseline irritants of close cohabitation at sea, placed that ideal beyond reach. The fleet festered with deep, guardedly touched resentments.

Downton's response the next day churns with consternation, sorrow, wounded pride, and suspicion: "Sir, Yours of the 23rd I have read, in which the bitterness, the unkind and strange construction made there of mine formerly, fills my mind with admiration and grief. I could readily answer every disjointed and cross point therein, but at this time I hold it better to forbear, being unwilling to grieve Sir Henry Middleton, as he, by other's device, doth wrong me. Sir, I can write nothing so plain . . . but malicious men when they list may make injurious construction, but evil come to me if I meant ill to Sir Henry Middleton or any part of the business" (*LR*, 1:81). As if hesitating to look him in the eye, Downton signals both alienation from and respect for Middleton by moving from the second to the third person, from "yours" to "he"—invoking the general as a figure who, like the monarch, a corporation of one, embodies two persons, one corporeal and presently captive, another perpetual and authoritative. Downton insists that his declared intent to take command of the fleet and blockade Mocha was a bluff. The crisis between them hinges on different ways of reading: Middleton fastens on content—literal statements—Downton on speech acts with situational interpretations. To steady himself, Downton again reads past Middleton's words to their rationale and plausible origin. "Sir Henry Middleton can do himself no right by wronging of me. God be judge between him and me, if ever I deserved the least evil thought from him, neither do I think Sir Henry Middleton did ever peruse or read this whole letter now sent me, else would I desire of God that he were so much himself, that he would neither be led nor carried by any injurious person to abuse an inseparable friend" (*LR*, 1:81). Refusing to accept that Middleton conceived and wrote the hurtful words, or perhaps even read them all before signing the letter, Downton, "an inseparable friend," invites Middleton to disavow the rebuke. Still, the ploy risks reaggravating the general by again positing him as a mouthpiece—earlier of the Turks, now of some "injurious person" (*LR*, 1:82)—not as a responsible author, the preeminent English strategist in the region.

The trouble between them inhered in their confinement to corporate discourse: to the letters necessitated by their separation. By putting nonciphered words to paper, one relinquishes control of their reception: "It was in private to Sir Henry Middleton to consider of," he complains, "not intended to the view of any malicious, snarling, nor fear-blasted fellow to coat, conster and cavil at, according to the weakness of their dejected spirits" (*LR*, 1:82). To suppress private scheming and foster shared interests, the East India Company desired its agents to produce texts with multiple authors and readers, but Downton—alert to other readers both foreign and collegial—now craves private communication with his general. Lacking that, one had best stop writing: "It is somewhat to be warned thereby, that there are snares set for me, which plot the better to prevent, I will henceforth be sparing to write, or not at all." His textual dependencies have fostered paranoid suspicions, and a quest for common ground with Middleton, in the supposition that others have conspired against them: "You are abused herein as well as myself." Once back at sea, the general will behold, face to face, Downton's submission to his authority: "I desire God to send you and all the rest into safety aboard, where you may satisfy your will on me as you please, since you may be assured I will not swerve a jot from your commands" (LR, 1:82). Erasing the defiant speech act of his prior letter, Downton expresses hope that their reunion will inoculate them against the pernicious counsel of unnamed colleagues. Rather than promising "love and kindness . . . on all sides" as their employers desired (Birdwood, 329), his capitulation factionalizes the Company.

Mollified by this letter, the general responded with an ameliorative message. He desired Downton "not to construe his last melancholy letter at the worst, informing me that he hath no doubt of the Turks' performance . . . when the westerly winds are come." He promised to make his escape if need be. In the meantime, he called for the hulls of the ships to be "made clean and trimmed" for readier sailing (D, f38, 6 April 1611). Enhanced speed would be useful if escape or blockade proved necessary. The fleet had been at sea for a full year now, their wooden hulls collecting sea worms, macroalgae, seaweeds, barnacles and other molluscs that slowed their progress and, over time, introduced leakage.[16] Under Downton's supervision, at a low island off the coast, they began with the *Darling*. Having carried foodstuffs, casks, and cargo ashore to lighten the ship, "by the continual attendance of all the boats manned out of the other ships" (LR, 1:85), they careened the hull, "trimmed to the keel on both sides," and rerigged the vessel (D, f38, 17 April 1611). The equivalent task on the *Peppercorn* took until 28 April, when that ship rejoined the others near the watering place on the Abyssinian shore. As they expected the western monsoon to begin any day and desired, with Middleton aboard, to follow it out of the Red Sea, full treatment of the flagship's massive hull surpassed them at this juncture. Downton had it "heeled and trimmed on both sides, so far as conveniently might be," on 30 April (D, f39v, 30 April 1611).

Amid these labors, the crews were not doing well. From the *Peppercorn*, Downton wrote to Middleton that they were bereft of candles and lamp oil, short of money to buy fresh victuals, their peas long gone, their wheat nearly spent, their bread "musty"; that "a great part of my men are sick" and they lacked the medicinal herbs to treat them because, the surgeon informed him, the "apothecary carried them ashore at Aden" and, when captured, lost them

(*LR*, 1:86; D, f38v, 20 April 1611). In the journal, Downton noted the deaths of two *Peppercorn* crewmen, John Scot and John Barber, formerly "betrayed at Aden" (D, f37v, 27 March 1611; f38, 19 April 1611). While noting the careening of the *Darling* and trimming of the *Trades Increase* (D in P, 3:240), the Purchas edition does not describe the protracted labors involved. Nor does it invoke the mortal hardships—the hunger, the sickness, the deaths in the fleet—during Middleton's resumed residence in Mocha.

Escape from Mocha

Upon their return, Middleton and Greene described the city that would hold them for the next two months. "The town of Mocha," wrote Middleton, is "unwalled, very populous, and seated close by the seaside in a salt, sandy, barren soil. The governor's house is close by the water's side, and here by the same is the quay or bridge which shooteth a pretty distance into the sea, to which quay all boats belonging to any shipping are enjoined to land for fear of stealing of custom. And close adjoining the quay is a platform whereon are planted some dozen of brass pieces [cannon]; at the western end of the town is a fort wherein is the like quantity of ordnance" (M in P, 3:152). Greene described Mocha as "a town of one thousand houses built of lime and stone . . . situated upon the seaside upon a plain and lowland." He explained the anchorage: "It hath a good road for small ships drawing but ten or twelve foot water. They may ride in three fathom in very smooth water with the land on both sides, on which the continual and firm wind doth blow." Larger ships had to exercise caution to avoid shoals, dropping anchor in less sheltered waters north of town. Greene took special interest in the mixed social order: "The inhabitants are Jews or Bannians who are merchants and artificers, and Arabs who are very poor and live by fishing and tilling and dressing their grounds; and the residue are Turks and Arabs who are soldiers that live by the labor of those whom I have formerly set down, not endeavoring themselves . . . to get their living by other means than by extortion, not caring how they come by it so they may have it, as partly by their entertainment of us may appear." Discerning common cause with those oppressed by the military class, Greene adds mordantly, "They told us [it] was a great favor that, notwithstanding they took our goods, that they took not our lives also, for so is their custom even with the very inhabitants themselves" (G, f3–f4, 5

March 1611). An upwardly mobile Englishman of middling station who valorizes the industrious groups that create wealth, Greene articulates his critique along proto-orientalist lines: Ottoman governance is a vast extortion racket.

Springtime was the season of arrivals from India. The great ships kept pulling in, disgorging merchants and passengers in civic festivities that, for East India Company spectators, drove home their own inconsequence. A captive witness to eastern opulence, Greene itemized with enthusiasm the cargo of the initial ship from Dabull, "pepper of Dabull which is as good as that of Priaman, also Musilpatan stuffs, sashes of all sorts, indigo of Golconda," coconuts and coconut oil, timber, "also great store of passengers, merchants and pilgrims, five hundred persons, those are the best soldiers of all India . . . the Nohuda [Melick Amber] had at his coming ashore to conduct to him one hundred small shot" (G, f4, 5 March 1611).[17] On 1 April arrived "a second ship from Dabull, burden 400 tons or thereabouts, laden with the like commodities as the first" (G, f4, 1 April 1611). Greene and Middleton tallied that month's arrivals great and small: a dozen vessels from Dabull, Achin, Ceylon, Cannanor, Calicut, Goa, Diu, the Maldives, Malabar, and a great caravan from Damascus, Suez, and Mecca "to trade with the merchants of India" (M in P, 3:155).

Like its predecessor, the second ship from Dabull was "full of people," noted Middleton, who added dismissively, "The Nohuda rid about the town in a painted coat, as the manner is. These coats are but lent them for the present, and afterward returned to the keeper of the wardrobe, to whom belongs a duty for the loan of them" (P, 3:154). "Painted" cues the reader to the defensive antitheatricalism of these remarks. Implicitly likening the ship's captain to a costumed stage player, Middleton frames the arrival as an ephemeral spectacle, a pompous show as insubstantial as his own hour in the sun there. But unlike the English, the Indian merchants brought cargoes coveted in Mocha and enjoyed durable favor with Ottoman authorities. Their receptions celebrated substantial commitments. In a further bid to salvage self-respect, Middleton then took up the orientalist critique of eastern potentates as, in fact, slaves. The three great ships of Dabull, he explained, were owned by that region's governor, "a Persian, and a great merchant, and hath many slaves, whereof Melick Amber is one . . . he is a negro born in Habesse, . . . and now never goeth out of his doors but with great troops of followers, like some great Lord" (3:154). Middleton's antitheatrical descants on the hollowness of Turko-Persian greatness defended against the stark recognition of England's utter marginality in this great Euro-Asian market.

Exhorted repeatedly by Pemberton and Downton to make his escape, as the seasonal shift in the winds approached, Middleton grew restless for his liberty. He understood that all the ships expected from India that year had come in. Yet, when he petitioned the aga for his promised release, reported Downton after the fact, "he had a harsh and careless answer" (D, f41, 13 May 1611). On 9 May, Downton wrote to inform him of a top-secret rumor from "one of the Budwees" (the people of the Eritrean coast) who had just heard from Arabs in Mocha "that the Basha had sent to Suez for twenty five galleys" and ordered Regib Aga to arrange for Indian mariners to arm their vessels to "surprise our ships, or at least to resist the further aid we might give to our general's enlargement" (D, f40, 9 May 1611). Hamet Aga and others likewise advised Middleton that fear alone would make Ja'far Basha "perform his word" (M in P, 3:156). He concluded that it was time to act.

Unsure of the hesitant Femell, before sharing the plans with him, Middleton "made him swear unto me to be secret and to use no persuasions with me to withdraw my mind from that I had resolved upon" (3:156). The scheme exploited the fact that Middleton was the only Englishman closely watched. While the others could walk about the town freely by day, "I never went out of doors, but two or three soldiers attended upon me" (3:157). Communal festivities on 11 May supplied the opportunity. Departing at dawn, Regib Aga and "all the chief men of the town were rid abroad in great state to his garden to be merry" (3:156). With the *Darling* anchored near shore, the general wrote to Pemberton to dispatch a boat for their rescue. He also requested wine and a potent bottle of aqua vitae.

After the boat's arrival, Middleton, like Odysseus in the cave of Polyphemus, graciously inebriated his keepers. By midday, his principal guardian the subbasha returned drowsy from "drinking hard" at an arack house (3:157), and the others, Downton adds, "were all retired their houses to rest" (D, f41, 13 May 1611). Middleton directed the carpenters to walk leisurely in twos and threes by different routes down to the waterside south of town "where lay a boat hard by the shore, with mast and sail ready fitted for their purpose" (3:156–57). Then he made his move: he hid in an empty barrel that crewmen carried out to the *Darling*'s boat. Meanwhile, Femell and several others made their way to the lee waterside where Middleton had promised to meet them. Femell reported that the armorer Thomas Eves, however, having carried goods out to the quay, returned to fetch more at "a swift pace till he passed the Aga's house, then he took off his shoes and ran through the streets with all the force he could, whereupon all the town rose after him" (*LR*, 1:97; cf.

91). With the pursuit up, the rendezvous failed. Initially "too slack in coming out of the town" (3:158), then frightened and slowed by sickly companions, Femell's party was, by Middleton's account, "too sudden entering into the sea, so that you could not come to us nor we to you" (*LR*, 1:98): they should have walked out nearer the boat. Hearing the story from Middleton, Downton caustically inferred that the cape merchant's "unwieldy fatness hindered his present enlargement and diverse others'" (D, f41v, 13 May 1611). Femell, by contrast, blamed "that idiot and white livered fellow the coxswain, who, seeing us hardly pursued, and we waving to have the boat sheer in, we being in the water up to the armpits, fell to leeward of us" (*LR*, 1:91).

While the blaming was mutual, so were the blunders. Moving leeward, Middleton had taken in several men when he witnessed the desperation of Femell's party. In the rush to reach them, he ran the boat aground "to the no little danger of us all." Panic ensued: "I caused men to leap overboard to rescue him, but before they could get a pike's length from the boat, he and those with him were all apprehended: M. Femell discharged a pistol in the face of one of them . . . and mortally wounded him before he was taken." Femell described two soldiers assailing him: "I placed two bullets in one of them, who lieth by it, as I hear. The second purposing to have cloven my head, I warded it with my pistol, the blow was so violent that his sword fell out of his hand into the sea. By this time there came a Turk who knew me and protected me from further harm" (*LR*, 1:91). "It booted me not to stay longer" (3:158), Middleton wrote, understatedly. Those already afloat made their escape. Aboard the *Darling*, he learned from the carpenters in the other craft that one of their group, Walter Talbot, had reached the beach after they had put off, plunged in to swim after them, and vanished. A few days later, his body washed up on the shore (3:159; *LR*, 1:97). Long postponed for fear of collateral losses, the escape from Mocha proved costly.

Once on the *Darling*, Middleton held a sound position from which to negotiate the release of the remaining prisoners. After reading Femell's account of their angry reception by Regib Aga—who was saddened and offended at the general's flight, with casualties on both sides, some ten or fifteen days before he was supposedly to be freed—Middleton took up the long-craved posture of retaliatory self-assertion: "I . . . sent the Aga word, that if he did not send me all my people, with those provisions of the ships which he detained contrary to the Bashaes order, . . . I would fire the ships in the road, and do my best to batter the town about his ears. Likewise I sent word to the Nohudas, that they should not send any boat aboard the ships without first coming aboard of me, . . . nor to carry anything out of them a-land without my leave and order" (3:159). He was claiming command of the harbor. His hand was soon strengthened by the arrival of the *Peppercorn* and *Trades Increase*. As the *Darling* approached the flagship on the morning of 14 May, almost six months after Middleton had left it, Downton orchestrated shoreward rounds of ordnance from all three ships to "salute the general" and "to see how far our shot would fly" (D, f41v, 14 May 1611). The general was received aboard the *Trades Increase* "with great joy of all my company" (M in P, 3:161), he wrote. Downton awaited him there, enormously relieved and heartened by their reunion. The two men "passed the night," the latter wrote, "not without much conferences concerning our ensuing business, and [my general] relating to me the manner of his escape" (D, f40v, 13 May 1611).

The English fleet held two major points of leverage: over other merchant ships in the road and over neighborhoods within reach of their ordnance—an area which, they hoped, included Regib Aga's mansion (D, f42v, 16 May 1611). On 16 May, Middleton sent Femell a bold message reminiscent of the "bragging or threatening" letters Downton had sent him for the aga's review. His overnight conversation with Downton no doubt warmed Middleton to arguments that his return to the ship enhanced compellingly. He cautioned Regib Aga not to "presume too far for having you in his hand, neither let him think that I will be tied to anything . . . which . . . seemeth not good to myself." He protested that he would "burn the India ships, which are my friends, rather than I will lose the benefit of a revenge upon so vile a traitor" as Regib Aga, whose government has "spoiled the scale" of Mocha "and before long will cost him his head." Confident in the superiority of his ordnance, Middleton declared himself ready to prove "that I am commander by sea, as Regib Aga is by land." He defied even the sultan: "Though I should fire the town and beat it smooth about their ears, whether it be pleasing or displeasing to the Grand Seignor, I care not, I am out of the reach of his long sword" (*LR*, 1:102–3). The boast put him beyond the reach of his employers as well. Numerous East India Company shareholders held interests in the Levant Company, a body utterly dependent on the sultan's favor, and would have deplored these incendiary words. Hesitant to offend "our countrymen who are merchants in Turkey," Greene noted anxiously that "part of them [are] adventurers in this voyage" (G, f5, 22 June 1611).

On 16 May, Middleton personally visited the Malabar ships at anchor, "all the way sounding the depths," Downton noted, to bring the *Darling* and

Peppercorn "nearer the town, to play upon the Aga's house if occasion served, if our ordnance would reach the same" (D, f42v, 16 May 1611). With the English fleet commanding the harbor, the nohudas mediated between Middleton and Regib Aga, bringing gifts to the flagship, conveying messages, advocating amiable relations on all sides; and Regib Aga, Downton reported, "began to sing a new song" (P, 3:240). Protesting that he would soon have released Middleton in any case, he observed that he could not now free the remaining Englishmen without consulting Ja'far Basha in Sana'a, which would require some fifteen days. Regib Aga's two surviving letters of the interval graciously itemize the return of "three anchors and three cables, five barrels of pitch and tar," surgeon's tools, several guns and swords, Middleton's "gilded poniard" (with a promise to look for his rapier as well), and the gift of "four hundred loaves of bread, one ox and two baskets of plantains" among other things. Middleton wrote back to Femell, "I have received the ox which our adversary sent you, and we are half in doubt to eat him, coming from so manifest a professed enemy" (*LR*, 1:117): they feared poisoning. Requesting Middleton to allow an incoming ship from Diu "quietly to land"—the vessel's owner was their benefactor Shermall—Regib Aga requested, "I pray you let things be referred, as they must be, to our betters in Constantinople, and let us part friends" (*LR*, 1:99–100, 112). Though displeased to surrender the completed pinnace to the English, the aga consented to do so.

The numerous letters that Middleton and Femell exchanged during this interval illuminate not only their power plays but also matters rarely noted in the journals: the personal properties, habits, and cultural practices of the English community ashore and at sea. A writer of authoritative dispatches, Middleton greatly missed his "seal ring, . . . a thing of such use as I always feel the want of." To stamp molten wax with his insignia was integral to his identity. He desired Femell to ask the aga to command one Emir Bahr to surrender the ring. (The errand failed: under summons, "the Emir Bahr . . . swore deeply he had it not, nor knoweth where it is" [*LR*, 1:99, 104]). While in Sana'a, he had built an astronomical instrument to measure the city's latitude (M in P, 3:137), and he kept a log of his sightings: he wanted back "my written book of the declination, which I left in my chair bed" (*LR*, 1:122). ("Declination" may also refer to the compass variation from true north, a crude gauge of longitude.) The English found Mocha's markets alluring: barred from trade, those who could went shopping. With an eye to his wardrobe for India, Middleton asked Femell to purchase "a very fine piece of calico to make me clothes, such as John Williams said he saw in the market"

(1:109). Having developed a taste for coffee in Yemen, he wanted Femell to "buy some coho pots" (aka, "caffao pots") for the ship (1:122, 125). He hoped for the return of "my plate and yours, my quilt and canopy [of blue damask] for my bed, mine and your Turkey carpets, livery cloaks, rapier, ready money and emeralds of drunken Cheluby" (1:126, 101); Cheluby had no news of them (1:127). He was anxious about religious, literary, and esthetic items left behind in the escape: "I pray you will [direct] my man to send me my prayer book with the velvet cover, . . . Mr. Bownes his bible, cornet, viol, and what other books and instruments are there" (1:112). He reiterated the request several days later: "If you hear of the cornet or treble viol hereafter you may send them, lay wait for them, for the concert is spoiled without them" (1:123). Edifying books and music were important to Middleton and his men. Tonics of morale, they eased the tedium of confinement whether ashore or on the *Trades Increase* at sea.

On 26 May, Middleton sent Regib Aga a letter invoking the abuses he and his men had suffered "as captives led in triumph, and not as innocents betrayed," yet assuring the governor that, upon receipt of his pinnace and his men, the general bound himself "not to meddle with any ships in this sea" (*LR*, 1:128). Regib Aga thereupon freed Femell and the other nine captives, who were welcomed aboard the *Trades Increase* near sunset that day. Femell, reported Downton, "seemed overjoyed" (D in P, 3:241). He and two others wore vests gifted them by Regib Aga at their departure—"paltry vests of little worth," the general sniped—and, by Downton's report, the others, who probably needed them, brought gift fabrics: "slight stuff to make them clothes." Wearing another vest from the aga, Nohuda Mahomet, the captain of a ship from Calicut (D, f42, 14 May 1611) who negotiated the transfer and brought the Englishmen aboard, then produced a gift vest from Ja'far Basha for Middleton—"in their esteem, a rich vest," Downton remarked. Loath to don this Turkish garment in his English theater of state, Middleton indignantly refused it, "telling him, I scorned to wear any thing that should come from so unconscionable a dog as my enemy" (M in P, 3:163). His aversion was visceral: the vest evoked the one worn at his disastrous landing six months before. Downton described the awkward scene that ensued, as Nohuda Mahomet refused to take the vest back. Cooler heads persuaded Middleton to let this icon of his betrayal remain aboard (D, f43v, 26 May 1611). The standoff was revealing. If meant to project self-assurance, Middleton's testiness equally expressed the emotional strain of his months of captivity. The stance of defiance intoxicated him now. Perhaps to make amends for the rudeness, he reciprocated the carceral exchange and surrendered to Nohuda Mahomet the Turk seized in the failed assault on the *Darling*.

The next day, the pinnace was towed out to the *Trades Increase* and brought aboard. The general proudly named the craft the *Release* and made George Jeffe its master (D, f44, 27 May 1611). Their prospects were improving decidedly—yet briefly. Two nights later, Lawrence Femell, the man delegated to take charge of the factory in Surat, suddenly died. Shortly before his release, he had dined with Regib Aga. At their parting, the latter amiably recalled Femell's prior speeches about resolving their differences at Istanbul and, "with a smiling countenance, told him that they might meet together" there now (D in P, 3:241). At 2:00 A.M. on his third night aboard the flagship, Femell succumbed to a delirious fever or "calentura" (M in P, 3:164). The surgeons who opened his body claimed he had been poisoned. Middleton did not know what to believe. But his ongoing negotiations with Regib Aga were darkened by the gravest suspicion.

CHAPTER 4

To India and Back Again

Middleton regained the *Trades Increase* in mid-May, as the eastern monsoon weakened. The next leg of the journey was to take the western monsoon, reaching full strength in mid-August, to Surat. As set forth in their commission, the voyage's primary aim was to strengthen the factory there. The man designated to direct that operation, Lawrence Femell, had just died; yet corporate bodies outlive their personnel, and, as stipulated in the commission, John Fowler, the principal merchant of the *Peppercorn*, succeeded him (Birdwood, 326). In the meantime, the fleet had unfinished business to consummate in Mocha: reparations for the losses and indignities lately suffered. To consolidate friendships with an eye to the future, to reward the critical interventions in Yemen of brokers and magnates from Egypt to India, was not Middleton's priority. Nor did the Levant Company's need to preserve friendly Anglo-Ottoman relations mitigate the outrage of Sixth Voyage mariners over their brutal reception in Yemen. At a deep level, they were still thinking like privateers—corporate raiders—not empire builders. Sustainability was the furthest thing from Middleton's mind. He craved immediate compensation to restore his honor.

An important transnational figure, their benefactor Shermall was a person worth cultivating. The shabander, a principal port officer of Mocha, was the Banian consul. In that capacity, he maintained vital connections in Cambay, their next destination. His interventions on their behalf were legion, as Downton observed: he "daily relieved our men in their misery with bread and other sustenance, not so much as our dog but also had daily allowance from him; so that always his presence administered comfort to our distressed people" (D in P, 3:242). Yet, when his ship arrived from Diu on 18 May 1611,

Middleton, in defiance of Regib Aga's late request, detained the vessel to leverage the return of the remaining crewmen and the pinnace. As the negotiations began, Middleton's threats of violence against the town of Mocha exposed Shermall, a leading advocate of lenity toward the English, to grave risk. A few weeks later, Middleton refused to render Shermall the sum they had promised Ja'far Basha upon his release. Having underwritten it, Shermall, unless he could persuade the caya to forgive it, would have to pay it himself. Consumed by his venture's frustrations, Sir Henry was resolved to assert English power at sea, to redeem his losses and depart for India, not to honor debts ashore.

Reparations in the Red Sea

At Shermall's entreaty, Middleton let passengers and pilgrims disembark from the former's ship but anchored the vessel near the *Trades Increase*, took down its sails, and removed its pilot to the flagship (M in P, 3:161–62; D, f42v, 20 May 1611). On 27 May, the morning after Femell and the others came aboard, the general called a tactical summit. With the prisoners returned and the pinnace under tow toward them, the principal mariners debated "whether [they] should release the ships according to promise or detain them till restitution were made." The council was divided. The English still had goods ashore, as well as Richard Phillips, Pemberton's boy, who had fallen ill in Tais on the march upland and remained there, "forced to turn Turk" (D in P, 3:237). Some believed it fruitless to demand his return until they seized hostages from a ship rumored to arrive shortly from Suez. Middleton preferred to bargain from their current position: to reward the nohudas' goodwill by allowing the Indian ships to unload some cargo, yet to keep them in awe. Having received and christened the pinnace, Middleton sent the Diu ship's pilot ashore in the craft that towed the *Release* to them. Then he directed Shermall's vessel to reanchor near the *Peppercorn* and the *Darling*, where the pair were poised, Downton explained, "to command all the ships in the road, or if need were, to play upon the Aga's house" (D, f44, 27 May 1611). It is worth noting that the deep draft of the *Trades Increase* removed its more copious artillery from any credible range on the town: as Raleigh argued to Prince Henry, sometimes great size was a deficit.

The first of June brought oppressive heat and a fierce onshore sandstorm that broke the land cable of the *Trades Increase* and drove Middleton into his

cabin (P, 3:164, 241). In more temperate conditions the next day, Allee Has-
kins, a Portuguese former captive and convert to Islam who had served as
Middleton's interpreter in Sana'a, came aboard the flagship with commendations from the capital.[1] He reported that the basha's gifts of a rich vest and a
horse were meant to dignify Middleton's open, not a stolen, departure; and
he conveyed the caya's hopes that Middleton would seek justice in Istanbul
before taking "any violent courses" here, which would cost him, the principal
advocate of Middleton's liberty, his head (M in P, 3:165). Allee had brought
Richard Phillips to Mocha and offered to deliver him the next day if Sir
Henry let the Indian ships unload their cargoes. Middleton refused. To free
the ships, the general demanded from Ja'far Basha the exorbitant sum of
70,000 rials of eight. Downton put the amount at 100,000 rials (P, 3:165,
241). The figure was rhetorical: a measure of honor.

Upon receipt of this demand, Regib Aga requested twelve days of peace
to consult Ja'far Basha and invited Middleton to document his losses. Gratified to rehearse these, the general indignantly maligned the aga as "a treacherous dog" who, having promised "kind entertainment and free and peaceable
trade, . . . without any cause or offense given, had cruelly slain divers of my
people and villainously imprisoned myself and others, and spoiled all he
could seize upon." Lacking full satisfaction, Middleton was prepared to "batter the town about his ears, take all the goods out of the Diu ship into mine
own, and burn all the ships in the road, and not depart thence till I were
sufficiently revenged: all which I could do without breach of promise, . . .
they not having performed covenants with me" (P, 3:165–66).

The suspected poisoning of Femell had clearly abrogated his vow of 26
May "not to meddle with any ships in this sea." Sir Henry was not in a
diplomatic vein. Likewise, Regib Aga's 6 June response was, as Middleton
put it, "peremptory." He demanded, "Who gave me leave to come into these
seas"; explained that their stern reception, which derived not from him but
from the basha, justly followed from his lawless arrival; and declared that if
displeased by the result, the general should refer the case "to the hearing of
our betters" in Istanbul, where the sultan "would be sure to be recompensed
for any harm" the English might inflict on the ships in the road or the town
of Mocha (3:166). In the meantime, if Middleton fired on the town, Regib
Aga would respond in kind.

Middleton answered by asserting the freedom of the seas—"to come into
this sea, I needed no leave but God's and my king's"—and insisted "I must
and would be paid" here and now: "even there where I had been wronged,

would I be righted: and if they found themselves aggrieved, they might go to the court of England to seek their remedy, for to Stambola I minded not to go" (3:165–66). For Middleton, the relevant arbiter of the standoff was not Achmed I but King James, who answered directly to God. With the dispatch of this reply, he went aboard the *Peppercorn* to confer with Downton about a show of force. Complaining that Regib Aga "did but dally with him," he commanded the lieutenant general to turn his ship broadside toward the town and prepare to fire on the aga's house. A cooler tactician, Downton cautioned against this. He feared that they might thereby betray "the insufficiency of our pieces to reach so far, which their silence kept them ever in [doubt] of" (D, f44v, 6 June). It was wiser to let the Turks fear their firepower than hazard a spectacle of insufficiency. The next day, the *Peppercorn* pulled back and anchored near the *Trades Increase*.

As a strange sickness spread among the crews, "a faint disease" that afflicted everyone and "went away in boils and scabs" (D in P, 3:241–42), Middleton, hesitant to resort to Mocha for fear of poisoning, sent the *Darling* to the opposite coast for fresh victuals (3:167). Word arrived on 15 June that, the basha having responded to Middleton's latest demands, Shermall would appear the next day to negotiate an agreement. When boats from the shore approached on the sixteenth without him, Downton learned that Shermall was delayed because tailors were making clothes "after the English fashion" for Richard Phillips, whom the consul intended to bring with him (D, f45, 16 June 1611). If Phillips was indeed "forced to turn Turk" (P, 3:237) in Tais, by gifting him "new clothes after the Christian fashion" (M in P, 3:167), Shermall graciously reversed that transformation to return the boy ceremoniously.

Downton described the scene on 19 June when Shermall, "accompanied with many of the chiefest merchants of the town, and the Alle Haskie and Tacaccee [aka 'Tocorsie, the Sabander's man' (3:169)], a Banian, came in state with diverse sorts of music" to the *Trades Increase* to negotiate an agreement (P, 3:242). The consul declared to Middleton that "he had always loved and favored me and my people" and was grieved by their injuries "as if it had been done to his own people." He explained further that his "love and pitying of me in my miseries" had put him in a precarious situation: the basha threatened now "to cut his throat, and seize upon his goods" unless he managed to placate Middleton and negotiate the fleet's peaceful exit from the Red Sea. The basha, that is, had passed to Shermall the burden of satisfying Middleton. No reparations would be forthcoming from the Ottomans. At least one of Middleton's colleagues, Greene, insisted that they had to protect Shermall. Greene argued that a violent course "might not only endanger our country-men who are merchants in Turkey, and part of them adventurers in this voyage." Thus to bring harm to Shermall could also blight their voyage's prospects and damage England's reputation in India. The shabander, "an Indian of Cambay, and the chiefest means under God for our delivery, should be sure therefore to lose his head, and all his goods to be confiscate, which would be blasted all India over to the great dishonor of our country and nation, as also prejudicial to our future pretences for trade in those parts" (G, f5, 22 June 1611). In Greene's view, both moral and strategic concerns demanded an irenic resolution.

Seeing it as a matter of personal honor, however, Middleton desired the Turks alone to render him compensation. He protested: "It was the Turks that had robbed me, and done me many injuries, and from them would I look to satisfaction, and not from any other." Shermall quietly requested that the general abandon such talk and enumerate his demands. When Middleton invoked his late hyperbolical request, Shermall answered, "It were but labor lost for have further conference" at that level (P, 3:167). So they began again. Haggling most of the day over the costs of commodities, Shermall induced Sir Henry to think more like a businessman than a dishonored knight. They settled on the substantial yet feasible sum of 18,000 rials, payable to Middle-ton within two weeks—"to come out of . . . our friend his purse," Downton noted (P, 3:242)—together with restoration of their lead and iron still ashore. Middleton also declared his willingness to sign a two-year Anglo-Ottoman nonaggression pact, "from the Port of Mocha to Cannanor" (3:168)—an agreement that Ja'far Basha never confirmed (3:169).[2] Shermall lacked the ready money, so he offered Middleton partial payment in goods from the Diu ship. By Downton's report, the English boarding party fastened on precious commodities: sixty bales of indigo and seven packs of "fine Indian cloths" (D, f46, 21 June 1611). This act of appropriation set a quiet precedent for more peremptory practice in the Red Sea the following year.

Shermall arrived with his final payment on 2 July, and Middleton "cleared all reckonings with him," both for money lent during Middleton's captivity and expenses since. His favor toward the English was proving costly. When Shermall asked for the 1,000 venetianos Middleton had promised the caya in Sana'a, the latter rudely refused, "although he much urged me with my word and promise, and that he should be forced to pay, for that he had passed his word for the same. I told him the caya had not performed what he promised me, in setting me and my people at liberty. How the caya and he will agree, I know not" (P, 3:168). The caya had not performed his promise because Middleton had made his own escape. He no longer cared about the consul's debts in Sana'a. Shermall's 18,000 rials covered the interim losses of the voyage's investors, and the fleet was on its way to India.

With another wave of sickness visiting the ships—"It began with a great pain in the head and stomach, bereaving them of sleep," and led to a fever that killed several (P, 3:168)—they departed for the Abyssinian coast on 3 July to find fresh victuals and await the monsoon. Ever suspicious, Middleton had the wells there "emptied and cleansed for fear of poisoning, for it was often told me at Mocha, the Turks practiced with the people of Assab to poison the wells" (P, 3:169). But they were graciously received. An embassy headed by Abdella, the nephew of the king of Rahaita, arrived on 13 July with "three fat bullocks" (3:243) and a letter of welcome offering "any thing I stood in need of and that his country did afford" and "rejoicing [in] my escape from my enemies" (3:169). Middleton feasted them aboard the *Trades Increase*, regaled them that evening with sweetmeats and wine ashore, thanked them for their kindness, and offered them "a present to the king their master: which was a vest of broadcloth and a fair looking glass" (3:169, 243). Thus the king might contemplate his image wearing a prime English export scarcely marketable in hot regions: broadcloth. They invited Middleton to relocate to a good harbor off their town near Bab-el-Mandeb, a place "more plentiful of refreshing," reported Downton, "where [the king] might better show his love unto the general" (3:243). The fleet remained in place.

A few days later, a jelba carrying Tocorsie and another Banian arrived with provisions Middleton had ordered, money owed him, and word that Ja'far Basha had not confirmed the proposed pact, "so that it was manifest he intended to keep no quarter with our nation" (3:169). The inference that their hostilities endured motivated Middleton, in evident unconcern for Shermall's danger from such behavior, to plot forceful action before they left the Red Sea. When the Banians departed on 19 July, Downton reported that Middleton, "carrying fresh in memory the murder of his men and hateful disgrace done to himself and his people by the bloodthirsty merciless Turks," called a council (D, f48). Somewhere to their north, a richly laden Turkish galleon, accompanied by a few galleys, sailed from Suez toward Mocha. On board were "many Turkish merchants on whom the general had hope to do himself right in the eye of the world, if God blessed him to meet her" (D, f48). He desired thus, Middleton declared, "to be sufficiently revenged for all my losses and disgraces offered me by the Turks" (P, 3:169–70). His understanding that "the traitor Jeffor Basha and his disciple Regib Aga had great adventures [investments] in her" (3:170) lent a distinct thrill to the prospect of its capture.

No one opposed the mission. Identifying his personal honor with the dignity of England, the general led the foray like a prototype of Captain Ahab. The hunt began on 24 July. Sailing by day, compelled to anchor at night, plying to and fro without a pilot through shoal waters in shifting, prevalently northern winds, Middleton put the *Trades Increase* to repeated and entire risk—"Many times [we] were like to have come aground, to the hazard and loss of all, had not God preserved us" (M in P, 3:170)—in the thwarted quest to intercept the galleon. On the *Darling*, Greene complained of the "many broken grounds, shoals, and sands" that made "the sea by night un-navigable," observing that "our Admiral, not long since, [was] like to come aground upon a rock of coral (as we supposed) out of sight of any land" (G, f5v, 1–2 August 1611). Having reached the Islands of "Juball Succor" (Jabal Zucar) and "Juball Arree" (Hanish al Kabir), they found shelter in deep water close to the latter, the southernmost, and waited. No galleon appeared.

Reconsidering the wisdom of his quest for vengeance, an aggrieved Middleton decided that it was, in Downton's words, "too much hazard to pursue things uncertain" (3:244), and he turned the fleet back toward Assab, where they regained safe harbor on the evening of 2 August (D, f49). On the fourth, conversing with men from a passing jelba who knew the island of "Cameran" (or "Comorinde") where they had hoped to find the galleon, Middleton called another council to consider whether they might, "without prejudice to our succeeding voyage," sail north again to avenge themselves. The proposal was soundly defeated. Greene for one feared that capturing the ship might precipitate "great losses" for their countrymen in the Levant, and he saw no point in putting themselves at risk with small likelihood of success (G, f5v). The western monsoon was nearly upon them. They needed time to stop in Socotra to buy aloes and leave a letter warning subsequent Christian mariners to avoid the Red Sea. So they prepared for the voyage east. The crews filled empty water casks, washed clothes, and readied the ships for departure. They set sail early on 6 August with a farewell visit to Mocha, whose anchorage they attained that evening. Moored near the town wall, emptied of its cargo, sat the coveted galleon. It had "missed us as we were entangled amongst the shoals" and arrived unmolested, Downton remarked (P, 3:245).

Though the English made no further demand for reparations from the Turks, tensions marked this parting visit to the site of their incarceration. Greene heard from Banian mariners that four galleys, "either tonight or tomorrow . . . would attempt all means possible, either by fire or otherwise, to do us some mischief" (G, f6, 6 August 1611). Having boarded the *Peppercorn*, Middleton brought it and the *Darling* commandingly close to the shore and the other ships in the road. There, "our old friend Taccacee and Sabrage, the Shabander's man, came aboard with a present from Shermall the Shabander," Downton reported (P, 3:245). Among the tasks at hand was the exchange of letters. From the nohuda Melick Amber of Dabull, they desired letters of introduction for that port on India's west coast. Though this individual did not appear, in his place several Banians boarded the *Peppercorn* with, Downton explained, "commendations to the general from diverse principal Turks of the town" and Melick Amber's letters. Middleton entrusted to Tocorsie a reciprocal letter, "in case he [Melick Amber] should meet at sea any of our nation." He also gave Tocorsie letters for Shermall to convey via Cairo to the East India Company in London. Among their guests were, by Downton's account, two "ordinary fellows" from the Indian ships who offered their services as pilots to Surat. Yet, when their lowest bid of 60 rials failed to meet the highest English offer of 50, "they departed as they came" (D, f50–50v, 8 August 1611). With the *Darling* and the *Release* advancing to sound the depths, the parsimonious English found their own way out of the Red Sea.

To Socotra and the Gulf of Cambay

The ships made a relatively easy transit on 10 August 1611 through the straights of Bab-el-Mandeb—the *Darling* and the *Release* by the wide western passage that the Turks, by Middleton's account, claimed unnavigable, the *Peppercorn* and the *Trades Increase* by the more fortifiable eastern channel (P, 3:170)—into the Gulf of Aden. There, with Mount Felix in sight on the Arabian coast, a swift current pulling southwest compromised their progress toward Cape Guardafui (3:171). Near the cape on 28 August in the *Darling*, Greene noted "a steady gale" from south-southwest and "a great sea, the current setting to the northwards." As conditions worsened the next day ("a great stress of wind and foul weather"), most of the *Darling*'s sails were blown from the yards (G, f6v), and on the *Peppercorn*, the main yard broke and the mainsail split. Driven by a "hollow sea" (post-gale waves) while the carpenter repaired the yard, Downton lost view of the admiral and feared being carried past Socotra altogether. In the meantime, he and his master's mates were at odds over their location. Recognizing landmarks, Downton "perfectly descried" Socotra in the distance, though it was partly obscured by fog. Others maintained they were not yet east of Guardafui; the land in view, they insisted, was either the cape or Abd-el-Kuri, an island west of Socotra. Taking quiet amusement at the divided views of his navigators, Downton offered to wager that it was indeed Socotra ("to confirm the former, it was not offered to lay £10 to 40 shillings" [f52–52v]), but he found no takers. Late that night, heading eastward with a southwest wind, they were greatly relieved to see, in the distance off their lee bow, the flagship's light.

With some difficulty, on 31 August the *Peppercorn* reunited with the fleet in Delisha, a bay on Socotra's northern coast where three Indian ships also rested. The nohuda of the largest—"a ship of Diu of some 400 tons, carrying, in merchants, passengers, and sailors, some 700 men" (D, f53)—had visited the *Trades Increase* the day before with their second notice of the *Ascension*'s loss, along with happier news of Englishmen in Surat and the good fortunes of Captain Hawkins of the Third Voyage (G, f7, 30 August 1611). Middleton learned that, as England's emissary to the Mughal court, Hawkins "was made a great Lord, and had great allowance from the king by the year." He also heard that Emperor Jahāngīr had given Captain Sharpeigh, late of the *Ascension*, "money to build a ship, which was then almost ready at Surat to be launched. This and many other things he told me," Middleton added, "which I doubted to be true" (P, 3:171). While skeptical of the captain's Panglossian reports, Middleton clearly did not anticipate the stunning reversals awaiting them in India.

With Downton and others on the thirty-first, "taking with him a good guard" (G, f7), Middleton went ashore to deal with the ruler over aloes, entrust to him a letter advising other East India Company mariners to expect courtesy in Socotra but to shun the Red Sea, and converse with Indian mariners about the seas and markets of Cambay. Mulli Hamour Bensaid, about to depart for Tamrida, received them in the pavilion of the Diu ship's captain, where Middleton gifted him, Downton detailed, "a vest of purple broadcloth." The nohuda and his company prepared a banquet, "which most consisted of preserved mangoes and mirablanes [myrobalan plums], as big as a great walnut" (D, f53v). The next day, Bensaid returned to Tamrida, and the English determined to press on to India. Greene reports that Middleton went ashore again on 4 September to take his leave of the "country people" and the Indians and to ask the Diu ship's captain for letters of introduction and a pilot for the bar of Surat. Middleton described this person as "a simple fellow . . . who took upon him to be a good coaster" (3:172), "who came with us," notes Greene, "of his free good will." Greene also reports a sad mischance: "Here we left a man in the river where we watered, being drowned carrying a cask made fast about his neck, and both sunk" (G, f7, 4 September).

Dated 1 September 1611, the letter Middleton left behind, a variant of which survives in the Company's correspondence, was copied by Captain John Saris of the Eighth Voyage upon his arrival at Socotra a few months later. In it, Middleton admonishes both English and Dutch mariners to abandon all hope of trade in the Red Sea: "Whosoever you are that shall come to view of this premonition, peruse it well, and use all diligence to escape the danger hanging over your heads. We give you hereby to understand that neither at *Aden* nor *Mocha*, nor any port under the Turkish tyranny in the Red Sea, there is not any trade for you. The *Ascension*, who was to seek trade first, was greatly injured, and we of the sixth voyage miserably misused." Middleton recounts the story of their betrayal. He reports that the sultan has directed the basha to disregard his own letter of protection for Yemen: "although he [the sultan] should give his license to come hither to any Christian, yet . . . here they should take their ships, kill their men, and confiscate their goods."[3] This bracing admonition clearly surpassed Ja'far Basha's similar warning to John Jourdain in 1609 "to come no more without order from the Great Turk" (J, 90).

Middleton's fleet left Socotra on 4 September 1611. The passage to India occupied just two weeks. Downton's log indicates steady winds from the southwest as the ships held northeast by east from 8 to 17 September (f54v). On the eighteenth, finding themselves opposite Diu at the tip of the Gulf of Cambay's western peninsula, they continued toward the bar of Surat across a perilously shoaled sea. Navigating the first English ship to reach the area in August 1608, Master Matthew Molyneux of the *Hector* had declared to Captain Hawkins, "It was a dangerous place, and . . . he durst [not] stir with the ship till he had a pilot from Surat" (Markham, *Hawkins*, 387). The *Ascension* foundered in these waters the following year. Now the pilot major of the Sixth fleet, Molyneux again desired local experts to intervene. The sea floor was unstable, tidal variations acute. As Greene observed, "This place is unnavigable without a pilot of this country, who always knoweth the altering of the sands" (G, f7v, 24 September 1611). The deep draft of the *Trades Increase* augmented its risk as they neared India.

On 21 September, contending with strong tidal streams, Downton anchored in "10 fathom muddy water" while his pinnace sounded a mere three fathoms in rippling water nearby (D, f55). The next day, Greene reports that they saw sailboats passing toward the bar of Surat south of them, "whereupon the general sent off his skiff and took a pilot of them" (G, f7v, 22 September 1611). Downton went aboard the flagship to consult with the general, "we being in an unknown coast, out of sight of land, in great streams, amongst shoals and uncertain banks which none of us know from former times how to prevent, but only by our lead to grope out the way" (G, f55v, 22 September 1611). Sounding regularly, "shunning diverse suspicious ripplings," they continued northeast along a steep-sided shoal "as against as wall," catching sight of "the trees of India" on the twenty-third, when Middleton secured another pilot from a boat out of Surat (D in P, 3:247–48). The *Darling's* pilot advised Greene that they were still a good ten leagues north of the bar. As they turned south with a new pilot the next day, the lost *Ascension* was on their minds (G, f7v, 23–24 September 1611). The pilot told Greene that water levels varied dramatically on the bar, running eighteen feet deep with the spring tide, "and that at low water, a man might wade upon it." The lowest stretch was only a musket shot wide (G, f8, 25 September 1611).

Outside the bar of Surat, reached on 26 September, three Indian ships lay at anchor. Closer in lay an altogether new impediment: a fleet of Portuguese warships, some twenty frigates, blocked their passage to the Tapti River (P, 3:172, 248).[4] The Portuguese had received word of an English voyage in the Red Sea headed for Surat. Commanded by Don Francisco de Soto Maior, captain major of the forces of Daman and Chaul to the south, they had arrived expressly to prevent the fleet from reaching or contacting Surat. "None could . . . come near us," Downton wrote, "but [the Portuguese] would narrowly search and see that they had neither letters nor other provisions that might comfort or relieve our necessities." Outbreaks of illness had plagued the crews for some time, and now, observed Downton, "our men grew to great weakness, and every day more and more . . . fell down with the scurvy" (P, 3:248–49). Yet "we dare put off none of our boats" beyond musket range for fear the Portuguese would capture them (D, f57v, 26 September). They desperately needed fresh foods. Their predicament was not long tenable.

The likeliest way to get a message ashore was by Indian mariners. "Paying them well for their pains," Middleton discharged the pilots and provided them with letters "to such of our people as they should find in Surat" (3:172).

He evidently hoped to reach a workable compromise with Soto Maior. He commanded the fleet, Downton reports, not "to shoot or use any violence to the Portugals" unless "present . . . danger did enforce the same" (D, f57v, 26 September). King James was formally at peace with other Christian powers, and the general had dealt more diplomatically with other Europeans than of late with Ottoman authorities. Early in the voyage, he had received the Alcayda of Cape Verde aboard the *Trades Increase* and won his blessing to fell trees for a new mainmast. On the twentieth-eighth, as the *Darling's* boat was chased by a frigate within musket shot of the *Peppercorn*, Middleton sent a letter to Soto Maior and flew a flag of truce from the flagship's masthead to invite a parley (G, f8; P, 3:173).

The next morning, a frigate with Indian rowers brought "one Portugal and his boy" to the *Trades Increase* with a stern response to Middleton's letter (3:173; G, f8, 29 September). The captain was pleased that their kings were friends. He declared himself, Middleton wrote, "ready to do me service in anything he might, provided I brought a letter or order from the King of Spain, or the Viceroy, for my trading in these parts." Otherwise, "he must guard the port." The absence of a royal pass was again the critical impediment. The general responded as he had in Mocha and Sana'a: he required no such pass, "for that I was sent by the King's Majesty of England with letters and rich presents to the Great Mogoll, and to establish the trade begun in these parts." There was "no reason why the Portugals should oppose themselves against us, for that [India] was a free country for all nations," not a vassal of Portugal. Even if they pretended to dominion here, the 1604 *Articles of Peace* required the Portuguese to provide safe haven and freedom of traffic for the English. That document, however, was drafted and signed on the far side of the world.

Middleton desired the messenger to tell his master, "in friendly manner," to allow Englishmen in Surat to come aboard in peace, and "not urge me to use force, for by the one means or the other, I must and would have them" (3:173). Declaring that Middleton "might use his pleasure," the envoy explained that the viceroy's commission required them to "attempt all the means they could to hinder us." He offered to provide them with water or other refreshment so long as they conducted no commerce. After he left, a boat arrived with word that Surat's governor Khwāja Nizām, who favored trade with the English, was detained at the bar in the effort to reach them (G, f8, 29 September 1611).

The fleets were at a standoff that the English could not long sustain. "The extraordinary diligence of the Portugals in their nimble frigates,"

Downton complained, "ever prevented or frustrated" their efforts to cross the bar (D, f57v, 26 September 1611). Yet Middleton refused to leave. By the shore boat of one of the local ships on 1 October, an Indian mariner, hiding it in a cane, brought to the *Trades Increase* a letter of "lame advice in a spacious paper" as Downton put it, from Nicholas Bangham, a joiner from the *Hector* left behind at the factory. (Bangham will reappear in the closing chapter.) The letter caused dismay—not least because it showed, "for want of sense, . . . that there was none of greater discretion at present" in Surat (D, f57). Downton's quick, class-based dismissal of Bangham was unfair.[5] The factory, the letter reported, was depopulated. A few days later, Bangham sent letters by Captain Hawkins in Agra and the chief merchant William Finch, whom they had expected to find in Surat. But Finch was in Lahore, homeward bound by caravan.[6]

Deeply pessimistic about England's prospects in India, Hawkins and Finch expressed "little hope . . . of any good for our nation in this country," Downton reported (f57). The letters advised Middleton "not to land any goods, nor hope for trade in those parts: for that the people were all fickle and unconstant like the king, and durst not offend the Portugals" (P, 3:175). Perhaps Middleton now grasped that a great, deep-drafted flagship—an icon of national power and prosperity—was not the tool he needed to circumvent his adversaries here. Whatever its efficacies in Europe, the Anglo-Iberian accord did not forestall hostilities in India. Jesuit fathers outflanked Hawkins at court, and swarms of frigates prevented new factors from entering Surat. The East India Company required a comprehensive, logistically feasible strategy that yoked rigorous diplomacy in Agra to substantial, highly maneuverable fleets in the Gulf of Cambay. The depressing news from Hawkins and Finch "was no small disturbance to Sir Henry Middleton and us all about him," Downton wrote. Most of their vendible cargo was intended for Surat, and they assumed it unmarketable elsewhere. What to do next was altogether unclear. The lieutenant general described Middleton to be, like the others, "not a little perplexed with swarms of troubled thoughts, our hopes . . . being dashed" in both Arabia and India (D, f57).

Soon thereafter, Middleton and his team were heartened by a second message from Bangham: Captain Sharpeigh and John Jourdain had left Agra and were expected daily in Surat (G, f8v; P, 3:175, 249). What to do next was suddenly obvious: they must bring these persons of discretion and the other remaining Englishmen aboard—"first," Downton observed, "to be fully informed the truth [of] what was to be expected by us in this country," and second, to remove them from India if need be (D, f57v). To protect his lines of communication, Middleton kept the Indian ships nearby. To compel their assistance, he informed the governor and shipowners "that their ships should not depart thence till I had all the Englishmen at Cambaya and Surat aboard of me" (3:175). In the meantime, as if persuaded that the English either feared to shoot or lacked powder, the Portuguese pestered them relentlessly. Their frigates came "so near us," Downton wrote, "as by night made us keep extraordinary watch in our smallest ships, to prevent whatsoever they might suddenly attempt." Middleton delivered a caveat to Soto Maior "that if he broke the peace between our princes, at his peril be it" (D, f58). The message went unanswered.

Exit from India

The factory at Surat had lost personnel since its inception late in 1608. English fortunes in India were not as reported to Middleton in Socotra. Of the original few factors who had disembarked, the merchant Francis Bucke was seized and imprisoned by the Portuguese as he petitioned for the release of his *Hector* shipmates captured in the ship's unarmed pinnace. When Hawkins demanded that the captain major release the men and goods, because "we were Englishmen, and . . . our kings had peace and amity together," that dignitary responded by "vilely abusing His Majesty, terming him King of Fishermen, and of an island of no import, and a fart for his commission." By his own account, Hawkins, "always wary, having a strong house with good doors," survived various Portuguese plots against his life, and in February 1609, left Finch in charge of the factory to depart for Agra.[7] After the abandonment of the *Good Hope* and loss of the *Ascension* in September 1609, the Portuguese prevented Finch from receiving all but three of the mariners. Jourdain was one of these; the others, sometimes unruly, camped among trees and tombs outside Surat and moved to a nearby village (J, 130). When Sharpeigh and many of his mariners left for Agra, Jourdain remained with Finch to manage the factory. Upon receipt of promising letters from Hawkins, in January 1610 Finch departed for Agra and left Jourdain in charge (J, 137). Eleven months later, at Hawkins's directive to sell off all their lead and carry the proceeds to Agra, Jourdain followed. He left only one man, a master's mate, in the idled house (J, 141).

Lacking a ship, Sharpeigh's authority was unclear. Once ashore, the Fourth Voyage mariners, who with Sharpeigh's blessing had divided the residue of the owners' capital when they abandoned the *Ascension*, went various ways.[8] In the eyes of the chief merchants, their countrymen's indiscipline embarrassed England. "The disordered carriage of the most part of our men," Jourdain wrote, "would make a man's ears to tingle to repeat the villainies that was done by them." Finch likewise complained of the "disorder and riot committed by some of them, especially one Thomas Tucker, which in drink had killed a calf (a slaughter more than murder in India), which made me glad of their departure" (J, 133, 135–36; Foster, *Travels*, 132–33). Disheartingly, Jourdain realized upon reaching Agra that the actions of England's leading representatives had likewise disadvantaged their nation at court. Reuniting with Sharpeigh there in mid-February 1611, he learned that Finch and Hawkins had quarreled and parted, with Finch already in Lahore. England's ersatz ambassador had enjoyed spectacular favor for a time: the emperor made him master of four hundred horses and gave him a bride, an Armenian Christian woman from the royal household. Recently, however, Hawkins "was in some disgrace with the king" (J, 154).[9]

The occasions of his disfavor were multiple. In a dispute over a debt Hawkins believed was due him, he had imprudently offended Mukarrab Khān, the powerful governor of Cambay and controller of customs there and in Surat; then troubling Jahāngīr over the matter, he alienated the chief vizier, Khwāja Abū-l Hasan (J, 154–55). When Hawkins later pressed Hasan for the land that Jahāngīr had promised him, the vizier put him off as a mere "merchant" who "might ply his merchandizing and not look for anything at the king's hands" (J, 155). Then Finch tarnished Hawkins's appeal by tactlessly outbidding the Queen Mother on a purchase of indigo intended for her Mocha-bound ship. Finally, the ambassador's disregard of drinking protocols at court unhinged his leverage there. Sir Thomas Roe later reported that Jahāngīr loved red wine and sometimes drank to excess, yet managed the consumption of his retainers arbitrarily. An invitation to drink after him was an obligation, yet "no man can enter the *Guzelchan* where the king sits, but the porters smell his breath, and, if he have but tasted wine, is not suffered to come in" (Foster, *Roe*, 199, 303–4). Violations provoked corporal punishment. Jourdain heard that the vizier, recognizing Hawkins's fondness for "strong drink," set him up: he had the porter smell the Englishman's breath upon his arrival at court, then haled him before the emperor, who, "considering that he was a stranger," forbore harsher measures but ordered him to depart. "So, being disgraced in public, he could not be suffered to come into his accustomed place near the king" again (J, 156–57). Hawkins's embassy was notable for its bluster and ineptitude.

During his five months in Agra, Jourdain did not warm to Hawkins. As the four principal Englishmen in India concluded that their errand had turned hopeless, they plotted homeward journeys. Jourdain declined Hawkins's invitation to depart with him. Implausibly, the latter hoped with Jesuit help to secure a pass from the viceroy to leave via Cambay and Goa to Lisbon and England. Jourdain mistrusted Portuguese promises and preferred other company. From Lahore, Finch invited him to join a caravan to Aleppo. But since Finch's departure, word of the Sixth Voyage had reached Agra. Jourdain, Sharpeigh, and their followers elected to rendezvous if possible with them in Surat, and if that failed, head for Masulipatam (J, xxxiv, 158), in hopes that an East India Company voyage was in progress to that city on the Coromandel coast—where, indeed, England's first ship, the *Globe*, anchored on 31 August 1611.[10] Leaving Agra on 28 July 1611, Jourdain and Sharpeigh reached Cambay on 30 September.

Their audience there with Mukarrab Khān, the viceroy of the greater region, proved decidedly helpful. Jourdain's syntax registers tacit concern about the man's good faith, but at this juncture Mukarrab Khān and his brother, Governor Khwāja Nizām of Surat, welcomed the English—perhaps, as Middleton and Downton believed and Foster speculates, to secure career-advancing novelties to present to Jahāngīr (*Travels*, 63); perhaps, more strategically, in hopes of destabilizing the dominant colonial presence in the region. Mukarrab Khān, in any case, "seemed to welcome us in good manner, although he were angry with Captain Hawkins" (J, 172), Jourdain wrote. He informed them that an English fleet had arrived at the bar of Surat, "seemed to be very joyful" of that, and offered to help them meet their countrymen. He sent word to his brother "to use us with all kindness." Sharpeigh and Jourdain having sold their horses, he provided them with two palanquins and a dozen men to conduct them to Surat (172–73). They arrived on 2 October and, with Khwāja Nizām's assistance, sent letters to Middleton. In his answer three days later, the general promised to be "ready at the water's side to take us in, if we did advise him of our coming" (175). To consummate that operation, the governor recommended a beach a league north of the main shoal outside Surat, an area later known to the English as Swally Hole, "where the ship might ride within musket shot of the shore, in eight fathom water." He offered to help them arrange a rendezvous there, safer for one than the both of them. Jourdain volunteered. Advising the Englishman to disguise himself as an Indian seaman, the governor directed a ship's master to take his full crew with Jourdain to the waterside near the ships, avoiding the Portuguese on the way (177). Jourdain would signal his presence to the ships with a fire by night or a white cloth by day.

Meanwhile, Middleton asked Soto Maior to permit his merchants and others ashore to reach him, promising "then, he would be gone from this place"; he was refused. Through a Portuguese intermediary, Sharpeigh likewise requested safe passage to the ships; the captain major wrote back "in scoff" that he would gladly pledge them safe conduct in his galliot all the way to Goa. On 12 October, Sharpeigh's food shipment to the fleet was intercepted, and Soto Maior mockingly thanked the English captain for "sending him fresh victuals for his supply" (D in P, 3:250, 252). On the same day, Middleton left the *Trades Increase* in the main road off Surat and boarded the *Peppercorn* to follow the *Darling* and *Release* filing slowly north along the shoal, their advance rowboats sounding regularly. Portuguese frigates kept abreast of them inside, "they all rowing in order of battle with their colors displayed," Downton wrote, "oftentimes making great shouts as in some great attempt, the captain major in a small frigate going from frigate to frigate throughout his fleet, encouraging them" (D in P, 3:252). As the *Darling*'s boat moved closer to shore "by occasion of a suspicious rippling," suddenly two small, swift vessels—"being overbold with our long sufferance," Downton remarked—accelerated to cut it off. Recognizing that "present danger" now required the move, the *Darling*'s master ordered the crew to fire on them. One frigate rowed clear of the shot beyond the boat; the other turned back and went aground, and "the men abandoning her ran away in the mud" (P, 3:253). Thus, as their sustained fire repelled the other frigates, the English came into possession of a useful vessel. It was in this craft two days later, with fifty men aboard, that Middleton spied Jourdain waving his unfurled turban on the shore. He had waited three nights in the fields there (D, f61v, 15 October; J, 178).

With Jourdain was the broker-translator Jaddow, a Banian entrepreneur who had worked with Captain Hawkins at court.[11] Middleton took them back to the *Peppercorn*, where Jourdain met Pemberton and Downton and informed them of the anchorage at Swally. This heartening news complemented their information from the day before, when they intercepted a frigate carrying servants and provisions for Mukarrab Khān, who they learned was traveling by land to Surat. Through the boatmen, Middleton sent word to him that he brought letters and presents from the king of England and "great store of commodities fit for this country" (D, f61, 14 October 1611).[12] English hopes were quickening: if they secured the described anchorage, trade could be possible here after all.

Over the next two days, Portuguese vessels continued to harass them, and shots were exchanged to no major effect as the English brought the *Peppercorn, Darling,* and *Release* to South Swally. Middleton took a skiff into the small river to catch fish and, on the evening of the seventeenth, bought milk and onions from a group who came down to meet them. The Indians said they would have done so that morning "had not the Portugals been in their town," and they promised to return with more and better provisions—"sheep, hens, and lemons"—from Surat. They also reported that Sharpeigh and other Englishmen were not far away (D, f62v, 17 October). For several days thereafter, landing parties in quest of Sharpeigh skirmished with Portuguese troops sometimes in the hundreds, found occasional Englishmen, and withdrew. By 24 October, however, Middleton lost hope of the rendezvous, and the crews weighed anchor to depart. As they were unfurling their sails, Downton wrote, "we saw a troop of horsemen coming from the northwards" (f64). They dropped anchor again and sent the frigate ashore. It was Sharpeigh. He appeared, unlike the camouflaged Jourdain, openly on horseback, surrounded by "an hundred horsemen for his guard, all armed with bows and arrows and swords."

In his company were Jaddow again, who facilitated both reunions, the captain's Indian servant, and a Hindu priest (D in P, 3:257). The bold arrival of this shipless captain demonstrated much more than his own well-bankrolled resourcefulness in an alien land. His retinue and Jourdain's concealment played out complementary modes of the corporate initiative they both advanced—one assertive, the other chameleonic. These musters of indigenous strength in the service of English reunions expressed the fundamental flexibilities of the East India Company outside England. Intricate local dependencies—on informants, collaborators, benefactors, potentates, and sometimes armed retainers—articulated every move the Company made in India and wherever else their ships lingered. Their opportunistic pursuit of two enormous challenges, survival and profit, freed these mariners from perpetual performance of the Jacobean identities and nationalist Christian agendas they periodically invoked to justify their actions and their self-regard. On unfamiliar shores, they understood the need to adapt and, where possible, collude with local powers of whatever ethical or religious persuasion.

That process hybridized both the methods and the demographics of corporate labor. By 1610, East India Company crews were made up of Dutch, Portuguese, Javan, and Indian, as well as English and Scottish, personnel.[13] They and the groups they joined ashore constituted a mobile, protoglobal workforce. Combatants intermingled as well, their affiliations surprisingly fluid. The Sixth Voyage mariners took in occasional deserters from the Portuguese camp, brought aboard a wounded soldier left on the beach after a skirmish ("Antonio de Sowso, a gentleman of Chaul"), tended to him, and buried him when he died. Several shipmates deserted them in turn, some to the Portuguese and at least one to Surat, who thereby joined the Fourth Voyage diaspora in India (D in P, 3:255–56, 261, 266, 268). Among the escapees were "John Coverdale, trumpeter of the Admiral" (3:266) and John Chambers, the *Trades Increase* quartermaster who came ashore to visit Middleton in a squalid cell in Mocha. A courageous, culturally inquisitive man, "upon what discontent I know not," wrote Downton, he "ran away to the Portugals" (D, f67v, 17 November 1611).

The English desertions expressed the toll of sickness, hunger, and blockade on the mariners' morale: for some, the need for fresh meals and free movement eclipsed national and corporate loyalties. As they awaited Sharpeigh, the mariners' relations with Indian authorities also took a troubling turn. Downton writes that, ashore on 19 October, Middleton was surprised to meet a former neighbor in Mocha, a Persian merchant and broker also named Jaddow, who reported that Surat's governor was coming to welcome him. They retired to the *Peppercorn*, where Middleton "kindly entertained" his party and prepared a present for the governor. But returning to shore that afternoon, they found that Khwāja Nizām had canceled the meeting—ostensibly for fear that his brother the viceroy "would take it ill, and think that he had received great and rich presents from us" (D, f62v). Middleton, "perceiving the distrust the governor had of him," in turn suspected "the perfidious dealing of this people." Through the Persian broker, he delivered the gifts anyway: a pistol, five sword blades, a gilt looking glass, and a bottle of rosasolis (an herbal liqueur).

Following the governor's apparent change of heart several days later, "the general [was] fetched on shore on a palanquin, borne on four men's shoulders, and . . . kindly entertained" as they sat together on a carpet to discuss business (D in P, 3:257). Khwāja Nizām tellingly suggested that the English would find a more accessible market across the gulf in Ghogha, "where he said we might ride with our ships in command of the shore" (G, f9v, 26

October)—much as he had described Swally to Jourdain. He had brought
pilots to conduct them there. A sudden downpour terminated the meeting
inconclusively. Middleton considered the move to Ghogha but remained
dubious. His reservations about Mughal intentions mirrored those of other
principal mariners at this juncture. Sharpeigh's 12 October letter to Middleton described the governor's "great joy" in reporting that the English "had
taken one of the Portugal's frigates and sunk another" only to conclude that
"these people doth but delay us with fair words, but they durst not displease
the Portugals" (*LR*, 1:138). Ironically, the remark echoed Jourdain's solitary
exasperation over English naivete in Arabia Felix (J, 99). By now, failure and
disillusionment had made skeptics of them all.

On the evening of 26 October, with everyone aboard from Surat but
Bangham, "who the country people would not suffer to depart" for payment
of English debts (G, f9, 24 October), they left South Swally to rejoin the
Trades Increase. Back aboard the flagship the following day, Middleton called
a general council to ponder their next move: return to sea and hope to come
back after the frigates perhaps departed for Goa? remove to Ghogha? assert
their presence at Swally? Some wanted to leave these shoal-infested waters
altogether and try their fortunes at Masulipatam, where, unbeknownst to the
discussants, the Seventh Voyage resided as they spoke (G, f9v, 31 October;
Moreland, *Floris*, 18–21). They settled on Swally, but with little hope of re-
establishing the factory. Middleton freed the Indian ships, and the fleet moved
north again. In the *Release*, he sent Thornton, who returned without success,
and the following day Pemberton, "in whose endeavors he had firm confidence," to seek the place Khwāja Nizām had described to Jourdain (D in P,
3:259). About two miles above their earlier Swally anchorage, Pemberton
found the area, where, Downton offered, at high tide even the *Trades Increase*,
"being a little lightened, might . . . go safely over the bar" (P, 3:259), and, as
Greene reported, "we might ride in ten fathoms within pistol shot of the
shore" (G, f9v, 3 November). To secure this harbor would thwart the Portuguese embargo. A day later, the *Peppercorn*, *Darling*, and *Release* crossed
inside as twelve hostile frigates anchored just beyond reach of their ordnance.
The *Trades Increase*, too heavily laden to follow, remained outside, formidable
yet exposed.

Thus began an edgy interval at North Swally. Gusted by successive
hopes, fears, and confrontations, English purposes wavered. The next day,
Bangham arrived from Surat with desperately needed lamp oil, candles,

"limes and other small refreshing for our sick company." Their Mocha food-stuffs were by then, Greene noted, "very much worm-eaten" (G, f10, 6 November; P, 3:260). Scurvy was spreading; several men had already died. Bangham brought news that Mukarrab Khān was in Surat and planned to visit them. In the meantime, there was urgent work to be done: its hull already "in a manner devoured by worms" (P, 3:260), the *Release* leaked dangerously. They beached the vessel for immediate repairs. Downton's men erected a tent and guarded the site against Portuguese interference; his full team of carpenters worked on the craft through the following day. But the villagers' report that evening of two galleys and eighty frigates on the adjacent river spurred Middleton to consolidate the fleet at once. He departed for the flagship and ordered the others to follow. Late that night with the tide, Downton's men refloated the pinnace and brought it beside the *Peppercorn*, and they all sailed back across the bar to join the *Trades Increase*. The following day, however, 9 November, brought contrary determinations. Middleton took the frigate ashore to meet Khwāja Nizām, who arrived with fifty horsemen and fifty soldiers to greet the general and talk business. The governor promised that, once the fleet held the anchorage, "he would bring down goods and trade with us." Villagers would sell provisions along the sea strand in the meantime. He reassured them that the Portuguese frigates in the river were not warships but merchant vessels headed for Cambay (G, f10; P, 3:176–77, 261).

The next morning, the pinnace and ships' boats sounded assiduously in search of safe passage for the *Trades Increase* and found nothing certain. Midafternoon on the eleventh, Pemberton in the *Darling* came from the flagship to Downton at anchor in the *Peppercorn* with word that Middleton desired the latter to escort the *Darling* across the bar immediately. Given "the fleet of frigates inside," the two vessels were to stay together. "This direction was some trouble to me, in regard the tide of flood was near spent," Downton admitted, yet a favorable wind prevented him from opposing the move. As swiftly as possible, they weighed anchor and pursued the *Darling*. But midway across the bar, the wind failed them, "leaving my ship to the mercy of the stream, which set us directly upon the highest of the shoal, where I in the *Peppercorn* stood fast, while the *Darling* drawing less water passed over. . . . With much pain, discontent, and troubles, we passed the time till it was within an hour of high water. [The] grounding broke two stanchions in the hold, our ship much arching by reason that the strong tide fretted away the sand from her bow." The ship damaged, their ordnance tied down and gunports sealed for sailing, anxiously they eyed the frigates inside, "riding still without molesting us" (D, f67, 11 November 1611).[14] Late that night—"God be thanked," wrote Greene—the cresting tide lifted the *Peppercorn* into the harbor (G, f10).

As they awaited the Mughal authorities' next move at Swally, for a fortnight the crews recuperated with abundant fresh victuals at hand. The fleet remained divided for the time being, the *Trades Increase* too heavily laden to cross the bar. Shore parties avoided sporadic Portuguese ambushes and, backed by ordnance, skirmished with troops in the hundreds. Disheartened by Khwāja Nizām's delay, Middleton suspected "all their former promises to be nothing but inventions to delude and weary me." Fear of the Portuguese prevented local merchants from offering him trade, he surmised, yet they were "loath to offend me with absolute denial." Having eluded the governor's watch, Bangham "stole secretly out of town" and arrived from Surat on 19 November (M in P, 3:177). Then two horsemen appeared to verify that Mukarrab Khān would arrive in a few more days—at which Downton remarked, "We had been so often deceived with their delays that we had little confidence therein" (f67v). But the report was true enough.

On the morning of 24 November, Jaddow boarded the flagship to announce that Mukarrab Khān would arrive before nightfall. Middleton took his midday meal and went ashore to find Khwāja Nizām, who confirmed that his brother was near. The general returned to the *Trades Increase* to equip himself with "a good present" (P, 3:178) for the governor of Cambay. He was still aboard when "the great man" (G, f10, 22 November) and his formidable train appeared. Downton detailed the grandeur: "one hundred horsemen, and many more footmen, five elephants, with diverse camels, carts, and oxen for transportation of his provisions, wherein he showed his greatness. Furthermore, he had diverse carts to carry his leopards, wherewith at his pleasure he useth to hunt." They pitched "a little town of tents" in the plain opposite the ships (D in P, 3:262; J, 180). As Middleton landed, the fleet answered the Mughal spectacle with a great volley of 160 muskets. Then, as he and Mukarrab Khān saluted each other and embraced, the ships, surely with ensigns and pennants flying, discharged rounds of ordnance "to bid him welcome": three from the *Darling*, five from the *Peppercorn*, nine from the flagship, "which," Middleton wrote, "he seemed to take kindly" (P, 3:262, 178). Though further offshore, the *Trades Increase*—material proof of English power and prosperity, the marine equivalent of a troupe of castled elephants—performed to its strengths now. Middleton presented his gifts, and they "sat down upon carpets spread upon the ground" to discuss business (3:178).

The great ship attracted Mukarrab Khān's curiosity. Near sunset, Middleton invited him to lodge that night aboard it, and against expectation he assented, bringing his own and Khwāja Nizām's sons and several other followers, though his brother declined. "He having all this part of the country under his command," remarked Middleton, "it pleased me well to see him so confident," the general's hopes for trade thus enhanced (3:178). Downton too was impressed that Mukarrab Khān "boldly accompanied Sir Henry Middleton aboard the *Trades Increase*" (3:262), a move Regib Aga would not have made. On board, a banquet was prepared, and the Indian entourage "fell roundly to" it (3:178–79). Then Middleton produced the royal letter he had brought to India for this occasion. In it, King James greets "the right Honorable the chief Commander of the great City of Cambaya" and declares that he has heard of the "great courtesies" his subjects have "received and do daily receive at your hands in their arrival and settlement of their trade." The English monarch offers thanks and expresses his hope that Cambay's ruler will confer his ongoing protection on Middleton and his men. Then, frankly invoking "the injury and loss which our subjects lately received by the Portingals of Goa (as is well known unto you)," he requests "your peaceable intercession for the redress thereof, before our subjects should attempt anything hostilely against them." While stating that they desired quiet trade, his majesty put the burden of maintaining the peace on the honorable addressee.[15]

Whatever Mukarrab Khān made of this message—it was not meticulously translated until 7 December (3:265)—he was pleased to inspect the ship. By Jourdain's report, "When he came aboard the *Trades Increase* he wondered to see her, affirming that he had been aboard many Portugal carracks and that they were nothing in respect of this; as afterwards he affirmed the same on land in my presence to many Portugals. In fine he liked the ship so well that he lay aboard her all night, with some dozen of his chiefest men" (J, 181). Before retiring to bed, he promised Middleton ample trade and supplies, a harbor wherever the English chose, and permission to fortify themselves there: "I not demanded him anything," Middleton declares, "but I found him as ready to grant, as I was to ask." Yet, as they toured the ship the next morning, the acquisitive vigor that his hospitality ignited in Mukarrab Khān gave the general pause. "Anything he liked belonging to the ship, he carried with him away gratis," even "toys" of the mariners that the general bought and gave him; in Middleton's cabin, "he needs would see all my chests, trunks, and lockers opened and searched. Whatsoever he saw there of mine that he took liking to, I gave him for nothing." After a midday meal, his guest left the *Trades Increase* to visit the other ships, "and there behaved himself in like sort" (3:179). The general suspected that he had been played.

Reconstructing the interval after the fact, Jourdain held a more positive view of the exchange. He specified both that Mukarrab Khān "paid well" for the knives, hats, looking glasses, "strong waters," and other items he took—"If it were a thing that liked him, he would have it whatsoever it cost"—and that the Indian dignitary produced gifts worth "five or ten rials worth of commodities to each" of the principal mariners, "which he brought for the purpose" (J, 181). The chief Fourth Voyage merchant recalled a felicitous moment of reciprocal courtesies. But the Sixth Voyage journalists, perhaps because their expedition carried more burdensome ambitions, viewed the visit with malaise. Receiving him aboard the *Peppercorn*, Downton dismissed the episode as a charade. The Mughal official took more interest in eye-catching personal effects than the commodities they chiefly wished to sell; "he bought up all our chests of sword-blades" only to return those he disliked, jumbled randomly (P, 3:263). While spying out their strengths, Mukarrab Khān acquired "all such fantastical toys that might fit his turn to please the toyish humor of the great king his master," Jahāngīr (3:262). Inviting Anglocentric scorn, the proto-orientalist trope of a decadent emperor's fondness for trifles deflected the writer's attention from the truth of England's utter marginality in India. For this defensive trope was of course ironically reflexive: the "toys" they carried expressed the East India Company's relevance to the Mughal Empire more precisely than the mariners preferred to admit.

Escorted ashore by Middleton, Downton, Sharpeigh, and Jourdain, the viceroy and his core entourage received them on carpets inside his tent. Middleton pressed the issue of trade and was put off till the morrow, and the Englishmen retired to their ships. The general returned in the morning to find, to his surprise, that Mukarrab Khān had departed to confer with the Portuguese forces—ostensibly "to make friendship between us." Khwāja Nizām remained at hand to express interest in the purchase of English commodities. But Middleton, suspecting betrayal, returned to his ship "laden with discontent" (D in P, 3:263). "Now our general was out of hope of any future good, thinking that all their promises were but delays," Greene ruefully observed, "seeing no performance at all touching our merchandizing," while Mughal authorities "fitted themselves with what they desired" to present to Jahāngīr (G, f1ov, 25 November 1611). The next day, two dignitaries from Mukarrab Khān appeared with a letter for the general, and Downton, assuming their mission "to be of import . . . to our commonwealth's business," sent them in his own boat to the *Trades Increase*. They had come merely to ask the general a second time for the perfumed jerkin and pet spaniel denied at Mukarrab Khān's initial request "when he begged his beaver hat." He also desired the carpenters and blacksmith "to make him the model of a chain pump," an apparatus evidently new to him (P, 3:264). Middleton surrendered his jerkin and his dog.

In mordancy and mistrust combined with shreds of hope, the mariners soon found their transactions with Khwāja Nizām deteriorating spectacularly. At a 27 November meeting, the governor again expressed interest in trade and promised to return from Surat with merchants and assorted cloths to barter for English commodities.[16] He left his son-in-law as a pledge of good faith. But the following night, this individual "dissolved his tent and departed," wrote Downton, "to no small disturbance to us, seeing none left to rectify any business" (3:264), and "leaving us destitute of any hope of good to be done" (G, f1ov). Protracted haggling ensued. Jourdain, Frayne, and Fowler fetched samples of cloth from a nearby village and brought them to Middleton, who recorded the amounts he would render for those he desired. The general sent word to the Indian merchants to do the like with English commodities. But on both sides, the quantities offered and demanded differed sharply. Then, Downton reported, a proclamation forbade villagers, on pain of losing their noses, to sell victuals to the English, "whereby they showed their desire to force us away by famine." Yet, on 6 December word arrived that Mukarrab Khān and Khwāja Nizām were again at hand. This time, however, their tents were erected more than a mile inland "and whether they came in peace or no, we knew not" (3:265).

On 8 December, the two brothers "came down with a great train to the waterside" and set up their tents (G, f1ov, 5 December), producing scores of packs of calicoes and pintados to exchange for English goods; "yet the sight thereof," Downton commented, "could not move all of us to believe [that] they meant faithfully to deal with us" (P, 3:265–66). Jourdain remained optimistic, for he had learned from Hawkins in Agra that Jahāngīr, while declining to grant a *firmaen* for an English factory in Surat, promised to direct Mukarrab Khān to trade with the ships of the Sixth Voyage (J, 182).[17] But the prevalent English suspicions precipitated a self-fulfilling crisis. Speaking for all the Indian merchants (the better to control prices, Middleton remarked), Khwāja Nizām expressed keen interest in quicksilver, vermilion, and velvet—not broadcloths—and, at English insistence that the desired goods were available only with concomitant purchases of lead, he agreed to proceed. As the mariners began to unload the latter the next day, however, a letter delivered to Mukarrab Khān "dashed all his mirth and our proceedings for that present," Middleton wrote. It was from the emperor: "He was very pleasant before he received and perused it; but afterwards became very sad. He sat a good pretty while musing, and upon a sudden riseth up, and so goeth his way without once looking towards or speaking to me, I being seated hard by him. Before he took horse, he better bethought himself and sent for me. When I came to him, he embraced me, telling me he was my brother, praying me to excuse this his sudden departure, for that he had earnest business and must be gone" (3:180–81). The letter had terminated his governorship of Cambay. Jahāngīr had appointed new governors for both Cambay and Surat. Mukarrab Khān's sole surviving office was the command of customs in Surat.

Khwāja Nizām continued, however, to manage the Indian merchants on this occasion. Lifting ponderous loads from deep in the hulls of their ships into successive shore boats, the crews had brought most of the lead ashore when, on 10 December, the process of weighing it triggered an ugly dispute. The Indians had acquired the velvets and other desired items, began to weigh the lead, and insisted on using their own scale. After a few passes, Jourdain's cohort called a halt and asked to calibrate the beam against their own. Having "found very great difference" (M in P, 3:181), they balked at the measurements. A translation problem agitated both groups. Their respective "maunds" clashed: the governor weighed by the "small maund," a local measure of some thirty pounds, the English by the "great maund," about fifty pounds. Furious that "we would not give him 46 kintalls for 36," Khwāja Nizām "in a rage said he would suddenly depart for Surat and not have anything more to do with us" (G, f10v, 7 December).[18] Likewise describing the late governor "in great rage" and packing up to depart (J, 182), Jourdain promptly went aboard the *Trades Increase* to inform Middleton of the crisis. Jourdain probably recognized with Downton that, "seeing the great pains and toil in landing" the lead, "intolerable disgust or discontent would arise among our people" at the Sisyphean labor of returning it to the ships (D in P, 3:266). The crews' morale had frayed severely by this time—Downton

notes three desertions on the evening of 9 December—and he for one feared
that the command to carry the lead back to the ships could prove incendiary.

Middleton was entertaining Surat's new governor, Hoja Nassan, and the
shabander, Hoja Assan Ally, when Jourdain reached the *Trades Increase*. The
news convinced the angered general that Khwāja Nizām, who had promised
"to take all of [the lead], and be as good as his word," was "going about to
delude me as formerly." So Middleton forced the situation: he told his guests
that they must remain on the ship "as pledges for the performance of the
bargain." The governor deftly offered an alternative: the general should go
ashore "and fetch the man himself" for that (3:182–83). Intrigued, Middleton
took them to the *Peppercorn* and consulted Downton, who seconded the
plan. Leaving his current hostages with the lieutenant general, he went ashore
with a substantial guard to confront Khwāja Nizām. Middleton explained
that the latter's "cross dealing" had compelled him to detain Hoja Nassan,
who came to his ship in good faith, and he insisted that Khwāja Nizām now
come aboard in place of the faultless governor. "Seeing no other remedy,"
Downton reported, Khwāja Nizām "with a grim look and sour countenance
came into the frigate," a hostage to the consummation of their earlier agreement (3:267). Barter by extortion was an art form increasingly congenial to
Middleton. The Sixth Voyage acquired some finesse in its practice.

Directed by the general to stay with the hostages, Jourdain was shocked
by Khwāja Nizām's extravagant distress that night on the *Peppercorn*. He was
"in such a rage," the merchant wrote, "that we thought he would have killed
himself; neither would he go into the cabin, but lay all night upon the deck"
(J, 183). Khwāja Nizām found the affronts of these clueless Englishmen insuf-
ferable. In the midst of the crisis, Downton reported, the fleet strengthened
its command of the occasion: at high tide on the next night, 11 December,
"to our great content," the lightened *Trades Increase* crossed over the bar,
thereby placing "all our strength together where our business lay" (D in P,
3:267). Yet, when the general wrote the following morning to bring the hostages aboard his nearby vessel, Khwāja Nizām refused to go. He declared that
they might carry his corpse, but "they would never carry him alive to a man
who had taken him prisoner in his own country for standing upon the buying
of his commodities." As Jourdain and Middleton exchanged anxious letters
over the situation, however, the shabander managed to mollify him, and he
consented to go aboard the flagship.

Then, by Jourdain's report, the great ship worked its magic even upon
this compelled guest: "And when he came aboard and saw the ship, and all

things in such good order, he embraced the general and told him that now his heart was merry, that he cared not to dwell in such a ship as that was.[19] Sir Henry used him very respectfully and told him that what he did was to avoid farther troubles . . . [and] therefore entreated him that the business might go forward in friendship like loving friends; which Hoghanazan [Khwāja Nizām] promised should be performed" (J, 183–84). Jourdain, who sailed for India before the flagship was constructed, observed that, as if in fulfillment of its builders' hopes, a visit to the *Trades Increase* inspired awe, respect, and consumerist desires in Indian hearts. For him, the great ship was the English traders's most compelling advertisement. Whatever its presence did for the current visitor's impressions of England, Khwāja Nizām graciously readjusted his tactics. Compliance was his likeliest way back to shore. He proposed that his son and son-in-law, a companion throughout the ordeal, remain aboard while he, Middleton, and the shabander went ashore to resume trading. Two Persian merchants were likewise willing to stand for the shabander. Middleton consented. Delegating two factors, John Williams and Henry Boothby, "to remain with them in their tents" as "pledges on our side" (D in P, 3:268), he received the volunteers, Jourdain reported, "very kindly." Over the next several days, while his sons were "making merry" on the great ship, Khwāja Nizām, Greene remarked, made himself "pliable to any reasonable demand for making a just weight for . . . our commodities," and the trading proceeded amicably (J, 184; G, 10v, 9 December).

Sporadic skirmishes with Portuguese troops continued, but the fleet's firepower kept them in the distance. On the twentieth, the *Peppercorn* was haled aground to clean and treat the sheathing on its hull. Accounts were cleared on both sides, and hostages returned, on 24 December. Three days later, a Jewish merchant named Maseno arrived from Masulipatam bearing a letter to Middleton from Peter Floris, who had heard of the misfortunes of the Sixth Voyage in the Red Sea and its arrival in the Gulf of Cambay. In his own journal, Floris indicates that he sent "letters overland to the English residing at Surat" (Moreland, *Floris*, 21). His surviving missive of 7 September to the merchants there sketches the progress of the Seventh Voyage from the Downs to the Coromandel coast in a mere six and a half months, "without the loss of any one man (thanks be given to God)"—a performance that should have rankled the haughty commander of a more ambitious mission distinguished by losses and delays. The letter also notes another fleet preparing "to depart two months after us, to wit, the *Hector*, the *Clove*, and a ship built in Ireland [the *Thomas*]": the Eighth Voyage (*LR*, 1:136–37). The letter

Maseno delivered specifically to Middleton, dated 8 September (3:184), has not survived. But by Downton's report, it recounted that at least one ship of that voyage "was to go into the Red Sea," a destination against which Middleton resolved to warn them. The disclosure was "very unpleasing to the general and us all, in regard of the danger we suspected they should fall into" (D in P, 3:269). This conversation marked the first tremor of the rancorous division that beset the Sixth and Eighth Voyages in the Red Sea and Bantam—a clash that tore the ligaments of the East India Company's corporate body.

On 28 December by Middleton's report (3:184)—30 December by Downton's and Greene's (P, 3:269; G, f11)—a letter arrived of more immediate concern from William Hawkins in Cambay. He had left the Mughal court in failure, without even a written response from Jahāngīr to King James's letter. His fortunes in Agra had risen again, and the emperor at last granted rights to a factory in Surat, only to collapse when "a great nobleman and nearest favorite of the king" persuaded Jahāngīr that "this would be the utter overthrow of his sea coasts and people, . . . and that it stood not with his majesty's honor to contradict that which he had granted to his ancient friends the Portugals." The emperor, though pleased to retain Hawkins in his service, decided not to grant the English "trade at the sea-ports" after all (Foster, *Travels*, 94–95; Markham, *Hawkins*, 415). Resolved no longer "to stay . . . amongst these faithless infidels"—"faithless," that is, both religiously and secularly—Hawkins departed in shame and disgust on 2 November and was en route to Goa with his wife, brother-in-law, servants, and plentiful possessions, in quest of safe passage in a carrack bound for Lisbon. By Downton's report, Middleton found the plan foolish: "If once he got to Goa," the general remarked, "his goods would stop his passage to England, if not shorten his life." By the same messenger, Middleton wrote back at once and invited Hawkins "to take his passage with us into England" (D in P, 3:269). Greene adds that Middleton updated him on the sorry fate of Anthony Marlowe and Francis Bucke, his former shipmates on the *Hector*, who "remained in Lisbon in prison, without hope of release." To sweeten the offer, the general also persuaded Pemberton, "an old acquaintance" of Hawkins, to draft a letter offering him and his wife the captain's cabin on the *Darling* (G, f11, 31 December 1611).

On 8 January 1612, Hawkins's man Nicholas Ufflet arrived from Cambay with word that the late ambassador welcomed their proposal. Concealing the new plans from his brother-in-law, Hawkins persuaded him to return to Agra. Meanwhile Ufflet, having returned to Cambay, turned back again and encountered Sharpeigh, Frayne, and Hugh Greet, whom Middleton had dispatched to bring the entourage to Swally. On 26 January, Sharpeigh and Hawkins reached the waterside there, having left the carriages and followers a few miles shy of shore. Middleton thereupon landed with a force of two hundred armed men and went personally inland "to meet and guard them from the Portugals," Downton wrote, "whose army was not far off" (3:269). Seeing no hostile troops, everyone reached the ships in safety (3:184).

In the meantime, on a commercial errand to Surat with Greene, Frayne, and Bangham, Jourdain met Mukarrab Khān to discuss, once and for all, the prospects for an English factory there, a development the latter had "always desired in outward show." Greene wrote back to Middleton that, "for settling of a factory, the people of the country were most willing thereunto" (G, f11v, 19 January 1612), and Mukarrab Khān ostensibly welcomed the proposal. Jourdain invited him to the waterside at Swally to confirm the arrangement with Middleton. They set a time for the meeting (J, 185–86). But the arrival of Hawkins, no friend of Mukarrab Khān, complicated the situation. As the latter explained, "He knew not in what sort" the English envoy left Agra, and "therefore he durst not treat of settling a factory until he had further order from his master" (J, 187). Moreover, he was then called away to meet the governor of Gujarat, Abdala Khān, passing toward Birampur with four thousand horses to renew his army following a major defeat in the Deccan.[20] Upon his return from that stressful encounter, Mukarrab Khān's "mind," wrote Jourdain, "was altered. . . . He demanded me when our ships would be gone, saying that our merchandizing was now ended, that we might depart, and the sooner the better." The English presence, he maintained, put fear in others and thus impaired the coastal trade, to their great loss in customs; indeed, merchants of the Queen Mother's ship bound for Mocha, the *Rehemy*, "would not lade their goods aboard until we were gone from the country" (J, 185–86). He refused to meet Middleton again. By Downton's account, they later learned that Jesuits in Cambay had persuaded Mukarrab Khān against the proposed factory by threatening that if Mughal authorities "gave place to the English in Surat, the Portugals would come with force, and burn all their sea towns and make spoil of all the ships" (D in P, 3:271). As Mukarrab Khān surely recognized, Middleton's fleet was not equipped to prevent that outcome.

Seconding Jourdain's message on 29 January, John Williams reached the ships with report of "an absolute denial of . . . any further dealing with our nation" in Surat. The merchants were commanded to depart at once, without even collecting monies owed them. Middleton directed everyone there "speedily to repair down to our ships," wrote Downton. On 31 January 1612, "all our people . . . from Surat, with all their goods" reached the anchorage. As they made ready to depart a week later, "a great caphala, or fleet of near five hundred sail" of Portuguese frigates passed by on the way to Cambay. The East India Company mariners surely felt rather small before a procession of such magnitude. On the morning of 9 February, "upon the top of a high water," wrote Downton, "the Admiral warped out over the bar, and anchored in the offing." The crossing was timely. "Had we not got over this tide," Middleton speculated, "we had lost the whole spring" (3:185), possibly stranding the *Trades Increase* at Swally for several weeks. The same day, Hawkins's servant Nicholas Ufflet, "left behind in pawn"—the East India Company's last employee in Surat—rejoined them. That evening, the others passed over the bar and anchored near the flagship (3:270). As they prepared to depart, Downton drew up their Indian balance sheet, "having continued here the space of an hundred and thirty eight days, in which we sustained many and sundry abuses by delays, breach of promises, withholding the country people from trading with us, and having exchanged a few commodities at very hard and unprofitable rates, withholding further trade, disappointing us of settling a factory, withholding some debts formerly, and commanding our merchants out of their town, and our ships to be gone" (P, 3:270). England's prospects in Gujarat had come full stop.

Decisions on the Malabar Coast

Stopping a ship inward bound from Callicut (Cannanore, says Downton, f75) on 12 February, Middleton secured a pilot for Dabull, the port city to the south where Nohuda Melick Amber's letter of introduction, obtained in Mocha, promised to ingratiate them to the governor. Not expecting much of the place, Downton wryly observed that Middleton "went [there] in hope to sell some of his English commodities, or (as it were) to shoot another arrow after diverse formerly lost" (P, 3:272). Sounding frequently along coastal shoals, they reached Dabull late on 16 February. The next morning, Middleton entrusted the letter to the pilot and sent him ashore in a fishing boat intercepted for that purpose. The initial response was felicitous: the governor, whom Greene names Abraham Adelshaw, and Melick Amber himself, having returned to Dabull, sent Middleton "a small present of refreshing, and many complements, offering me anything the country did afford" (M in P, 3:186–87; G, f12).

Yet the ensuing business proved unenticing. Jourdain and Fowler went ashore the following day with musters of cloth in which the governor expressed small interest, desiring only, Downton wrote, "some little broad-cloth and kerseys of our best colors, as stammels, popinjay green," and Venice red. He purchased bars of lead but, upon delivery, refused all the red lead "because it had been wet," Jourdain explained. The crews were compelled to carry it back to the ships (G, f12, 17–23 February; D in P, 3:273; J, 195). Opposite Downton's conclusion, "the governor dealt double with us, grant-ing free leave to sell, yet underhand had men in wait to restrain or beat away such as came to buy," Purchas added coyly, "Dabull, double dealing" (3:273). Unable to sell much, they nonetheless bought foodstuffs and water at reason-able rates and secured much-needed "cable of eighteen inches, and ninety-six fathom of the country stuff, worth eight pound sterling, for one of the *Dar-ling*'s anchors"—a bargain. Downton wondered whether a habitual kindness to strangers or the fleet's reputation preceding it from Mocha, "that we endeavor to right what wrongs any should impose upon us," motivated the Dabullians "to make the best shows unto us" (D in P, 3:273–74). Middleton concluded their business here within a few days. By Jourdain's report, the general, perhaps anticipating Portuguese countermeasures if he proceeded, respectfully declined the governor's offer to establish a factory in Dabull, "saying he was not provided for it," though by "some other voyage it might be effected" (J, 195).

They were amply provided, however, to renew their reputation for right-ing wrongs suffered elsewhere. The need to balance one's accounts justified opportune predation, a tactic whose appeal had increased with the frustra-tions of the voyage. Yet pillaging introduced volatilities that challenged the authority of the principal mariners and, as the next chapter details, subverted the strategic aims and structural integrity of the corporation that they served. In transit to Dabull, from two Indian frigates they had taken assorted goods in ostensible exchange for bills due Hawkins in Surat (D in P, 3:271). Off Dabul on the night of 26 February, not molesting the Malabar merchant ships anchored near them, at Middleton's command the *Peppercorn* and *Dar-ling* sailed off to arrest a Portuguese ship and its attendant vessel and bring them to the *Trades Increase*. The 300-ton *St. Nicholas* of Cochin and its 60-ton frigate were proceeding to Chaul and Ormus laden with tin, China dishes, "and other gross commodities" (G, f12v; D in P, 3:276). As frigates from the *Peppercorn* and *Darling* helped bring the Portuguese vessels near the admiral in the dark, however, their excitable crews ruptured the decorum of the process. Downton firmly "intended [that] Sir Henry Middleton should be the first Englishman should enter" (3:274) the *St. Nicholas*. Yet, as Downton met with Portuguese detainees in the *Peppercorn*'s cabin, mariners in the ships' boats, "more greedy of prey than careful of credit," boarded both Portuguese vessels: "Like disgoverned pilfering people, they ran all into the ship, not forbearing to break open chests . . . and make spoil of all things that liked them, forbearing no ill language to such as I had sent to restrain them" (D in P, 3:275).

If hard service, long privation, and a suppressed tradition of self-interested opportunism understandably motivated the sailors' looting, their actions shredded the facade of corporate legitimacy and embarrassed the principal mariners. Having arranged for his Portuguese guests to observe the process, Downton appointed a few trusted men with the purser to wait "at the ladder with a lantern and candle to search them one by one" as the crewmen climbed aboard from the ship's boat, and they retrieved and returned the stolen goods (D in P, 3:275). Thereafter, the "legitimate" inspections and appropriations unfolded for several days. It amounted to a modest haul: balls of raw silk, cloves, chests of cinnamon, bags of rice, "and some wax to make us candles: all which was as it were but a mite in comparison of the damages done us by the Portugals," Downton observed. They returned to the frigate the several Portuguese who had deserted to them at Swally, and, in a gesture of reciprocity, Middleton gave "a fine broadcloth" to the merchant who owned the silk and "a fine kersey" to the captain of the frigate where they found the rice (D in P, 3:276–77). Like Downton, Greene explained that these goods were seized "in recompense of former wrongs done unto our nation, I mean for goods which they have taken from us" (G, f12v). Middleton likewise specified the justifying provocation: "former injuries offered me by the Captain Major Don Francisco de Soto Maior at the bar of Surat, as namely, taking my goods, and hindering my trade" (P, 3:188).

The thought of former injuries returned the general's mind to the Red Sea. Having given up on Dabull and wrung from the *St. Nicholas* "but a mite" of satisfaction due from Soto Maior, Middleton pondered the ways to right the balance sheet of his ubiquitously thwarted expedition. What to do next was again unclear. The next stop on their received itinerary was Priaman on Sumatra, yet the prospect that the Seventh Voyage should precede them there, with fresher commodities more apt for that market, discouraged them.

In the opening labyrinthine sentence of a despondent letter to the Company composed between 24 and 26 February 1612, Downton articulated their discontent:

> Environed with swarms of perplexed thoughts by present likelihood of the ruin or overthrow of this our journey begun with glory (which drew great expectation in all estates), set out with great charges; now after two years travel our victuals spent, our ships, cables, and furniture far worn, men's wages for 24 months already past, ourselves deluded and abused in most places we have come, whether to repair [where to go] to lade our ships not yet known, or by merchandising to recover former damages is beyond expectation; now rests, whether better we wish a languishing end, or a shameful return, God only direct, for our counsel is weak and our case doubtful. (*LR*, 1:155)

The Company required profits in order to pay wages, and to date the expedition was two years in arrears. The stunning contrast between the unprecedented expense and great expectations that launched the voyage, and the sad saga of its ensuing journey, was so disheartening to contemplate that Downton wondered whether a languishing death in the East were not preferable to a shameful return to London. Captive for six months in the Red Sea, they had come away without reparations from the Turks and but partial compensation from the Banian consul; after minimal marketing in Surat, they had shut down the factory and exited with England's disgraced quasi-ambassador and all the former merchants there but Finch, homeward bound by caravan. The East India Company's only extant hope on the Indian subcontinent was lately ignited by the solitary *Globe* at Masulipatam—on a voyage proposed and managed by Dutchmen.

Middleton's journal typically represses the dismay and self-doubts that permeate Downton's. But the shame, sadness, and perplexity that gripped the *Peppercorn*'s captain was likely shared by the other principal mariners as they met off Dabul on the *Trades Increase* on 4 March to plot the next leg of their costly voyage. "We rest near worn of all things and in manner as far from our ladings as when we were but newly come from home," Downton complained. Both their earnings and their honor were compromised. While he felt "the common sort of us"—the sailors—to be "neither sensible of shame or infamy" over the voyage's humiliations, "yet the general, on whose

shoulders the greatest burden lies, can never avoid an unremovable imputation, nor we about him an incurable disgrace," unless they managed "to do
our country, company, and ourselves right on them which have wronged us"
(*LR*, 1:159). Mere marketing, a dilatory process with at best incremental gains,
could not now redeem their time and honor lost. The predicament
demanded forceful action.

In his letter to the Company, Downton surveyed the groups that had
offended them: "as first the Turks, who began in hateful treason, continued
it by murder, robberies and other cruelties"; then "the Moors [Indians],
[who] first by show of welcome and kind usage, invited our merchants to
bring them variety of goods" only to expel them from the country, "to our
great loss, by delays and otherwise"; finally, "the Portugals, [who] by open
hostility . . . both robbed us of our goods, spoiled and took prisoners our
people, and continually lay in wait for our farther destruction, in another
king's country." Posing the question "from which of the said nations we
should soonest wish to recover our losses," Downton found it "all one in
conscience" to target any of them. They sought the likeliest way to swift and
substantial rewards by concentrating their power at sea. The Turks, being
"too far out of our reach," with "neither men nor goods passing in these
seas," were unassailable. To pursue those "most hateful to us of all others,"
the Portuguese, would necessitate a sustained presence on the Malabar Coast,
exposing ships and crews to inordinate wear and tear and possibly organized
attack. Thus, the selective seizure of the *St. Nicholas* set a pattern that beck-
oned them back to the Straits of Bab-el-Mandeb: "In my opinion," Downton
concluded, "our best way is to lie in the way of the Red Sea," where richly
laden ships from all of India converged—like the enormous *Rehemy*, lately
departed from Surat with pilgrims for Mecca (D in P, 3:271). To remove
regionally vendible cargoes from such ships would sting the Ottomans by
reducing their customs revenues. And although such extortion "may be
thought a great scandal to our nation over all India amongst those which are
Mussulmen [Muslims]," the English could salvage their honor by allowing
ships of Diu and Malabar to pass by while concentrating on the "subjects of
the great Mughal," Jahāngīr, who had denied them trade. "They will see that
we only endeavor to recover our loss on them which have wronged us" (*LR*,
1:160–61). As Greene put it, this course will "make them know we make a
difference between our friends and our enemies" (G, f13, 5 March).

The council on 4 March (24 February in Middleton's account) concluded in strong support of Downton's plan. Observing that, because "the

ships, men, and victuals were very far spent," they were presently "unable to proceed for the Moluccas, as he determined" (G, f12v, 5 March), Middleton first proposed to take their demand for reparations directly to the viceroy in Goa. There, no doubt invoking the 1604 treaty with Spain, he would offer to return the goods seized from the *St. Nicholas* if granted compensation for damages suffered at the hands of Soto Maior. If denied the same, he would threaten to prey at will on Portuguese shipping off the Malabar Coast (D in P, 3:277; J, 198). But the hazards of that option—"the variety of delays, and treacherous plots we were to expect, to our further abusing" (D in P, 3:277)—loomed larger as they discussed it. As Greene succinctly concluded, "Going for the Red Sea was less dangerous and held greater hope" to enrich the voyage. Goods taken from Cambayan ships would be of far greater value in London than the pepper they might later buy in Java and the Moluccas (G, f13). Middleton especially liked the idea of imposing his own ratios of exchange of English broadcloths for Indian calicoes, pintados, and indigo, "we having come so far with commodities fitting their country [Cambay and Gujarat], nowhere else in India vendible. I thought we should do ourselves some right, and them no wrong, to cause them [to] barter with us" (P, 3:187). Beyond presenting them as gifts, the most direct way to unload woolens and worsteds in the East was by extortion.

So, determined to restore England's honor and redeem, in Downton's words, "our manifold wrongs and ruin of our journey," on 5 March 1612 they turned back toward the Red Sea (*LR* 1:177). The errand took peculiar urgency from a further consideration: the news of an East India Company ship in progress to that sea. Middleton was resolved "to save that ship, men and goods" from falling into "the like mishap as we did" (P, 3:187, 277). Captain Saris and the Eighth Voyage, however, did not want saving.

CHAPTER 5

Corporate Strife in the Red Sea

Entering the bay of Tamrida on Socotra on the afternoon of 18 February 1612, the East India Company's Eighth Voyage (1611–14) saluted the town with rounds of ordnance, and Captain John Saris dispatched a landing party to pay respects to the island's ruler, Hamour Bensaid. His cape merchant Richard Cocks returned with assorted gifts and two letters, one being Middleton's admonition to English and Dutch mariners to "use all diligence to escape the danger hanging over your heads" in the Red Sea. The sultan, Middleton declared, had countermanded his own letter of protection for Christians with an express order to "take their ships, kill their men, and confiscate their goods" for trespassing "so near their holy house" in Arabia.[1] The news gave Saris pause. They clearly did not expect Middleton to reappear in the Red Sea. The Sixth Voyage was plotted from there to India, Sumatra, Java, and the Moluccas. The Eighth Voyage mariners had no desire either to divide the fleet or remain in Socotra for several months awaiting favorable winds for Surat. The Company's commission advised them to proceed to Aden and Mocha if they reached Socotra far in advance of the western monsoon (Birdwood, 403). Nor did Bensaid wish them to linger. He had complained to Middleton that the English ships in his bay discouraged others from entering; his unease was evident in his request that Saris not trade with any ships from Gujarat "without his privity and consent" (S, f53v, 19 February 1612).

Saris knew that Middleton was not carrying Achmed I's pass—a fact that Sir Henry's letter did not divulge. He wondered whether the Company's interests would be better served by crediting Middleton's report or by repeating the experiment with a difference: presenting the pass in Mocha (fig. 10). At a meeting on 27 February, having weighed the warnings, the voyage's

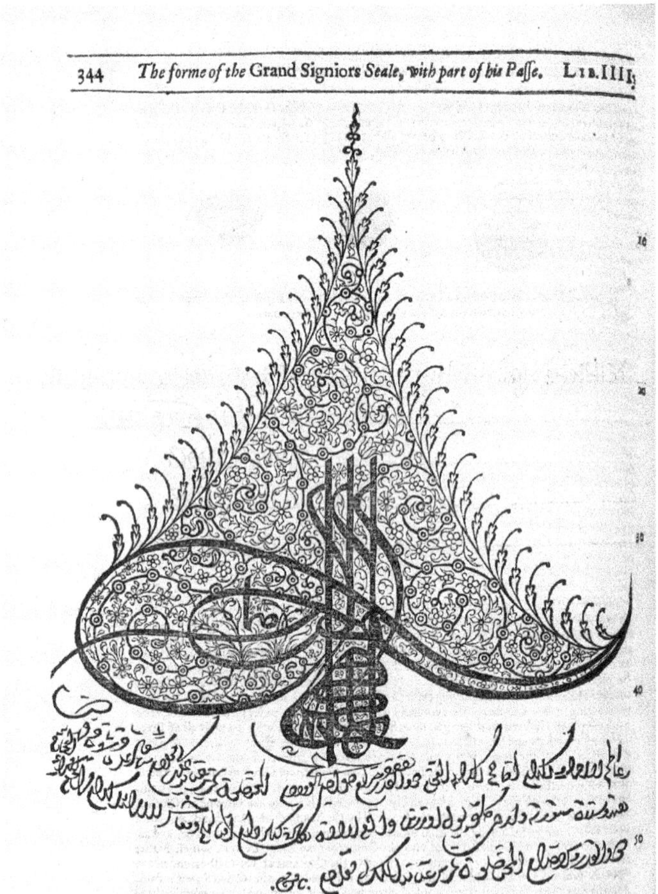

344 *The forme of the* Grand Signiors *Seale, with part of his Passe.* LIB. IIII.

.&c.

The Great Turkes *Letters Patents Englished.*

YOU *that are My most Laudable, Fortunate, Wealthie, and great* Vice-reys *and* Beglerbeys, *that are on the way from My most Happy and Imperiall Throne (both by Sea and Land) vnto the Confines and Bounds of the* East-Indies: *Owners of some part of Dignitie, and those vnto whom belongeth to giue aide, helpe, and succour in* GODS *cause, and* Mussulmanicall *Religion, vpon thier Emperours becke, The Wealth and Greatnesse of whom let it continue for euer. Likewise vn-*
to

FIGURE 10. Achmed I's insignia on letter of safe conduct. Samuel Purchas, *Hakluytus Posthumus* (1625), 1: 344. Courtesy of the Huntington Library.

chief merchants voted with Saris to try their luck in the Red Sea. They had "the Grand Signior's pass, which the former ships never had, yet was it demanded by the Turks." They wagered that their voyage would find a warmer reception than Middleton's and were prepared to retaliate if not. "For thereby shall we ascertain [for] the company what benefit there is to be made thereof, [while] standing upon our guard." They would not send anyone ashore "without good pledge" (hostages), confident that "we may ride securely and obtain trade aboard, though none ashore, our force being able to defend and offend upon occasion the greatest power that port can make." His reflexes resembled Middleton's: if denied trade, Saris would invoke the damages inflicted on the prior fleet to justify an enforced exchange with incoming ships of English for eastern commodities, or even to blockade the port. "But until then, I shall be very unwilling to offer any violence to them" (S, f55v; cf. S in P, 3:372). Departing from Socotra, he left a letter explaining the decision, "the monsoon not serving me to go for Surat," to go instead for the Red Sea: "Having the Grand Signior's letter which the former ships had not, with sufficient force to defend ourselves, I have resolved to make trial of the uttermost benefit [that] may be had by the letter aforesaid" (S, f56v, 29 February 1612).

The two generals pondered similar tactics yet operated from contrary assumptions. Premised on hopes of trade, Saris's course put him in direct opposition to Middleton's quest for reparations. The voyages' convergence thus precipitated a crisis in the East India Company's maritime governance. The strain of their conflict weighed heavily on both generals: Saris's defiance ignited post-traumatic stresses already triggered in Middleton by the return to the theater of his betrayal and captivity; and Saris, a former subordinate to Sir Henry, nursed his own insecurities in a paranoid vein. He had ample provocation, for the division between the fleets destabilized the command of the Eighth Voyage. Exposure to Sixth Voyage protocols and practices disturbed the fealties of Saris's mariners and provoked a mutiny on the *Hector* in which Saris was nearly slain. The arguments between Middleton and Saris—"these two ill met captains," as Downton described them (*LR* 1:168)— were rancorous, recurrent, and volatile. Institutional stimulants of egotism— each general presuming himself to be the personification of his voyage and the principal steward of its capital—aggravated their conflict, repeatedly igniting rage in Middleton and suspicions in Saris. With the latter threatening to sink the Indian ships in their custody if denied his demands, and Middleton threatening to sink Saris if he tried, the spring and summer of

1612 devolved into a dark, bewildering interval for both fleets.[2] As Downton observed, the conflict damaged and dishonored all of them: "A long while we spent in wrangling and discontent," he wrote, "to the shame of our nation, and to the spoil of our business with the Turks" (*LR* 1:168; D, f87, 15 May 1612). A few months later, to the detriment of an already fractious English community there, their quarrels resumed in Bantam.

Trying the Sultan's Pass in Mocha

That the voyages operated from distinct musters of joint stock sharpened the tensions between them. As generals, Middleton and Saris had both invested considerable ego and personal funds in their ventures. Middleton claimed in a letter to Emperor Jahāngīr to have "adventured in these ships my whole estate"; T. K. Rabb documents Saris's investment.[3] For his part, Saris believed the pass was indispensable, and he took due measures to secure it. Shortly before his fleet sailed, the London executives appointed Edmond Camden, a merchant assigned to the *Hector*, to carry the pass to Saris on the *Clove*. The errand failed ignominiously: while drinking with friends at Gravesend, Camden lost the papers. He "acquainted me," Saris writes, "that making merry amongst his friends, it was stolen from him, desiring me to stand his friend. Upon which unwelcome accident displeasing me beyond measure, knowing well how much that pass concerned the good of my voyage, where-upon my credit and welfare wholly depended, I sent the said Camden instantly with my letter to Sir Thomas [Smythe] acquainting them thereof, and if they had a duplicate, to send it with speed, soliciting a favorable censure of Camden's negligence" (S, f5, 7 April 1611). Fortunately, the Company possessed a copy. After two days, Camden returned with the duplicate and a translation (S, f5v). Ten months later in Socotra, Saris refused to assume these papers useless in Mocha.

Saris had served under Middleton before. Shipping out as a merchant on the East India Company's Second Voyage (1604–6), he had disembarked to become a factor in Bantam. There, to invoke Arthur Miller's Willy Loman, he was evidently "liked, but not well liked"—at least not by Middleton, who in 1605 placed him fifth in the chain of command below the chief factor Gabriel Towerson, resident in Bantam from the outset.[4] Yet, possessed of the durable constitution vital to advancement at this malarial outpost, and

promoted by the deaths of superiors, Saris became the chief factor at Towerson's departure late in 1608. He sailed homeward the following year, reaching
England in mid-1610. Having learned the Malayan language and a great deal
about commerce throughout the East Indies, he won the attention of Company magnates with a lengthy memorandum, "Observations on the Eastern
Trade," a Dutch-informed treatise that expounded markets, commodities,
and exchange rates across wide regions, including Japan.[5] The document
probably helped persuade the Company to make Saris the "captain and chief
commander" (Birdwood, 396) of the Eighth Voyage, the East India Company's first to Japan. The appointment elevated him above his former superior, Towerson, who became the captain of the well-traveled *Hector*, which,
along with the flagship *Clove* and the *Thomas*, made up the fleet. It also cast
Saris opposite Middleton.

On 1 March 1612, four days before Middleton's fleet left the Malabar
Coast, the Eighth Voyage sailed for the Red Sea. Anchoring near Mocha on
the sixteenth, they were visited by "a poor old slave in a small canoe" sent by
the governor to ascertain their intent. He informed Saris that Regib Aga had
been cashiered—ostensibly for mistreating the Sixth Voyage mariners—and
that the new governor, Ider Aga, "a Grecian by birth," was "very kind to
strangers, and a great friend to merchants" (S in P, 3:377).[6] Having dismissed
the messenger with a request to see a person of greater dignity, they were
next visited by "an Italian turned Moor, well clad," who asked to see the
sultan's pass. Denying this request, Saris explained that he had both the pass
and a letter from King James I and that, to honor the former, he would
discharge fifty-one rounds of ordnance. Giving the messenger time to return
and announce the same, the fleet made its show of force, and the town
"answered with five pieces of excellent ordnance, and two galleys three a
piece." Saris admired these versatile vessels, "five and twenty oars on a side,
and well fitted, yards up" (S in P, 3:377–78).

The Eighth Voyage clearly hoped to make a new beginning in Mocha.
Visited by the governor's secretary, Saris explained that he knew of "the
wrongs done by Regib Aga unto Sir Henry Middleton his countryman and
his company" yet was willing to forgive and forget these offenses, "if we
might now have quiet trade" (S in P, 3:378). The secretary, "fearing that he
was come to take revenge of them," asked if Saris were a kinsman of Middleton and was reassured to the contrary (3:379). On 20 March, taking aboard
several high dignitaries as pledges, Saris accepted Ider Aga's invitation to go
ashore. While the fleet discharged another thunderous fifty-one rounds, he

and his merchants set off in three handsomely outfitted skiffs and landed to
a crowded, festive, musical reception. They were escorted in full state to
the governor's house. Inside, Ider Aga, whom Cocks described as a "gallant
gentleman" (*LR* 1:218), emerged to lead Saris by the hand to a bay window
where they sat on a silk quilt and cushions to exchange courtesies. Then Saris
produced the letters from their respective monarchs. Cocks first read King
James's declaration of amity, which, in a translation relay, "[Nicholas] Boulton our linguist interpreted to the captain of the galleys, and he to the Aga";
then Saris "delivered him the Grand Signior's pass, which he gave to his
secretary to read, which done, he took it, kissed it, and laid it upon his head
without further ceremony" (S in P, 3:381). This looked to Saris like an auspi-
cious start.

Ider Aga informed him, of course, that they could not engage in substantial trade until permission arrived in ten or twelve days from Ja'far Basha, to
whom he had already written. In the meantime, the English were welcome
to come ashore to buy and sell "small matters," for such evidence of amity
would reassure the local population and incoming mariners, who might avoid
the harbor if they suspected trouble. Saris welcomed the arrangement. He
had anchored the fleet near the shore, so that "no laden ship could come
in, but that she must perforce ride within call of us." With their ordnance
commanding the town, their skiffs could come and go at will, and they could
conduct trade "either ashore or aboard the ships" (S in P, 3:385). An elaborate
feast followed the meeting, after which Saris, who declined an offered "horse
richly trapped, the . . . bridle all of silver," and his entourage were conducted
on a foot tour of the town. They viewed a likely house for their factory,
visited the home of a former governor, Hamet Bey (S, f63v), and paid parting
respects to Ider Aga on his stairway before, "accompanied with a great train
of the best of the town," they all returned aboard, to a salute of another
fifteen rounds from the ships (S in P, 3:386–87). Their employers might have
complained that the fleet was squandering its gunpowder, but Saris believed
otherwise. He remained wary, displayed power, and held clear hopes of establishing substantial trade and an English factory here.[7]

The next day, Saris learned from Richard Cocks that, evidently in 1610,
Hamet Bey had traveled from Istanbul to Mocha "with a letter to the Aga
not to permit any Christian to trade here upon his life." This troubling news
confirmed Middleton's report and raised urgent questions. Did their letter of
safe conduct supersede this letter? Bey speculated that it should. He told
Cocks that he left Istanbul six months before the date indicated on their pass

(c. 18 February 1611), and "ours being of a later date, there was great hope we might leave a factory." Yet he could not be sure. The "letter," he remarked, bore a "date upwards of two years" (S, f64, 21 March 1612). Which, if either, document held currency? Bey recommended in any case that Saris quickly hire a house in Mocha "before the India ships came in" to drive up prices and leave "few or none to be had" (S, f64v, 22 March 1612). What neither of them knew was that Mocha's housing market that season would be slowed by an English blockade of the Straits of Bab-el-Mandeb.

Saris learned on 31 March that the governor had received the basha's letter granting them safe trade; yet Ider Aga did not show them the letter, and they remained jittery. Nor had Ja'far Basha, as a Turkish confidant of Femell cautioned them, yet received from the governor their copy of the sultan's pass. Advising Saris not to go ashore without "good pledges as formerly" (S in P, 3:388–89), this discrete friend, "Hosoroofe," shared with Cocks and Saris Femell's 30 April 1611 letter, which turned out to be a copy of the one Sir Henry left at Socotra (S, f66v, 28 March 1612). When Ider Aga invited him ashore again, Saris sent instead his "brother" Towerson, who was eager to perform the errand, with the request to see "the translation of the Basha's letter." Yet no such document was produced. Instead, the governor suggested that the English should "send up a couple of men of good fashion up to the Basha" with the sultan's pass and a suitable gift, "and then speedy dispatch would be made to my liking" (S, f67v–f68v, 3–5 April 1611). As they pondered whom and what to send on this mission, however, letters arrived from Middleton and Sharpeigh to announce, stunningly, that the Sixth Voyage was anchored in the straits. Middleton "was come back to be revenged of the Turks," and he desired Saris "to get his goods and people aboard with all speed" (S in P, 3:389–90). The message instantly obliterated their plans for Sana'a. Once word had reached Mocha that Middleton was arresting ships at Bab-el-Mandeb, any envoys sent inland would become hostages.

"These Two Ill Met Generals"

Readers of *Purchas His Pilgrimes*, still the primary printed source for the journals of Middleton, Downton, and Saris, and Satow's edition of the last, miss Downton's depiction of Middleton and Saris as "two ill met generals" and earn scarcely a glimpse of the rancor between the fleets in the Red Sea.[8] A supporter and paid beneficiary of the East India Company, which awarded him £100 upon the massive work's publication in 1625, Rev. Samuel Purchas enjoyed privileged access to the papers archived at Sir Thomas Smythe's house, and he edited them with an eye to the Company's reputation.[9] Major controversies over the eastern trade and the East India Company's monopoly agitated Parliament and the press during the years Purchas was assembling his volumes, and his great collection constituted an act of advocacy in these debates. Fervently desiring the Company to endure and grow, he conceived its captains as merchant-soldiers of heroic stature and minimized the intracorporate conflicts, the embarrassments of command, documented in the manuscripts he redacted. Many of these journals, like Middleton's, have not survived. But Downton's and Saris's do. They, along with Greene's, Jourdain's, and the candid letters preserved in the Company's "Original Correspondence" (printed in *Letters Received* in the late 1890s), enable us to reconstruct a damaging interval of conflict between the Sixth and Eighth Voyages in the late spring and summer of 1612. The problems were both structural and personal.

Following his months of incarceration in Yemen, Middleton was in no mood to accede to a protrade agenda. In progress toward the Red Sea, he dispatched Pemberton in the *Darling* to Socotra for news of the East India Company ship rumored to be headed there, "even into the mouths of the wolves," as Downton put it, "which by God's mercy we have escaped" (D in P, 3:280). Near Aden on 2 April 1612, Middleton's fleet reunited. Carrying a copy of the letter Saris had left in Bensaid's care, Pemberton boarded the flagship with the distressing news that Saris and his full fleet, having appraised the warnings, sailed on in hopes of "better entertainment than I had," Middleton wrote (M in P, 3:189). This course, which struck Sir Henry as dangerously naive, directly threatened his designs. He had come to rescue these men, and if they were already active ashore, he could not initiate a blockade without provoking the wolves to bite.

He called a council that swiftly concluded there was nothing for it but "to proceed as formerly we had determined," fixated on honor and reparations, "for back we could not return till the Westerly wind were come, which could not be before middle May" (M in P, 3:189). Saris's delusional hopes for trade and a factory in Mocha would have to be abandoned. He sent Downton in the *Peppercorn* to blockade Aden and direct its traffic toward the "two-fold entrance" of Bab-el-Mandeb, where the *Trades Increase* and the *Darling*, one poised in each passage, would intercept vessels entering the Red Sea (P, 3:189, 280). Anchored on the side nearer Arabia, the flagship was visited on 4 April by a party of guards from an adjacent fort who offered to send a foot post to

Mocha with answering correspondence within three days. Jourdain reports that when these men, who had mistaken the two vessels for Indian ships, found themselves aboard the *Trades Increase*, "they were in great fear, because some of them were actors about the imprisoning of our men with Sir Henry Middleton. But the general gave them good entertainment and sent them ashore with letters to the English at Mocha" (J, 204–5). This was the summons that interrupted Saris's plans.

Flummoxed, Saris wrote back to report his progress. However ominous their welcome looked to Middleton, Saris argued that the case was altered: the new governor, he insisted, operated in good faith. Ider Aga offered "solemn words, that if what hath been already committed by Regib Aga against you might be forgotten, I shall not only trade peaceably, but upon them and their children's heads be it if the like be committed again" (S, f68v, 5 April 1612). He elided their uncertainty over the precedence of the sultan's pass or its countermand and the content of the basha's letter. In mingled concession and complaint, Saris declared that Middleton's arrival has blasted his hopes for trade: "Some hope I have had, but the coming of your worship hath made it of no effect." He explained that he had sent the factor Richard Wickham to Middleton with this letter "to understand further from you" what their combined fleets might do for their employers.

Then, in an ingratiating bid, he segued to a prospect of mutual advantage. He reported his strength: "I have at this present 221 men in my three ships which, I thank God, are for the most part in good health, so that I stand in less fear of their villainy." He concluded with reflections heartening to his fellow general: "I do wish the time would permit me to come unto you, for if I deceive not myself, here is more benefit to be made by virtue of his majesty's commission, so great an injury having been committed, than otherwise may be expected . . . by way of commerce" (S, f69). Saris declared himself open to a campaign of barter-rationalized pillage. They had goods to sell by one means or another and needed eastern cargoes. Together, their fleets might adapt the venerable English habits of privateering to their current predicament. Yet critical impediments loomed: the separate funding of each voyage; the grudging ambivalence and indecision of Saris; and the fierce resolve of Middleton, determined to restore his fortunes and personal honor, to dominate their collaboration. Sir Henry, Saris came to understand, inexplicably believed himself to possess "a larger commission" than his fellow general—an egoistic conviction that Saris, while honoring Middleton's superior social status as a knight, refused to concede (S, f81v, 16 May 1612).

While suggesting to Middleton that he was amenable to a blockade, Saris did not "get his goods and people aboard with all speed." He vacillated and temporized on both fronts. Hoping for some reward from the promising negotiations with Ottoman authorities, on 6 April he wrote to "my approved good friend Captain Mame," the captain of the galleys in Mocha, that he was "very busy in clearing my ship" and needed a few more days to retrieve the gifts he planned to send to Sana'a. He exhorted Mame and the governor "not to fear the arrival of Sir Henry Middleton, who was so grievously wronged here and his people murdered." He promised to persuade Middleton "to so reasonable conditions as shall be for the good of the town and all those merchants which are or shall hereafter come to this place, to pass . . . without fear" (S, f69–69v). Returning with Mame's written reply, Boulton reported that the governor wished to reassure Saris of his good will, for the basha had instructed him to "permit me trade and use me kindly." Ider Aga "cared the less what he [Middleton] did," for Saris would be witness to that conduct. Middleton should be advised that all of them answered to a higher power: If he were to "shoot into the town, [and] take and burn the junks, he might. But there was an ambassador at Constantinople [who] should pay for all, for their master would not be wronged" (S, f69v). The English nation would perforce compensate the sultan for any damages Middleton inflicted.

In a following letter, Ider Aga gratified Saris's request to see a translation of Ja'far Basha's response to their petition for trade. "You have writ me," the basha reportedly began, "that three English ships are come to Mocha to trade in merchandise with the Grand Signior's pass. Give them faithful promise from me to come ashore, buy, sell, and take a house till the monsoon be passed. You have likewise written me that they will send two men up to me. Give them all things fitting for their journey, etc. That what I [Saris] would propound he and the Aga would underwrite. That for bartering, they would do something of love but not of force, and were willing to lade all three ships as well as one" (S, f69, 7 April; cf. S in P, 3:391). These were reassuring words. Yet Middleton's blockade had created such a stir in Mocha that Saris dared not send a skiff ashore with goods to sell (S, f69v, 7 April). Observing that the basha's letter "makes no further mention of [a] longer stay than for the monsoon" (f70v, 8 April), Saris answered that he no longer desired a factory in Mocha. Instead, he requested the governor's blessing to barter with Indian ships offshore, proffering that once Middleton heard he had thereby laden one of his ships with "their commodities at reasonable rates, . . . I know he will not persist in anything that shall be prejudicial to you to the hindrance of my business" (S, f70). Saris was claiming more than he could deliver. Yet Ider Aga promised to grant him a warrant to "fetch in" junks to Mocha that would otherwise, upon sight of the *Trades Increase* or *Darling*, go elsewhere if they could. Before letting them land their goods, Saris might "have all such [of] their commodities which I shall find fitting my use in barter, . . . paying the Grand Signior his customs, and . . . keep them by me till this be performed" (S, f70v, 8 April). Saris was thinking along Middleton's lines here: not precisely blockading Mocha but securing prior access to whatever he desired from the incoming vessels in order to make exchanges in kind— English broadcloths for Indian calicoes and indigo.

Another letter from Sir Henry reached him on 9 April. This time Saris's response was less conciliatory. He explained that his prior declaration of openness to combine forces in a blockade expressed, not his desire, but the "honest disposition and love I bear you": to adopt such a course would be a favor to Middleton. Where Middleton insisted that the basha meant to make hostages of any merchants Saris sent to Sana'a, "I have no such thought," the latter replied, "having hitherto had good entertainment with promise of trade." It was Middleton, not Saris, who had engineered that risk:

> But this course which you have taken is the cause I dare not credit them [the Ottomans] and hath overthrown the benefit I should have made by the Grand Signior's pass. And however you have been persuaded [that] here is little benefit to be made, our commodities not vendible, I am well assured if a factory were settled, whereof I had great hope, we should not only vent cloth, iron, and tin to the India merchants in good quantity and per reasonable profit, and better cheap than those that bring it out of the Mediterranean, but also procure indigos, bastas, cotton yarn, and other India wares fitting our country at reasonable prices and at the first hand. (S, f71, 9 April)

Saris understood eastern trade networks and made a valid point of major consequence: a factory in Mocha should provide cheaper, more direct access to Indian goods than the Levant Company enjoyed at Mediterranean ports serviced by caravan. A permanent house in Mocha should have compensated the East India Company for the present loss of its factory in Surat. Saris suggested, in short, that Middleton's return to the Red Sea was a strategic blunder for the East India Company, damaging the corporation's long-range interests. "I would to the Almighty you had been better persuaded than to have come hither," he vented.[10] Seconding the sentiment, Cocks later complained to East India Company directors that, had Middleton conducted himself "in such an indifferent sort as he ought to have done"—that is, in pursuit of legitimate trade—"it would have been much for our ease, but much more for your Worships' profit" (*LR* 1:220).

But Middleton had forced Saris's hand. The latter's negotiations in Mocha soured on 10 April, as news of further seizures in the straits arrived: "There was neither merchant nor broker [who] would come aboard us as I desired, the knight's taking of the junks had so discontented them" (S, f72, 10 April). Cocks delivered the governor's unwelcome message that a judge had deemed his late promises impossible to perform, for they exceeded the terms of Achmed I's letter of protection. Saris would win no warrant to "fetch in" Indian ships after all. A meeting of his merchandizing council the next day concluded that, given Middleton's activity in the straits, their "hope of trade here is very little." They should "continue friendship" in Mocha if possible yet consider forceful means to secure rich cargoes. Wickham's reminder of Sir Henry's earnest desire "that I would come unto him, with promise that he would do more for me than for any of his acquaintance" (f72v, 12 April), persuaded Saris to sail with the first wind to Bab-el-Mandeb.

On the friendly pretext of delivering Ider Aga's admonitory letter to Middleton ("I have no occasion of my own to go to him," Saris lied to the governor [S, f72v]), the *Clove*, *Hector*, and *Thomas* left Mocha on the evening of 13 April 1612. As they reached the *Trades Increase* the following morning, the fleets exchanged salutes of ordnance, and Saris went aboard the great ship. The generals talked into the night. Sir Henry described the meeting as cordial and productive: "We spent all that day in friendly communication." The conversation continued aboard the *Clove* the next day, where Saris "kindly entertained" (M in P, 3:191) Middleton's party—which included Sharpeigh, Hawkins, Jourdain, and other principal mariners—for dinner (the midday meal). Middleton hinted at some disagreement—"Many words passed betwixt us, he promising to himself much good trade at Mocha if I had not come, which my experience found to the contrary"—but did not elaborate (M in P, 3:191). Jourdain remarked more candidly that Middleton and Saris again talked until "ten at night, but they did not well concur together about their affairs" (J, 206).

The measure of this understatement comes clear in Saris's manuscript.[11] In their first exchange, the latter declared his willingness, "our hopes of trade being cut off" by Middleton's return, to detain Turkish and Indian vessels if doing so did not violate his royal commission. In conference the next morning before Sir Henry arrived, he, Towerson, and Cocks concluded that they might proceed. But the expected consensus failed. After dinner, Middleton declared that he could not countenance an equal division of the spoils. Fixated on the insolvency of his own voyage, "he said he would take out of all the India ships which should come in here what he thought fitting, and then, if I would, I might have the rest." Saris objected that this was grossly unfair and that, if Middleton insisted on proceeding thus, he would depart. The threat outraged Sir Henry:

> He asked me whither I would go. I told him to windward [to] try my fortunes; whereat he swore most deeply that, if I did take that course, he would sink me and set fire [to] all such ships as traded with me. But not willing to put flax to fire, I sought by mild speeches to win him to remembrance of the love he had borne me, and not to fall out with me in this action, seeking but to advance the benefit of the undertakers of my voyage, his unexpected return having much impaired the same; and for himself, I honored him as one that had and shall command me, desiring that as I was come unto him to confer and contrive what shall be fittest to be done, so that he would be pleased not to be offended if I shall not assent to unprofitable projects. He told me I should not meddle with any ship that came in here, neither go to windward of him; and so parted.
> (S, f73–f73v, 15 April; cf. J, 206n)

Poised to perform synchronous mutual service of the "body corporate and politic" that launched them both, the voyages found themselves at cross-purposes. To go to windward would allow Saris's fleet to arrest incoming ships before Middleton's could. Sir Henry would not suffer it. Despite the likelihood that his precedence would encumber their tactics, he held firm: his men, not Saris's, would first ransack any ships detained.

Middleton's ireful threats exposed critical flaws in the East India Company's systems of finance and command. Each general fixated on the earnings of his own expedition. Their commissions offered no protocols to arbitrate between them. As during the late Red Sea crisis between Middleton and Downton, it was up to the persons on the scene to negotiate a solution. In this instance, the more prudent Saris, "not willing to put flax to fire," backed down. As a knight, Sir Henry outranked him socially; and deference to Middleton was familiar to him. The following day, they hit upon an agreement that the Sixth Voyage should possess two-thirds, the Eighth one-third, of the take from any detained ships. Yet the concession to Middleton galled Saris and eroded his authority in the eyes of his own men. Towerson too had once outranked him. Would Eighth Voyage crews believe the *Hector*'s captain better suited to Saris's office? If Towerson deferred to Middleton over Saris, whom would they follow?

Mutiny on the *Hector*

Saris hosted Middleton to dinner the next day—"Sir Henry came aboard and protested great friendship," he wrote (S, f75, 18 April)—and they drew up papers of agreement that he delivered to the flagship the following morning (J, 207). Then, in an act of damaging indecision, Saris made a tactical blunder: in hopes of purchasing promised indigo, on 19 April he departed in the *Clove* for Mocha. Plotting to exercise his authority from a distance, drafting careful instructions to send his way, not Middleton's, any great ships they detained, he left the *Hector* and *Thomas* to patrol the expanse southwest of the "Habesh" Straits while Middleton's ships kept the narrow northeastern passage (J, 208). He left his informant Wickham aboard the *Trades Increase* to report any "private conveying away of the richest goods" (S, f75, 19 April) by Middleton's men. But Saris, the prolixity of whose journal bespeaks his faith in the social efficacy of texts, put too much trust in penned directives. His departure left Middleton in tactical command of both fleets.

Mariners on the *Hector* took quick advantage of these circumstances. Prone to curtail expenses and preserve victuals for the return voyage, Saris had enforced a relatively austere, legume-based regimen for his crews. Resentments over their lean rations had long festered among the *Hector*'s mariners, and the crewmen, who saw no point in refraining from meats likely to rot unconsumed, now appealed to Middleton for help. The sailors of the Sixth Voyage, they had learned, dined better. Two days after Saris sailed for Mocha in the *Clove*, tumult erupted on the *Hector*, and a large party of crewmen took a boat to the *Trades Increase* with a petition for Sir Henry. They had arranged their signatures in a circle or "round-robin," Jourdain reported,[12] so that "it should not be known who was the principal of the mutiny. The effect of their petition was to have more victuals, for that they were almost starved, and some had already perished for want of food; and rather than they would endure it any longer they would run to the Turks. Presently after, Captain Towerson sent the skiff aboard the *Trade*, with a letter to Sir Henry entreating him to come aboard the *Hector* to pacify the company; which presently Sir Henry performed" (J, 208). Sir Henry duly boarded the *Hector*, promised the crew that Saris would bring them "redress" on his return, and calmed the company. That evening, Towerson returned with the general to the flagship (J, 209). One wonders what thoughts they shared about Saris. Listening to the crew's litany of complaints, Jourdain, for one, faulted him for dealing "so hardly with men, having such plenty of victuals in his ship, . . . and the men starve for want thereof, being forced to eat the tallow from the ties with hunger; with many other tyrannies which I cannot believe that so wise a gentleman would do to Christians" (J, 211).[13] Upon his return to London, Saris was indeed compelled to answer for his parsimony. Drafted in his own hand probably during his residence at Sir Thomas Smythe's house while the Court of Committees took up these and other charges, the prolix British Library manuscript of his journal constitutes a sustained brief in his defense, as the author specified each day's allotment of victuals and detailed the myriad urgencies he addressed as general.[14]

As these events transpired, incoming ships busied the blockaders. There was no time to dispatch any ships to Saris, who, given the mutiny, would have to return at once in any case. Middleton and Jourdain note the interception of a ship of Cananor on 18 April; two of Surat the next day, one of these the *Hasanni*, "belonging to Abdelasan [Khwāja Abū-l Hassan], Captain Hawkins's friend, and the other to Hoghanazan [Khwāja Nizām], our old friend the governor of Surat" (J, 208);[15] a ship of Diu on 20 April; and three days later, the prize they most eagerly sought—the Queen Mother's ship, the *Rehemy*. Larger than the *Trades Increase*—over one hundred fifty feet in length and forty-two feet at the beam—it carried rich cargo and some fifteen hundred pilgrims toward Mecca (S in P, 3:396; M in P, 3:193). To arrest this great vessel, noted Downton, "would most have touched the Great Mughal [Jahāngīr], so she would best have pleased us in meeting her" (D, f83, 15 April 1612). This ship "was the principal mark we aimed at," he elaborated, "that thereby the Great Mughal may sooner understand how un-patient the subjects of the king of England (whom he in his pride so much despiseth . . .) are, both for the dishonor done to their king and wrongs to themselves" (D, f85, 7 May 1612). With its capture, report of English sea power would permeate India's highest echelons.

Jourdain notes that the combined fleets moved on 24 April to consolidate their gains: "Having now as many ships as we could well tell what to do withal, we set sail towards Asabb" (J, 210).[16] The *Hector* followed the *Trades Increase* while the *Thomas* and the *Darling* remained in the straits. The news that the two fleets functioned as one in his absence stunned Saris. He suspected the worst: that Middleton flouted their late agreement and had harnessed the *Hector* to the aims of the Sixth Voyage. "Wherefore I hold Sir Henry hath molded him [Towerson] for his own use. God direct me, for help have I none but Mr. Cocks and my purser" (S, f75v, 23 April 1612). The next day, a sheaf of letters from Towerson and Middleton arrived with report of the mutiny and the departure of the *Trades Increase* and *Hector*, in convoy with the captured Indian ships, to Asab Bey. The crisis on the *Hector* demanded sudden remediation. The next day, Saris abandoned his hopes for Mocha's indigo and sailed back to reassert his authority.

Middleton's journal, indicating that "we fetched good store of indigos out of the ships of Surat and Diu"—the irony would not have been lost on Saris—breaks off with notice of the *Clove*'s approach on 27 April 1612 (M in P, 3:193). Between that date and 15 May, when Downton and Greene rejoined them in the *Peppercorn*, Saris and Jourdain provide the only eyewitness accounts of the ensuing troubles. (Purchas's edition omits the mutiny and effaces scenes of strife between the generals.) Anchoring near the others on the evening of 27 April, the *Clove*'s captain was visited by Towerson, Wickham, and Camden, who reported that sixty bales of indigo from the junks had been removed to the *Hector* and that the decks of the *Trades Increase* were encumbered with "goods out of diverse junks, most confused." The next day, the *Clove* received a boat from the *Trades Increase* carrying Captain Sharpeigh, who invited Saris to meet with Middleton, and Towerson, who escorted two detained leaders of the mutiny, Evans and Morrideth. Meaning to accept Sharpeigh's invitation before intervening on the *Hector*, Saris consigned the two men to the bilboes without questioning them.

Learning that disorder persisted on the ship, however, he postponed the confrontation with Sir Henry. Worked up by Master Thomas Fuller and his son, a boatswain's mate, the crew now threatened to abandon the *Hector* or storm the *Clove* to free Evans and Morrideth. When Saris requested that young Fuller, "a chief actor," be sent to him "to know the reason of [the] distraction," Towerson wrote back that "the gentleman denied to come" (S, f76v, 28 April). Saris would have to intervene directly. Accompanied by his cape merchant, Richard Cocks, and the *Clove's* master, James Foster, and carrying the papers of his royal commission, he climbed into a turbulent scene:

> I found the company in most confused disorder, the master [Fuller] upon the half deck looking furiously upon me, and after comes in the waist where I was and stands with both his arms akimbo, rousing himself up against me, but said nothing.[17] I asked what he meant to do to use this action towards me. He said I cannot tell. Wherefore noting this passion in him, [I] went upon the half deck [away] from him, where he followed me and stood by me in the like manner again. I commanded the boatswain to call up the company, and opening his majesty's commission, charged them to be quiet and show me the reason of this disorder. (S, f76v, 28 April 1612)

Ranked immediately beneath the captain, a ship's "master" directed the daily labor of sailing it.[18] That this officer so blatantly challenged Saris marked the severity of the situation: he and Towerson had lost command of the vessel.

Saris heard the crew's complaints and promised to augment their food portions. He assured them that they might have negotiated the same "by a more direct way" (S, f76v): simply by asking. They grew milder. But, to the alarm of Cocks and Foster, Fuller still stood out menacingly against the general. At that, Saris commanded him aboard the skiff for transport to the *Clove*, "for I would confer further of this business with him there." The order proved explosive:

> He said he scorned my command and would not go, instantly flung into his cabin, where he brought out a broad bladed falchion or brewer's bung dagger, naked.[19] Holding it by his side in the one hand, [he] took me by the throat in the other, wherefore I craved aid of the officers to apprehend him. He still continued holding me forcibly by the throat, myself commanding him to obey, having nothing but his majesty's commission open in my hand, Capt. Towerson pulling me away, desiring me not to trust him. He offered to strike at me, and loosing his hand from my throat in most base fashion, scorning my authority, thrust me from him and struck his majesty's commission against the mizzen mast. (S, f77, 28 April)

The sheaf of royal paper was nothing to Fuller. As officers approached, he stabbed at Saris, missed, and again bolted toward his cabin. Saris pursued him to the doorway just as Fuller, moving to shut it, stabbed at him again. The coxswain and Towerson pulled Saris free of the thrust, and the blade struck the cabin's beam. At that, Fuller kicked Saris clear of the door and barricaded himself inside.

Shaken and enraged, Saris insisted that he would have Fuller aboard the *Clove*, and he huddled with the others to plot the man's removal. "They said it would cost bloodshed, yet the abuse being so great, they would assist me so far as their lives would go. I told them they should need to go no further than I went myself, for I would lead the way" (S, f77). Saris offered to carry no weapon, simply the commission. Towerson and Cocks convinced him that they should try persuasion first. They returned with a report of Fuller's defiance: "They could get nothing of him but [that] he would be the death of him who should first come in, and of as many as he could" (S, f77). When Saris told every man to arm himself for the assault, Towerson beseeched him to send for Middleton instead and offered to fetch him. "Not willing to use violence if persuasion might serve" (S, f77), Saris relented. But the plan's implications were humiliating: if, before the eyes of the *Hector*'s crew and other witnesses, Middleton mollified Fuller, Sir Henry would demonstrate his supremacy over Saris in the office they shared.

Thus it happened. Coming aboard with Captains Sharpeigh and Hawkins, and the *Trade*'s Master Giles Thornton, Middleton persuaded Fuller to leave his cabin and surrender himself, with his son, to Foster's custody for conduct to the *Clove*. In exiting the scene, however, the *Hector*'s master openly insulted Saris: "Before them," Saris reports, "he gave me such base, reviling speeches [that] Sir Henry reproved him and protested that, if he had been under his command and used the like, he would have killed him" (S, f77). Thus Middleton, containing the mutiny, schooled Saris in the management of men. The exercise insinuated that his fellow general lacked both the tact and the rigor to command a fleet. Saris was, indeed, a milder-tempered man than Middleton. Even now, had the humiliation not been public, he might have forgiven a repentant Fuller: "Yet had all these gross abuses been offered privately, I could for my own part [have] let it pass. But in the knowledge and sight of so many, it is not to be endured. And should I let it pass, it might encourage others to do the like" (S, f77). The severity sometimes requisite to his office wore awkwardly on Saris.

Forced Exchanges and a Bid for Reparations

The following day, Saris went aboard the *Trades Increase* to confer with Middleton over the disposition of ships in their custody. The two argued bitterly. Their approaches to Ottoman authorities and Indian mariners were diametrically opposed: Saris desired good relations with the former and maximal profits from the latter; Middleton preferred moderate extortions from the latter and spectacular compensation from the Turks. The dispute played out with disheartening variations for several weeks. Jourdain omits the "many unkind words" that passed between them on 29 April yet notes Saris's insistence that the Indian ships remain in custody until he agreed to release them and his threat to detain them again otherwise (J, 212). In his account, Saris objects to the Sixth Voyage's prior access to the Indian ships: choking the decks of the *Trades Increase*, disorganized heaps of "huge packs of cloth" impeded their own inspection, for "there was not any room" to do so. The monsoon might call the fleets away before they could sort through the packs. Saris proposed that mariners from both voyages should collaborate to streamline the thus-far chaotic unlading of the Indian ships, whose decks might serve, in a more rationally disposed process, as inspection sites. Unmoved, Middleton maintained that there was ample time for the tasks at hand, for he wanted only indigo, a dye destined for the home market; once securing that, he would free the ships. Desiring regionally vendible cloths as well as indigo, Saris demanded his right to a full third "of all such goods as should be" in the junks, and he meant to verify such division with bills of lading taken from the Indian vessels. But Middleton resented Saris's move to acquire cargo marketable in the Indies. He was indignant that the Eighth Voyage, having sailed a year after him, was "further forward in [its] lading than himself" and readier to proceed to Sumatra, Java, and the Moluccas. He swore "deeply," Saris wrote, "that I should have no cloth to spoil his market in places where we shall come. I desired him not to continue that opinion, neither once to think that any one junk should depart out of this road before I had exchanged as much of my English commodities with them as I thought fitting or [as] my third part would yield" (S, f77v, 29 April 1612). As the generals argued, the sorting of indigo and cloth went forward. The Indian mariners, Jourdain observed, "stood by to see their goods parted before their faces, and knew not whether they should have anything for it or not" (J, 212).

Within a few days, Middleton assented to a mutual division of cloths. Perhaps he was persuaded by Saris's demand for that material (rials evidently being nonnegotiable with the local tribesmen) to buy fresh meat for the company of the *Hector*, who "are ready to arm and come against me again . . . and will have goats as Sir Henry his men have." Saris speculated darkly that Middleton "doth deny me cloth to stir up my company to molest and vex me" (S, f78v, 2 May 1612). Their collision elicited suspicions and indignation on both sides. Yet the essential trouble between the generals was of the Company's making, not their own: the East India Company's investment in a single voyage at a time. "Yet do I heartily wish, Saris expostulated, "that it had pleased God my fortune had been better than to have met with him here" (S, f77v). Middleton likewise confided to Downton that his plans to take "sufficient revenge" on the Turks "should have gone forward . . . had it not been his ill chance to have met him [Saris] here" (*LR*, 1:167). That both Middleton and Saris regretted the meeting points up a pivotal irony of the East India Company's predicament at this juncture: the occasion to deploy unprecedented strength at sea—their great new flagship in fortuitous convoy with the vessels of combined fleets—devolved instead into a spectacle of division with marginal gains. The clash between the voyages offered an important object lesson to the London Company: that each expedition conducted itself like a petty commonwealth compromised their strength at sea and stunted corporate growth in London. The East India Company would not implement long-range strategies of capital accumulation so long as voyages moved at cross-purposes—so long as one general schemed to block another from taking on goods whose sale might "spoil his market" at subsequent ports of call.

Whatever Middleton chose to do, Saris resolved to claim his share from the Indian ships. On 30 April he warned the nohudas not to depart without his leave.[20] The detained mariners replied that they risked losing the monsoon to Jedda unless the work of bartering quickened considerably, and they offered to facilitate the process: "to bring aboard our ships what packs we would to be opened there, and to carry back what we refused" (S in P, 3:396). The next morning, Saris sent Cocks, Towerson, and—flouting Sir Henry's directive that, having served as Saris's spy, Wickham was not welcome on the *Trades Increase*—Wickham to induce Middleton to accept the nohudas' offer. They reminded Sir Henry that discord between the fleets would invite "the Moors [to] deride us both," squandering any respect earned by the *Rehemy's* capture. In a vile humor, Middleton agreed to the process. Angered that Wickham had reported his outbursts, Middleton ordered the man out of his sight, and Thornton "reviled him in his [Middleton's] presence, telling him he was a lying knave, Sir Henry not once reproving him" (S, f78, 30 April, 1 May). It was an ugly scene—remotely orchestrated by Saris by including Wickham in the party. Saris duly noted the incident in his journal. He was keeping score.

Saris lamented that his troubles with Middleton were infecting the crews. Having heard report of raucous complaints against him and his mariners among Middleton's men, on 3 May Saris went to the *Trades Increase* to object to Sir Henry "that his people in general . . . did in their drunken meetings make a common course of cursing me and my voyage, . . . reviling my people also." He declared that he feared "there would be bloodshed on both sides" if Middleton did not discipline his men at once (S, f78v, 3 May). The next day, Middleton duly admonished his crew; on 5 May, he and Saris agreed to add cloth to the commodities divided from the Indian vessels (S, f79). The concession generated further uproar. The next day, Jourdain witnessed a heated exchange of "very gross speeches" between the generals, "not fitting for men of their rank. They were from this time forward so cross the one to the other as if they had been enemies" (J, 213). Saris's repeated complaint that their cumbrous protocols of inspection brought "much trouble and hindrance to the company" so angered Middleton that the latter, within earshot of Cocks and Wickham, declared that he had arranged the process explicitly "to cross me, once more repeating that he scorned that my voyage should be affore him, coming twelve months out after him" (S, f79v, 8 May).

On 3 May, two jelbas had reached the *Trades Increase* with gifts and comestibles for the generals and letters from Governor Ider Aga and Mame, the captain of the galleys, requesting an agreement to bring the Indian ships to Mocha and commence peaceful trade with the English (J, 212). Several days later, with Shermall and "diverse other Turks" in company, Captain Mame stopped at the *Clove* and took Saris to the *Trades Increase* for plenary negotiation (G, f16, 16 May 1612). Declaring his ignorance of any current injury done to Middleton, "and for the former they had satisfied him before his departure," Mame asked Middleton to clarify his demands. Having garnered just 18,000 of the 70,000 rials demanded the year before—a sum surrendered, not by the Turks, but by Shermall—Middleton was decidedly not "satisfied." He now demanded 100,000 rials of eight in "satisfaction for the loss of his men's lives and for his time spent, having lost his monsoon to the overthrow of his voyage" (S, f79v, 11 May). Mame indicated that if these demands were put in writing, he should have Ja'far Basha's answer within two weeks. Departing with Sir Henry's letter the next evening, as Mame paid his respects at the *Clove*, Saris surprised him by declaring that his voyage too "had an interest in the junks and would be satisfied" before their release (S, f79v, f80, 11 and 12 May; J, 213). Inferring that any such sums would derive from surcharges on the Indian mariners, Saris concluded, "It stands to reason that we should have one-third of whatever shall be received. Otherwise, the company may hold me very simple" (S, f82v, 18 May).

On 15 May, when the *Peppercorn* rejoined the other vessels at Asab Bey, the king of Raheita appeared on shore attended by two hundred armed men (J, 214). Accompanied in turn by one hundred fifty men in arms, the principal English mariners—Middleton, Saris, Sharpeigh, Hawkins, Downton, Towerson, and the "masters and merchants of all the ships"—landed to meet the entourage and exchange gifts (J, 214; S in P, 3:397). The king desired the Indian vessels in the road to pay him tribute; Middleton answered that he could not command but would ask them to be "liberal to him" (J, 214). While these negotiations transpired ashore, the merchant Benjamin Greene went from the *Peppercorn* to claim two-thirds of the cloth deposited on the *Clove*. Having heard of "much discord" between the generals, he found himself in sudden "quarrel and debate": "For only seeking our due, [I] was by Richard Wickham stroocken such a box under the ear that I never received the like before nor since, as also diverse times misused by the said Wickham in most vile and intolerable speech, as calling me son of a whore, and many more vile speeches hard for flesh and blood to endure, but that for the good of the business I bore all this reproach" (G, f15v, 15 May 1612). While the Sixth Voyage writers concurred that the Eighth Voyage mariners behaved badly on 15 May, two of the former also expressed concern for their commander's state of mind. At supper that evening on the *Trades Increase*, Jourdain noted "bitter words" between the generals and took offense at Saris's inflated valuation of English goods up for barter, "contrary to the agreement made between Sir Henry and him. . . . This contention lasted till midnight, with most vile words betwixt them" (J, 215–16).

Upon arrival at Asab Bey on the morning of 15 May, Downton learned from Thornton that Saris had greatly vexed their general: "To my grief, he told me Sir Henry Middleton was put so far out of quiet by the pride, turbulent and cross dealing of Capt. Saris his countryman, the Indian company servant, as formerly by the treacheries, cruelties, and disaster imposed on him by the Turks, yea and as an attorney general pleaded the Turks' cause against him" (D, f86v, 15 May 1612; cf. *LR*, 1:165). While condemning Saris's willfulness, the passage radiates concern for Middleton's mental balance: the general's vexation evokes his distress the year before. Middleton made the connection for Downton, declaring, "the disturbance of mind which by the other's [Saris's] cross-dealing he sustained . . . was not inferior to that which was by the Turks imposed on him" (*LR* 1:167). Downton found him "most impatient at his continual misfortunes, that in the place where the Turks have done their worst for his overthrow, that in the same place, his employers should send servants to plead the Turks' cause and keep him from satisfaction" (*LR* 1:180). The bitter ironies of his situation wore on Middleton. Downton expresses "grief," presumably, because he cared for Middleton, had felt his wrath, and feared it would impair the general's judgment. For Saris to reignite traumas of betrayal and entrapment in Middleton was a development with unsettling consequences for them all. With an anxious eye on his commander, in measured praise Downton sought reassurance of Middleton's self-control: "Though I cannot by commendation place Sir H. M. amongst the most patient men, yet in these extraordinary trials . . . his patience and forbearance, for the company's sake, made me esteem of him more than an ordinary conqueror over his own passions" (*LR*, 1:170).

Forewarned by Thornton, Downton made himself an unobtrusive witness at supper on the *Trades Increase* that evening. "Making more use of my ears than my teeth," he wrote, "supper in a quiet calm grew to an end. Soon after, began some gusts of contestation." The fundamental division hinged on two concerns: Saris, "seeming to know that he [Sir Henry] should never recover any" damages from the Turks, desired to minimize the Company's offense to Ottoman authorities and maximize their earnings from the Indian mariners. "Sir H. M. on the other side," wrote Downton, "would have what he demanded of the Turks, or else have none at all." Further, unlike Saris, he distinguished between "our friends of Dabul and Malabar" and the "Guzerats, by whom we had been wronged," and he preferred to appear equitable toward them all—in order, Saris explained, to preserve "a future hope" of trade in India (S, f82, 18 May 1612). Middleton therefore meant to appraise the bartered English commodities, "which we know not how anywhere to vend," at rates they might have fetched in Cambaya (D, f87, 15 May; cf. *LR* 1:166). Saris, "in consideration of the great charge" and risk incurred in their transport to the Red Sea, insisted on far higher estimates (S, f80, 12 May).

As the evening wore on, the arguments degenerated. Saris, preferring the term "junks," objected pedantically to Middleton's usage of "ships" for the Indian vessels, "for so the ships of China are so called at Bantam. . . . As if," Downton objected, "a galleon, argosy, or carrack might not without some man's leave be called a ship." For Downton, the occasion epitomized their predicament in the Red Sea: "This night's cavil, for brevity's sake, might serve as a glass to show how by fits, for a long while, we spent in wrangling and discontent, which was made so apparent to all that we had to do withal, to the shame of our nation, and to the spoil of our business with the Turks" (D, f87, 15 May; *LR* 1:166).

Saris's account of the evening imputes to Middleton the "vile words" that Jourdain declared mutual. Bypassing argument over the valuation of bartered commodities, Saris focuses on his claim, given the loss of hopes for trade in Mocha, to a third not only of goods lifted from the Indian vessels but also of any reparations from the Turks. The latter demand stunned and enraged Middleton—who, by Downton's account, had already received Saris's promise "to further him all he could . . . and no way hinder" the blockade, whose purpose, Sir Henry had then clarified, was to compensate the Sixth Voyage for wrongs inflicted by the Turks (D, f87, 15 May; *LR*, 1:165). Saris's threat now to sink the Indian ships "if they offered to go away without his leave," Downton reported, "did infinitely disturb Sir H. M., who could not release them without danger of civil broils in defending them" (*LR*, 1:170).

Middleton answered Saris's threat of "civil broils" with bracing ferocity. Quoting him at length in the journal, Saris depicts a haughty, scornful, volatile interlocutor whose hubristic resolve threatened to detonate their corporate endeavor. As the shore party concluded that afternoon,

> Sir Henry entreated me to go aboard with him, where he gave me good cheer but most vile words, telling me he marveled I would be so saucy as to stand out with him for the advancing of my voyage, asking me if I thought myself as good a man as he, saying that the king of England knew me not, etc., with many other strange words in his choler, so that Capt. Towerson and Mr. Cocks, who were in hearing thereof, would have replied. But I entreated them to silence, being willing to forbear him as my better, only answered that what composition was made or money paid for the release of these India ships, I would have at least the one-third thereof, or I would carry one-third of the junks out of the Red Sea with me. To which he swore he would thrust his dagger into my throat before, protesting he would lose all before my voyage should get a penny. Notwithstanding, in mild speeches I took my leave of him, entreating him

not to be offended, for till I were satisfied, they should not set sail, and that I had the company's right. He protested that when he had given them leave to depart, if I shot at them, he would shoot at me. I said he might do what he thought good in that, but I would not shoot at him; and so took my leave. (S, f81, 15 May 1612)

As Saris shortly explained to Towerson and Cocks, unless he relinquished any claim to a share of Middleton's Turkish settlement, "I shall barter no longer with the Indians. If I did, he would do his best to sink me" (S, f82v, 18 May). Drafting the journal for the Court of Committees in London, Saris wrote to justify himself and expose his fellow general as a grave risk to the Company: a leader whose embattled egotism obliterated corporate fealties and damaged earnings.

The witnesses from the competing voyages differ predictably in their assessments of Middleton and Saris. Without prioritizing anyone's situated testimony, it is fair to say that their division awakened demons in them both. Each suspected the other of violating their agreements, seizing cloths and indigo without compensating the Indian merchants or notifying rival factors. Saris's inference that Middleton's inquiry about his preferences in calicoes cloaked a desire to dispatch the *Darling*, appropriately laden, to Sumatra at once—not, as earlier given out, to London (S, f83, 18 May)—proved prescient. Packed with Indian cloths—"as many callicoes as she was able to stow" (G, f16, 19 May)—the ship stole off "with all secret and expedition" (J, 218) at 3:00 A.M. on 19 May (D in P, 3:288; J, 225). Not to be outdone, Saris sent the *Thomas* in pursuit four days later. Sailing with Captain Pemberton on the *Darling* was the invaluably sane John Jourdain. Depressed by the incessant strife—"weary to see and hear daily such controversies between the two generals" (J, 218)—he had earned Middleton's reluctant blessing to depart. Jourdain's exit offered a choric lament on the breakdown of corporate fellowship in the Red Sea, where occasions for collaboration had devolved into rancor, threats, and self-interested improvisation.

Exit Plans

Among those on the *Thomas* was the *Hector*'s mutinous master. Delegating young Fuller to the *Clove*, Saris was nearly thwarted in his plan thus to divide the pair when father and son went aboard the *Trades Increase* and were, Saris testifies, warmly received by Middleton: "*Sir Henry*, who before scorned [Old Fuller] for his base behavior, now made very much of him, and Thornton vowing to assist him in what he could." When he heard that Middleton had requested that Towerson come to the flagship and speak with them, Saris, alarmed that in the captain's absence the pair might return to the *Hector* and reignite trouble, directed Towerson to stay put. He dispatched Foster and Cocks to ask Middleton "to be advised what he did and not to harbor or countenance such a disordered person." On arrival, they indeed found the Fullers departing for the *Hector* and prevented that. Saris inferred darkly that, by releasing the Fullers, Middleton hoped to provoke a crisis of command in the Eighth Voyage that would delay the *Thomas*'s departure.

Whether delusional or shrewd, the suspicion expressed the pathology of the corporate body at this hour. "But God I trust will deliver me out of the hands of this great man with whom no reasonable acknowledgment will take place," Saris vented, "who, by working my trouble ever since I unhappily met with him, hath sought to purchase himself fame by defaming me and to advance his own business by hindering mine" (S, f84v, 22 May). By Saris's account, that "hindering" included the subversion of his authority. In April, Saris had complained that Middleton "moulded" Towerson "for his own use" (S, f75v, 23 April). Now, as Towerson conveyed Middleton's request to meet Saris alone onshore to determine their shares of extorted cargoes (*LR* 1:182), Saris found that Middleton had poisoned his relations with the *Hector*'s captain: "*Sir Henrie* doth now set abroach new matter to cause breach of ancient amity between Capt. Towerson and me, persuading him that the company did him great wrong not to make him chief, with many other speeches stirring him to self-conceit, so that many unkind words passed, which till this present, all the voyage hath not happened in the least between us" (S, f87, 25 May 1612). Saris's superior in Bantam, Towerson had presumably suppressed overt resentment at the former's appointment over him on the Eighth Voyage—until Sir Henry took up the theme. Saris's painful quarrels with Towerson continued during the combined fleets' negotiations for release of the Indian ships in Mocha (S, f94v, 29 July 1612).

Middleton's plot to restore his honor by wringing compensation from the Turks had imploded the year before. He might have suspected that it would fail again. Saris clearly found the plan naive: "the Basha would never give him an asper," he maintained (S, f82v, 18 May 1612). Any sums Middleton gleaned would derive from surcharges on "our friends" the Indian merchants. The Sixth Voyage mariners, however, saw this prediction as evidence of Saris's collusion with the Turks "to draw it to that end," so to enlarge his third of the take from the Indian ships as per their prior agreement (*LR* 1:180). It must have been in a spirit of déjà vu that Shermall and Captain Mame had arrived at Asab Bey on 3 May 1612 to discuss the terms for freeing the ships for the season's trade. Their departure "within two or three days," by Greene's report, "without doing anything" (G, f16, 20 May 1612), indicated the need, prior to any settlement with Ottoman powers, not only to consult Ja'far Basha in Sana'a but also to resolve their own disagreements. Downton, for one, saw that their division invited both Ottoman and Indian actors to play each voyage against the other: "They became so well informed of the difference, contention, and division between Sir H. M. and General Saris, these two ill met captains, so that in discretion they informed themselves, that to flatter on both sides for serving of turns (which they can well do), they may hold their own and care for neither" (*LR* 1:168).

Following their fiercest argument to date, on the morning of 16 May Middleton sent John Fowler to demand that Saris abide by their former contract, or "he [Middleton] should have nothing to do with him in the business" before them (D in *LR* 1:167). He enforced the point by prohibiting Saris's men from unloading cloth from the junks that day (S, f81). At Saris's protest, Middleton "returned me word that he had a larger commission than myself" and that Saris "must of force be contented . . . with . . . his pleasure" (S, f81–81v, 16 May). Middleton indeed commanded a larger salary than Saris.[21] But the claim to superior authority expressed rather self-conceit than Company policy. Neither his knighthood, his greater compensation, nor his grander flagship granted Sir Henry interfleet dominion. At this impasse, Saris sent Cocks and Towerson to propose that "some principal men of both the Sixth and Eighth Voyages" arbitrate the matter of shared compensation from the Ottomans, "which speech gave Sir H. M. good content" (D in *LR* 1:167). With the principal antagonists absent, Downton and Towerson led a "troublesome and tedious dispute" to a provisional compromise: if Ottoman reparations were indeed forthcoming, then three-fourths should go to the Sixth Voyage, one-fourth to the Eighth. They would refer the matter of any further adjustments to London (G, f16, 16 May). Premised upon an outcome that never materialized, the agreement soon gave way to further disputes, as negotiations with Mame, Shermall, and the agitated nohudas evolved. But the pact held a useful lesson: reconciliation between the fleets would depend on deputies like Downton, Frayne, Cocks, and Towerson, whose offices curbed their egotism and habituated them to compromise. As Downton confided later to Cocks, it fell to them to collaborate for "the company's good, which we were more to covet than the pleasing of our displeased captains" (*LR* 1:172).

On 30 May 1612, with the principal mariners of both fleets in attendance, Captain Mame, Shermall, and a messenger from Sana'a arrived at the *Trades Increase* off Asab Bey with Ja'far Basha's response to Middleton's demands "for satisfaction of our former abuses" (D in P, 3:289). Declaring that the 18,000 rials dispensed the year before was sufficient, the basha refused any further payment. Yet he was willing to allow an English factory and "any other courtesies" in Mocha if desired. This was a pivotal concession—an opportunity to cultivate the peaceful trade the East India Company had sought in Arabia Felix from the start. Ja'far Basha had by now seen Achmed I's letter of protection and was willing to proceed. But Sir Henry, terminally mistrustful, angrily fixated on reparations, insisted on his 100,000 rials. Then, as in the year before, Shermall intervened: he requested an abatement of the sum and promised payment once the detained ships had reached Mocha (S, f88, 31 May 1612). Middleton offered to accept the compromise if the Turks would declare that the money came "from them for injuries done him, and not for the release of the ships" (S, f88, 31 May 1612). Shermall doubted that this condition would be granted. The compensation would likely not, as Middleton's honor required, derive even ostensibly from the Ottoman treasury. The financial deficits of the voyage, however, might be corrected by other means. The visitors departed to discuss with the mariners detained in Asab Bey the prospects of raising cash for the English.

These talks went poorly. Annual visitors, the Indian mariners enjoyed long-standing, mutually profitable relations in Mocha, and their voices carried more durable impact than Middleton's in negotiation with Ottoman authorities. The English fleets might bend to their will the ships in custody, but not the landed powers. Their primary leverage ashore was the blockade, which reduced Mocha's customs revenues and hurt its tradesmen; but it was temporary and porous. Two of the six English ships had left the Red Sea; the remaining four were overtaxed with vessels already detained. The *Rehemy*'s nohuda, Mir Mohamed Tooke, confided to Saris that jelbas routinely conveyed the "principal and best goods" from their ships to Mocha without interference (S, f89, 9 June 1612). Having erected a pavilion on the shore, the Ottoman entourage conferred there with the nohudas and their principal merchants about elevating their customs fees in Mocha to satisfy the English. The proposals were roundly rejected. Several nohudas refused even to meet with them. The *Rehemy*'s captain, for one, insisted that he, bound for Jedda, would not pay taxes in Mocha (*LR* 1:167–68). Nothing accomplished, on 9 June Mame and Shermall departed to consult Ja'far Basha again. (Saris, pretending to serve Middleton's directive, rudely intercepted and searched their jelba yet found little to seize; advised of the intervention, Middleton returned his share of Saris's take to the owners [S, f86v, 9 June].) Each errand to Sana'a and back could take up to one month. In two more months, the Indian and English ships would have to depart with the monsoon or keep to the Red Sea for another season. The Sixth Voyage's cables were frayed and breaking, their victuals low (*LR* 1:170).[22] Desperation likewise festered among the Indian vessels. Mocha's authorities knew that time was on their side.

Recognizing this predicament, the English made the most of it. "All this time" at Asab Bey, wrote Downton, "our people were employed in rummaging,[23] opening, packing, and repacking of Indian cloths fit for our turns, giving them of our English commodities in lieu thereof" (D in P, 3:289). The latter goods were "with no willingness by the Indians received, but have it they must, at such rates as we [English] had agreed upon" (D in *LR*, 1:169). Their fierce quarrels over the values to assign else-unmarketable commodities—their attempts to put a fair face on compulsory exchange—held transparent ironies. Transferring to recipients the burden of realizing any claimed values, the process was inherently exploitative. Downton, moreover, concedes that the prices the English put on their own goods, should the recipients ever manage to earn the same, were "not half the value they [the Indians] would here make" by marketing their own cargoes ashore. In one contradictory sentence, he describes "this forcible trading" as a process of "mutual consent" among the "merchants of both sides" (*LR* 1:165). This was privateering with a difference: the English prepared not letters of marque, but bills of sale, to justify the thefts. "And by this way, we put off all the remains of our goods brought out of England, exchanging it only for Indian wares without disbursing of any money" (*LR* 1:169). The near-term economies of the exchange were compelling. Yet the entire process marked a regression to rationalized pillage by a Company that, while founded by late-Elizabethan privateers, continued at the pleasure of a peace-loving king who desired them to proceed at home and abroad as a trustworthy institution of legitimate and sustainable commerce.

Having seized what they desired—with a commission of four (Downton, Frayne, Cocks, and Towerson)[24] allotting three-fourths to the Sixth Voyage (Middleton insisted on four-fifths) and one-fourth to the Eighth, referring further adjudication to London, and bonding Middleton and Saris at £1,000 to honor the same—the combined English fleets escorted seven remaining vessels to Mocha on 11 July 1612 (S, f93, 8 July; S in P, 3:399). Among them was the *Rehemy*, whose captain, desperate to deliver his pilgrims to Jedda, "wished diverse harms to himself rather than he would go to Mocha" (*LR* 1:183)—a fruitless protest. As the Indian vessels sailed faster than the English, the *Trades Increase*, *Hector*, and *Clove* were "constrained," Saris explained, "to shoot diverse pieces of ordnance at them . . . to keep them together" (S, f93, 11 July). Downton followed the next day in the *Peppercorn* with "a small ship called the *Jungo*, into whom I re-delivered all the goods that I had formerly taken out of her" (D in P, 3:289). Not that the act assuaged any plausible regret over their abuse of the Indian merchants: the goods were "not fit for our use, but for some jars of butter and lamp oil, . . . but they thought themselves kindly used" (*LR* 1:184).

Having arrived at Mocha, Middleton received a letter from the governor delivered "in a canoe by an Arab . . . in the carelessest manner that might be." The message rebuked him for presuming to demand "satisfaction for wrongs formerly done us in another man's government" (*LR* 1:185). Shermall's prediction was correct: the Ottoman powers refused to grant any compensation. Middleton told Saris of this and other letters "of defiance . . . from the Turks, wherein they used him with very vile speeches, saying he was a robber, and that they would have recompense three for one in Constantinople" for his depredations (S, f92v, 15 July). He responded by threatening to carry "all the Indian ships away out of this sea" (*LR* 1:185) unless satisfied—unless, that is, Ottoman authorities "fathered" the payments he took from the Indians. In the meantime, the *Peppercorn* and *Clove* anchored near shore to "keep all the road in awe" (*LR* 1:185) and prevent smuggling. Though within range of Mocha's ordnance, they fired on smaller transports many times "so as the men forsook both the junks and jelbas and swam ashore, the castle nor town not once shooting at us" (S in P, 3:400). They later charged one of the captains for the powder and shot spent preventing him from landing his goods (S, f95v, 3 August; G, f16v, 2 August). The English threats and demands put intolerable stress on the captive merchants, who feared being effectively "sold to the Turks," Saris reported: "To have the Turks to undertake the payment of it for them were the next way to make them slaves," they complained, "weeping very bitterly. . . . The poor men stood like bodies without souls" (S, f93, 17–18 July).

On 26 July, "to avoid debate in Captain Saris's ship, or frivolous contention" on the *Trades Increase*, the principal English and Indian mariners convened on the *Mahomudy*, "a great ship of Dabull, . . . a sober place for that purpose," to settle their affairs (*LR* 1:186). Five Indian cohorts were party to the talks. Middleton explained to them "as often times before," Downton reports, the damages he had suffered in Yemen compelling him to prohibit trade until the Ottomans compensated him; and although the business lately transacted at Asab Bey satisfied him for his "injuries sustained in India," he was now forced to conduct them all out of the Red Sea "that this year by them the Turks may receive no benefit." He possessed "no means to force satisfaction from the Turks" without further harming his listeners. They capitulated. Rather than carry their remaining cargoes home again, "they desired to make composition with Sir Henry Middleton and Captain Saris, every ship severally to pay a certain sum of money, and we to forbear to hinder their quiet trade" (D in P, 3:290–91). They were loath to borrow money in Mocha but would do so to make the payments. "But then grew as much trouble in agreeing on the sums which every ship should give," Downton explained, that it was "a heart-relenting business in regard of the outcries of the poor people, and the difficulty, according to our haste, for them to get the money, and that which they had from the Turks was hired at a most excessive rate" (*LR* 1:185).

As these negotiations transpired, the governor canceled Ja'far Basha's offer to make peace with Middleton. In doing so, as Downton had predicted, the governor and Captain Mame exploited the generals' division, bitingly. Their surviving letter of 28 June 1612 to Middleton was clearly informed by one from Saris to the governor (copied in the journal) two days before. Saris's message bizarrely invokes "my great hindrance sustained by them [the Indians] in their country"—as if the Eighth Voyage had suffered the Sixth's frustrations in India (S, f91, 26 June). Presumably, he floated this conceit to present a united front with Middleton. But Ider Aga and Mame seized upon the claim to justify their refusal to settle with Middleton: "Very Dear Sir Don Henrico Middleton, we advise you that we had order from the Basha, for to accord a peace with your Worship, and we were ready to make the peace. . . . And by the coming of Captain John Saris demanding that he will have money for hurts that he hath received, of which his demands and loss we know nothing, for he hath received no other than honor and courtesies from us. . . . And because of his demands, we cannot conclude the said peace with your Worship: for he demands false demands" (*LR* 1:196). While puncturing Saris's account of his "hurts," the letter endorses Saris's equation of the two voyages to stain Middleton with the former's bad faith. The rhetorical move makes the closing statement, which echoes Middleton's own scorn for Saris's "false demands," deftly inflammatory.

The strain between the generals increased with the winds. Saris grew so fiercely protective of his interests that he refused to give the Sixth Voyage even urgently needed cables he might have spared, as Downton noted: "We were troubled with stormy winds and a high sea, to the great straining of our weak ground tackle, which Capt. Saris, though oftentimes thereunto requested by Sir H. M., would in no wise yield us any relief therein for money, though he had more than he needed" (D, f89, 2 August 1612). Sixth Voyage mariners therefore "peeled the Indian ships of all that possibly we could of their best cables," neither as strong nor as durable as their own (*LR*, 1:191). As arguments over extorted sums flared between the generals, the intractable pair, sick of the "confused rabble of wrangling contestations . . . in this tiring, hot place" (*LR*, 1:188), named Downton and Towerson to negotiate the payment from each vessel (D, f89, 27 July 1612). The captain of the *Rehemy* settled for 15,000 rials; the *Hasanni*, 10,000; the *Salametee*, 8,000; the *Mahomudy*, 2,000; the *Cawdrie*, 5,000, totaling 40,000 rials. Petitioning over the next several days lowered all but the *Rehemy*'s payments, bringing the total to 32,000 rials (S, f94v, 28–29 July; f92, 31 July 1612). This outcome was nowhere near the 100,000 rials Middleton sought to restore his honor and fortunes, nor even Saris's rider of 50,000 (*LR*, 1:168). Middleton's share fell to 24,000, Saris's to 8,000, rials. A few payments were made in kind. A merchant of the *Rehemy*, weeping with distress at his inability to secure a loan in Mocha, visited Saris on the *Clove*, begging the general to accept cloth instead of money. Saris took the offer (S, f95, 31 July).

Imagining themselves to treat their captives fairly—Saris saw fit to invoke his "kindly courtesies unto" the mariners of Dabull, Deccan, and Malabar "as a well-wisher to the hopeful trade expected in those parts" (S, f99v, 13 August)—the English fleets threatened violence and took what they could get. Their conduct held clear genealogical links to the long tradition of Elizabethan privateering, a business model premised upon force and open to improvised collaboration, like James Lancaster's lucrative 1595 assault on Portuguese Pernambuco in Brazil. Lancaster's squadron was bolstered fortuitously by two English vessels met in Maio, five French ships arriving later in

FIGURE II. Capture of *Santo Antonio*. Johann Theodore de Bry, *Indiae Orientalis Pars Septima* . . . (Frankfurt, 1606), plate 12. Courtesy of the Huntington Library. East India Company ships are above the carrack: the *Dragon*, Lancaster's flagship, upper left; *Hector*, upper right; *Ascension*, center left; Dutch vessels are below their mutual target, with Admiral Joris van Speilbergen's *Schaep* at lower right.

Pernambuco, and three Dutch ships riding in the harbor there. All took shares of the action. In 1602, Lancaster turned a handsome profit on the East India Company's commercially thwarted First Voyage by pillaging a Portuguese carrack in the Straits of Malacca, the *Santo Antonio*, again with Dutch assistance (fig. 11).[25] The East India Company's renewal of this pattern of opportune coercion in the Red Sea ten years later, however, differed in at least two respects: in its need to frame the action as legitimate commerce and to depict the fractious participants as the servants of a well-governed corporate body. The provisional agreements between Middleton and Saris were far more volatile than Lancaster's with French and Dutch collaborators.

An apostle of English maritime expansion, Samuel Purchas labored to burnish the East India Company's public image. As already noted, the journals printed in *Purchas His Pilgrimes* omit the quarrels between the two generals. Purchas also obscured the aura of privateering manifest in their conduct. In their manuscripts, as we have observed, Downton and Saris document injustices visited upon, and agonies suffered by, the nohudas and their merchants. Purchas effaces them. Moreover, to solemnize the legitimacy of the Red Sea transactions, his edition of the Saris journal inserts documentary proof of "mutual consent": bills of exchange between Saris and two of the Indian captains. The latter's signatures, presented in their original script, and one of their seals, are attached (S in P, 3:401–3). The first begins "Memorandum, That I Mahomed Hashen Comall Adeene Ashen, Captain of the *Hassanee* of Surat, have bartered and sold unto Captain John Saris, . . . for the sum of seven thousand four hundred rialls of eight and 11/48 of a riall in these goods following." The equivalency of "bartered and sold," of course, begs major questions. To each item is affixed a surreally precise figure. Indigos valued at 3,046 7/48 rials, "Cambaya Cloth" at 4,136 rials, and a few incidentals make up the list. Totaled, the items achieve exactly the sum attained in the sequel. The page continues, "And I have received in payment thereof these goods following." Broadcloths, calibrated at an impressive—indeed, implausible—4,574 19/48 rials, eclipse the other items in Saris's inventory: kerseys, lead, iron, tin, and fifteen fowling pieces. The signature and seal attest the equal value of both batches, down to 1/48 of a rial. Nohuda Assan of the *Cawdrie* similarly endorses an exchange of goods worth 2,947 9/16 rials.

In a volume dominated by English voices, these documents earn notable status and persuasive impact as instances of non-English testimony. Purchas took pains to secure and duplicate them. Like the sultan's pass, also printed in the Saris chapter, they appear in neither surviving manuscript of his journal. Yet, as the forced exactitude of the sums implies, the documents retain traces of the events Purchas has suppressed. Read in the light of Saris's and Downton's full manuscripts, the memoranda offer proof, not of "mutual consent," but of English coercion passed off as equity: a trick of protocolonialist ideology. The nohudas consummated their release by endorsing their own subjection: ventriloquizing English appraisals of relative worth. In historical hindsight, these documents, like the redactions they joined, set a weighty precedent. They justified the exploitation of mariners from the subcontinent over which Britain, several generations later, came to exercise imperial sway.

An engine of capital growth deeply ingrained in the English maritime psyche, privateering, by which a marginal island nation challenged larger powers through the opportune assertiveness of ad hoc coalitions at sea, held the germ of the subsequent land-based imperialism of this demographically challenged nation, which augmented its holdings by mobilizing some indigenous groups against others.[26] Moreover, legacies of privateering and its public rehabilitation persist in the acquisitive behaviors and cosmetic publicity of multinational corporations to this day.

The Indian mariners concluded their payments on 6 August. That accomplished, the English fleets did not linger. On 8 August, to the surprise of the Sixth Voyage, the *Hector* sailed for Sumatra. Towerson offered a salute of five rounds to the *Clove* (S, f98v, 8 August) but made no "show of courtesy or leave taking of Sir Henry Middleton" (D, f89, 6 August). Middleton invited Saris to spend the next day on the *Trades Increase*, and they shared both dinner and supper in evident amiability. Saris's "demeanor," Downton noted, "void of many caviling arguments (his accustomed manner), gave good content" (D, f89, 9 August). Yet, four days later, the *Clove* departed for Socotra and Bantam "with as little courtesy as his Vice Admiral," Downton noted (D, f89, 13 August). The rude departure, "without taking any leave of our general or once bidding him farewell," vexed Benjamin Greene. He found the snub "very strange, if but for our country's sake, much more for that we are all servants of one master" (G, f16v, 13 August). The *Clove*'s exit quietly declared that the troubles between the fleets did not conclude with this separation. They would meet again in Bantam.

CHAPTER 6

The Final Transit

On 16 August 1612, the *Trades Increase* and *Peppercorn* departed the Red Sea for Sumatra, Java, and the Moluccas. It was the last leg of the great ship's journey. The *Darling* alone traveled farther east than Bantam. Of the three, only the *Peppercorn* returned to England. Almost two and a half years at sea, the vessels were seriously weathered—cables and hawsers frayed or replaced with weaker ones, anchors lost, rigging worn, sails degraded, barnacled hulls infested with worms—and their progress was slow. Middleton was perturbed that, though the *Darling* had sailed before the *Thomas*, the heart of his fleet followed in the wake of an expedition that left England a year after theirs and vexed their efforts to redeem their "every way thwarted journey" (D in *LR* 1:259). Although their route since expulsion from Surat had diverged from that proffered in their commission, they resumed it now: Priaman, near Tiku, just below the equator on Sumatra's west coast, followed Surat on the itinerary (Birdwood, 338). In 1602, Sir James Lancaster secured trading privileges in the region from the king of Achin (aka Kotaraja, Banda Aceh), the capital on Sumatra's northernmost tip, and the directors took pains to equip the merchants, like those of the Third and Fourth Voyages, with a copy of the letter (Birdwood, 321).[1] Yet, inexplicably, just as Middleton failed to produce the sultan's letter of protection in Mocha, so the *Darling* evidently carried no copy of the king's letter, nor did Middleton bring one with the gifts he carried into Tiku. Perhaps the document was among Lawrence Femell's effects abandoned in the escape from Mocha.[2] Their trade here, in any case, suffered for lack of it. And, as they excoriated the Turks for their misfortunes in Yemen, so they slandered the Sumatrans for commercial frustrations largely of their own making. Among other things, they arrived off-season for pepper.

The passage to Tiku was documented by Downton and Greene on the *Peppercorn* (Middleton's account breaks off months earlier). The two ships made faltering progress eastward between the coast of Arabia and the Horn of Africa for the rest of August. After several days of "close weather" in the Arabian Sea, by mid-September, at 14° northern latitude (D in P, 3:293), they "saw diverse snakes swimming on the top of the water, . . . an apparent sign of being near the coast of India." When the sky cleared on 14 September, they spied land to the northeast and turned south to follow the Malabar coast into the Indian Ocean. The ships lost each other in a storm early on the seventeenth but reconnected as the day cleared. They passed Cape Comorin, India's southernmost point, on 22–23 September, and Ceylon on 24–25 September (D in P, 3:293, 294), adjusting their course there against a strong current carrying toward the Bay of Bengal. Viewing it from the *Peppercorn*, Greene described Ceylon as a lowland, "except for one great high peaked hill like that of the . . . Straits of Gibraltar" (G, f17, 24–25 September 1612).

On the final day of September, following recurrent bouts of heavy rain, Downton discovered that much of the wheat in the breadroom was soaked, and twenty pieces of sail canvas stored there "for most security" had rotted with the damp (D in P, 3:295). Through warm windless downpours that likewise soaked the sails on the yards, and "a tumbling sea like to raise the ship spooning" into oncoming waves (D, f91v, 5–6 and 11 October), they crossed the equator and headed east in mid-October. When a "vehement . . . gust of wind and rain" hit them, he feared that "our rotten sails" would be carried off "before we could stow them" (D, f92, 13 October). Storms and currents continued to vex their progress near Sumatra. They made several attempts to weather the north end of a large "savage island" (D, f92, 11 October), probably Siberut, whose thick tropical forests unnerved Greene: the island, he wrote, was "all covered with trees, . . . like a wilderness, for nothing is to be seen but trees: the very hills are all covered" (G, f17v, 16 October). On 15 October, they passed to its south and made their way northeastward toward Tiku, initially mistaken for Priaman to the southeast (G, f17v, 18 October).

Arriving on the afternoon of 19 October, they met the *Thomas*, which was returning from Priaman, and anchored near the *Darling*, which had awaited them in Tiku since July (D in P, 3:295). As Saris had hoped, the *Thomas* made swifter progress than the *Darling* and had already visited both ports when the latter ship met them in Tiku on 7 July. In the absence of their testy generals, William Pemberton and Tempest Peacock, the *Thomas*'s chief merchant, agreed not to "spoil one another's market," Jourdain explained (J, 232): they would remain in contact while the *Darling* worked Tiku and the *Thomas* Priaman. Having broken the seal and made a copy, Peacock shared with the *Darling*'s merchants a letter from Middleton. Saris was sorely displeased when he learned of this disclosure,[3] but the act instilled good relations when performed: "We proceeded in our business like loving friends," Jourdain remarked (J, 232).

The arrival of more ships renewed the cynicism between the fleets. The *Darling*'s hull was so compromised—"so leaky, eaten with worms" (J, 234)—that its merchants, awaiting the balance of their fleet, anchored near an island and stored purchased pepper ashore rather than load and risk sinking the vessel—"our men," Jourdain explained, "being so weak that they were not able to search for" the leak (J, 234). To find it would have required exhausting rearrangements of cargo. Many had died, many were sick, and their food-stuffs had dwindled. When the *Hector* turned up late in September, Captain Towerson suggested that Pemberton sell him their pepper, since Middleton was not to be expected: the *Trades Increase*, he lied, was headed for Dabull and then for England. Refused, the *Hector*'s captain declined to share his victuals or other supplies with the *Darling* and, on 9 October, sailed for Bantam with the *James*, the flagship of the East India Company's Ninth Voyage (1612) under Edmund Marlowe (J, 234; Birdwood, xiv).[4] Ten days later, when the *Thomas*'s merchants confided to those of the *Peppercorn* and *Trades Increase* that, knowing the *Darling* to be "very leaky and in some distress," they had come to render assistance, the account was heard with skepticism: they came "most likely for love of her pepper," offered Greene (G, f17v, 19 October). Downton concurred: finding "as slender success" in Priaman as the *Darling* had in Tiku, the *Thomas* arrived "in hope, by the continuance of our *Darling*'s leak, to have bought all such pepper as Mr. Pemberton had provided against our coming" (D, f93, 19 October). Reunited, the Sixth Voyage merchants were pleased to thwart that intent.

Jourdain offered a more charitable view of the *Thomas*'s actions: with most of the *Darling*'s small crew ill, they had come "to buy our pepper," abandon the "unserviceable" ship, and "carry us to Bantam" (J, 234). The supply of pepper in question was modest—some eighty tons, Greene reported (G, f17v, 19 October). Sad news beset the reunion: they had buried a number of men in Tiku, including the merchants John Fowler, Femell's successor as the voyage's chief merchant (Birdwood, 326), and William Speed, a sometime geographer and member of the East India Company's inner circle who had transcribed Anthony Marlowe's Third Voyage journal in London during the weeks before the voyage (D in P, 3:295; Birdwood, 328).[5] Greene reported that they and "Mr. Glanfielde died here in September of a fever or ague, which disease all them that lay ashore had, or for the most part. Few or any that had it escaped" (G, f18, 31 October). A civil war inland had stunted the pepper market, which was off-season in any case and would not resume until April or May. Moreover, the merchants and civic authorities hesitated to proceed until the English had displayed regional credentials (J, 232). When, two days later, Middleton went ashore bearing presents for the governor, "with Captain Downton, Captain Sharpeigh, Captain Hawkins, and forty shot," he learned that their trade was hitherto constrained, and their costs inflated, because "we brought no letter from the King of Achin" (G, f17v, 21 October).[6]

The disclosure should have come as no surprise. Yet none of the journalists say anything of such a letter once in Femell's charge. The impasse marked yet another breakdown in the East India Company's disposition of corporate knowledge: another critical failure of the paperwork. Documents disappeared, institutional memory lapsed, and the fleets improvised as usual. Their own unpreparedness, which the committees tried to forestall, created frustrations that provoked the mariners to fault the Sumatrans. Taking umbrage at their reception, Downton observed of Tiku's authorities, "Between their uncivil blockishness and pride together, they scarce gave him [Middleton] thanks for the presents" (D, f93, 21 October). Having worked with the traders there for several weeks, Jourdain too condemned "these unseasoned Mahometans. Although they are all bad enough, yet these are the worst that I have seen" (J, 236). As in Arabia Felix, rejection ignited ethnocentric defensiveness: stereotypic scorn and dismissal of their desired partners in trade.

Rumors from reunited comrades and mariners on Chinese junks (G, f17v, 19 October) abounded: Sir Henry's brother David prospered on the East India Company's Fifth Voyage to Bantam, Banda, and the Moluccas (1609);[7] the *Dragon*, on the East India Company's Tenth Voyage (1612), was proceeding to Socotra and Surat; Greene heard that the *James* had sailed, not for Bantam, which two of the Ninth Voyage's ships had already reached (D in P, 3:295),[8] but toward Masulipatam, following the *Globe*'s late trajectory (G, f17v, 19 October);[9] the *Pearl*, an English interloper commanded by Captain Samuel Castleton (J, 233),[10] two French traders, and a formidable Dutch fleet of fifteen sail were active in Sumatran waters—"all which," Downton concluded dispiritedly, "quell the life of the present hopes of our out-tired,

crossed, and decayed voyage" (D in P, 3:295–96). With no occasions of assistance or advantage there, the *Thomas* returned to Priaman on 20 October.
Nor did Middleton linger. The reports of his brother's success, the competing
traffic in the region, and the prospects of sickness and scant trade in Tiku
sharpened his urgency to turn a profit, at last, in Bantam. Finding "cold
comfort at this place" (D in P, 3:296), and anxious to reach the Java factory
before others, including Saris, marred his market there, he exchanged commands with Downton and, on the evening of 22 October, hastened south in
the *Peppercorn*.

He took the midsize ship primarily because it was fit for the journey.
The *Trades Increase*, like the *Darling*, was in "some distress." Downton's
immediate duties aboard his new command included stopping "a great leak
in the ship, which would require much time in rummaging, lading, and re-
lading of goods." Unfortunately, the leak proved irremediable from within.
Downton believed the source might be located forward in the hull, but
"when trial was made [there], small means to ease the pump was found": the
leakage continued. Lacking time and manpower to clear, inspect, and treat
the rest of the hull from the inside, they gave up and simply kept pumping.
A few days later, with great labor, they shuffled cargo to tilt the ship laterally
and deployed a "floating stage" outside by which to inspect and treat exposed
sections of the hull; then they repeated the process for the other side. Thereby
"they stopped diverse suspicious places which the worm hath ruinated,"
Downton detailed. Yet substantial areas nearer the keel eluded their reach.
They lacked the time, tools, and infrastructure to consummate the repairs:
"Neither are we furnished with timber, planks, boards, nails, nor other ironwork to effect it" (D, f93v, 3 November).

The interval in Tiku proved crushingly laborious for the crew and disheartening for the merchants of the *Trades Increase*. Middleton desired them
to follow by 20 November (D, f93, 22 October), so while diagnosing problems and making repairs, they hastened to load pepper from the islet and
whatever more they could purchase ashore. "As the wind and rains permitted,
and our rotten tottering boats prepared," Downton "kept them ever
employed" (D, f93v, n.d.). They took down masts for inspection and repair
on the island (D, f94v, 13 November). Rearranging packs of cloth deep within
the *Trades Increase*, crewmen found many of their Indian fabrics damp and
degraded, while those from the *Darling* had rotted more severely, given "the
extremity of rains since their [the *Darling*'s] arrival" (D, f94, 3 November).
The same held for the *Darling*'s pepper. Piled in leaky tents on the island,

many sacks had rotted with "the continual rains . . . before our coming" (G, f18, 31 October). To the merchants' dismay, the minimal market ashore broke off on 2 November when "all the men of sort in Tiku went with Raja Boonsoo to the wars." What fitful commerce resumed was fueled by bribes and inflated costs and sometimes involved spoiled or garbled goods, rice or rocks filling out the bags (D in P, 3:296). Downton complained that the merchants of Tiku "play fast and loose at their pleasure, so that our trading with them must be, as it were, to devise a trap to catch a fox" (D, f94v, 11 November). Their chief solace in this predicament was likewise compromised: carrying up wine from below, they found "by the rottenness of the cask, . . . great leakage" from the barrels (D, f93v, 2 November). Images of porous vessels, seepage, dampness, and rot permeate the Sumatran passages of Downton's journal.

While these labors proceeded, the *Darling*, presumably after similar repairs, tried its luck in Pasaman, a village at the mouth of the so-named river some nine leagues to the north (J, 235; D, f93, 22 October). Greene transferred to the ship for the mission. They sailed on 1 November and, after three days, had "much ado, although we had a pilot, to find the river." Finally locating it, they discovered the river's mouth to be "very dangerous": incapable of oared headway against a current so strong it carried fresh water three fathoms deep beyond the bar, they had to hale up their boats by ropes from the shore. The *Darling* anchored two miles offshore in eight fathoms of water—an exposed position. "God be thanked," Greene remarked, "we had . . . good weather" (G, f18, 1–3 November). On 4 November, with supporting crewmen, he, Pemberton, and the merchant John Staughten carried gifts into the town and presented themselves to dignitaries. "We were very kindly entertained with promise [that] if we tarried but four or five days, we should have a good quantity of pepper" (G, f18, 4 November). The governor advised them, predictably, that more abundant supplies were not available until April or May and that a letter from the king of Achin would be vital for any ongoing business. Nevertheless, "for this short time, he had ventured upon his own head" to proceed, "not knowing whether he should well answer [for] it or not, but he hoped he should . . . as well as his neighbors" (f18). Greene suspected that "the depth of their meaning . . . was only to delay us with good speeches, and to fool us with fair promises, until such time as they had what they looked for": more presents and high customs (G, f18, 4 December). "These people are a miserable poor people and are very desirous of our trade," he concluded. "I told them I was in doubt" of substantial commerce, for by "bringing quantity of goods with us, we should not be in safety" against the river's "forcible current" (G, f18v, 4–7 November). Indeed, laden with pepper on departure, Greene's boat nearly overturned crossing the bar (G, f18v, 8 November).[11]

The governor and townspeople clearly wished them well: "They were very careful of us[12] . . . coming at all hours of the night to visit us. . . . They brought us buffalo hides to lie on. To conclude, they entertained us with all the kindness that might be, but with a caveat at last" regarding the vital letter (G, f18v, 4–7 November). They shared copious information about pepper markets on nearby islands, its production inland, and its delivery by prows on the river. "Here is to be noted, where there is no river, there is little quantity of pepper, for . . . they cannot bring it down by land. . . . Many others . . . bring down gold, which they find washing down the mountains" (G, f18v, 4–7 November). The business consummated in the meantime, however, was marginal. The English purchased "but twenty-eight bahars" of pepper—not enough to justify the trouble taken (G, f18v, 8 December; D, f94, 11 November; J, 236).[13]

More important, the visit's toll on personnel was devastating. Priaman, like Tiku, proved "a very contagious place for our men," Jourdain observed of the *Darling*'s return: "Many of their men [were] sick, so that within short time they all died, as many has had lain a-land at Pasaman. Only Benjamin Greene remained sick until he came to Bantam, and there died" (J, 236). The last two leaves of Greene's roughly scrawled, degraded, often-illegible journal narrate the errand to that town, the return to Tiku, and the passage to Bantam. While the entries thin out toward the end, the copious detail he offers on Pasaman holds poignancy. From his conversations with the governor and others, he delivers data on regional markets. From his own observations, he describes the environs: navigational hazards; landmarks; the water's depth across the bar (reportedly two fathoms "at a spring tide, . . . but we found no more than five and a half foot and six foot"); the village's "fifty cottages built . . . upon the river side"; the water's depth through town ("nine or ten feet"); and, with a vivid familiarizing simile, the force of its current—"the river runneth down as swift as the tunnels under London bridge" (f18v).[14] He was the only journalist to document these moments, and he felt his own evanescence acutely. If little else, the visit to Pasaman might yield information of value to the "Worshipful Company"—but only if he wrote while he could. Though never mentioning his sickness, several times in the last few paragraphs, he invokes God's mercy on them all.

Back in Tiku, the *Darling*'s merchants bought eighteen bahars of pepper from a junk of Andripura (G, f18v, 14 November); those of the *Trades Increase* negotiated ashore for 110 bahars at rates lowered by their imminent departure (D, f94v–f95, 16–17 November). They sailed for Bantam at midnight on 20 November, navigating by moonlight. Reversing their route upon arrival, they took care "to avoid the two known rocks, three leagues" outside Tiku (D in P, 3:296). Yet, in that area around 3:00 A.M., the great ship ran hard aground, leaking dangerously as the hull's stranded midsection flexed against the floating bow and stern (J, 296). As if to justify his conduct of the vessel, Downton noted the precautions taken: adjustments to wind and current complicating their plotted course, repeated soundings; the rock, he added, was indiscernible even by daylight. For his part, Greene faulted the "careless negligence" of Master Giles Thornton, who "had been at Priaman, and viewed the coast along, and acquainted himself with all the shoals between Tiku and that place," yet who had not seen fit to send "any other ship or boat ahead" to measure depths. Indeed: Why had they not followed the *Darling*? By Jourdain's report, that vessel was "half a mile astern" (J, 236). "God forgive them their pride, which was the cause thereof," Greene wrote, adding, "God forgive me if I think amiss" (G, f19, 20 November).

This was the second serious grounding of the already leaky *Trades Increase* on record, and the predicament was critical. "The water did so increase," wrote Downton, "that both our chain pumps with painful labor" scarcely kept pace with it (D in P, 3:297).[15] "We thought all of us never to have seen our ship again in safety," Greene declared (G, f19, 20 November). Yet the wind abated, and the sea remained calm. "Our general endeavor, with most expedition possible," Downton reported, was to carry an anchor astern by boat, drop it in deep water, and pull the ship back off the shoal by the cable at the capstan. They were amid these labors, and had begun to tighten the cable, when, at 5:00 A.M., "the gracious Lord so blessed our endeavors" that the vessel floated free with a gust of wind that carried them safely westward. A mile off, they anchored to assess the situation. Their "exceeding desires and haste for Bantam" (D in P, 3:297), which likely motivated a midnight departure through shoals in the first place, urged them onward. Yet, beyond the magnitude of the leak, which kept shifts of twelve men on two pumps working continuously, "which caused all w[ho could?], . . . master, preacher, etc., all night and day to take their turn" (G, f19, 20 November), a range of other concerns—the pumps' recurrent breakdowns, their irreparability without new iron fittings, the exhaustion and demoralization of the crew, the need to protect their cargo, and the late loss of Sharpeigh's flagship in the Gulf of Cambay—all mandated immediate return to Tiku. There, they could off-load precious indigo and calicoes and try to stop the leak (D in P, 3:297–98). Anchoring near the island at sunset, the interim commander of the *Trades Increase*, haunted by the specter of Middleton awaiting them in Bantam, ached with guilt at the damage and delay: "Notwithstanding the exceeding cause I have to rejoice for God's most merciful help and present deliverance, yet feeble faint wretch that I am, [I] cannot remove the remediless sorrow for this further addition of the damages of this our troublesome journey, with deep feeling of S[ir] H M's grief, in long wearisome looking for us, deeming every hour a week that he is hindered in the proceeding of his journey" (D, f96, 21 November). Purchas omits this despondent testimony.

Among Downton's paramount concerns was the condition of the crew. Without constant working of the pumps, "which often break or . . . slip to our great discomfort," the ship would sink. To demand such exertions all the way to Bantam—to expect recurrent heavy labor from men exhausted beyond care—was delusional. Downton decried "the desperate carelessness of many of our people" at moments of "greatest need," and expressed exasperation at "their faint weakness and inability to hold out labor (by coarse diet as they pretend)" (D in P, 3:297). Yet he had to respect their limits—like Middleton and Keeling on prior voyages, who heeded crews' demands to override their commissions and put in at the Cape of Good Hope. As Keeling's men reminded him then, "without them, he could not perform his voyage."[16] Hard on himself, Downton expected as much of others. But he had to allow for the needs and desires of "our people" and countenance their potential noncompliance or volatility. The reports of "Captain Sharpeigh's misfortunes, and the lewd demeanors of his people" (D in P, 3:298)—the tales of panic and confusion at the *Ascension*'s foundering, when "there was no respect of persons . . . it was every one for himself," and Jourdain nearly drowned (J, 118–19)—confirmed the decision to return to Tiku.

The occupants of the *Trades Increase* now faced a double bind. To maintain the crew's health and morale was a paramount concern. To that end, it was imperative to find and fix the leak, and leave this "infectious place" as soon as possible. But to do so required exertions that threatened to overtax them. To the relentless pumping, new labors were added the next day: to elevate the stern, they removed heavy goods, including their chests of money in the aft breadroom, from the rear to the forepeak, leaving "but light goods in her mid-ships" (G, f19, 21 November). Two days later, they began off-loading many materials—"all our timber," casks, cables, anchors, hawsers, calicoes, indigo, cinnamon, pepper, and other spices—to the island, where carpenters erected tents from sails to dry out dampened cargo. Not without "discontented clamors and murmurings," half the men worked the pumps, the other half the cargo (D, f96v, 21 November). The labor of pumping "indeed is so extreme," wrote Downton, "that it can but little while . . . be continued. . . . It tires all our people" (D in P, 3:298). As the days advanced, they limited each shift to four hundred strokes (G, f19, 30 November). They tried to find a hundred workers ashore to relieve the crew but discovered that "none of this country people . . . will be hired for any money." Likewise frustrated in their initial efforts to provide fowl or other meat, "to sustain or enable them to hold out their great labor," Downton distributed rials of eight "for their extraordinary expense for a week in fruits or what else liked them" (D, f96–96v, 21 November). Meanwhile, men were dying. Among those who perished on the *Darling* were the ship's surgeon and the factor John Staughten, who had gone ashore with Greene in Priaman (D, f97v, 29 November). The *Trades Increase* lost one Edward Courtney a few days later (D, f97v, 4 December).

Having removed the last of the pepper from the after section of the hull on the twenty-ninth, crewmen of the *Trades Increase* discovered "a great leak . . . right under the end of the keelson,[17] . . . an open seam six inches long, and twenty inches above the keel on the larboard side" (D, f97–97v, 29 November). They had to cut off the keelson's end to reach it. Greene observed that "in the very bilge abaft by the keel, a plank rent, wherein it ran so fast and forcible that we had much ado to stop it" (G, f19, 30 November). Divers slung a double rope woven with oakum beneath the hull, then workers inside pulled it into the leak to slow the water sufficiently for the pumps to make progress (J, 237–38). With the water mostly cleared, they placed a plank treated with tar and hair over the opening, sealed it with a lead plate, and added another plank, "whereby (blessed be our merciful God)" Downton expostulated, "at present, to our great joy, we had no more such use of our pumps" (D, f97v, 29 November). The next day, while carpenters refloored the aft section, others shifted cargo forward to further elevate the stern, whose timbers or "fashion pieces" near the waterline they caulked (D, f97v, 30 December). These were temporary fixes.

For the next week, interrupted by downpours, they reloaded the *Trades Increase* from the island, purchased cows, hens, and another fifty bahars of pepper on the mainland, outfitted a newly purchased pinnace, and repaired their longboat, "broken in diverse places in the blustering weather" (D, f97v, 3 December). On 7 December, as the last load of pepper was consolidated ashore for loading that evening, they weighed the heavy anchors—a slow, laborious process: "We could not get up our anchor, he was so fast in the ooze" (G, f19v, 7 December)—and secured the ship between a light "stream anchor" and a cable tied to a tree for quick departure at first light (D, f97v, 7 December). Their second exit from Tiku was, like those of subsequent English voyagers forewarned by the inhabitants,[18] markedly cautious. At 5:00 A.M. on the eighth, with a "faint gale" from the shore (D, f97v, 8 December)—"being now taught not to work by night in so dangerous a place," noted Jourdain (J, 238)—behind boats sounding depths, they set sail again. At midday, "by estimation . . . near the rock we had sat upon, we used great diligence with boats ahead, but could discern no show of it" (D in P, 3:298–99). A fisherman came aboard to caution them against a westerly course here, "for, said he, . . . both a seaboard and to the landward, were many dangers not seen." Jourdain reports, "This poor fisherman told us that there were between Priaman and Pasaman (which is not above 13 leagues distance) more than 60 shoals, most part under water, some seen. I take this to be the most dangerous place that is in all the Indias," he concluded (J, 238–39). Indeed, the *Darling* had struck a coral bank on arriving in these waters (J, 231). The folly of their first departure, driving a deep-drafted vessel through submerged reefs, by moonlight, without a local pilot or forward escort, was now numbingly clear. It had nearly sunk the ship.

Its final resting place was now but two weeks' sail away. Through rains, lightning, and fickle winds, they continued south toward Java into a current that prevailed against them when the wind slackened, the "high land of the main of Sumatra" visible to the east (D, f98–98v, 9 December 1612). As the days advanced, their progress turned disorienting. They passed islands so thick with trees that "we can see no ground, neither have [we] ground with our lead" (D, f98v, 14 December); several days later, with "a thick sky on head, and a huge gale astern," a large hill looming darkly in the mist, uneasily they opted to lie ahull overnight rather than put in someplace unknown (D, f99, 19 December). The next morning, their "best pilots of former experience"—navigators with prior knowledge of the region—argued over whether mountains visible to their north were the tip of Sumatra or the "Salt Hills" further east, the Krakatoa group in the Sunda Straits. Downton put his trust in a former *Peppercorn* master's mate, Thomas Herrod, who placed the ships near "the main of Java. . . . He showing me a hill over Bantam, as he thought, whither I desired to make all haste possible. [I] therefore directed our course with it, running in" that evening (D, f99, 20 December). Before long, however, the deep bay shallowed to prove Herod wrong. When the *Darling* ahead measured but four fathoms and the *Trades Increase* seven, they anchored overnight and, in the morning, found themselves, Jourdain explained, "the wind hanging in our teeth, . . . within a mile of a lee shore, with shoals and rocks within two cables length" (J, 240)—a very precarious situation. Downton had twice put the *Trades Increase* at risk in his urgency to reunite with Middleton. Bantam, they perceived, was many leagues beyond the intervening land. As they had striven to pull the ship off the rock in Tiku, so they laid out two hundred fathoms of cable astern; and again, "our merciful God favored us with a gust of wind from the south, whereof we haled off NW to get sea room" (D, f99v, 21 December). In mockery of the overconfident master's mate, Thornton named the place "Buzzard's Bay."[19]

Sailing northeast fourteen leagues along the mainland, they anchored that night "at the point of Java," a league and a half shy of Pulo Panjang, an island at the entrance of Bantam Bay where the English serviced their ships (J, 240n) (fig. 12). Also at anchor outside the island were three great Dutch vessels, homeward bound awaiting a wind, whose flagship saluted them with three rounds of ordnance. Saving powder as per the Company's strictures, Downton answered with just one. He sent a messenger aboard "to inquire of our friends at Bantam, by whom to my content I was informed that Sir Henry Middleton was in good health, but much grieved for my long absence from him." At the grounding off Tiku, his own "remediless sorrow" at their delay (D, f96, 21 November) had deepened with personal guilt for prolonging Middleton's now confirmed agony of expectation. Their sorrows of separation indexed an emotional codependency forged, at least in part, by persistent failures to consummate the grand ambitions of their voyage—designs and damages materialized in the great ship as it neared Bantam now. Middleton needed Downton's incisive support, as Downton Middleton's, to resist despair.

The messenger reported further that the *Solomon*, *Hector*, and *Thomas* were preparing to sail homeward and that the *Peppercorn* was "upon the careen"—its hull under repair—at Pulo Panjang (D, f99v, 21 December). Early the next morning, Downton sent presents to the Dutch commander to excuse his parsimonious ordnance the evening before, and they made sail for

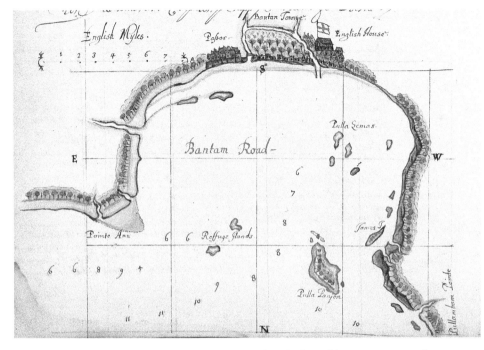

FIGURE 12. Map of Bantam Bay. Drawing by Charles Wilde, 1651. Courtesy of
the British Library Board. Sloane MS 3231, p86. A surreally enlarged "English
House" appears at upper right across the river from "Bantan Towne."
Note "Pulla Panjon" along the right entrance of the bay.

the mainland. As they rounded the island, the *Peppercorn*'s pinnace, carrying
the ship's purser and Master John Davis of the *James*, approached them with
word that Middleton was in Bantam and would be pleased if Downton edged
the *Trades Increase* into Pulo Panjang, where the *James* also lay, to join the
labors on the *Peppercorn*. Waiting out adverse winds, the *James* remained there
"of purpose . . . to assist the *Peppercorn* with the help of their people" (D,
f99v–f100, 22 December 1612). They made way for the island while the pinnace
delivered word of their arrival to Bantam. Before long, in company with Captain Edmund Marlowe and one Mr. Petty of the *James*, whose material assistance had renewed his hopes of collaboration among East India Company
voyages, the general boarded his flagship. He and Downton sequestered themselves in the cabin to share their sorrows and recalibrate their expectations.
During an emotionally labile "private conference," Downton wrote, "I relat[ed]
my misfortunes, by great troubles, dangers, and damages, and he his grief by

my long absence, so on either side turning both griefs unto one." Their griefs
rehearsed, Downton was relieved to hear of the "great kindness diverse ways
found, both for the furtherance of his [Middleton's] business and comfort of
his person by the two friends present," Marlowe and Petty, "wishing me to
take notice thereof and give them thanks, which report gave me no small cause
of rejoicing that, once in our long journey, we had met with our honest and
kind countrymen, whose feeling was such as did add comfort and not grief to
our distress, which till now we could never meet any but that showed us no
less malice than the Turks" (D, f100, 22 December 1612). The news came as a
great comfort not least because General Saris, having reached Bantam before
Middleton, was active there as well. Sad reports, however, also accumulated:
"To my grief I understood that Thomas Glenham, factor, and diverse others
were dead, and that Hugh Frayne, the principal factor, was very sick" (D, f100,
22 December). Their shared comfort in reunion was laced with gloom and
anxiety. Downton admired Frayne, having worked closely with him to forge a
compromise between the fleets in the Red Sea. Bantam's mortality had commenced its work on the mariners of the Sixth Voyage.

CHAPTER 7

Catastrophe in Bantam

An urban enclave within the Sundanese kingdom of Pajajaran since the eleventh century, Bantam grew into a great mercantile center long before English ships arrived. Traders called here from the Arabian Peninsula, Persia, the Malabar and Coromandel coasts of India, Malaysia, Sumatra, Thailand, the Moluccas, China, and Japan. Europeans found the open port well situated for staging voyages to the Spice Islands. The city grew in importance after the Portuguese captured Melaka (Malacca) in 1511 and, like the Chinese before them, worked both sides of the Straits of Sunda. With help from the sultan of Demak in central Java, converts to Islam established a kingdom with a capital on the coast that won independence by 1570. The sixteenth-century pepper boom, notes Anthony Farrington, "quickly made the city one of the largest in Asia."[1] When Sir James Lancaster reached Bantam in December 1602, merchants from Arabia, Turkey, Persia, Gujarat, Tamil, Bengal, Malaysia, China, and Holland were active there. Flanked by two small rivers, the city's central district was bounded by walls five miles in circuit that contained the court, the main mosque, and the homes of Javan nobility. The great market convened daily outside the walls to the east (fig. 13). To the west was the Chinese quarter, where the English established themselves (Farrington, *Trading*, 34). The monarch, Pangeran Ratu (r. 1596–1651), was still a child, and the government was managed by the protector (governor), a position that changed hands shortly after Lancaster concluded his agreement.[2]

The factory at Bantam was the East India Company's first trading hub in the East Indies.[3] The nascent Company needed settlements with warehouses overseas, not only ports of call, to develop corporate efficiencies: to offset the inflation triggered by a fleet's arrival, shorten processes of lading, and prolong

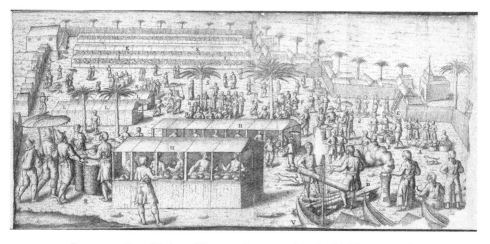

FIGURE 13. Great Market of Bantam. Courtesy of the British Library Board.
Willem Lodeswijckszoon, *Historie van Indien* (1598), shelfmark 1486.gg.18.
Indexed locations offer melons and coconuts; pots of sugar and honey;
beans; bamboo and rattan; swords, lances, and helmets; men's clothes; women's
clothes; spices and drugs; meat; fish; fruit; fresh vegetables; pepper;
onions and garlic; rice; jewelry; poultry; stalls for Bengalis and Gujaratis,
Chinese, and a zone for merchants in general; and a site for mooring boats
(Farrington, *Places*, 39).

those of sales. In principle, resident merchants stored incoming cargoes, sold
them opportunely, and purchased goods at advantageous prices in advance of
a ship's arrival or return. But as rifts between competing East India Company
voyages in Bantam proved, the separate funding of each expedition undermined the factory's institutional integrity. More crippling, residence here
took a staggering toll on Company personnel. This richly trafficked city
proved lethal to all but the heartiest of Englishmen, many of whom arrived in
poor health and lacked innate resistance to the diseases—malaria, dysentery,
typhoid, cholera, the plague—endemic to the low, hot, swampy region. Sexu-
ally transmitted infections were evidently rife here as well. "He that escapes
without disease from that stinking stew of the Chineseas' part of Bantam,"
Nicholas Downton declared after some experience of the place, "must be of
a strong constitution of body, or else of a temperate and well governed life."[4]
Within a few months of Lancaster's departure in February 1603, the factory's
initial agent, William Starkie, and his second, Thomas Morgan, both perished. Edmund Scott then took charge through late 1605, when he returned

with Middleton, then the general of the Second Voyage, to London. Scott's account of his tenure there, *An Exact Discourse of the Subtilties, Fashions, Policies, Religions, and Ceremonies of the East Indians*, was published by Walter Burre, Middleton's brother-in-law, in 1606.[5] Having just produced an anonymous account of Middleton's expedition, *The Last East-Indian Voyage* (London: 1606),[6] Burre intended these publications to enlist support for the financially stressed East India Company, then raising funds for the Third Voyage. Yet, while endorsing patriotic visions, Scott's treatise depicted Bantam's English community as a haunted settlement poised, perhaps like Virginia's Roanoke Colony, at the edge of extinction.

Writing of Lancaster's arrival, Sir William Foster declared Bantam "*destined* to be for a long period the centre of English trade in the East" (*Lancaster*, xxxi; emphasis added). His phrasing minimized the outpost's precarity. Bantam was abandoned for Jakarta in 1619, resumed in 1629, and following a few turbulent decades, as English interests consolidated on the Indian subcontinent, lost in 1682, when the Dutch, active in Java since 1596, drove out the English.[7] To frame the East India Company's arrival in Java, with Foster, teleologically, as the onset of a predestined reconfiguration of power—to foreground promises of imperial achievement in the work of the founding generation—is anachronistic. Teleological thinking elides the radical contingency of historical process, overstates the solvency of imperial systems, and thereby justifies the losses suffered in the labor of building them.

The most elemental threat to London's plans was the mortality of Englishmen in the East Indies. The narrative of Lancaster's voyage, *A True and Large Discourse* (London, 1603), names the dead on each ship as the fleet departed from Achin in Sumatra: sixty-six on the *Dragon*, thirty-seven on the *Hector*, thirty-eight on the *Ascension*, thirty-nine on the *Susan*. A subsequent letter from the *Ascension*, homeward bound at Saint Helena, lists more: in all, one hundred eighty-five men, probably over half the complement of the voyage, perished—months before the ships returned to London (Foster, *Lancaster*, 141–43, 147). The voyage's final death count is unknown. Nor do the above figures include those lost at the factory after the fleet's departure. When Scott landed, he was one of twenty-two persons assigned to Bantam—a place, in Scott's words, of "low ground [that] is very unwholesome and breedeth many diseases, especially unto strangers which come thither" (Foster, *Middleton*, 168). In April 1604, Scott noted that "of seven factors left there, . . . we were now but two living"; their full complement at that hour was "ten living, and one boy" (Foster, *Middleton*, 85, 111). In fourteen months, their numbers had dropped from twenty-two to eleven. Scott's "extraordinary great joy" at the arrival of the Second Voyage that December turned to consternation at the sight of "their weaknesses. . . . It grieved us much, knowing that Bantam is not a place to recover men that are sick, but rather to kill men that come thither in health" (Foster, *Middleton*, 15, 147). On his return in October 1612 (S, f104v, 24 October 1612), John Saris, a survivor of the place, observed a striking pattern: undernourished seamen on crowded, unsanitary vessels survived at rates higher than those of Englishmen in Bantam, where "[our] people, through great disorder ashore, died" (S, f111, 11 December 1612). When at anchor, mariners typically moved sick men ashore to recuperate. Not in Bantam. The *Clove* lost six crewmen while anchored there from 24 October 1612 to 14 January 1613. Saris left ten men at the factory when he departed for Japan. At his return one year later, only five were living: 50 percent mortality within a year. By contrast, of the eighty-one who sailed with him for Japan, twelve perished in that span—five within a month of leaving Java (S, f114, 15 January 1613; f116v, 2–4 February 1613; f117v, 11 February 1613; Satow, 85, 194).

Scott's Regime in Java

As Bantam's microbial environment mowed through English immune systems, its social milieus, laced with collusion and strife among multiple ethnic groups, posed existential challenges as well. The English surfaced in a world destabilized by conflict between the Portuguese and Dutch trading empires. Their arrival, Michael Neill explains, "further complicated already violent rivalries . . . between Chinese, Indian, and Javan merchants, while it added to the tensions created by local power struggles, including ethnic, factional, and dynastic rivalries that the newcomers did not well understand" (Neill, 290). Dependent on groups whom they mistrusted, skeptical of the guarded advice they took from the Dutch, Scott and his fellows tried to secure well-placed fixers, trusty servants, and obedient workers from among neighbors whose quarrels perplexed them. Living in perpetual and justified "fear of fire and thieves" (E. Scott, *Discourse*, 91), they maintained their perimeter with paranoid intensity. Lancaster had negotiated their "authority to execute justice" not only "on their own men offending" but also "against injuries from the natives" (Foster, *Lancaster*, 99). In August 1603, when stones were thrown at their windows as they sang a psalm at the change of a watch, they burst out in pursuit, broke down the door of a nearby house, and threatened its occupants with rapiers. "We terrified those that dwelt about us so," boasts Scott, "that never after we had that abuse offered again" (Scott, 93). The little band was truculent. Yet, without volleys of new personnel from London— moreover, without the labor of workers hired locally, the blessing of Javan authorities, the intervention of various brokers and translators, and the assistance (storage, counsel, sometimes protection) of the Dutch neighbors with whom local groups identified them—the English factory would not have endured.

A small, fearful, dwindling encampment, the "*English* Nation at *Bantam*," as named on Scott's title page, was about the size of a troupe of players; and like Shakespeare's company in *Henry V*, "ciphers to this great account" (Prol. 17), they imagined themselves to represent a nation. Operating far beyond the territorial horizons of the English state, they became more than a band of merchants: Scott's group self-consciously constituted the English government in this place.[8] Moreover, they epitomized England not only in such theatrical presentations as the musketry and parade on Elizabeth's (unknowingly posthumous) Accession Day, orchestrated to distinguish themselves from the Dutch (Scott, 99–101), but also in addressing a problem that, in Linda Colley's terms, beset Britain's imperial efforts perpetually: "their own, incurable limits." Without the widespread collusion of indigenous groups, Britons lacked the demographic strength to impose their will on Asian populations. "The logic of all this was clear to the Company from early on," writes Colley. "If it was ever to control substantial tracts of India, the bulk of its manpower would have to be Indian" (Colley, 258, 259). For his part, Scott hoped to control not "substantial tracts" but a compound of two houses, and he could not do that without outside help. They leased space in the Dutch warehouse. The dust and fumes of milling and chuting pepper so sickened Scott's men "that . . . we were forced to hire Chineses to do that work, and our own men to oversee them only" (Scott, 104). Toxic processes and their own low numbers made foremen of the English and expendable laborers of the Chinese. Likewise, East India Company ships, their crews decimated, required fresh mariners to complete their voyages: "We were . . . constrained . . . to hire so many as we could get of Gujarats and Chinese to help bring home our ships" (Scott, 150).

But English relations with these indispensable groups remained volatile. When their warehouse caught fire in May 1604, they hurriedly enlisted forty Chinese neighbors to help remove the goods, and Scott and Towerson soon found themselves enforced "to stand by with our swords to keep them from throwing them [the packs] over the pales" to thieving accomplices outside (115). Afterward, they learned that some of these men had inadvertently set the fire: over two months, they had tunneled in from the adjacent grounds of a grocery and arak brewery and, once beneath the building, set a candle under the floorboards to break in quietly. Throughout the crisis precipitated by this discovery, armed Dutchmen came to their aid: "doubting [suspecting] the Chinese would rise against us," swearing "they would live and die in our quarrel" (117). With the government's leave—in a sadistic tone of coy self-congratulation, Scott details his vengeance—the English tortured and executed three plotters.[9] The protector endorsed their conduct by ceding them the brewery property.

This expansion of their real estate triggered further acquisitions. After they reconstructed the fire-damaged main house, Scott purchased another nearby, "so that now we had a very spacious yard." To store more pepper, he "hired another house right over against us . . . and some other houseroom was lent us by our friends" (Scott, 128–29). Under his watch, the Bantam properties accumulated by various means: gift outright, purchase, lease, and loan. As Bantam's conditions eroded the Company's discursive regime and degraded institutional memory, the passage of time lent some confusion to these arrangements. Disease and depression compromised the documentation of events; multiple deaths silenced oral histories; entropy unraveled resolve. Middleton's parting "Instructions Left at Bantam" in 1605 complained that "not any of the deceased have left any writing concerning their own estates behind them." He duly insisted that each merchant henceforth keep "his particular estate in writing" (Foster, *Middleton*, 197). But the directive made no discernible effect. The disposition of goods in Bantam, person to person and voyage to voyage, became a perpetual muddle. Further, as noted earlier, the rationale of the factory—to serve multiple expeditions—contradicted that of the separately funded ventures staffing the facility. Factors ashore lacked the capital and storage to treat voyages indifferently. With warehouses full of goods committed elsewhere, incoming expeditions had to rent new houses and purchase commodities post arrival. Over time, this process fractured the community and introduced multiple inefficiencies, like inflationary competition among East India Company merchants from different voyages.

Near the close of *An Exact Discourse*, Scott expressed his concern that the settlement he had vigilantly maintained might fail. That it should continue, despite harrowing losses in personnel, was for him a patriotic imperative: "If we give over our trade there, it will purchase more infamy to our nation in all those parts and in China than ever we have hitherto gained credit; for it will be thought . . . that either poverty is the cause, or that we dare not come there for fear of the Hollanders" (Scott, 165). Rationalizing relentless sacrifice, Scott's anxious nationalism burns with emulation of the Dutch, those better-equipped neighbors who rallied to defend the English from local mobs, who outmaneuvered them at court, and whose "baser sort" (Scott, 165) brawled with English sailors in the streets. Scott's peroration, of course, was framed for readers and investors in England. Locally, Middleton, the factory's interim decider, held a more nuanced view of Anglo-Dutch relations. Having formerly navigated between warring Dutch and Portuguese factions in the Moluccas, he advised the factors that overt affiliation strengthened both the English and the Dutch in Bantam (Foster, *Middleton*, 197). Before sailing homeward in October 1605, leaving Gabriel Towerson in charge of the factory and Saris fifth in succession, the departing general feasted the principal Dutch mariners and merchants. "We were all exceeding merry," Scott recounts, "and great friendship was made between us; and I pray God they may still continue it which are there resident, for they shall be sure to find dangers and trouble enough besides" (Scott, 165). Fixated on extramural threats, Scott probably did not foresee that factionalism and self-interest among Company personnel would disrupt the factory almost as severely as literal undermining and fire had done.

General Saris Returns to Bantam

When Saris, having directed Towerson to meet him there around 1 January, reached Bantam road on 24 October 1612, he was displeased to find the *Hector* and the *James* already at anchor, near a few Dutch ships with whom they had sailed in the day before. All answered the *Clove*'s salutes of ordnance. Their collective arrival, Saris discovered, had tripled the cost of "all requested goods" overnight (S, 104v, 24 October 1612). That the arrivals of the *Thomas*, *Trades Increase*, and *Peppercorn* would soon augment the problem exasperated Saris: "So many ships in the road . . . will make all things so dear as we shall make little profit," he complained. His mood did not improve when Augustine Spalding, whom he had left in charge of the factory three years before (Satow, *Saris*, ix), boarded the *Clove* to pay his respects. Having shipped out as a youth on Lancaster's voyage, Spalding, an accomplished linguist, was weary of his decade-long assignment and not helpful. Inquiring "what store of lading he [Spalding] had in readiness, how the state of the country stood, and what store of cloves were in town," Saris learned that nearly all of the ten thousand sacks of pepper in storage were spoken for. As instructed "by advice from the Cape Bon Esperance," Spalding had purchased most of them on credit for the Sixth Voyage; the remainder, to be shipped in the *Solomon*, a vessel of the Tenth Voyage, were dedicated to the Third and Fifth Voyages. The interest due on these purchases accrued at four percent monthly. Saris faulted Spalding for his "evil husbandry" and proposed to discharge the debt immediately; the latter demurred, "saying it would not be long before he [Middleton] would come" (S, f104v, 24 October). Spalding then declined to help Saris purchase cloves forthwith at preinflated prices. The chief factor was resolved to return to England and not "meddle further with the company's business. . . . No persuasions will induce him to hold the governance of the house ashore" (S, f105). It was a bracing return to a grudging English settlement whose governance had slackened under Spalding's charge.

The Eighth Voyage, Saris realized, would have to shift for itself. With the approval of Towerson and Cocks, he appointed Edmund Camden, long forgiven for having lost the sultan's pass on his way to the *Clove*, "to take the business of the Eighth Voyage in hand and to see to the ordering of the house" (S, f105, 24 October). Saris was anxious to sell calicoes seized in the Red Sea before Middleton arrived to complicate their marketing. Yet, when he raised the issue with Spalding the next day, the latter again declared himself unable to help: "The warehouses were full, and no goods could be put in there." Thwarted by his countryman, Saris earned a more heartening welcome on the morning of 26 October when "diverse Javans of account and of my old acquaintance came aboard to visit me and . . . manifest their loves to me, according to the compliment of the country, which I took kindly and gave them many thanks with some feeling" (S, f105v, 26 October). Cheered by the meeting, he went ashore to reconnoiter the situation. After dining at the English house, he and his merchants, hoping to secure the "speedy landing of certain goods" (S, f105v), carried gifts of cloths, firearms, a barrel of gunpowder, and a "Turkey carpet" to Governor Pangran Chamarra, whom they understood "to continue the rule of all, and the king as nobody" (S, f105). Upon the governor's request that "his officers might be acquainted first" with the goods in question, the calicoes again became a problem. The following day, "I went to the court to confer with the governor about the custom and found that our swarts [blacks] brought out of England had told him that we had stolen our cloth from the Guzerats and all the holy men of Mecca. He was awhile silent, seeming much discontented and speaking doubtfully whether he might take custom thereof with a safe conscience" (S, f106, 27 October). Undermined by Muslim solidarity and subaltern witness to English predation at sea—the "swarts" were dark-skinned mariners likely hired in Bantam on prior voyages at lower wages than their English shipmates—Saris found some hope in his embarrassment: perhaps the governor would exempt the cloth from his customs. "But upon his better bethinking, he said he would have three percent to be paid in cloth" (S, f106, 27 October), about half the usual rate.[10] Pangran Chamarra proved flexible, his concerns of marketing counter-balancing those of piety.

Compelled to rent their own warehouses, the Eighth Voyage hired two on 3 November (S, f107, 3 November). As for the cloves, Saris soon regretted having raised the issue with Spalding. Rated at sixteen rials per pecul at the *Hector*'s arrival, their price quickly rose, Spalding reported, to "forty rials the pecul" (S, f106, 28 October).[11] Saris suspected that the veteran factor had plotted to enrich himself at their expense. When Spalding, having promised to rejoin them, failed to appear on 28 October, Saris and Richard Cocks went to the great market without him. They contracted with one Keewee, a Chinese merchant, to purchase the cloves in his possession, and "all he could get," for thirty-eight rials a pecul. Saris suspected that a good portion of these came from Spalding's "private account, . . . the only cause of this intolerable exaction and reason he would not go along with me" that day (S, f106, 28 October). "I am credibly informed," he wrote a week later, "that the cloves we bought were Spalding's, who bought them after the arrival of the *Hector* for sixteen rials per pecul, and sold them to the company at thirty-eight rials per pecul, and allowed the China merchant for his pains in selling them for him" (S, f107–107v, 6 November 1612).[12]

Saris's suspicions may have been unfounded; Jourdain later inquired into the matter and found no persuasive evidence of guilt, "only . . . suspicion because of his familiarity with the Chineses" (*LR*, 2:278). Mistrust pervaded the factory. On 21 December, Saris advised Camden to distance himself from the veteran agent: "Make no respect of Spalding but carry yourself well." That their lead factor was rumored to be pocketing personal gains from corporate accounts confirmed the London office's accusation in a letter carried by the Sixth Voyage to the Bantam factory: "Those who have had the managing of the business have had more care to enrich themselves than to seek our profit" (Birdwood, 313). Not that the reproof changed anything. A letter reached London in July 1614, for instance, with complaints against several Sixth Voyage personnel (including Robert Larkin and John Williams) "for purloining the company's goods, and appropriating them to their own particulars, deceiving many private men in their estates, with their insolent behaviors in those parts, and vanity and pride in wearing buckles of gold in their girdles, and making known the great wealth which they have suddenly gathered together, . . . whereas they came very bare thither, without any means at all" (*Court Book* B/5, 161, 12 July 1614). Suspicions of graft in the factory's principal agent motivated similar sleights among others in the household—men who, watching one another succumb to wasting diseases in the service of investors in London, resolved to compensate themselves where and while they could.

Residence in Bantam, in short, corroded corporate resolve. Shareholder earnings and factory governance suffered together. Having noted an alarming lack of discipline at the factory—the collective temperance that Saris, Downton, and other East India Company leaders understood to protect both personal health and corporate profits—Saris found himself helpless to arrest a contagion of recklessness among his men: "The place here unwholesome and our people dangerously disordering themselves ashore with drink and whores, making jest of fair entreaty or punishment, both [of] which hath been used, but to little purpose" (S, f105v, October).[13] When the *Solomon* arrived on 4 November, "her people all sick" (S, f107, 4 November), Saris befriended its captain, Robert Ward, who joined him ashore.[14] The day before, Saris had received a petition for back payment of wages from seven Englishmen left behind by their voyages, now two years "idle in the house to the company's charge, living very lewdly and without order, not once assisting the merchants." At this juncture, the East India Company had no formal provision for displaced sailors. The men lived outside the disciplinary regimes set forth in their voyage commissions, and their presence destabilized the factory. Spalding had promised them wages but never delivered. Saris offered them employment on the *Clove* or *Hector* and, after much haggling and "turbulent" exchange—one man protesting that "he would be satisfied for the time he had served or he would seek entertainment of the Flemings"—came to terms with five of them, Spalding agreeing to pay half their back wages (S, f107, 3 November; f107v, 8–9 November). Witnessing the negotiation, Ward "much admired[15] the state of the business here, the people without government, and every one of those sailors doing what he listed" (S, f107v, 8 November).

English indiscipline in Bantam offered early proof of a pattern N. A. M. Rodger finds in the Georgian navy: "Ships in port . . . were like little towns without a police force" (*World*, 207). At sea, everyone understood that their survival depended on their coordinated efforts; not so in harbor. Visited on the *Clove* by Captain Edmund Marlowe and Master John Davis of the *James* on 3 November, Saris heard complaints of further disciplinary problems in town: Marlowe's merchants were defying him. Acting as if his ship-based authority were null on land, the merchants "had so misused him [that] he was constrained to read the king's commission openly" to them, to minimal effect. Marlowe asked Saris to read the commission himself "and see what authority he had over them."[16] But as Spalding had lately refused to help him, so now Saris demurred, protesting, "I had business of my own and would not meddle in other men's matters." As noted in the prior chapter, Middleton took heart from his conversations with Marlowe and other "honest and kind countrymen" of the *James* (D, f100, 22 December 1612), who offered him sympathetic collaboration, not conflict. Saris, by contrast, perhaps sensing trouble, held off. After supper, Marlowe and Davis, a reputable, seasoned navigator,[17] departed, "to my thinking, friends," Saris writes. But on return to the ship, Marlowe, a heavy drinker, quarreled with Davis: "The master and captain fell from words to blows, [and] Davis was soundly beaten," Saris reports. "And the sailors much rejoiced to see their weakness, none assisting, but looking and making a jest of their disorder" (S, f106v, 1 November 1612). Jourdain likewise wrote scathingly of Marlowe's command: "In all places where they have been, they have left themselves famous with infamy to our nation, what by fighting, brabbling and contention amongst themselves, troubling all men where they come, . . . both strangers and others are weary of their company; and he that should govern all is chief cause of these disorders" (*LR*, 2:274). Pace Middleton, the *James* was a demoralized vessel, not an icon of corporate solidarity.[18]

Rival Voyages in Residence

While enduring conflict and disarray within their household, the "*English Nation at Bantam*" strove to present a unified front to Javan authorities and other outside groups. Formal public displays constituted prime occasions to do so. To ingratiate themselves with authorities ashore, East India Company mariners regularly doubled as itinerant showmen; and ever since Scott's grandiose parade on Elizabeth's Accession Day, a tradition of English self-display, often augmenting Javan occasions, had taken root. When, at the close of

Ramadan, the governor "importuned" Saris "to let our people come ashore with their furniture" (in armed regalia), the Dutch declined, yet the resident East India Company voyages delivered a procession to consolidate good relations within the city. The *James* having departed the day before, "I appointed forty men out of the *Clove* and *Hector*, Sir Henry thirty out of the *Peppercorn*, and Capt. Ward ten out of the *Solomon*. [They] joined together and were led by Capt. Cox," coxswain of the *Hector*.[19] Saris reports that "the governor took it kindly and returned many thanks" (S, f108v, 15 November 1612).

Ironically, such cooperative displays reinforce the overriding impression carried by Saris's testimony ten years into the experiment in Bantam: corporate solidarity—the performance of group personhood by embedded servants of the Honorable Company—was an evanescent achievement here. Riven by fealties to subsidiary coalitions—including one's voyage, one's shipmates, one's immediate superiors, one's work cohort—and to one's self, the East India Company's nominally perpetual "body corporate and politic" was a fugitive, intermittently confirmed fiction in Bantam. Middleton's arrival on 9 November deepened the factory's divisions. A second general on the scene, a proud man of high temper overstressed by captivity and pervasive frustration on a "journey begun with glory . . . [and] great expectation" (D in *LR*, 1:155), perplexed the factory's governance. Hastening south in the *Peppercorn* lest Saris precede him to "spoil his market" there (S, f77v 29 April 1612), Middleton was no doubt displeased to find the *Clove* and *Hector* riding at anchor in the bay, two weeks into their stay. Learning that Sir Henry had arrived, Saris sent Cocks to greet him, and at Middleton's request, visited him on the *Peppercorn* the following day. The meeting began cordially but quickly devolved: "His desire," Saris reports, "was to have me discharge all the *Hector*'s goods into the *Trade* for England and to let him have her to dispose of." Perhaps Middleton strategized to deploy all available ships to the maximal advantage of the Company—as if they all served the same joint stock. But he tended to identify East India Company interests with those of his own superiorly furnished, and hitherto unprofitable, voyage.

Saris abruptly terminated the meeting. He saw the proposal as a transparent bid to harness the *Hector* to the aims of the Sixth Voyage, a move he believed Middleton had already attempted in the Red Sea. "I was not a little ashamed," he wrote, "to hear such a motion proceed from so wise a gentleman. I desired him not to misuse me in this fashion and took my leave" (S, f108, 10 November 1612). Undaunted, resolved to widen his reach, two days later Middleton floated the proposal past mariners of the Tenth Voyage:

"Now Sir Henry labors to get the *Solomon* of Capt. Ward, purposing to be at Japan before me" (S, f108–108v, 12 November), Saris mocked. Middleton's grand designs provoked Saris's parsimony. When Cocks and Camden reported that Sixth Voyage personnel dined at the house in such numbers that the cook frequently lacked food for Camden's staff, "I acquainted Sir Henry therewith, desiring reformation, but he made light thereof." Differences of class inflected the misunderstanding, Middleton assuming an aristocratic code of reciprocal hospitality, Saris a bourgeois frugality. Saris advised Camden to order victuals solely for the twenty-six persons in his charge and not to let men from other voyages dine with them unless their commanders covered the bill (S, f108, 12 November). East India Company personnel divided even at the dinner table.

"I have much marveled," Camden wrote in a 15 January 1613 letter to the Company, "what the reason" might be that "Sir Henry should be so addicted to the hindrance of our voyage." Camden speculated that personal hatred, umbrage that Saris no longer conducted himself deferentially, or the knight's conviction that Saris held an office beyond his desert, could have been involved. Camden, to the contrary, believed Saris to be "a man worthy of far greater employment" (*LR*, 1:228). The relations between the two generals remained volatile. Sometimes they collaborated: on 20 November, for instance, acceding to Middleton's request to share a purchase of pepper from Keewee, Saris fronted the Sixth Voyage half the money, 2,000 rials—a courtesy for which Middleton, Saris reports, "gave me more thanks than I expected or he was accustomed, for greater kindnesses shown unto him" (S, f109, 20 November).

But four days later, an ugly scene erupted as Eighth Voyage personnel moved to store several packs of Cambayan cloth from the lately arrived *Thomas*: Middleton blocked the door. The building in question was the "old warehouse"—reportedly full at Saris's arrival, yet presumably a shared facility—not one of their own. "Sir Henry stood in the door and denied the entrance thereof, protesting it should not be brought in there, for he had hired warehouses, and so should I," Saris reported. The pillaged callicoes continued to vex Saris and his men. Towerson and Cocks protested that rain, which would ruin the exposed textiles, was imminent, but Middleton refused to step aside until Sharpeigh and Hawkins arrived to talk him down. "And instantly," Saris continued, "there fell such an extreme shower of rain" that Cocks had to hire the crowd of bystanders drawn to the confrontation to hustle the merchandise inside (S, f109v, 24 November). General Middleton's will to curb Saris flouted corporate solidarity and, on this occasion, publicly embarrassed the Company.

They contended further over housing, "the old mansion so pestered [crowded]" with goods from multiple voyages (S, f110, 2 December). Saris's men found a promising location, "Sinsan's house . . . by the waterside, adjoining to the Flemings, and most convenient and spacious for the company hereafter." Saris expected the Company might "build a fair house" there (S, f110, 5 December 1612). Their shared need for such a place, however, ignited competition, not collective action. Cocks wrote to Saris on 14 December "that Sir Henry and Mr. Jones were again very busy about the bargaining for the house, and that he doubted [suspected], if they were not prevented, we should have all our goods thrown into the yard." Suspecting that Middleton created confusion to delay the departure of the *Hector* and *Thomas* for England, Saris advised Cocks to ignore them: "I wrote him to follow our business and not to esteem what they did or said in this matter" (S, f111, 14 December). When Saris subsequently booked "Sinsan's house and ground by the waterside . . . for £100 per year," Middleton worked with "the governor's minion" to acquire it for the Sixth Voyage instead. Pangran Chamarra responded in vexation: he "would let neither of us have it but said he would pull it down" (S, f112v, 2 January 1613). On the street and at court, internal rivalries repeatedly embarrassed the Company.

It was by now obvious to most Englishmen on the scene that the factory required a unified command structure. But in the absence of directives from Smythe's office, how to reorganize the factory and compensate a supreme officer—all raises, by recent Company stricture, being awarded exclusively in London—remained unclear.[20] At Spalding's refusal to continue as chief agent, Saris, the sole general then at hand, had assigned command of the house to Camden. Middleton found this arrangement unacceptable and evidently preferred to install an overseer from neither of their voyages. In a salutary effort that Saris took as a direct challenge to his authority, on 13 December Middleton called a meeting at Pulo Panjang to propose the creation of a consul, an office familiar in the Levant Company. Significantly, he did not invite Saris, nor did he propose that the Eighth Voyage contribute a share of the salary: "Sir Henry caused a meeting . . . for the displacing of Mr. Camden and placing a consul in the house to command the merchants and merchandize as well of the Eighth Voyage as of all the rest. But no man was nominated for the consul this meeting, only a writing drawn, subscribed by Capt. Ward, Mr. Jones, and Capt. Marlowe, appointing £120 a year wages to this unknown consul *to be paid to him here*, viz. £80 out of the Sixth Voyage and £20 a piece per year of the *Solomon* and *James*" (S, f111, 13 December; emphasis added).[21] The consensus achieved here illuminates Middleton's praise of Marlowe and his officers as "honest and kind countrymen" (D, f100, 22 December 1612) with whom he could work to the Company's benefit. For his part, Marlowe found in Sir Henry, as opposed to Saris, a general committed to clear and comprehensive lines of authority in Bantam.

Six days later, Middleton confronted Saris with the proposal. The latter took predictable umbrage. He framed Middleton's proposal as an arrogant usurpation of London's authority. He deemed Camden fit to direct the factory and refused to underwrite, without London's approval, an ad hoc appointment whose salary, derived locally, would enlarge the Company's expenses:

> I entreated him to pardon me. I had very sufficient merchants of the company's appointing in England for the managing of all such businesses as they had committed to my charge. And Spalding having refused the further service of the company, I had, according to the company's order, being here before he [Middleton] came, appointed one for their business. Which if he pleased not to hold sufficient for the business of the Sixth Voyage, I desired him not to be offended with me, [for] I knew him to be very sufficient and worthy for what I should leave in his charge. And that I had no order to put the company to frivolous charge [expense], and to the discouragement of their servants, by appointing any other to command over them than they had made choice of at home. (S, 111v, 18 December 1612)

Saris's intransigence, piously justified as fidelity to London's will, infuriated Middleton, who sought creative efficiencies of command to enhance the factory's utility to multiple voyages in the Company's service. In the event, he flatly ignored Saris, who was soon to depart for Japan anyway as the *Thomas* and *Hector* sailed homeward. Anticipating a longer stay for repairs on the *Trades Increase*, Middleton and his team simply took over the house and elected a consul themselves. Two days before the *Clove* sailed, Cocks protested, "Sir Henry hath proceeded according to his own determination without advice of our general" (*LR* 1:221, 12 January 1613). Jourdain clarified the arrangement: "Sir Henry delivered me the charge of the house and goods and presented me to the King of Bantam as chief factor, and Mr.

Jones as deputy to Captain Sharpeigh, who was elected to stay as consul or governor over all the English; the which the king accepted and took notice thereof" (J, 241).

In an environment less lethal to Englishmen, once Saris sailed away, Middleton's consular initiative might have taken hold. But it came to naught.

Repairs and Deliberations on Pulo Panjang; a Death in Bantam

When the *Trades Increase* anchored at Pulo Panjang on 22 December 1612, the timely repair of the fleet was a paramount concern. Crewmen of the *James* had joined those of the *Peppercorn* to careen the latter's hull. Careening, an intensive process, required a ship to be grounded ("in harbor, where the slower the tide runs, the better," explains Henry Manwayring) and emptied of most cargo and ordnance. Then, with ropes and pulleys above, and ballast strategically arranged on deck and within the hull, the ship was lowered onto one side to allow workers on scaffolds to scrape the exposed areas clean of invasive organisms, recaulk the seams, and sheath and tar the hull. That done, it was brought over to the other side for the same treatment. As Manwayring explains, the procedure facilitated vital repairs in locations lacking the naval infrastructure of Deptford or Woolwich:

> It is most commonly used in such places where there are no decks
> to trim a ship in, nor no good places to grave[22] a ship on. . . . For
> the manner of careening, . . . is thus: they take out all, or leave but
> little of the provision, ballast, ordnance . . . in the ship; and you
> must have a lower ship by her, with which she must be haled down
> on a side, and righted again with tackle (yet with the weight of
> ballast above, or below, they do effect the chief force of the business,
> and so never strain the ship's masts much). Note that all ships are
> not of a like condition to careen; for some ships will be very hard to
> come down, though they have no ballast in them, and those are the
> Flemings . . . and yet these will right themselves very easy, and
> therefore need not much in hold to right them. Some, as our English
> built, . . . will come down easy, and be hard to right. . . . Some will
> do neither, so that there is not one way for all, but as we see the
> condition of the ship, we fit things and work accordingly.[23]

One notes again, as in the opening chapter, the disposition to improvise: like shipbuilding, early modern ship repair was not an exact or altogether predictable art. Crews and carpenters did what they could with the conditions and materials at hand. The process concluded with the sheathing of the outer hull "with thin boards, and hair, and tar. . . . This is done only under water, or a very little above; the use whereof is to keep the worms from eating through the planks, . . . for . . . the worm . . . cannot abide" the tar (Manwayring, 92–93).

At the close of his reunion with Downton on 22 December, Middleton called for "the people of the *Trades Increase* to assist them of the *Peppercorn*" in this process straightway. Whether the weakness of the latter's crew or the need for haste dominated Middleton's calculations, he clearly found more help necessary. He instructed them "to bring her down and pump when she is down, and right her again as the carpenters' work shall direct us," explained Downton, who duly consecrated "all our own carpenters" to the project. "The great ship's company at present," Middleton observed several days later, "cannot be spared from helping the *Peppercorn*" (D, f101, 27 December). There, in a clear example of corporate solidarity and local outreach, they collaborated with "the carpenters of the *James* and *Solomon*, [and] with diverse Chinese hired from Bantam for more expedition." The urgencies of repair brought crews from various ships, voyages, and ethnic communities together.

Notwithstanding the resourcefulness evident here, the convergence of workers from several sources multiplied microbial exposures exponentially; and the deployment of combined forces to fix a vessel about one-fourth the tonnage of the *Trades Increase* held troubling implications for the latter's repair, once its fleet mates had departed. Extraordinary labors would be demanded of a crew attenuated by sickness, the late pumping and repairs in Tiku, and recent work on other vessels. Their health and morale were pressing concerns, as Downton understood. While praising "one Day, the carpenter of the *James*" for his "true labor, few needless words, and honest behavior," Downton deemed those from his ship "for the most part clamorous fellows, not satisfied with treble the allowance of other men" (D, f100, 22 December). But the crew's discontent was not irrational. Recognizing their limits, the great ship's carpenters evidently preferred to save themselves for the ensuing enormities of repair on which their own safe passage home depended. No one yet knew that the *Trades Increase* would prove irreparable. A Marxist critique of Downton's complaint would find him, with the wage bonus, complicit in the alienation of their labor: redirecting their life-sustaining energies from the maintenance of their own vessel to the preservation of the corporate person. Soon enough, while the *Peppercorn* sailed home with profitable cargo, most of them perished in Pulo Panjang and Bantam.

Late the next day, Middleton, having sent for the ship's surgeon that morning to tend to Hugh Frayne in Bantam, returned to the *Trades Increase* to plan the construction of a storehouse on Pulo Panjang and review their next moves. Both fleets readjusted their plans, perpetually improvising ways forward. On 24 December, they generously loaned the Eighth Voyage the pinnace Downton had purchased in Tiku, so that Saris could send word to the outbound *Hector*, "at the watering place at the south end of Sumatra, called Marigobrough" (D, f100v, 24 December), to turn back and await the *Thomas* for the homeward journey. Huddled to discuss "our ensuing business of no small import," Downton and Middleton foresaw critical impediments at every turn: "To all our wished endeavors, we found ourselves contradicted." At this attenuated hour, the voyage's master narrative of great expectations thwarted, high ambitions crushed, looked unalterable. In hopes of better cheer the next day, that evening Middleton invited "all our friends at Bantam" to join them on the *Trades Increase* on Christmas morning (D, f100v, 24 December). Saris notes no such invitation: passing the twenty-fifth on the *Clove* off Bantam, he feasted his crew with "twenty-five hens, four ducks, and a goose" and ordered "certain chambers to be discharged at the house and answered . . . out of the ships" in celebration (S, f112, 25 December). Middleton's gathering included "Capt. Marlowe and his merchants, Mr. Petty, Capt. Hawkins, and Augustine Spalding" (D, f100v, 25 December). The divided feasts marked the Eighth Voyage's alienation from the rest of Bantam's English community.

A sad summons reached the *Trades Increase* early the next morning: Frayne was dying. He "desire[d] the general to come over to him, if ever he desired to see him, at which was no small grief," Downton wrote. "Instantly the general sent for me and Mr. Adams the preacher to accompany him." This was Downton's first entry into Bantam. As they arrived around 9:00 A.M., an ominous stench beset them: "We were encountered with most noisome smells." The swampy urbanized region, rife with mosquito- and waterborne infections, reeked with noxious effluents as if to verify the miasmic theory of disease transmission. ("The water of Bantam is very vile, as hath been oft proved," confirms a mariner of the *Solomon*, explaining why they went elsewhere to fill their casks).[24] Downton disembarked in full awareness that this errand of farewell imperiled him. The stink, he wrote, "bred a conceit in me that it was hard and doubtful for any newcomers to continue their health, until they had made it familiar unto them." They reached the compound at a critical hour. "At our coming into the English house, we found Hugh Frayne in good memory, but his extreme parts [were] growing cold. Till noon, the general and he was dispatching diverse business, which being dispatched, about two or three a clock, he gave up the ghost." For both the writer and his subject, the mixture of intimacy and duty in this entry—dread, pathos, and flat documentation—is striking. On his deathbed, Frayne, the chief surviving money manager of the Sixth Voyage, troubled himself to clarify their affairs for Middleton while he could.[25] Downton depicts the dying man, his extremities growing cold like Sir John Falstaff's in Shakespeare's *Henry V*, not babbling "of green fields" (*Henry V*, 2.3.16), but taking leave of friends and "dispatching . . . business"—identifying his personal and corporate functions—to the end. In Downton's eyes, he died as he had lived: an exemplary servant of the Company. Though anxious to avoid the stench, they stayed to bury him in the morning (D, f100v–f101, 26 December).

Middleton remained to find a warehouse for the Sixth Voyage, "a good way from the English house" in town; Downton departed to erect a "spacious storehouse for our goods and a chamber for me to lie in" on Pulo Panjang. Projects there proliferated, including, over time, the construction of a "little new built village" to serve the repairs (*LR*, 1:260). To coordinate work on the three vessels, he took the *Darling* and the *Trades Increase* into "the narrow neck, or sound, where the *Peppercorn* lay on the careen" (D, f101, 27 December). They leveled ground for a house, established the requisite dimensions, and set to work briskly. "Finished by six men in five days" (D, f101, 28 December), the house was then filled with "all the packs . . . out of the *Trades Increase*" to empty it for work on the hull, inside and out. The initial plan was to send the great ship home with cargoes topped off with the pepper Middleton had purchased in Bantam; the other two ships would make opportune forays to Amboyna, Banda, Borneo, and the Moluccas. There, they expected resistance from Portuguese and Dutch fleets, whose superior strength, Downton confessed, "indeed, makes our hopes extreme doubtful" (D, f101v, 28 December).

Middleton had taken the *Dragon* to Ternate and Tidore on the Second Voyage, and a plenary meeting on the island nominated him to command the *Peppercorn* to those parts again (D, f101v, 28 December). Maintaining to the contrary that the general was better employed "managing the company's great business at Bantam," Downton offered to lead the quixotic expedition himself. He explained, perhaps more explicitly in the journal than to his colleagues, that he desired thus to free Sir Henry for the more promising duties that would insulate him from the damages, reputational and psychic, attendant on the errand's likely failures:

> When question was moved for deciding our business, and what ship and what principal commander to employ either way, my speech and request was that, howsoever hazardable and hopeless, I offered myself to undertake the same, to the end that whatsoever casualty, imputation, or disgrace by not achieving what was sought for, . . . might light on me and not on Sir Henry Middleton. . . . This motion of me not proceeding of any desire . . . to be employed in any hopeless or desperate business, but if of necessity, by the company's direction, . . . one must try the fortune of that doubtful way, I wish rather to be employed therein than my commander, who is to carry and sway all the whole business.

This masochistic plea met some resistance ("by diverse, for private respects, contradicted," Giles Thornton for one). The meeting, like many others, ended inconclusively, "my motion neither affirmed nor denied" (D, f101v, 28 December).

Given his satiric naming of the place, Thornton was likely displeased when Downton, seeking entry into Bantam road, had followed master's mate Thomas Herrod's advice into "Buzzards Bay." The *Trade*'s master, in any case, evidently took a dislike to the lieutenant general, for he opposed Downton's motion, the latter came to understand, so as to return to service under Middleton while Downton stayed with the great ship. To that end, and perhaps to evade the burdens of overseeing its repair, in concert with the carpenter George Collinson and others who should have known better ("to my great wonder," Downton wrote), Thornton maintained that the *Trades Increase* was "very sufficient and firm to go home." Downton suspected otherwise: "The *Trades Increase*, after she had beaten upon the rock, and when by great industry her leak was stopped, . . . every man's conceit in reason was that she was not to be adventured home without seeing her keel, and securing of all doubts" (D, f101v, 28 December). He took Thornton's surprising claims of its fitness "to be but loose dealing," yet said little, trusting that soon enough

Middleton would examine more carefully the condition of the vessel on which "the safety of so many men, and so much goods as she would contain," depended. Indeed, as work on the *Peppercorn* wrapped up, closer inspection of the *Darling* raised concerns about the flagship: "When the *Darling* came on the careen, discovering how dangerously she was eaten . . . put doubtfulness of the *Trades Increase* might be as bad, he [Middleton] resolved in no case to hazard her without seeing of her keel, and firmly making her outside by sheathing and otherwise, himself apprehending this to be a business of necessity, and that she could not return this year with any assurance of safety" (D, f102, 28 December). Given the protracted duration of the Sixth Voyage, the only move consonant with company interests was to send the *Peppercorn* "with most expedition home for England" (D, f102, 28 December), richly laden, while work on the other ships advanced.

Thus Downton resumed his former command—not on a sacrificial errand eastward, but on an exhausting, death-punctuated journey home. The *Peppercorn*, "laden with indigo and other rich commodities" (J, 242), sailed from Pulo Panjang on 4 February 1613. Three days later, Middleton ("my general," Downton calls him fondly) met them in his pinnace as they took on wood and water at the northwest point of Java. He had come to deliver letters for England and bid farewell. "The next morning, our people were employed stowing down all things we could and making ready the ship; which done, and the general business dispatched, about noon, the wind northerly, we set sail. And soon after, the general departed: whom I desire almighty God to bless with a happy conclusion to this our backward journey. And at parting, I shot off five pieces of ordnance for a farewell" (D, f102v, 8 February 1613).[26] They never saw each other again. Two years later, Downton too would die at Bantam. Like Sir Henry, he was probably buried in the English plot on Pulo Panjang. In the meantime, his departure in the *Peppercorn* removed the voyage's most exacting commentator from the terminal agonies of the great ship's brief career.

His departure was one of several that season. Captain Hawkins, whom Saris described as "much depressed" while living on the *Trades Increase* (S, f112, 23 December 1612),[27] sailed with his wife for England on 12 January 1613 aboard the *Thomas*, which joined the *Hector* awaiting it in the straits (S, f112, 30 December; f110v, 12 January). Saris sailed for Japan on 14 January; he passed through Bantam again one year later, homeward bound. Hawkins died as the disease-infested *Thomas* reached Ireland, the return from Bantam having killed "most of the people in that ship," Downton reported (*LR*, 2:209). In London, Towerson, who captained the *Hector* home, married Hawkins's rich widow, Mariam Khān, early in 1614. They returned together to the East Indies in 1617.[28] Towerson was tortured and executed by the Dutch at Amboyna in 1623, a patriotic death that earned him a literary afterlife more glamorous than those of his companions on the Sixth and Eighth Voyages: as a heroic factor in John Dryden's *Amboyna* (1673).

As for Middleton's consular initiative, English mortality erased it. The indeterminate longevity of a corporate body could be brief in Bantam. Sharpeigh, sailing in a small junk to Sukadana in Borneo as Middleton's team met in mid-December (S, f111, 10 December 1612; J, 241n), was named consul in absentia. He never returned to assume the office. His deputy Mr. Jones soon died (J, 241n, 312). The resilient Jourdain—who fell finally, not to disease, but likely to a Dutch sniper's bullet at Patani in 1619 (J, lxxii, 368–74)— might have stepped up; but as one of the few veteran leaders remaining, he was given command of the refitted *Darling* on a voyage to Amboyna and beyond instead. This came about because Master William Pemberton, whom Middleton meant to captain the ship, had instead to supervise repairs on the *Trades Increase* after Thornton, who should have performed this charge, "not being sick to any man's seeming" (J, 243), as Middleton and Downton bade farewell at Palembam Point, suddenly died.[29] Though Thornton had alienated Downton and been chided by Middleton, "Sir Henry was a very sorrowful man for him and knew not whom to make master of the ship, demanding my opinion whom I thought fit. I answered him that I thought Mr. Pemberton to be the fittest man for that great business of careening the *Trade*; whereunto Sir Henry answered that . . . he had none to send in the *Darling* for commander of that business, except I would take it upon me; to which I answered that I was not wedded to Bantam" (J, 242–43). Reluctantly, Middleton dispatched his most trusted counselor at hand to Amboyna.[30] Jourdain sailed eleven days after Downton, on 15 February 1613 (J, 244). His journal long neglected, Greene "lay sick aboard the *Trade* of his Pasaman disease," Jourdain reported on 9 February (J, 243), and soon died. Given these departures, no eyewitness testimony of the effort to repair the *Trades Increase* survives. Presumably, Middleton kept a journal at Pulo Panjang while he could, but it vanished.[31] Among the collateral breakdowns of the great ship's loss are regrettable lapses in the record.

The Demise of the *Trades Increase* and Its Crew

Summarizing the situation at his departure for Amboyna, Jourdain wrote that Middleton, for "the most part of the time of his being"—that is, for the balance of his life—"remained at the island of Pulo Panjang about the sheathing of the ships. The *Peppercorn* being ended, the *Darling* was laid in the careen, the *Trade* being also within the two little islands where the ships were careening, to take her turn when the others were ended; so that Sir Henry had much travail about it" (J, 242). Jourdain's bare phrase, "much travail," is an understatement. The day before the *Darling* sailed, however, and the flagship's repair commenced, Middleton orchestrated his vessel's final performance as a transcultural theater of British hospitality and power: "The king of Bantam and the protector his uncle, with many of his nobles, came to the island to see the *Trade*, and brought with them above fifty great proas or frigates armed. The king and the governor came aboard the *Trade*, where he was afraid to stay long, not being used to see such ships. The general gave him a good present and took it for a great favor of the king to adventure to come aboard his ship, knowing that none can come to talk with him but whom the protector pleaseth" (J, 244). It was a grand occasion, and Middleton expressed due gratitude at the honor of the visit; yet the young king, intimidated, broke off the event prematurely. There was evidently no dinner shared. Advised that large ordnance frightened him, the English waited until he was "out of sight" of it before saluting his fleet's departure with "all the ordnance of the *Trade* and the *Darling*, which the king and the protector took very kindly" (J, 244). If delivered in single rounds, the reports from so many cannon would have produced an impressively sustained farewell. Yet Jourdain may have erred to suppose that the royal party enjoyed their thunderous departure. The monarch's unease at the size, bearing, and formidable armaments of the *Trades Increase* may, in fact, have figured in its eventual fate: burned to the waterline by persons unknown.

But it was the irreparable hulk, removed with difficulty from Pulo Panjang to Bantam, that was thrice the target of arson there. The repairs commenced in the shallows at Pulo Panjang, where the *Peppercorn* and *Darling* had been careened. As Manwayring explains the process, "You must have a lower ship by her, with which she must be haled down on a side, and righted again with tackles." But the need to inspect the keel may have motivated them to beach the ship altogether, rendering the placement of another ship nearby, if the *James* was still at hand, perhaps more challenging. Manwaring notes that well-situated ballast should "effect the chief force of the business, and so never strain the ship's masts much" (21). Yet the broad beam of the *Trades Increase* would bring major stresses to the masts in any case, especially if the ship had been beached; and a leverage point lower than another ship—perhaps a tree at the edge of one of the "two little islands" Jourdain describes (242)—would increase these forces, steepening the angle of the ropes, pulling more directly toward the hull. Whatever their method, it malfunctioned.

They managed to careen one side of the hull. Then, in the struggle to hale it over to the other side—the procedure that Manwayring declares more difficult on "English built" ships—the mainmast broke. Had William Burrell secured the massive Latvian timber he desired for the masts, perhaps the *Trades Increase* would have endured. But the vessel's earliest mishap at sea, the fracturing of the mainmast, had prefigured its death knell. Without a mainmast, the careening stopped. They lacked the infrastructure, the leverage, and, as the work advanced, the manpower to consummate mission-critical repair. Crewmen, weakened by the lengthy voyage, sickened and died at the site in droves. Infections spread wildly. As the crew dwindled, the survivors hired Chinese laborers who likewise died in large numbers—up to five hundred by one report.

Among the casualties was Middleton, sick at heart to view the ruin of the magnificent vessel in his charge. Immobilized on the beach, the *Trades Increase* emblematized at once King James's and the Company's grand ambitions for the voyage and the relentless setbacks suffered in their attempts to realize them: their captivity with loss of life in Mocha; their expulsion with all resident factors from Surat; their damaging clashes with the Eighth Voyage in the Red Sea; their inability to wring substantial reparations from the Turks while extorting marginal gains from Indian vessels there; their small yields of pepper from Tiku; their ongoing divisions in Bantam; their impotence to bring the great ship home with a full and splendid cargo; the many deaths along the way, deaths that quickened now. For almost three and a half years, they had displayed heroic resilience and determination, but circumstances finally overwhelmed them. As Downton, who tried repeatedly to protect and comfort his general, understood, Middleton ached with the personal burden of responsibility for their failures. Brooding on this sad trajectory, grieving at the loss of his ship and crew, he succumbed to disease and despair on 24 May 1613.

Some three weeks later in Patani, Peter Floris reported the sad news:

> They say . . . that the fair and costly ship, the *Trades Increase*, lyeth
> a ground at Bantam, without mast, with thirty-three men, the great-
> est part being sick. The ship is doubled [sheathed] on the one side
> but not on the other. In the said ship are deceased some 200
> Englishmen,[32] and more Chinesians, which wrought for daily wages,
> as also eight Dutch, some plague or other mischievous sickness being
> come into the ship; and, as it is reported, the Devil hath kept a foul
> rule there. Sir Henry Middleton died the 24th of May, most of
> heartsore. This in truth is a grievous news, the death of so many
> men, and the perishing of so costly and famous a ship. (Moreland,
> 83–84)

The *Trades Increase*, while active, may have ignited intracorporate rivalries; yet the shock among East India Company personnel at the news of its loss—Saris perhaps excepted[33]—galvanized emotional bonds confirming their identity as members of the corporate body. Carried by mariners of various origins, as word spread from Bantam to Patani to Tiku and beyond, expressions of alarm echoed among Company agents. In Tiku on 25 August 1613—by which time the wreck had been moved to Bantam for disposition of its cargo—General Thomas Best of the Tenth Voyage reported: "There came in a junk of Bantam, the owners Chineses. They confirmed unto me the death of Sir Henry Middleton, with the loss of most of her men and mainmast, which brake with forcing her down to careen her: and that now she was gone from the island Pulo Panjang to Bantam: that 300 Chineses died in work on her" (Foster, *Best*, 65–66). These details confirmed rumors Best had already heard from officials in Tiku, reported by Ralph Croft on 8 July: "They did certify our general of the death of Sir Henry at Bantam . . . with many or most part of his merchants and mariners. They did affirm Sir Henry's death to be after a very strange manner, which to describe it, it would seem incredulous [incredible]" (Foster, *Best*, 177–78). A month later, Croft conveyed a more straightforward account of Middleton's death, as reported to Best by Tiku's governor: "not in such manner as was first reported, but only upon grief and sorrow for the death of his merchants and mariners, that, having brought his voyage to such effect, [he] could not accomplish it for want of men" (178).

Foster speculates that the "strange manner" earlier reported may allude to the diabolical apparitions Floris mentions—a tale that, along with the numbers of the dead, magnified with retelling. Arriving in Bantam in February 1615, John Milward reports what he heard from "Mr. Baily merchant and Mr. Samon master of the *Globe*":

> The *Trades Increase* being brought on ground on Pulo Panjang, all her men died in the careening of her; and afterwards it stood them in five hundred rials of eight a day to hire Javans, of whom five hundred died in the work, before they could sheath one side; so that they could hire no more men, and therefore were enforced to leave her imperfect, where she was sunk in the sea, and after set on fire by the Javans. The Chineses also reported that the devil appeared on Pulo Panjang island, signifying his offence that the Chineses would undertake such a business on his ground and give him nothing (for they were the workmen), whereupon one of the chief Chinese carpenters came to Sir Henry Middleton and reported it, desiring to have a buffalo for sacrifice, who denied, yea forbade him when he would have done it at his own charge, esteeming the want thereof cause of their evils. (P, 4:283–84)

By 1615, the catastrophe had earned mythic elaboration in Bantam. Milward's account is puzzling: initially, he conflates Javans and Chinese, then specifies that the workmen were the latter. Whatever the details behind the story, the report indicates that the factory's relations with the Chinese community remained both cooperative and turbulently conflicted; that each group misunderstood and resisted the other's beliefs and superstitions; and that the effort at repair, costly in rials and terribly wasteful in human lives, collapsed in a crisis between the Chinese workers and their English paymasters. Middleton's labor problems blew up because his Company was committed to a lethal business.

The most haunting account of the aftermath was Jourdain's. Returning from the Spice Islands with an incomplete cargo of cloves and copious resentment of the recent Dutch monopoly there, he entered Bantam Bay on 18 August 1613. A fisherman lately met had informed them of Middleton's death, but they knew nothing of "the laying up of the *Trades Increase*" (J, 301), a ghost ship mudded at Bantam. To display good will, the *Darling*, like any ship entering a friendly anchorage, announced itself with rounds of ordnance and awaited a kindred salute, if only a pennant raised in the yards. But from the *Trades Increase* and the English house near shore, no one stirred in response: "Approaching near to the road, we might discern the *Trade* to ride near the shore, which seemed much for so great a ship; but coming to anchor within call of them, in fourteen foot water, we might easily perceive that she was aground. We hailed them, but could have no answer; neither could we perceive any man stirring her ordnance (the most part thereof mounted). I saluted them with three pieces, but [received] no answer, nor sign of English colors, neither from the ship nor from the town" (J, 302–3). Jourdain suddenly suspected foul play: perhaps the Javans, "knowing of the great store of wealth that was in her," had seized the ship and plotted to ambush them now. Observing that the Dutch house raised and lowered its flag twice, perhaps in warning, he readied the *Darling*'s ordnance. But then a proa put off from shore and made its way toward them. Entropy and division, not a plot by strangers, explained the silence. The boat carried four survivors, "all of them like ghosts or men frighted. I demanded for the general and the rest of our friends in particular; so that I could not name any man of note but was dead, to the number of 140 persons; and the rest which were remaining, as well aland and aboard the *Trade*, were all sick, these four persons being the strongest of them, who were scarce able to go on their legs" (J, 303). Sounding a sad litany of names, all deceased, Jourdain absorbed the enormity of the loss. Beyond Middleton's, he does not cite names in the journal entry. Yet one such "man of note" would have been Pemberton, the *Darling*'s hitherto impervious master, with whom Jourdain had sailed from the Red Sea to Tiku: the fleet's first escapee in Yemen who fled the forced march to Sana'a, stole a boat, made a sail of his shirt, and drank his own urine to endure; who survived the visit to Pasaman lethal to Greene and the others who slept ashore there; and who lately supervised the inspection and repair of the *Trades Increase*. He too was gone. Only twenty-one members of Middleton's large crew lived to sail homeward with Thomas Best of the Tenth Voyage (*Court Book*, B/5, 122, 17 June 1614).

The deaths and departures had bewildered the factory's governance. There were three thinly staffed English houses in Bantam now, each at odds with the others. Those founded by Saris near the harbor and Middleton uptown had distanced themselves from each other and the original compound that Scott, Towerson, Saris, and Spalding had managed. The rents for multiple facilities inflated the Company's expenditures. Preparing his report of the great ship's loss and of fires in warehouses, Floris marveled at the confusion of these "three English houses: the one hath nothing to do with the other, and all three vent cloth, which seemeth very strange to me, for each spoileth the other's market as much as they can, being the right way to be made to forsake the Indies. . . . God give them joy," he concluded (Moreland, 84). Floris was a veteran of the Dutch United East India Company, which had long since brought once-rival ventures into a single consortium. In 1598, five Dutch companies sent ships to Indonesia; in 1601, there were fourteen distinct expeditions, and Bantam held four competing Dutch agents. Having endured the confusion of these numerous " 'wild' or 'unregulated' voyages (*wilde vaart*)," in 1602 the Dutch consolidated their finances into the Vereenigde Oost-Indische Compagnie (VOC), a development that strengthened them substantially (Ricklefs, 24–25). The East India Company's discord in Bantam struck Floris as absurdly self-defeating.

Middleton's consular initiative strove to mitigate these problems, and one of the persons elected at the mid-December 1612 meeting was still living. Jourdain expected to resume his office as chief merchant in Bantam upon return. But aboard the *Darling*, one of the four ghosts from the proa, Robert Luther, whispered in his ear that "they did not greatly care for my coming aland and . . . were not determined to receive me as principal merchant." "Well perceiving that their sickness was not the only cause that they showed no colors" (J, 304), Jourdain hastened ashore. He was met there by two factors from the Eighth Voyage house, George Ball and Richard Wesby. Jourdain does not mention Camden, who must have died in the interim. Ignorant of the ongoing "civil wars" (J, 304) between the Eighth and Sixth Voyage compounds, he accepted Ball's invitation to visit the lower house before continuing uptown, not anticipating that his escort from the other cohort would take umbrage at the stop. Following brief pleasantries there, in a bid for unity he invited the Eighth Voyage merchants to accompany him to the other house, and they did. "Boldly coming in," they were met by an enfeebled figure, Robert Larkin, "not able hardly to stand on his legs," who presented himself as the chief merchant. He refused to defer to Jourdain. The servant of a text-dependent Company, Jourdain recognized that, in the absence of a voyage general, an official paper must resolve the crisis of authority. He demanded to see "Sir Henry's will and what order he had left for the disposing of the Worshipful Company's affairs. Whereunto he [Larkin] answered that Sir Henry made no will" (J, 304–5). Perhaps this failure bespoke something beyond technical difficulties: Middleton's despair. Given his insistence eight years before, that every principal agent in Bantam should keep "his particular estate in writing" (Foster, *Middleton*, 197), the lapse held tragic irony. Even the most resolute of English designs unraveled here.

Larkin claimed, however, to possess "a writing (which he knew not where it was) which tended to that purpose" (J, 305). Awaiting the discovery of this document, Jourdain excused himself and toured the town with the Eighth Voyage factors. Returning to the upper house for supper, he asked Ball and the others to stay with him, which they "were loath to do, in regard that there was great enmity betwixt them ever since the death of Sir Henry." Larkin was not at table, but his deputy John Williams, when Jourdain asked to see the paper Larkin had described, erupted, "What hast thou to do to demand any writing of us, who are the company's factors, and thou a neuter?" As Jourdain responded in some heat, Larkin "came running forth like a madman, asking for the bilboes, threatening that if I would not be gone out of his house (as he termed it) he would set me into them" (305). Jourdain retreated to the ship. Returning in the morning with the Eighth Voyage merchants, he commanded Larkin and the others to deliver him the keys and monies, "according to Sir Henry Middleton's order. But they, being armed with guns, halberds and swords, came out against me as in defiance, saying that they knew me not for chief factor, neither should I have anything to do in that business; John Williams running at me with his naked sword that I was fain to put the point thereof back with my hand, which if he had been strong, he might have slain me" (J, 306). Protesting that "it would be a great scandal to our nation to fall together by the ears," he managed to pacify them. Arms set aside, Jourdain requested again to see the document naming Larkin. Upon its delivery, he discovered "that it was framed before Sir Henry died, but he would not sign it." Someone had forged the signature, "a scratch" (J, 307), postmortem.

Jourdain had had enough of Bantam. Convinced that the Company should challenge the Dutch in the Moluccas rather than malinger in this "most unhealthful country" (LR, 2:16), longing to return to England, he departed in the *Darling* with a cargo of cloves and Chinese porcelain for Masulipatam on India's Coromandel coast. Near Tiku, however, they encountered the *Dragon* and *Hosiander* of the Tenth Voyage. Apparently coveting the cloves (J, 311), General Best insisted over Jourdain's objections that the *Darling* accompany them to Bantam. Jourdain's return distilled the East India Company's ambivalence about this outpost: the site of a reluctant, divided, entropic, exhaustingly renewed commitment. In Bantam on 14 November 1613, having learned of the "disorders and controversy . . . betwixt the factors of the Sixth and Eighth Voyages, as also of the other voyages formerly," and finding it a "great disgrace . . . to our nation and the Honorable Company . . . to have so many houses in one place" (J, 312), Best convened a General Court to unite the factory. Over

Jourdain's protests, the general named him chief factor. Best departed on 16 December 1613, and upon reaching London six months later, reported that he had unified the factory's accounts and governance: "He hath reconciled the former division that was, so that they join in love" and dine together, though lodged still in "three several houses yet kept by three persons" (*Court Book*, B/ 5, 123, 17 June 1614). The *Clove's* return to Bantam on 3 January 1614 threatened to disrupt the new regime, but Jourdain mollified Saris, who, without Middleton to provoke him, saw the wisdom of the factory's reforms and consolidated them by lodging everyone in a single facility. Henceforth, wrote Jourdain in a 31 January 1614 letter carried home in the *Clove*, the factors were, "per appointment of General Saris, to be all in one house both at bed and board, not doubting but we shall hold that decorum . . . and not scandalize our nation as formerly it hath been." He hoped soon to "bring all the loose goods into one warehouse" as well, "for it lies most confusedly and in great danger, both for thieves and fire" (*LR*, 2:15).

Unbeknownst to those who with Best's guidance forged the new arrangement, the London office had introduced kindred reforms in 1613. Emulous of their more potent Dutch rivals, contemplating the dysfunctions of the Bantam factory and probably the recent strife between the Sixth and Eighth Voyages, the London merchants followed the VOC beyond the single-venture financing that perplexed corporate growth. With the Tenth Voyage in progress, the East India Company raised its first truly joint—that is, ongoing—stock, which ran until 1621. A second, initiated in 1617, continued until 1632 (Chaudhuri, 45, 209). At the Cape of Good Hope in May 1614, the homeward-bound Saris met the first ship outward bound under the new system, the aptly named *Concord* (Satow, 197). This decisive move toward capital consolidation was vital to the Company's coordination of multiple voyages; organization of traffic in Indian, Indonesian, Persian, Arabian, African, and European markets; strength against Dutch and Portuguese fleets; and overall growth. The Bantam factory stabilized under Jourdain's reluctant leadership, which continued until 1617.

The Problem of Tenure in Bantam

Despite regionally grounded arguments to move the factory to Jakarta— "where the air [is] very healthful, and the king very desirous of them, proferring all kindness" and, Best added, requesting lower customs (*Court Book*, B/

5, 123, 17 June 1614)—the Company's commitment to Bantam persisted. A range of concerns motivated this resolve: the port's cosmopolitan purchase on traffic throughout the East Indies; its supplies of pepper and spices from the Moluccas along with goods from so far impenetrable China; its usefulness as a staging ground for regional voyaging; above all its provocative status as a focus of nationalist pride—in the charter's phrase, "the honor of this our realm of England"—distilled in emulation of the Dutch, robust there. To abandon Bantam would, in Scott's opinion, bring "infamy to our nation" (Foster, *Middleton*, 165). Viewing it as foundational, the East India Company made Bantam its principal settlement in the East Indies. By 1617, it oversaw the other English houses in Sumatra, Borneo, Banda, Japan, Thailand, and India.[34] But the commitment to Bantam was historically capricious, arbitrary, and in Jourdain's view, altogether irrational. The new chief factor believed Bantam was neither an optimal site to manage regional trade nor to contest the Dutch, who challenged the Portuguese throughout the Spice Islands and even in Japan. Why commit to this lethal place, whose chief commodity, pepper, already gluts England, when more lucrative cloves and other spices might, if the Company resolved to assert itself there, be purchased directly in the Moluccas—"a very healthful place, and the people willing to trade with us" (*LR*, 2:16)?

However brisk the business, one overriding problem of the Company's persistence here was its toll on morale and reputation. Deployment to Bantam greatly accelerated the defining tendency of the corporation to outlive its personnel. The differential longevities of East India Company constituents in London and Bantam disclosed a deeply troubling tendency within the corporate body: when stratified by grotesquely imbalanced ratios of risk and reward, it became self-parasitic. Mariners and factors on fixed salaries were far likelier to lose their lives in Company service than London's shareholders their high-yielding speculations. Bantam's lethality, then, not only compromised local morale; it also generated terrible publicity for the Company in London—particularly after the magnificent *Trades Increase* joined the region's casualties.

The indignities visited upon that vessel had not concluded when Jourdain assumed leadership of the factory. He was there to document them. For one thing, many of the ship's goods were "embezzled and stolen away" (*Court Book*, B/5, 194, 9 August 1614). More strikingly, in humbling material testament to English incapacity, the proud ship was cleared of its ordnance: the cannon forged with the East India Company's seal on the barrels (*Court*

Book, B/3, f135, 30 August 1609). It and the ship's gunpowder were "disposed of," Jourdain reported in a nonextant letter to the Company, "amongst the Hollanders and the king of Bantam" (*Court Book*, B/5, 157, 11 July 1614; Foster, *Best*, 275). At his arrival in London, Best somewhat differently explained "that he hath brought home in the *Dragon* six pieces of the *Trades Increase*, and the Hollander hath three of them to be paid for in [*phrase missing*] or else to deliver as many for them to the English, weight for weight, which was the rather done because the king of Bantam was earnest for them" (*Court Book*, B/5, 122, 17 June 1614). However many pieces the king obtained, the English factors, loath to lose their ordnance, preferred to sell them to Dutch rivals in hopes of restoration, "weight for weight," than to the Javan government.

Finally, English anxieties over fires in their warehouses soon spread to the vessel idled in the mud of Bantam Bay. It was targeted by arsonists three times in 1614, the terminal conflagration with accelerants in late October or November. A summary section of Jourdain's journal alludes to "the setting on fire of the *Trades Increase*" (J, 318). His 2 January 1615 letter to the Company elaborates:

> Now concerning the *Trades Increase* that was laid up on the ooze as
> . . . your Worships have at large understood: about two months past
> she was fired by night suddenly from stem to stern, [so] that none
> could come near to quench it, which we suppose was done of pur-
> pose by the Javas, because formerly she had been set on fire twice,
> and by great help we quenched it again, which now was impossible
> to do, because she was, as we suppose, laid all fore and aft with . . .
> pitch, otherwise she could not have so suddenly taken fire. Which
> we suspect was done by the better sort of Javas by instigation of a
> renegado Spaniard which is turned Moor, putting them in the head
> that in time she might serve in lieu of a castle. She was burnt in one
> night close to the water, and what remaining of her it is sold for
> 1,050 rials. (*LR*, 2:279)

In the end, the salvage from the cindered wreck of the costliest merchant vessel yet built in England amounted to the cost of two days' hired labor during its failed repair. Jourdain's uncertainties over the identity, methods, and motives of the arsonists recall those of his predecessor Scott, likewise tormented by fire and confusion. The mysterious Spaniard "turned Moor," a convert to Islam like the governors of Aden and Mocha, epitomized the ethnic and affiliational fluidities that vexed English efforts to distinguish allies from enemies in Bantam and throughout the East Indies. Jourdain suspected that this adaptive individual convinced "the better sort of Javas," the ruling elite, to incinerate the wreck so as to prevent the erection of an English fort from the timbers—a garrison whose potential armaments had already been "disposed of," some to the king.

As he wrote this letter, Jourdain negotiated with Pangran Chamarra over the construction of "our new house in the place where now we make our abode," on land the king had granted them "near the river," where the protector insisted, "We may not build above three fathom high." There would be no towering walls. The restriction galled Jourdain, urgent to fortify the compound against fire and thieves, and quickened his interest in Jakarta, where a more compliant king "hath given us leave to build at our pleasure" (*LR*, 2:15, 276). In his will to grow the business and contest the Dutch, Jourdain had begun to think like a colonizer. But Bantam's authorities, anxious about English ambitions in the region, resisted the consolidation of outwardly projected East India Company power on land. Perhaps the young king's brief reception aboard the *Trades Increase* persuaded him to countenance a plot to burn the ruin to the waterline. Fortresses were one thing afloat, another on land. Ironically, its final performance as a theater of power may have confirmed the great ship's fiery extinction.

CHAPTER 8

Controversy over the
East Indian Trade, 1615

Report of the loss of the *Trades Increase* and nearly all its people was formally received in London the day the *Dragon* anchored in the Downs, 8 June 1614. Hastening inland with the terrible news was a survivor of the great ship, Nicholas Bangham. A versatile, well-traveled man, Bangham had sailed as a carpenter on the *Hector* in 1607, worked at the Surat factory, joined Hawkins in Agra in 1610, returned to Surat, was the last Englishman to flee that city, and rejoined Hawkins and Jourdain aboard Middleton's flagship; he also accompanied John Jourdain on the *Darling*'s errand to Amboyna (J, 244). Well received in London, he shipped out the following year with the nation's first genuine ambassador to India, Sir Thomas Roe, and became the director of the East India Company's factory at Burhānpur (Foster, *Best*, xli, 92n). In company with William Carmichael, the first Scotsman to reach the East Indies, Bangham brought news of the *Dragon*'s arrival and letters for the Court of Committees.[1] Among those in attendance was the shipwright William Burrell, whose fellows, earlier in the meeting, "held him worthy to be well chidden for his carelessness" in making ships' boats too long to be stowed aboard "without cutting."

Bangham's presentation of General Thomas Best's letter proved far more disturbing for the builder of the *Trades Increase*:

> One Nicholas Bangham presented himself in court (in company
> with a Scottishman, who hath served the Portugalls these thirty-two
> years in the East Indies) and brought news of the safe arrival of the

> *Dragon* into the Downs, with letters from Captain Best of the 7th
> of this instant, . . . whereby they understood of the great loss of the
> *Trades Increase,* which miscarried near Bantam whilst she was careen-
> ing, Sir Henry Middleton and most of his men being dead, but yet
> all her goods on shore at Bantam, and only the bare ship perished.
> (*Court Book,* B/5, 117, 8 June 1614; Foster, *Best,* 263)

Tolerance for calamity—the capacity to absorb catastrophe and carry on—
was vital to the growth of England's East Indian trade. This note captures
the Court of Committees in a pivotal moment of that career: giving witness
to "great loss," then inoculating the terrible news with germs of redemption.
The flagship that, a decade into the trade, embodied the quickened hopes of
the founding generation, "a ship of wonderful importance" (*LR,* 1:43), was
gone, along with its distinguished commander and some 90 percent of those
who sailed it. But "only the bare ship perished" with them. The objects of
their quest, "all her goods," awaited shipment to London. The *Peppercorn*
had reached England with rich lading, and more would soon arrive. Shareholder profits, though staggered by this grievous loss, would remain intact.
The corporation would endure.

Given early modern marine technologies, everyone knew that the risks
of England's East Indian traffic were grave and irremovable and that it took
a robust organization to endure them. The collective strength of such a company shaped the mentality of its investors: resilience against trauma belonged
to the psyche of the corporate person. Institutional durability hardened the
group's mentality, blunting responsiveness to counsel honed by suffering
abroad—like Jourdain's argument that Bantam be abandoned. This chapter,
addressing the ideological stakes of the great ship's loss, juxtaposes two pamphlets published in 1615: one, anonymous, that leveled a range of damning
accusations against the Company; the other, penned by the East India Company's chief apologist in 1615, Sir Dudley Digges, refuting these charges. A
crucible of nation-based argument over the nature and consequences of the
East Indian trade, the debate articulated emergent, tenacious, and increasingly consequential divisions over the moral, social, economic, and environmental consequences and responsibilities of corporate power.

The mentality evident in the 8 June 1614 *Court Book* entry manifests the
paradoxical early modern intuition of what Valerie Forman calls the "produc-
tivity of loss," an ideological construct germane to joint-stock investment in
East Indian voyages. Beyond the loss of ships and personnel, the traffic's costs

included spectacular outlays of the nation's bullion. The Company's export of precious metals to import perishable exotica provoked insistent complaint against the East India Company as a business whose enrichment of an elite few impoverished England. The founding generation's justifications of its economic practices took mature form in the work of the East India Company magnate Thomas Mun, who in the 1620s theorized the overall cycle of investment and reward as a positive balance of trade: gains earned through multiple transformations of initial outlays of goods and capital.[2] Yet if monetary balances were rationally accountable, other operating costs proved less amenable to financial justification. The ghastly human toll of the business posed, for investors, ethical and temperamental challenges which prompted defenses of a different order. These emotional and ideological justifications took impetus from the patriotic applications of the traffic: in Queen Elizabeth's charter phrase, "the Honor of this our realm of England" (Birdwood, 166). Rationalizing their monopoly of the trade, East India Company magnates identified the Company's capital growth with the wealth and reputation of the English nation.[3] That equation, of course, invited blistering critique from antimonopolists and all who suffered from the Company's inequitable distributions of risk and reward. The East India Company's financial, ideological, and patriotic orders of defense interpenetrated, and all met resistance catalyzed by the tragic losses attendant on the material transformations of globally mobilized capital in the early seventeenth century.

How was it that God-fearing men of conscience like Sir Thomas Smythe found themselves advancing businesses that lethally exploited the mariners in their service? While they took measures to foster the health of crews, they remained committed to a traffic whose somatic insults to personnel overwhelmed current nutritional and medical knowledge and practice. Profit-driven alliances enabled them to carry on despite the carnage: with others who could afford it, they forged societies that accepted losses to be inescapable and instrumental to earnings. With the exception of such principal mariners and craftsmen as Middleton, Saris, and Burrell, as a group, shareholders differentiated themselves from their wage earners in dockyards, at sea, and in factories abroad. To stay in business—to sustain the collective personhood recognized in the charter—required them to perpetuate both gains and losses while securing positive returns on capital. Although irregular and slow to accrue, the profits of the East India Company's early voyages—with the stark exception of the Fourth Voyage, a total loss—were substantial. The First and Second Voyages together earned 95 percent; the Third and Fifth together, a heady 234 percent. Our focal concern, the Sixth Voyage, earned almost 122 percent. Saris's voyage to Japan did far better: 211 percent.[4] Such earnings proved irresistible. Moreover, the pool of expendable labor in London was large and growing.

In *Moral Man and Immoral Society*, the theologian Reinhold Niebuhr described contradictions between individual and group morality and theorized the "moral obtuseness of human collectives": "As individuals, men believe that they ought to love and serve each other and establish justice between each other. As racial, economic and national groups they take for themselves, whatever their power can command" (Niebuhr, 272, 9). Niebuhr found the group ego, perpetually reinforced by its own plurality, less disposed to altruism, and more tolerant of collateral damages in pursuit of its aims, than the morally grounded individual. His argument illuminates the mentality of those coalitions of mercantile elite who propelled England's maritime expansion. In the estimation of the East India Company's founders, inaction, a corporate failure of nerve, weakened and dishonored the nation more consequentially than did losses incurred in overseas campaigns that brought reputation, reward, and maritime power to England. Beyond the lust for profit, nationalist emulation of Portuguese and Dutch trading empires urged them to press on: to carve out market shares in the East, eventually to colonize where possible. Inevitably then, as the East India Company accumulated capital, it learned to exploit incommensurable orders of risk and tolerate disasters. In subsequent generations as a colonial and imperial power, the Company bequeathed this model of collective achievement, and the ethical latitude of the profit-seeking corporate person, to the world. A formidable legacy of the East India Company, the amoral resiliency of joint-stock corporations persists, greatly enlarged and accelerated, today. It has contributed substantially to the construction of a risk-saturated global economic order that produces, along with stratospheric payoffs for inside financiers, attractive earnings for general investors, and other divisions of great but inequitably distributed wealth, widespread poverty, major demographic disruptions, and unsustainable environmental damages—losses more devastating by many orders of magnitude than those, severe as they were, documented in this microhistory. To return to the controversy ignited by the loss of the *Trades Increase*, I suggest, clarifies the stakes of our ongoing arguments over transnational corporate power.

Although the charter defined it as "one body corporate and politic, in deed and in name really and fully" (Birdwood, 167), and although many of its sworn brothers and bonded servants maintained solemn fealties to the Company, the East India Company was, as noted throughout this study, riven by multiple divisions of personnel and interest. The fundamental chasm, bridged by a few, separated the shareholders from the salaried ranks who materialized their designs. Both groups were populated by replaceable individuals, but mortality rates among mariners far exceeded those of investors. Mistrust and evasion held between these groups: often with good cause, investors suspected their agents of self-enrichment at the Company's expense. Earning fixed wages in the pursuit of geometric returns for shareholders whom they might not live to answer to, agents in the field sought their own advantage beyond the reach of their commissions. In a telling testament to the anarchic effects of such employment, in November 1612 one merchant wrote to Smythe of another in Bantam, "Mr. Wilson hath been too often in the India voyages ever to be good—he that will make your commission to be mutinous if it be read" (*LR*, 1:203). As we have seen, to brandish papers of London's authority could inflame conflicts that these documents were designed to quell.

Hierarchies of authority bred ill will, particularly among those on assignment. The protracted trials of voyaging chafed relations between master and common mariners, as the pressures of dislocation, opportunity, disease, and mortality destabilized the landed communities. Principal mariners complained repeatedly of the willfulness of crewmen. In letters to Edmund Camden, for instance, Captain Saris vented impotent vexation at the many "loiterers" from his fleet in Bantam: "For aught I see, the number increases. It is a matter fit to be thought of by you, and to keep the folks so about you employed, as upon all occasions they give you account where they spend their time" (*LR* 1:200). The thought of untasked sailors disporting themselves into wasting diseases obsessed him: "the men dying so fast by surfeit and most filthy abusing of their bodies, which by all means of mild or strict course cannot be helped" (S, f112v, 30 December 1612). Downton, plagued by leaks and split sails, depressed by deaths and missed rendezvous—having united with and then lost the *Hector* and *Thomas* off South Africa, then bypassing vital refreshment at Saint Helena to avoid Portuguese carracks anchored there—sailing homeward with a dwindling crew, Middleton's lieutenant general lamented the *Peppercorn*'s precarity. He excoriated the Company's negligent, leaky carpentry and provision of inadequate "sails, ropes and cables for your ships. . . . God forbid that the ship's goods (with the lives of men, which are rated at least value) should perish in the sea for want of supply" (*LR*,

1:262). With bitter sarcasm, his parenthetical parallel between goods and lives assails the Company's perverse valuation of cargo over human beings.

Yet Downton also recoiled from the unruliness of the crewmen whose welfare so concerned him:

> I have extreme doubt[5] that my poor out-tired and long unrefreshed people will fall into great mortality and weakness, yet if they come at last home, you shall find them very scandalous and troublesome people. . . . They are grown careless of observing any command, and we dare not inflict any punishment lest the scurvy join with it in the overthrowing of their healths, to the further scandal and discontent of the Indian Company. For, unless you procure an alteration by stopping the success of idle complaints, and get them contradicted by a contrary precedent, *I hold it more vain for you to adventure such wealth in these long voyages.* (*LR*, 1:267–68, emphasis added)

Describing entropy at sea, crewmen so bruised by scurvy that the lash might maim or kill them, Downton ached at the collapse of health and discipline on his ship and the wanton wastefulness of the Company's entire eastern enterprise, epitomized in the plight of his vessel. Unable to maintain the lives and loyalties of personnel on assignment, the East India Company, he finds here, produces fatalities and anarchic breakdowns too consuming to justify, either as operating costs or patriotic sacrifices. Incalculable human losses disappear into commodity-indexed account balances; confusion and disorder, inevitable "in these long voyages," bring shame to the entire endeavor. Pace Purchas, who describes the sea as "a school of sobriety and temperance" (in Neill, 332), for Downton, the East India Company's overlong voyages foster insubordination among surviving crewmen and thereby undermine respect for authority in England. Ominously, Downton suggests that the Company's heavy outlays of capital demand protection in more severe regimes of discipline. For lack of adequate control over their exploited mariners, he implies, London's investors would do better to seek reputation and profit nearer home—perhaps in privateering, a more egalitarian business model that divides profits among crews as well as investors. When lodging these sweeping accusations, Downton did not yet know that Middleton was dead and the *Trades Increase* rotted mastless in the mud at Bantam. By no surprise, his letter of 20 June 1613 remained sequestered in the corporate archive, unpublished until 1896.

The Company was vigilant to suppress or neutralize adverse publicity. But the loss of their greatest ship on its initial voyage ignited just that. One of those driven to reexamine his support of the Company was Sir Henry Middleton's brother-in-law, the bookseller Walter Burre, who also published several of Ben Jonson's plays. As the Second Voyage concluded and the cash-poor Company recruited funds for the Third, Burre had marketed two above-noted pamphlets "clearly intended," observes Michael Neill, "to stir up nationalist feeling in the interest of an expanded East India trade": *The Last East-Indian Voyage* (1606) and Edmund Scott's *An Exact Discourse of the Subtilties . . . of the East Indians* (1606).[6] But early in 1615, Burre's shop at the sign of the crane in London's bookselling hub, St. Paul's Churchyard, introduced another patriotic work of contrary import: a pamphlet whose title ironized King James's hopeful speech act on a doomed vessel. *The Trades Increase* (fig. 14) assailed the East India Company's lethal profiteering: what the traffic increased, along with handsome returns to monopolists in London, were shipwrecks, the felling of English forests to build more ships, the dispersal of stout vessels into remote seas, and the loss of mariners fit to defend England's shores. Burre was taking risks. He had lately published Sir Walter Raleigh's *History of the World* (1614), a book that offended King James for "too free censuring of Princes" and provoked George Abbot, the archbishop of Canterbury, to order that it "be suppressed and not suffered hereafter to be sold."[7] The briefly anonymous 1615 pamphlet proved likewise inflammatory, again prompting the archbishop's intervention, an inquest by the king's Privy Council, and brief imprisonment of the exposed author, "I.R.," Robert Kayll (or Keale).[8] With friends in high places, the East India Company moved swiftly to punish the offending pamphleteer and produce a comprehensive refutation, *The Defence of Trade* (1615). Both treatises are of compelling historical and ideological interest.

The Trades Increase

Declaring himself "a fresh-water soldier" whose "estate is but mean" (1), Kayll opens his critique by endorsing Tobias Gentleman's thesis, in *England's Way to Win Wealth* (1614), that great potential for nationwide prosperity lay in the herring fisheries in adjacent seas—a resource assiduously cultivated by the Dutch. With Gentleman, Kayll maintains that development of the herring industry should stimulate shipbuilding, enrich coastal towns throughout

THE

TRADES

Increaſe.

LONDON,
Printed by *Nicholas Okes,* and are
to be ſold by *Walter Burre.*
1 6 1 5.

FIGURE 14. *The Trades Increase* (1615), title page. Courtesy of
the Huntington Library.

Britain, grow the ranks of mariners available to defend the nation at need, and distribute wealth widely without substantial loss of life and shipping at sea. It was a populist argument. "The sea is large," wrote Kayll, "and hath room enough to make us all rich: . . . a man may run a course this way to enrich himself, to strengthen his country, [and] to enable his Prince more honestly than many late sea-courses can warrant us in" (1). Unlike the eastern trade, the herring fishery, conducted by ships of modest size ("Busses, Pinks, and Line-boats"),[9] is not capital-intensive: not dominated by London's mercantile elite. Its material and mortal risks are limited, its earnings sound. It traffics in nearby waters, not through the protracted, deadly, demoralized voyaging that the homeward-bound Downton held "vain" in his letter of June 1613. Gentleman and Kayll saw the herring fishery as a potent way to spread wealth, foster widespread demographic vitality,[10] and enhance England's maritime power. Moreover, their argument gained traction from the same motive that precipitated the East India Company's creation and commitment to lethal zones like Bantam: emulation of the Dutch. As a spur to patriotic readers, Gentleman's title page promised "a true relation of the inestimable wealth that is yearly taken out of his Majesty's seas, by the Hollanders." A "true relation" of incalculable sums may prove slippery, but one took the point: the Dutch have enriched themselves near England's shores while Englishmen sit idle.

Kayll did not oppose maritime trade. What troubled him was trafficking on the far side of the world. He lamented that England's first joint-stock consortium, the Muscovy Company, had failed to exploit its advantage in Russia—"We have in a manner lost that trade" (3)—and left room for the Hollanders to traffic there in strength. He attributed this lapse to the gravitational pull of the East India Company, which bled the former of investors and resources: "The *Muscovy* merchant . . . I fear can scarce hear me, being (as I said) gone so far as the *East-Indies*; and if I should send to him, I fear I should not find him at leisure, having thither transported much of the *Muscovy* staple" (5). Likewise the Levant Trade, "a very material business of merchandise" that built large ships "of defense and renown to the kingdom," has been "lessened by the circumvention of the *East-Indie* navigation" (5–6). Later in the treatise, he tightens the link between East India Company gains and Levant Company losses by claiming that Middleton's blockade of Mocha had put English vessels at risk in the Mediterranean: "Diverse durst not go presently after to the Straits [of Gibraltar] . . . out of rumor of revenge for violence offered by our Indian men to the Turks in the Red Sea" (32).

Mercantilist critique of the eastern trade often fixated on the "transport of treasure" (Kayll, 32): the export of the precious metals that constituted the nation's wealth. Kayll echoes this complaint by citing Emperor Charles V's remark on Portugal's trade to the East Indies, "that they were the enemies to Christendom, for they carried away the treasure of Europe to enrich the heathen" (32). It was a basic tenet of mercantilism that resources were finite and that trade, as Stephen Pincus summarizes the traditional view, "was a zero-sum game" (Pincus, 14). In such a framework, different parties—be they nations, corporations, commercial emporia, or separately funded expeditions of a single Company—strove for earnings at one another's expense. Kayll duly observes that, like the Russia Company, the Levant Company has ceded opportunities to the Dutch: "They coming in long after us, equal us in those parts in all respects of privilege and port; that have devanced [outstripped] us so far in shipping, that the *Hollanders* have more than one hundred sail of ships that use those parts, continually going and returning, and the chiefest matters they do lade outward, be *English* commodities" (7).[11] Commitment to the eastern trade, Kayll insists, has foreclosed opportunities nearer to hand. With irony equaling that of his title, he maintains that the East India Company magnifies the very inequities the Company's founders had striven to redress: Dutch hegemony in markets of English opportunity. Kayll's complaint touched a nerve not only because London's Dutch merchant community, which had built one of the triumphal arches for King James I's royal entry into the city, enjoyed considerable influence at court but also because, when *The Trades Increase* reached Burre's bookstalls, in the Netherlands, where the pamphlet duly turned up, the Vereenigde Oost-Indische Compagnie (VOC) and the East India Company were negotiating a possible merger. King James favored the union.[12] Though this initiative eventually came to naught, the winter of 1615 was an impolitic hour to foment resentments toward the Dutch.

As Pincus and others have observed, the mercantilist view of totalized, state-regulated, pugnacious commerce, a theory long held hegemonic for the seventeenth and eighteenth centuries, was not shared by all players in the emergent global economy.[13] The name that King James I, for instance, an ardent pacifist, gave the East India Company's great new ship in December 1609 held no hostility toward England's rivals in the eastern trade. Implicitly rejecting the vision of a finite world system, the name postulated vistas of perpetual growth: of absolute increase untethered to the market shares of other actors. To declare that "the trades"—multiple trades—"increase," one clear reading of the phrase, is to affirm that the global economy is expanding. As agricultural labor adds value to land, and fishing gleans value from the sea, so the work of deep-ocean commerce—the purchase, transport, and profitable resale of goods in markets of demand—generates new wealth. So long as consumers abound at home and abroad, more such traffic (and more goods crammed into larger vessels) will produce more wealth, open-endedly.

Fully cognizant of arguments that the eastern trade enhances England's strength and prosperity, Kayll reviews the mediocre state of the country's traffic in various sectors. Then, with mocking repetition of the term "increase," he invokes this claim: "It hath . . . begot out of all callings, professions, and trades, many more new merchants. Then where there is increase of merchants, there is increase of trade; where trade increaseth, there is increase of shipping; where increase of shipping, there increase of mariners likewise: so then rich and large *East Indies*" (14). Introducing these clauses as "the singing of swans, which so many journey so far to enjoy," only to find instead "greedy ravens and devouring crows," he sets about to dismantle them. Numbering twenty-one "goodly ships" of eighty to eleven hundred tons deployed by the East India Company—a group person whom he addresses as "you"—he concedes, "at first appearance you have added both strength and glory to the kingdom. . . . But where I pray you are all these ships?" he asks. "Four of these are cast away, . . . two more are docked up there as pinnaces to trade up and down: the rest are either employed in the trade in the *Indies*, or at home out of reparations; which if true, if the kingdom should have need of them on any occasion, it shall surely want their service" (15). Sunk, under repair, or deployed to distant seas, East India Company vessels will offer small help to the Admiralty at need.

Kayll then segues to an important ecological critique: vast woods have been cut down to build vessels that are now "either lost, or not serviceable. . . . Our woods, I say, cut down in an extraordinary manner . . . in regard of the greatness of the shipping, which doth as it were devour our timber" (16–17). The construction and repair of the East India Company's large vessels have so depleted forests and inflated costs that timber is "almost not to be had for money" in England (17). Kayll no doubt exaggerates the East India Company's responsibility for this predicament; the *Trades Increase* was one of the Company's first two purpose-built ships, and, as noted in Chapter 1, Burrell had difficulties securing sound timber for it—particularly mast timber. Nevertheless, the construction of large ships, Kayll maintains, has consumed great swaths of forest. Although Henry VIII, Queen Elizabeth I, and

King James legislated to preserve England's woods, they did not anticipate "that a parricide of woods should thus be committed by building of ships . . . and therefore there was no proviso for it" (18). Indeed, "our said famous princes have provided clean contrary, . . . having encouraged by reward out of their own purses the builders of great ships" (18–19). Without naming Phineas Pett or the *Prince Royal*, Kayll maintains that the Crown and London's mercantile elite have colluded in extravagancies of shipbuilding to consume England's forests, "to the hurt of the kingdom" (19). The forests of England, a common inheritance, have been depleted by royal and private interests. While humbler local operations thus find themselves unprovided for, the East India Company now builds ships in better-forested Ireland, he observes (17).

Although faulting the London Company for problems of wider causation, Kayll's complaint about the lack of English timber holds historic gravity, for it demonstrates that the tendency of aggregated capital to consume natural resources in one region and move on—to tolerate local losses in a globalized quest for gain—was already manifest, and resisted, during the East India Company's first generation. "I heard a shipwright say on the loss of the *Trades Increase*," Kayll reported, "that if you ride forty miles from about *London*, you could not find sufficient timber to build such another" (19). The ship's fate summed up the East India Company's tragic wastefulness: woods that might never regrow were felled to build a magnificent vessel lost on its initial voyage. "But alas! she was but shown; out of a cruel destiny she was overtaken with an untimely death in her youth and strength . . . and brake many a man's [heart] withal, memorable in her misfortune" (19). The loss, he observes, impacts the commonwealth more severely than it has the saddened merchants of the East India Company, "for all their goods were on shore, and she had brought abundance out of the *Mocha* fleet" to earn them consolation (19).

Kayll's fixation on the *Trades Increase*—his brooding on the inequities between shareholder profits and permanent widespread losses epitomized in the ship's destiny—expresses something beyond mercantilist reflexes. The critique, I suggest, marks the emergence of ecological and class-based anxieties about the disruptive effects of profit-driven, state-sanctioned corporate expansion: a dawning awareness of long-range social and environmental dislocations typically effaced from boardroom reckonings of financial viability. These concerns speak directly to us today. The vestigial mercantilist understanding of the earth as a vast haven of finite resources, not a myriad network of opportunities for perpetual growth, has returned with ominous force to the residents of a biosphere whose cumulative degradations—atmospheric and oceanic pollution, aquifer depletion and contamination, widening deforestation and desertification, warming temperatures, frequent severe storms and wildfires, rising seas—phenomena propelled in part by the work of multinational corporations, now threaten modern civilization.[14] An advocate of local and sustainable industry, Kayll expressed alarm at the environmental toll of capital-intensive corporate activity as it first went global from England.

Kayll concludes his counterintuitive complaint, that the eastern trade degrades English shipping, with a meditation on the deaths of ships in remote seas: "I may justly say that they die not the ordinary death of ships, who commonly have some rest, and after long service die full of years, and at home, much of their timber serving again to the same use, besides their ironwork, . . . and not in this bloody and unseasonable fashion, rather indeed as coffins full of live bodies, than otherwise as comfortable ships" (20). Unlike coffin wood cut for single use, ship timber, if fit, should reincarnate in other vessels and thereby mitigate the demand for logging. In its hard use of large ships—as in its marketing of imported luxuries—the East India Company, by contrast, accelerates consumption. Those vessels that manage to return, "come home so crazed and broken, so maimed and unmanned, that whereas they went out strong, they return most feeble," requiring wood-hungry repairs (20).

The haunting image of ships as "coffins full of live bodies" anticipates Kayll's next major theme: the extraordinary mortality of mariners in the eastern trade. He introduces the complaint on a jingoistic note: "Whereas they [ships] were carried forth with Christians, they are brought home with Heathen" (20). Eurocentric anxieties exacerbate his concern: that this commerce kills so many English mariners as to bring numerous "heathens" into England troubles him, on both counts. Yet, while insular and protoracist, his alarm at the deaths of seamen holds class-based concern that warrants emphasis. All the writers who sailed with the Sixth Voyage, the mariners whose voices shaped the corporate narrative, were principal personnel of the Company: managers. Kayll, by contrast, a patriot whose "estate is but mean" (1), identifies with and speaks for common mariners. As he declares at the pamphlet's close, "I was born in the City, and live amongst seamen" (56). "It is the good pilot that bringeth the ship to the haven; it is the wise master that governeth the men in the ship. But without men the master cannot govern, nor the ship go. What is the leader without an army, and that of soldiers? The same reason of seamen in a ship: the body must have life, blood, and flesh; the same are seamen in a ship" (22). Recommending proximate markets and sustainable modes of gain, Kayll condemns the lethal exploitation of able seamen—the "life, blood, and flesh" of England's ships—by London's global investors.

Voyages to the East Indies carry a distinctive burden of mortality, he explains. In the Mediterranean, "all in general commonly went and returned in good health, a ship seldom losing a man on a voyage. I heard a proper master of a ship say that in eighteen years, wherein he frequented those parts, he lost not two men out of his ship" (23–24). From the East Indies, by contrast, "though ships come home, yet they leave the men behind" (27). As for the pious excuse that sailors precipitate their own demise by "incontinency" and congress with "unwholesome . . . women" in the East Indies, Kayll flatly observes, "I hear the common sort of women to be as dangerous, and the generality of our men as idly disposed" (24) in the Levant as in Java. He refuses to fault lax sailors or "dangerous" women, exoticized or "common," for the terrible English mortality specific to tropical and subtropical regions.[15] Recent research confirms that the East India Company's long voyages—given nutritional regimes adequate in calories yet disastrously low in scurvy's antidote, vitamin C—typically killed far more mariners than shorter ones.[16]

By Kayll's estimate, well over two-thirds of the persons who shipped out with the East India Company perished abroad. "In the adventure of some three thousand that have been employed since that voyage began, we have lost many above two thousand" (27), he asserts. Shaming the supposedly God-fearing Company, he invokes King David's refusal "to drink of the well of *Bethlehem*, which the strong men had fetched, when he thirsted and longed, because it was the price of blood. This trade, their commodities are at a far dearer rate, being bought with so many men's lives" (27).[17] As for the Company's argument that mortality has abated in recent voyages, he invokes the late harrowing experiences of Middleton; of Downton, who departed with seventy and returned with "some twenty" on the *Peppercorn* (28); of Towerson, who lost eighty-five of his complement of "some hundred and twenty" (29); of Saris, who sailed with "some ninety odd, not having brought home above two or three and twenty" (29); and of Best, whose "Indian vengeance haunted his ship even to our coasts," taking more than one hundred of the hundred and eighty men in his charge. Best, moreover, "made the voyage in shorter space than any other ordinarily; the dogged star of those climates, the stench of those countries, were his fatality" (30). As for Middleton,

> His ship was that famous and infortunate vessel of eleven hundred tun; his company in that ship some two hundred and twenty men. After four years' errors up and down the sea, wherein he underwent many constructions at home, and overcame strange difficulties abroad; having, to his eternal reputation of policy and courage, outgone the perfidious Turk, and revenged their barbarous wrongs, to the merchants' gain and the kingdom's repute: After he and his had, I say, been accompanied with many sorrows; with labor, hunger, sickness, and peril; That worthy commander, with many a sufficient mariner, with the whole number (ten excepted) of his live *cargazon* [cargo], perished in that Acheldama, that bloody field of *Bantam*. (28)

The lament honors the heroism of Middleton and his crew—their resilience throughout protracted suffering, their courage, their high achievement—tragically squandered in the deadly destination ordained by their employers. To rename Bantam Acheldama drives home the gravity of the sacrifice, the evil of the Company's greed. Acheldama, "the field of blood" (Acts 1:19), also named the potter's field, was the foreigners' burial ground in Jerusalem purchased with Judas Iscariot's thirty pieces of silver: "And he cast down the pieces of silver in the temple, and departed, and went and hanged himself. And the chief priests took the silver pieces, and said, It is not lawful for to put them into the treasury, because it is the price of blood. And they took counsel, and bought with them the potter's field, to bury strangers in" (Matthew 27:5–7, KJV). "The price of blood," refused on principle by David and the temple priests yet accepted by the "Worshipful Company," resonates damningly across these accounts to give the lie to the East India Company's pretensions to Christian charity.

Having assailed the East India Company for robbing England of forests, ships, and mariners, Kayll maps the manifold benefits of intensified commitment to the herring industry in "our seas" (37). These include the reduction of poverty and the "sordid idleness" (34) of unemployment: the desperation that drives mariners to piracy and high-risk labor on East Indian voyages. He concludes the treatise by denouncing monopolies and advocating "freedom of traffic for all his Majesty's subjects to all places" (51). By restricting access to markets and information, monopolies inhibit industry, he maintains. For the good of both the nation and the royal exchequer, King James should abrogate the charters of the East India Company, the Virginia Company, and others: "Hereby his majesty's customs will increase, the navy and seamen will receive nourishment out of more employment, the whole incorporation of merchants reap comfort, in that they may communicate with all adventures, and the universal body of the subjects of the land content, in that they may become merchants; being very ready in this adventurous world to make new discoveries" (51). For Kayll, the commonwealth and the great body of its citizens prosper from the protection of individual rights and widely shared opportunities against consolidated private interests that warp markets to their own advantage. He articulates what Phil Withington describes as a Ciceronian ideal of the commonwealth as a *res publica*, "the public life and participants of a society broadly defined, as well as the affective obligations that citizens or subjects owed it."[18] Being "subjects and equal citizens" of one monarch (*Increase*, 52), merchants should not be constrained "into those limits that private orders tie them in" (51), "tied and subject one unto the other" (52). Corporate monopolies engross their members' money, constrict their options, and fix prices at high levels, "either by sending forth most part of the commodities abroad, or else by buying all others into their hands. . . . The commonwealth being made private," he concludes, "suffereth by all" (52). As societies of private interest—corporate persons who hoard secrets and exercise greater public sway than do most actual persons—joint-stock monopolies operate antisocially. Their claims to speak for the full commonwealth are specious. "Society first began, and knowledge and civility, by communication. But if the world in his infancy had been resolved to have held private what they had in possession [in common], and to have concealed what they knew, there had not only been no civility, but no society" (55). For Kayll, civil society thrives on the open exchange of information—the freedom of public discourse that Milton would defend in *Areopagitica* (London, 1644)—incompatible with the mysteries of state and commerce variously articulated by the Jacobean Crown and London's mercantile elite.[19]

Punishment and Retraction

Living "amongst seamen," Kayll presumably learned in conversation with East India Company mariners sensitive information whose documentation

Smythe and the committees supervised as corporate secrets. They published such records only selectively: to promote their interests. The first great publicist of East India Company papers, Samuel Purchas, aptly termed himself the Company's "orator and patron."[20] When, in 1622, he requested access to archived journals to compile "a great volume of all their voyages," *Purchas His Pilgrimes*, he promised to publish "but the historical part" and to "meddle with nothing else," tactfully emending, for instance, accounts of "broils between the English and Dutch." The Court of Committees duly advised their clerks to see that "nothing be taken out of their journals but that which is proper to a history and *not prejudicial to the company*."[21] The 1615 Court of Committees, in turn, viewed *The Trades Increase* as an outrageous violation of corporate privacy—its disclosures toxic, its arguments anathema, its timing, amidst merger negotiations with the VOC, infuriating. Learning of the pamphlet just four days after Burre and the printer Nicholas Okes listed it in the Stationers' Company register (Ogborn, 113), they swiftly penetrated its anonymity and moved against the author.

Conjecturing him to be "one Mr. Keale," Smythe informed the court on 16 February 1615 that he had written to the archbishop of Canterbury—an East India Company shareholder whose brother Maurice Abbot, a charter member, was negotiating at The Hague[22]—"concerning the suppressing of the said book." Archbishop Abbot sent his chaplain Dr. Neede, who had authorized the publication, to advise the Court of Committees that, while willing to issue a warrant for suppression, he preferred that the book "be suffered to die, rather than a stop to be made, which will cause many men to seek after it the more earnestly." Censorship would advertise the text. But Smythe and his colleagues were adamant. They meant to make an example of Kayll: "to have the author rather punished, which will quickly be bruited abroad, and thereby discover the dislike the state hath to such pamphlets that shall tax what the state hath approved" (*Court Book*, B/5, 370, 16 February 1615). They delegated the charter members Nicholas Leate and Robert Bell to confer with the attorney general about haling the offending author before the Star Chamber. Kayll and his sympathizers would learn the folly of his effort to divide the Jacobean state, and the better interests of the commonwealth, from the East India Company.

At the court's next meeting on 22 February, Leate and Bell reported that the attorney general "and another lawyer much esteemed for his judgment" found *The Trades Increase* to contain "some points very near unto treason, and all the rest very dangerous." Thus encouraged, the committees resolved to press their case: "to prosecute such courses as by learned counsel they shall be directed unto." No doubt recognizing that censorship and punishment should quicken interest in the pamphlet, Smythe informed them of Sir Dudley Digges's proposal to commandeer the controversy—indeed, to reiterate and vanquish Kayll's accusations—in a public refutation: "to have a book set forth in defense of the East India trade, and to make known the benefit that it brings to the commonwealth" (*Court Book*, B/5, 373, 22 February 1615). Digges was game to undertake the task.

On 29 March 1615, a meeting darkened by Smythe's sharing of pessimistic letters from The Hague, the Court of Committees returned to the matter of Kayll. Smythe had spoken with Sir Ralph Winwood, the secretary of state, who, like Smythe, was in receipt of Commissioner Clement Edmondes's 21 March letter confessing that the negotiations "would be a long business." England's posture had been weakened by, among other things, "a book published in England against" the East India Company that had surfaced in The Hague. Winwood took this news to the king, who referred the matter to his Privy Council. Key figures of the Jacobean state were thus duly apprised of the stalled negotiations and presumably of Kayll's argument that England could earn windfall profits by dissolving the East India Company, stop buying fish from the Dutch, and ramping up the domestic herring industry.[23] These developments raised concerns about the Crown's support for the East India Company and induced the angered governor "to consider what wrong and scandal the Company is subject unto by the envious eyes that do depend upon them, . . . notwithstanding the great hazards they run, the profits they bring in to his Majesty, and the great burdens of charge that fall upon them. Yet the malice of some is ready to take advantage upon the least occasion to disgrace either the principal members of this body or the whole Company itself" (*Court Book*, B/5, 400, 29 March 1615). The chief offenders named on this occasion were one Mr. Newman, who had arrested Deputy Governor William Greenwell in Southwark "only to have disgraced and discredited him," and Kayll. Smythe "hoped to find redress for some of these injurious courses." In its next item of business, the court duly denied Newman's petition to become a "free brother" of the East India Company. For Kayll, who had "so maliciously and unjustly written in public disgrace of this Company," harsher measures were afoot. Praising the rigor of the Dutch, "so jealous of their trade in the Indies as that they have given special commandment for none to be so bold to dare to make any invectives against the same," Smythe advised his fellows to speak no further of the offending author and to await "the event with patience" (*Court Book*, 400–401).

The wait was brief. On 4 April, in a decisive show of support for the East India Company, the lords of the Privy Council summoned Kayll to appear before them to answer for his "late treatise." His answers failed to satisfy, and he remained unrepentant: he had not "demeaned himself as he ought," they observed afterward. So they lay "just correction" upon him: indefinite commitment to Fleet Street prison.[24] Stunned by incarceration, over the next several days Kayll reconsidered his arguments published in futile anonymity and his manner under questioning. He drafted a petition to them to express "his humble submission and acknowledgment of his offence" (*Acts*, 107). In strong formulae of self-abasement, retraction, and apology, he begged for release: "Now may it please your lordships, upon this his humble suit and submission, wherein he very justly condemneth himself, to pardon these his transgressions and to release him of this his deserved punishment and imprisonment, whereby (but chiefly by your lordships' most wise and just reprehensions) he is truly and, as he hopeth, sufficiently admonished both of his duty to the commonwealth and your lordships, to whose mercy he most humbly submits himself" (108). His voice of protest silenced, his "duty to the commonwealth" and its privileged echelons numbingly internalized, on 17 April they ordered him, upon his payment of prison fees, set free. One major takeaway from this sequence of events is that Governor Smythe had moved the Privy Council toward much harsher measures than the archbishop initially felt either necessary or advisable. Kayll's punishment and retraction set a troubling precedent. The Company's retaliation demonstrated the power of a well-connected capital-intensive corporation to manipulate civic authorities, constrain public discourse, and, in so doing, to consolidate proprietary business strategies in defiance of popular complaint that its commerce damaged the land and the people. By a hurtful irony, Kayll's victimization confirmed his argument that joint-stock monopolies, superpeople of the commonwealth, prevented individuals from exercising the freedom they might otherwise inherit as "subjects and equal citizens" (52) beneath one monarch, the supposed guarantor of their liberty.

The Defence of Trade

The editorial reprogramming of Kayll's voice fell to Sir Dudley Digges (1582/3–1639), a Kentish nobleman consummately equipped to speak for the corporate elite on England's oceanic achievements. His godfather was Robert

Dudley, the Earl of Leicester, under whom his father, the mathematician and military theorist Thomas Digges (c. 1546–1595), served in the Netherlands. The eldest surviving son, Dudley was senior to Leonard Digges, a poet who contributed encomiastic verses to William Shakespeare's First Folio (London, 1623). Their stepfather Thomas Russell was a friend of Shakespeare; the playwright named Russell an overseer of his will and left him £5.[25] In 1601, Dudley received a BA from Oxford University, whose master George Abbot, the future archbishop of Canterbury noted above, introduced him in 1602 to Sir Robert Cecil, who likely mentored Digges in political pursuits. He traveled to the Continent, earned a knighthood in 1607, and was elected to Parliament in 1610, where he became an ardent advocate of merchants' rights, offending the Privy Council for his anti-Spanish convictions and attacks on royal impositions. He joined the Virginia Company in 1609, the East India Company in 1611 (a candidate for its governorship in 1614), and the Northwest Passage Company in 1612 (Rabb, 280), publishing in its advocacy a treatise on the earth's circumference.[26] His Protestant politics and maritime investments likely associated him with Prince Henry's court at St. James's Palace, several affiliates of which contributed, like Digges, to the "Panegyrick Verses" prefacing *Coryat's Crudities* (London, 1611).[27] Many of Coryat's contributors belonged to the galaxy of wits and luminaries who frequented the Mermaid Tavern, a loose fraternity of poets, court dignitaries, scholars, and parliamentarians including John Donne, Ben Jonson, Thomas Campion, Michael Drayton, John Harrington, Hugh Holland, Lionel Cranfield, Richard Martin, Henry Goodyear, Henry Peacham, John Hoskyns, and the royal architect Inigo Jones.[28] Digges commissioned Jones to design his still-extant castle at Chilham, a magnificent home near completion as he penned *The Defence of Trade* (fig. 15).

Printed for the bookseller John Barnes by William Stansby, who produced the great folio of Jonson's *Works* the following year, the treatise offers itself as a letter to Sir Thomas Smythe, "Governor of the East-India Company, etc., from one of that society."[29] Unlike other letters so addressed in the Company's archive, however, this one was penned explicitly for print. On the title page, Digges presents himself as a Company man, unnamed until the letter's signature page (50). The Latin tag "Vexat censura Columbas"—from Juvenal's maxim "Dat veniam corvis, vexat censura columbas," "the censor forgives the crows and harasses the doves"—anticipates Digges's contention that the author of *The Trades Increase*, "some unknown busy person" (1), like a wrongheaded censor, has attacked a benign society

THE
DEFENCE OF
TRADE.

Jn a Letter

To Sir THOMAS SMITH Knight,
Gouernour of the EAST-INDIA
Companie, &c.   *by Smelley Sigges*

From one of that Societie.

——*Vexat censura Columbas.*

LONDON,
Printed by *William Stansby* for *Iohn Barnes*, and are to
be sold at his shop ouer againſt Saint *Sepulchres*
Church without Newgate.
1615.

FIGURE 15. *The Defence of Trade* (1615), title page.
Courtesy of the Huntington Library.

whose endeavors benefit the commonwealth. The tag also offers an implicit rebuke to Kayll's likening of the eastern traders to "greedy ravens and devouring crows" (14) who masquerade as swans. By restoring the author's anonymity, in class-based scorn Digges drives home the "unknown" writer's unfitness to speak of the matters he presumes to diagnose. Digges by contrast enjoys privileged access to East India Company records, has consulted "our committees best experienced in that business" (2), and addresses "the Right Worshipful Sir Thomas Smythe" (1) as a "friend and kinsman" (50). An unpaginated "Post-script to the Reader" boasts Digges's "love to the *East-India Trade*" and again stipulates that his sources are sound: "The substance of this which you have read, was taken out of custom-books, out of the *East-India* Company's books, out of grocers', warehouse-keepers', merchants' books, and conference with men of best experience."

At the outset, the writer admits to some ambivalence in taking up the pen: to dismiss Kayll's accusations, he must reiterate them. For Digges, the East India Company's benefits to England are so manifest as to require no justification. To reprint libelous allegations perpetuates a material afterlife they do not deserve. Yet, having "perused" the contemptible pamphlet, he has discovered that, under cover of its "pleasing title of *Increase of Trade*"—an inexact rendering by which Digges obscures the actual title's evocation of the great ship lost—and sensible advocacy of the herring industry, the book induces readers to swallow "pills . . . that perhaps may work weak stomachs to distaste our course of traffic" (1–2).[30] The more he read, "though the author handle the particulars with such confused *contradictions*, as assure me he conceived not what he writ" (2), the more clearly Digges saw the danger of, and the need to refute, such arguments. The East India Company, "like *Hercules* yet in the cradle, in the infancy hath been assailed by serpents' sly aspersions" (3) and must defend itself to grow and thrive.

Early in the treatise, Digges quotes uninterruptedly from *The Trades Increase* for several pages (6–15); then he takes up brief extracts answered point by point. He sets off Kayll's text in archaic black-letter type to insinuate, as Withington observes, "his own modernity at the expense of his opponent's conservatism" (*Society*, 228). He further corrals Kayll's voice with annotations in the outer margins: answers, clarifications, elaborations, points of fact, rhetorical questions, zinging put-downs. His vexation with the task resurfaces in the postscript, where he wittily invites readers to tear up both pamphlets, using pages from *The Trades Increase* "to wrap up fish, and this *Defence of Trade* to wrap up spice: a couple of ink-wasting toys indeed, that if my hearty wishes could have wrought it, should have seen no other light than the fire" (n.p.). This trivializing conceit would have the reading of his treatise to consume the both of them—twin controversialist texts reduced, in readers' minds, to embers of faith in the East India Company and its secrets.[31] But to the contrary, the two books, by putting proto-environmentalist, insular populist, and global corporatist ideologies into vituperative exchange, ignited disputes that became inextinguishable as capitalism consolidated its grip on world economies: intractable arguments over the nature, aims, consequences, national and transnational obligations, and ethical burdens of corporate power.

Digges approved of Gentleman's argument that England should grow its herring industry, but he condemned Kayll's use of the theme to bludgeon the East India Company. He mistrusted Kayll's animus against the Dutch and suspected that the latter's preference for regional European over more remote commerce served a pro-Spanish agenda. An ardent antimonopolist in the 1620s, he ignored Kayll's argument against monopolies and concentrated instead on the East India Company's benefits to England. His fundamental rhetorical challenge was twofold: to diminish the allure of Kayll's Anglo-and Eurocentric fixations while still appealing to English patriotism; and to justify the human and material damages of the eastern trade—the consumption of English forests for shipbuilding, the recurrent shipwrecks, the deaths of swarms of English mariners—as sacrifices to the higher aims of England's prosperity, maritime power, and reputation. To this end, early in the treatise he attaches parasitic imagery to insular economies and heroic imagery to overseas trade. He associates the former with "idle *Drones* and greedy caterpillars" who practice "eating usury and harmful arts," and (in a glance a Kayll) to "a spider in a corner [who] spends his fruitless days perhaps weaving weak objections against" England's deep-ocean traders. The latter, by contrast, "from furthest parts abroad, . . . fetch and bring the honey to the hive, laborious bees, they clothe and feed the poor, and give the willing man employment to gain with them" (2). A learned writer who invokes Tacitus and quotes Virgil repeatedly, by comparing them to "laborious bees"—a stock Virgilian simile for imperial industry—Digges deftly heroizes East India Company mariners. Aeneas witnesses the builders of Carthage in book 1 of the *Aeneid*,

As hard at their task as bees in early summer,
that work the blooming meadows under the sun,
. . . .
The hive seethes with life, exhaling the scent
of honey sweet with thyme.
                                    "How lucky they are!"
Aeneas cries, gazing up at the city's heights.
"their walls are rising now."
(Fagles, 62)

The epic allusion associates East India Company traffic with inspirational imperial labor. Digges energizes an informing nexus of Jacobean mythology here.[32]
The Trojan Aeneas sired the race that founded Rome, which defeated Carthage;
and early modern London styled itself as the inheritor of classical Rome, King
James being the new Caesar Augustus. The conceit gained traction, in part,
through the efforts of England's mariners to translate London into a world city.

Digges's investments, like those of his nominal addressee, were indeed
global. Their mutual involvement in several major trading companies invited
deft refutation of Kayll's mercantilist complaint that the growth of the East
Indian trade has blighted English ventures elsewhere. Regarding the "Muscovy staple," Digges coyly observes that "Sir Thomas Smythe, an honorable
gentleman, whose constant and continual readiness to spend both time and
money in any action that may good the commonwealth, . . . hath been long,
and is still, governor of the *Muscovia* Company" (16). Though not mentioning that Smythe had served as King James's ambassador to Russia (1604–5),
Digges notes that, although the trade had declined "by reason of the troubles
of that land," the business was resuming: the Russia Company has covered
the expenses of "a *Muscovite* ambassador all the last winter here, and Sir *John
Merrick*, one of ours now there, in hope to settle once more privileges for our
nation" (17). For Digges, the premise that commitment to the East Indies
has obviated business elsewhere simply does not hold. English merchants, he
points out, routinely invest in multiple companies. Lapses of trade with any
given country, he implies, derived rather from regional turmoil and Dutch
or Portuguese competition than from swings of capital in England.

As for the Levant Company, Digges concedes a decline occasioned by
Dutch interventions in the Mediterranean and their import of spices via the
Cape of Good Hope. The latter development was a call to action. "And then
our merchants (that whatever ill men say, do scorn to wear the shoes of other

nations) resolved upon an *India Voyage* for themselves" (18). Once consolidated, Digges maintains, East India Company traffic in fact rejuvenated the Levant trade by enabling the profitable reexport into Turkey of Asian goods at costs lower than those achievable by caravan. "Our overplus"—eastern imports unsold domestically—"hath served the Turks with spice, and carried in one year much more into the *Straits*, then ever was imported thence" (18). The implications of this claim were clear: England's trading companies did not contend against each other in a capped economy of investment. Rather, they operated synergistically within a global environment of opportunities for open-ended returns on mobile outlays of capital. It was an insight to inform the designs of imperial capitalism.

As a learned spokesman for the early modern nationalist elite, Digges aligns his classicism with the emergent field of statistics. He assembles data ostensibly more exact and comprehensive than Kayll's to argue that the latter inflates the damages of the trade; then he justifies these lesser losses by infusing them with a classical ethos of imperial striving. Naming but a handful, Kayll numbers twenty-one large ships deployed since the East India Company's inception; three more in the offing; thirteen voyages completed or in progress; and, to date, four vessels "cast away" (*Increase*, 15). Digges marshals a "truer catalogue" in response. His figures are not far from Kayll's: twenty-four ships, two under construction at Deptford, seventeen voyages. He faults Kayll, of course, for counting just thirteen voyages (22). The greater detail of his catalog, in any case, establishes Digges's authority. Opposite the name of each ship, he notes the tonnage and attaches a bracketed précis of the vessel's genealogy and status. Thus their first flagship, "*The Dragon*, 1,060: An old worn ship bought by the Company, but by their cost made so strong, that she is now gone her fifth voyage to the *Indies*" (19); and "*The Trades Increase*, 1,293: New built, and overswayed as she was careening at *Bantam, &c*" (20).

Addressing Kayll's lament that "four of these ships are lost," and that among them, "the *Trades Increase*, that gallant ship, was overtaken by untimely death in her youth and strength,"[33] Digges reflects,

> And is four of so many ships, so long at sea, so great a loss, especially in fourteen years of our yet infant and discovering trade, while in the farthest and unknown parts of the world
>
> ——————*Ignari hominumque locorumque*
> *Erramus, vento vastis & fluctibus acti,*
> *Incerti quo fata ferant, ubi sistere detur,*

while we seek for traffic with strange nations? Surely we esteem it
God's great blessing, that we lost no more, and we are thankful for
it. (22; *Aen.* 1:331–33)

Book 1 of the *Aeneid* permeates Digges's meditations on English questing at
sea. The quotation above makes Aeneas the seafarer, driven by Juno's ire to
an unknown shore, into the prototype of East India Company mariners who
suffer protractedly in unfamiliar waters for England's greater good:

> Castaways,
> we know nothing, not the people, not the place—
> lost, hurled here by the gales and heavy seas.
> (trans. Fagles, 59; *Aen.* 1.403–5)

To have lost but four ships in fourteen years of such extremities is a measure
of achievement, not failure. *The Aeneid* valorizes the rigors of self-discipline,
the agonizing labors, the tremendous hardships suffered in the creation of the
new Troy, the great imperial city. The proem announces the epic's ruling
theme: "Such a long hard labor it was to found the Roman people" (Fagles,
48, l.41). Foundational effort of great magnitude justifies great sacrifice. Digges duly praises the late Sir Henry Middleton in language echoing Virgil's: a
modern Aeneas, he "made the beginning, [and] laid the true foundation of
our long desired *Cambaya Trade*" (23). Such framing of the Sixth Voyage,
with all its heartfelt losses, as a foundational achievement anticipates the
enthusiasms of Samuel Purchas and the many generations of editor-
publishers since who understood the charter generation of the East India
Company as seminal agents of England's imperial expansion.

Readers of this book will recognize, however, that Digges's boast of Middleton's signal accomplishment—on a voyage that the East India Company's
apologist elsewhere declares "one of our worst" (40)—distorts the facts. The
author substitutes the primary *aim* of Middleton's commission, which pro-
poses Surat to be "the main and principal scope of this our voyage" (Birdwood, 333), for its outcome. But Middleton did not found, rather his voyage
closed and abandoned, the factory there. The *Trades Increase* exited Cambaya,
not with a grant of expanded trading privileges, but with a disgraced ambassador and the full cohort of merchants from Surat. Middleton *lost* England's
first foothold in India. It was Best's and Downton's unexpected victories over
larger Portuguese fleets, in December 1612 and January 1615 respectively, that

reopened Gujarat to the East India Company, the latter clash sparking the interest of Emperor Jahāngīr.[34] The primary takeaway from the Sixth Voyage was not a revitalized emporium in Surat but the recognition that the East India Company's enhanced presence in the Indian Ocean required, as Sir Walter Raleigh would have advised, not more massive ships to make intimidating displays of hospitality, but more fleets of stout, well-armed, yet moderately proportioned vessels likelier to complete their voyages. The hubristic size of the *Trades Increase* was its *hamartia*: a tragic miscalculation. By representing Middleton to readers as a Virgilian originator, Digges imparts a recuperative telos to events that the principal mariners themselves witnessed as agonizing collapses of the great expectations that distinguished their expedition. This trick of Digges's argument—the neo-Virgilian determination to infuse breakdowns and tragic losses with an aura of foundational promise—became instrumental to the imperialist mythos that, until recently, shaped the authoritative view of the East India Company's early voyages.

Rationalization and minimization of catastrophe mark Digges's treatment of the wrecks of the *Trades Increase, Ascension, Union,* and *Susan.* Observing that these losses have after all been moderate—that God dealt more cruelly "with some other nations. Look on the *Portingal* or *Dutch* beginnings"—in an act of projection, he demeans Kayll as a "vulture that thus follows wrecks and dead men's bodies" (23), as if to document and decry the disproportionate mortality of East India Company seamen were to feed upon carrion, yet to profit from those deaths remained somehow laudable. He explains the shipwrecks, insofar as possible, as outcomes of preventable error, bad luck, and immoral or mutinous behavior, not of flaws in the Company's plans, equipment, or diligence. He avers that Middleton chose to careen his flagship in Bantam "more for providence than need"—as if, contrary to Downton's informed conviction, the vessel might have sailed home without repairs to the hull. There, in an accident of bad timing, "while a mortal and infectious sickness raged then among the natives, . . . and fell on him and many of his people unto death," the ship was "overswayed . . . by the breaking of a cable, . . . [and] left half ruined above water, for want of skillful hands to help her" (23–24). By reducing the critical failure to a snapped cable—a mishap, we recall, also incident to the ship's launch— Digges reduces the structural severity of the impasse: the fractured mainmast. This was not a proper shipwreck, he suggests: the *Trades Increase* never sank and might have been restored with adequate manpower and technology. By fixing on an infection that happened to spread from the natives to the crew,

Digges elides the constancy of such danger for mariners who lacked immunities to tropical diseases. Labor was always going to be a problem for the English in Bantam. Finally, in a telling gesture of recuperation, at the close of the paragraph on the *Trades Increase*, Digges adds a marginal note: "Yet the goods were safe" (24).

Equivalent moves to fault flawed personnel, exonerate the Company, and justify optimism characterize the accounts of the *Ascension* and *Union*. Digges neglects to note that these vessels comprised the entire fleet of the disastrous Fourth Voyage. The first was "run aground upon the shoals of *Cambaya* . . . by the willfulness of a lewd master" (24) who refused to await the assistance of a local pilot. This preventable outcome, the author suggests, was engineered by a bad actor atypical of the East India Company. Digges hesitates to unpack the suggestive term "lewd"; yet those familiar with Robert Covert's *A True and Almost Incredible Report of an Englishman* (1612), an *Ascension* shipmate whose account of "our willful master" (23) possibly influenced Digges's phrasing, may have recalled the book's lurid finale: "For, *Philip de Grove* our master being a *Fleming*, and an arch-villain, who was not only accused, but it was (by the boy with whom he committed the fact) confessed to myself, that he was a detestable buggerer: So that had not God's mercy been the greater, it was wonder that in regard thereof, and of others being offenders in the like, that our ship had not sunk in the ocean" (68).[35] Sir Dudley's treatment of the wreck, while avoiding mention of buggery, nevertheless suggests that the fault for the loss lay, not with the Company, but with reckless and immoral personnel. Characteristically, he reports that "all the men, with the best merchandise, were saved." He neglects to note that the salvaged goods and bullion disappeared in India.

Turning to the *Union*, Digges explains its demise as the last of an improbable sequence of accidents that the East India Company had done what it could to prevent. The captain and eleven principal men were slain going ashore incautiously in Saint Lawrence (Madagascar) "through foolish breach of their commission" (24). The directors had indeed exhorted them to stand "upon your guard in every place, without yielding any trust to those people" in Saint Lawrence (Birdwood, 244). "Yet she had come richly laden home, if first a mutiny had not fallen among those new unfit commanders, and then fourteen of her ablest men had not forsaken her distressed to go for [*La*] *Rochelle* with a ship of *Alborough*. And yet, good ship, almost at home upon the Coast of *Brittany*, where she drove in with her weak men, the lewd inhabitants first drew her on the rocks, then bored her full of holes, and . . . made a wreck" (24). The result, the ship's cargo pillaged in Brittany, was by this account the unlikeliest of outcomes and not the Company's fault. The sole calamity that Digges concedes to have been a true shipwreck was that of the *Susan*, "an old rotten ship . . . ready to have been broken up for firewood" (24). Rebuilt by the East India Company, it completed the First Voyage but, homeward bound on the Second, foundered somewhere in the Indian Ocean. "This only one ship properly was lost," he declares (25). For Digges, the corporate person does not fully own a shipwreck unless the vessel and its precious cargo sink with all hands.

Arguing that the anonymous writer greatly exaggerates the time generally required to refit ships returned from the Indies—that East India Company vessels are therefore available "to serve the state at home upon our coasts" (26)—Digges next addresses the complaint that shipbuilding initiatives, motivated by royal extravagance and corporate greed, have committed a "parricide" (*Increase*, 18) of England's woods—for Kayll, a shared patrimony of the English people (27). Digges insists that Kayll overstates the depletion of forests, and he scoffs at the notion that the East India Company has independently precipitated sharp increases in the costs of timber and foodstuffs. Given the enrichment the Company brings to England, inflation does not strike him as a pressing concern anyway (29). He views English patriotism as a global project that overruns the defensive insularity of Kayll's vision.

The cultural divisions over England's proper functions within the great world turned largely upon the neoclassical trope of English exceptionalism. As explained by William Camden in *Britannia* (1586), the topos valorizes both insular and expansive energies. Camden invokes the Roman view of Britain as a separate world, citing Virgil's phrase "*Et penitus toto divisos orbe Britannos*: And Britons people quite disjoin'd from all the world besides" (Camden, 1). In nostalgic praise of England, Shakespeare's John of Gaunt evokes the precious insularity of the conceit:

This other Eden, demi-paradise,
This fortress built by nature for herself
Against infection and the hand of war,
This happy breed of men, this little world,
This precious stone set in the silver sea,
Which serves it in the office of a wall
Or as a moat defensive to a house,
Against the envy of less happier lands.
(*Richard II*, 2.1.42–49)

The neofeudal vision of a regal and pastoral England blessedly environed by the sea speaks to Kayll's desire to preserve native forests and limit the influx of "heathens" into the land—as, by extension, it resonates in arguments over immigration and Brexit today. Yet the sea, of course, is both barrier and thoroughfare. Along with its isolation, Camden praises Britain's openness to the world, "disjoined from those neighbor-countries all about by a convenient distance every way, fitted with commodious and open havens for traffic with the universal world, and to the general good, as it were, of mankind, thrusting itself forward from all parts into the sea" (1). Camden's Britain holds itself as an intact, androgynous, sexualized body: its harbors open to penetration, its promontories extended in phallic longing. In this construct, Britain is distinguished by the separation that motivates promiscuous extraterritorial exchanges that work "to the general good . . . of mankind," enhancing both Britain and the other lands within its reach. Camden espouses thus a confident, outward-looking Anglocentrism that thrives by transoceanic commerce.

In like manner, speaking for the corporate elite of a growing maritime and industrial metropolis, Digges finds preposterous Kayll's complaints about the depletion of England's forests—as if the measure of the nation's greatness lay in the extent of its impenetrable woods rather than the strength of its fleets in seas near and far. The globalized cycle of investment, return, re-export, and reinvestment that, he argues, widely benefits England, depends, as Withington notes, "on the unprecedented exploitation of natural resources for commercial ends. Trees were no longer the symbol of Saxon resolution in the face of would-be conquerors" (Withington, 229). Digges writes, "Thinks he, these royal princes cared to keep their woods for any nobler use, than to build gallant ships, and those not to lie still and rot his ordinary death, but such as round about the world disperse the honor of the crown they serve, and then return with wealth for king and kingdom, and for those that set them forth, instead of wood?" (*Defence*, 27). Trees exist, not "to look upon" until they rot (28), or to build and heat houses for the poor, but to generate honor and wealth through shipbuilding. Digges approvingly cites King James's desire to prevent good timber from going to the construction of "beggars' nests (that growing scurse [*sic*] upon this City), new tenements, whose rotten rents make many gentlemen before their time, or that our woods should be consumed in fire and furnaces for glasses and such baubles, when God hath blest us with a fuel in the bowels of the earth" (28), coal. Suburban London had endured metastatic growth for decades as the enclosure and land reform movements threw tenant farmers off the land and drew legions of wage-earning poor into the capital.[36] As the historian Francis Shepherd notes, James I was one of a sequence of rulers who strove vainly to contain that growth: "a long series of proclamations . . . issued by Elizabeth, James I, Charles I, Cromwell, and Charles II," aimed "to prevent the inexorable expansion of London" (Shepherd, 175). If decried by court and civic authorities, however, London's unstoppable growth provided abundant cheap and expendable labor to large employers. Substantial numbers of those who crowded London's tenements found their way into East India Company vessels. Digges's urban and protoindustrial vision comprehends the laboring poor as a consumable resource, like England's forests—to be harvested before they rot. In his view, the East India Company mitigated the problem of London's idle poor both by gainfully employing them and, in the process, also removing a good number of them from the world.

How many in fact perished in East India Company service was another matter of dispute. Denying "the extraordinary death" (23) alleged by Kayll, Digges faults his adversary's estimate that, "in the adventure of some three thousand, . . . we have lost many above two thousand" (*Increase*, 27; *Defence*, 33). For one thing, he finds that the pamphleteer has inflated the employment figures: "Unto this day, there were at first set forth but three and twenty hundred, thirty and three men of all conditions." He therefore concludes, "There will not rest much likelihood of many above two thousand cast away" (33). Mocking Kayll's reliance on "wise masters, his informers," not East India Company papers, to generate his numbers (35), Digges also proves impossible the former's estimate of four hundred fifty deaths on the *Trades Increase*, *Union*, *Ascension*, and *Susan*, when these vessels employed but four hundred thirty-five persons from the outset (33). He notes that some whom Kayll presumed dead remained on assignment abroad; and he quibbles over the death counts for Downton's, Towerson's, Best's, and Saris's ships. Yet his more detailed parsing of supposedly more accurate data cannot refute the fundamental pattern that Kayll decries: a disturbingly high percentage of deaths in East India Company service. For lack of an alternate sum to propose, Digges's opening rebuttal, "not much likelihood of many above two thousand cast away," is not reassuring.

Yet the Company's apologist remains sanguine about the mortality of common mariners. Bold initiatives that enable members of the commonwealth to bypass European and Asian middlemen and reach markets of desire directly—"fetching from the well-head" (5), the East Indies—magnify the

honor and prosperity of England. To go beyond mere well-being, he maintains, "to flourish and grow rich, we must find vent for our abundance, and
seek to adorn us out of others' superfluities" (41). This "we" deftly identifies
the corporate person with the commonwealth at large. Digges represents the
former as a benevolent body that, at its own expense, benefits the public
weal both by employing "shipwrights, smiths coopers, ropemakers, porters,
lighter-men, etc. and such like infinite number of laborers which they have
continually in pay," and also by bringing home "more than two for one" in
profit over the last two years (41–42). During that span, Digges estimates
"above two hundred thousand pounds sterling added to the commonwealth"
by the Company's efforts "to proceed for the enriching of the kingdom" (43).
Running the figures, he shows further that the East India Company has
lowered the domestic costs of pepper, cloves, nutmegs, and mace (42); to
Kayll's claim that victualing their ships inflates the prices of foodstuffs
(*Increase*, 32), Digges answers that their mariners would eat food at home if
not at sea, that the Company husbands its victuals carefully (46) (as Saris's
provocative parsimony on the Eighth Voyage testifies), and that, in any case,
many of their victuals come from France, Spain, and elsewhere. Without
quite formulating Thomas Mun's subsequent theory of a favorable balance
of trade, Digges maintains, finally, that the East India Company's material
operations and financial profits increase the circulation of money within the
commonwealth, to everyone's benefit. The argument constitutes an early version of the "trickle-down" theory of economic prosperity.

Public comfort with this formulation demands evidence of measures to
mitigate damages as well as an anesthetic ideology: a nexus of beliefs to ease
the consciences of shareholders and public over the widespread suffering and
death built into the Company's business. Conceding that Bantam is indeed
"unhealthy to our people," Digges indicates the directors' goodwill by pre-
dicting, "We therefore change our factory from *Bantam*" (36)—presumably,
a proposal at the Court of Committees that, like many others, met with
mixed results. As noted above, the factory removed to Jakarta in 1619 but
returned to Bantam, for many decades, in 1629. He further evokes the Company's anxieties and solicitude for employees:

> It is the merchants' grief (and he that knows what hazard they do
> run, that have their goods in Heathen Countries, in the hands of
> dying men, that must expect rich ships to come from places so
> remote, so weakly manned, through seas of dangers, besides pirates,

will believe it is their grief) unspeakable, that hitherto they cannot absolutely clear themselves from this (to them indeed great) mischief. . . . They provide what ere it cost, all that the wit of man, helped by continual experience, can invent, for victuals, clothing, physic, surgery, to keep them in good health, besides good preachers, and the best commanders, all that may be to preserve them. (36–37)

The Company, Digges insists, is saddened, charitable, systematically attentive to mariners' needs. This was a credible claim. Shareholders recognized that their returns rode upon the survival of crews—the *Union*'s fate being a lamentable case in point. As Cheryl Fury notes, the East India Company was "an employer well known for its concern for shipboard conditions and the health of its seamen"—a solicitude that, notwithstanding the risks of its long voyages, enhanced the East India Company's appeal to mariners seeking employment (Fury, 170, 183). From the start, all East India Company ships carried surgeons and surgeon's mates; and in 1613, the Company appointed a surgeon general to standardize medical practices across the fleets, select ships' surgeons, and provide them with well-stocked chests. The accomplished John Woodall assumed the office and, in 1617, published *The Surgeon's Mate*, a manual whose publication eased his labor of "writing for every ship the same instructions anew" (Ded. to Reader, n.p.). Described as "the first good medical textbook of its kind in English," it recommended among other things lime juice as a tonic against scurvy.[37] In the dedicatory epistle to his "singular good patron" Smythe, Woodall praised the governor's "especial providence and great care for the health and preservation of such as have been or hereafter may be employed in your services" (2, 2v). Nevertheless, the carnage, while likely lessened by these efforts, continued. Significantly, moreover, in the passage above, Digges links the merchants' concern for the lives of mariners to their anxieties over the storage and transport of goods: the shareholders' grief attaches equally to personnel and cargoes—perhaps, as Downton damningly insinuated in his letter above, more acutely to the latter.

To defend against this "grief unspeakable," Digges advocates stoic acceptance. Mortal hazards pervade the world; substantial achievement demands great sacrifice. Such an attitude clearly informed the courage of mariners like Middleton, Downton, and most others on early modern sailing ships, who knew themselves to be, as John Huyghen van Linschoten observed, "always within two inches of their death" (Burnell, 1:xlix). "To stay from the sea for fear of death, and starve at home, or pine away in poverty, were foolish superstitious cowardice. . . . Living bodies, unemployed, are nothing. And if unhealthiness or danger of mortality should keep us from a course wherein we may enrich us, or our masters, or serve the king, or good the common-wealth, who then shall live in Rumney-Marsh,[38] or Holland, or our Cinque-Ports, or Cities visited with sickness, or go unto the wars?" (32). The fear of death does not prevent people from living where they must or advancing their own and their country's interests. Yet this meditation on the life worth living, be it long or short, then takes a heartless turn: "Besides, the common-wealth esteems not the life of any but good men, such as do good; the rest are *Tacitus* his *Purgamenta Urbium*,[39] their death to her is nothing but an ease. Nay, mariners themselves . . . were better die in the *East-Indies*, than here at home at Tyburn or at *Wapping*, for want of means to live" (32–33).[40] Such dismissal of the idle poor is not idiosyncratic to Digges. Thomas Mun, notes Ted McCormick, likewise criminalizes "unemployed seamen" as "not merely idle but treasonous: 'Take them from their laudable and accustomed employments . . . we see what desperate courses they do then attempt, by joining even with *Turks* and Infidels to rob and spoil all Christian nations.' "[41] For these and other merchant magnates, ordinary sailors are human refuse refined by East India Company employment and better carried off by sick-ness abroad than by the hangman in London for theft or piracy. The Com-pany does the state a service in removing them. Walter Peyton's journal on the voyage that took Sir Thomas Roe to India indicates that the fleet carried, along with eleven Japanese and fourteen Indian sailors, "nineteen condemned persons out of Newgate, to be left for the discovery of unknown places, the company having obtained the king's pardon for them to this purpose" (P, 4:289). Digges's treatise effectively erases Peyton's distinction between the crews and the convicts they transported in 1615. In a striking testament to the chasms of mistrust dividing investors from common mariners, he conceives the Company's ships as mobile colonies of preventive detention.

Most English deaths in the East Indies, Digges further insinuates, must be charged to the victims themselves—men who might have saved themselves by Christian self-restraint. An insidious privatization of responsibility excul-pates the corporation. All who die on East India Company voyages volun-teered to go: "For my part," Digges writes, "I that often visit *Philpot Lane*, profess, I meet few sorrowful *East India* clients, but such as are refused to go the voyage" (38). The investors having provided the vessels, victuals, surgeons, discipline, and spiritual counsel to sustain them, most who perish in the East

Indies invite their own demise, "through their own abusing of themselves, with the hot drinks[42] and most infectious women of those countries" (37). Digges fully endorses the racist-misogynist rationale that Kayll resists: the stereotypic early modern notion that immoderate sexual congress with women drains one's manhood and that, in particular, the intoxicants and "most infectious women" of the East Indies pose a graver threat to intemperate sailors than do crowded, unhygienic ships, protracted heavy labor, exhaustion, malnutrition, spoiled victuals, bad drinking water, scurvy, and serial exposure to tropical and other diseases on voyages of inordinate duration. While a corporation outlives its members, the investors also constitute, for Digges, a body more principled than most of those dying in its service. He frames the appalling death rates in the East Indies as measures of recklessness and depravity among mariners and factors, not of a force more sinister: corporate resilience at financing, equipping, and staffing highly attritional voyages to lethal destinations whose factories endured only by perpetual renewals of personnel.

Closing Thoughts

Published during the emergent years of global capitalism, the pamphlets of Kayll and Digges divided sharply over the nature and propensities of state-sanctioned corporate power. These epistolary adversaries—one, an "unknown" Londoner who lived among seamen and found himself imprisoned for speaking his mind; the other, an Oxford-educated nobleman and parliamentarian who, in 1616, took up residence in the neoclassical splendor of Chilham Castle—articulated ideological convictions whose deep differences remain unresolved today. Indeed, arguments over corporate power have elaborated and intensified into questions of civilizational and planetary scope over the four centuries since Kayll and Digges publicly disputed the loss of Jacobean England's greatest merchant ship. In reconstructing that vessel's long-neglected story, characterizing the generation that built and sailed it, describing the material and imaginative life of its journey, and postulating the ideological stakes of the controversy ignited by its destruction, I offer *The Loss of the Trades Increase*, not as a neo-Virgilian valorization of foundational sacrifice, but rather as a cultural-materialist critique of the "body corporate and politic" that the founders built.[43] Enduring financial crises at home, and political and strategic setbacks and grievous losses in men and materiel abroad, the early East India Company modeled a pattern of self-righteous yet ruthless resilience for subsequent generations of joint-stock investors: they demonstrated the capacity of the transnational corporation to turn tragedy into an engine of capital accumulation. While the practical immortality of the corporate person set preconditions for this development, it was the distinctively damaging conditions of trade between England and the East Indies that educed and consolidated it.

When reconsidered from the twenty-first century, the work of the nascent East India Company, whose survival was clearly not inevitable, did not intimate that England was destined to hold, for a considerable span, imperial rule in Asia. The Company's tenuous endurance did, however, prove that seeds of the reckless, world-altering interventionism that Naomi Klein has provocatively termed "disaster capitalism" (*Shock Doctrine*)—the exploitation of crises both engineered and unforeseen that weaken opposition to the deliberate implantation of neoliberal economies—existed from the East India Company's inception in privateering's legacy of opportune aggression and the corporate body's amoral tolerance for catastrophe. The charter generation starkly implemented patterns of development critiqued by thinkers today who challenge orthodox economic theory, like those academics who in December 2017 posted "33 Theses" on the doors of the London School of Economics in hopes of widening the civic and moral scope of economic discourse.[44] The capitalist fixation on perpetual growth that David Pilling finds delusional gathered decisive impetus from the East India Company's emulous striving against the Dutch and Portuguese trading empires (Pilling). And as I write, arguments hauntingly reminiscent of those between Kayll and Digges on the relative importance of lives and revenues fuel controversies over when and how to "reopen" public schools, universities, and local, regional, and national economies during the COVID-19 pandemic.

Multinational corporations have grown by many orders of magnitude greater, richer, and more intrinsically manipulative of public polities around the world than was Smythe's East India Company over Jacobean England. As a literary scholar, I have labored in this study to excavate and critique the internal and public discourses attending a voyage that epitomized the great strivings and tragic limitations of the founders of a corporation that evolved into a principal agent of imperial capitalism. It is my hope that the narrative will provide insights and suggest historic points of leverage to those who would, by persuasion and regulation, move joint-stock corporations, and the financial industries that attend and motivate them, to tame the profit principle: to uncouple it from catastrophe; to harness it to the robust service of workers and communal well-being as well as the interests of investors; to cultivate, rather than perpetual increases in market exposure, sustainable sufficiencies; and to prioritize the human, ethical, and ecological needs of a postimperial world. It is time we lost trust in the trade's increase.

NOTES

INTRODUCTION

1. Downton, "Journal," f101, 26 December 1613. Hereafter cited as "D."

2. On the theory, legal history, variety, and political work of corporations, see the important study by Turner, *Commonwealth*.

3. Stern, *Company-State*, examines at length the East India Company as a crucible of transnational government: a colonizing state.

4. Van Linschoten (1598). An earlier English attempt by the southern route was decidedly unpromising. James Lancaster, later the general of the East India Company's First Voyage, captained a privateering venture to the East Indies (1591–94), then lost his vessel to a mutinous crew in the Caribbean. A castaway, he returned to Europe in a French ship. See Foster, *Lancaster*.

5. On the ethics of commerce, see Turner, "Corporations," 155.

6. Quotations from early modern sources are modernized in spelling, punctuation, and some capitalization.

7. The charter thus engages the English pluralists' argument "that so-called sovereign authority can be said not to create a fictional legal person but rather to *recognize* a real association of persons whose practical activity preexists legal formalization" (Turner, *Commonwealth*, 21). The 1600 charter constitutes a strong royalist version of this model, for it recognizes an association whose practical activity of voyaging had not yet begun.

8. Turner, *Commonwealth*, 14; cf. Stern, *Company-State*, 7.

9. Stern, *Company-State*, 9; Turner, *Commonwealth*, 11, 13. On dual body theory, see Kantorowicz; and Turner, *Commonwealth*, 10–18. I thank Joel Altman for suggesting the parallel between the monarch's and the East India Company's two bodies.

10. Foster, *John Company*, 4; Bruce, 1:156–57.

11. Morgan, "Smythe, Sir Thomas (*c.*1558–1625)," *ODNB*, accessed 14 August 2016, http://www.oxforddnb.com.ezproxy.proxy.library.oregonstate.edu/view/article/25908.

12. Prockter and Taylor, 25 (5R).

13. Foster, *John Company*, 12. The *Court Book* names the committees present at each meeting; see also Sainsbury, 151 (#368).

14. *Court Book*, B/3, f37, f98, f129v. Cashier and treasurer were different offices: a note on 18 August 1609, during Farrington's tenure, identifies the cashier as Richard Atkinson (f134).

15. On Staper and Osborne, see A. Wood, 7, appendix 4; on Smythe, 31; see also Stevens, 1, 245.

16. On capital accumulation from privateering, see Andrews, *Privateering*; and Andrews, "Sir Robert Cecil."

17. Andrews, *Privateering*, 117; Foster, *Middleton*, xv–xvi; Barbour, *Orientalism*, 88–89.

18. For overviews, see Rodger, *Safeguard*; and Wernham.

19. Hakluyt (1598–1600), 3:708; Beeching, 375. On Lancaster and Pernambuco, see Andrews, *Privateering*, 209–13; Foster, *Lancaster*, xx–xxiii, 31–74; and Beeching, 375–85.

20. See, for instance, Bawlf, 106, 144.

21. Mun, *Discourse*; Mun, *Treasure*.

22. Misselden, 20; cf. Malynes. For discussion, see Wright, *Culture*, 453–58.

23. On Anglo-European competition in the East Indies, see Innes; Furber; on Dutch influence, Neill, 319–22.

CHAPTER 1

1. See chart of East India Company investments in Chaudhuri, 209; tonnage in Farrington, *Catalogue*, 502, 657.

2. On naval technology and tactics, see Parry, 53–68, 114–27; Ricklefs, 20–28; and Lavery, esp. chap. 1.

3. Lawson, 19, 21–23. Evidently misconstruing the first generation's understanding of the term "committee"—a person to whom a particular charge, trust, or function is "committed"—Lawson envisions an order of twenty-four "individual Directors" each of whom supervised a dedicated "committee" (21). But Smythe's East India Company held no such plenitude of standing offices. The twenty-four committees—that is, the full Court of Committees, an electoral body whose members convened in smaller groups for specific tasks (Chaudhuri, 32)—*were* the twenty-four directors. On the usage of "committee," see Birdwood, 171.

4. Michelborne in Purchas, 2:347–66; on the Scottish initiative, see Lawson, 33–34; on relations with the Crown, Chaudhuri, 23–31.

5. Sainsbury, 129 (#295, #296), 130 (#297); Bruce, 1:150–51.

6. Profits surveyed in W. R. Scott, *Constitution*, 2:124; note of *Ascension*, *Dragon*, and *Union* in Sainsbury, 193 (#459, #460), 225 (#577). On the Third Voyage, see Barbour, *Journals*.

7. See Wright, *Religion*, 84–114.

8. See Wright, ed., *Voyage*.

9. See, for example, Stromberg, "Starving Settlers," http://www.smithsonianmag.com/history-archaeology/Starving-Settlers-in-Jamestown-Colony-Resorted-to-Eating-A-Child-205472161.html. Cf. John Smith's account in *The Generall History of Virginia* (1623), in P. Barbour, ed., *Works*, 2:232–33; Bernhard, esp. 95–115.

10. Jenner, "Myddelton, Sir Hugh," *ODNB*, accessed 17 August 2015, http://www.oxforddnb.com.ezproxy.proxy.library.oregonstate.edu/view/article/19683.

11. Spence, 179 (launch, 127); Andrews, *Privateering*, 70–79; Barbour, *Journals*, 5; on tonnage, Farrington, *Catalogue*, 168.

12. See Barbour and Klein, 150–68.

13. On the *Ascension*, see Andrews, *Privateering*, 76–77; Stevens, 13–14, 16–20; and Farrington, *Catalogue*, 31. On the *Hector*, see Farrington, 310; and *Diary of Thomas Dallam*, in Bent, *Early Voyages*. On the *Susan*, see Farrington, 633.

14. As Chaudhuri explains, the "committees initiated policy which was either ratified or altered by the General Court . . . which also elected the Governor, the Deputy, and the members of the Court of Committees" (Chaudhuri, 32).

15. Letter of 10 March 1600, *Sainsbury*, 104 (#266); printed in Bruce, 1:121–26 (who mistakes the recipient for Walsingham, d. 1590).

16. Birdwood, 217–18, 219–20; Barbour, *Journals*, 10–11.

17. *Court Book*, f120v; cf. Sainsbury, 185 (#443).

18. £100 is the minimum pledged by initial subscribers (September 1599) in Stevens, 1–4.

19. See "Voyage of M. David Middleton," in Purchas, 3:51–60.

20. Raleigh, *Observations*, 8–9. *Maineable*: flexible, workable.

21. "You are to fire your bow pieces upon her, and then your full broadside; and then letting your ship fall off with the wind, let fly your chase pieces, all of them, and so your weather broadside. The which being done, bring your ship about, that your stern pieces may be given also" (Perrin, *Dialogues*, 296–97); Lavery, 15.

22. Rodger, *Safeguard*, 386–87.

23. McGowan, 91, 98; Barbour, *Journals*, 13, 38; Rabb, 256; Sainsbury, 124 (#288).

24. "A Proclamation for Preservation of Woods," in Larkin and Hughes, 1:207; *Oxford Scholarly Editions Online* (Oxford University Press, September 2013), 1.

25. *House of Commons Journal*, vol. 1 (1395, 394), http://www.british-history.ac.uk/report .aspx?compid=8722; *Journal of the House of Lords*, vol. 2 (13 June and 2 July 1607, 22 October 1610), http://www.british-history.ac.uk/search.aspx?query1=timber&rf=pubid:117.

26. The decree excepts, "necessary uses . . . lawfully warranted," but neither specifies mills and shipping nor stipulates the cutting seasons (Larkin and Hughes, 1:208).

27. Saris, "Journal," f44 (9 December 1611), hereafter cited as "S"; on the *Thomas*'s construction, see Danvers and Foster, 1:137.

28. Moryson, *Itinerary*, qtd. in Hinton, 4; *Petition* in Hinton, 168.

29. "Mr. Sheriff Cockaine" was nevertheless in honorary attendance at the prelaunch Court of Committees, 29 December 1609 (*Court Book*, f163).

30. The "Exchange": likely the Royal Exchange, a wholesale mart and financial center, or perhaps Cecil's recently opened New Exchange.

31. *Court Book*, f98v (1 July 1608); Foster, *Lancaster*, 85–86.

32. "David Middleton," Purchas 3:90.

33. On the compensation of wives and widows, see Fury; Christensen; and Barbour, "Desdemona."

34. S, f5v (9 April 1611); Sainsbury, 357 (#839), 401 (#956). Piloting the *Hector* with Downton's outbound fleet in 1614, Poynett was accused of misplacing a buoy in the Channel "to disgrace others that should undertake to conduct the ships" (Sainsbury, 282 [#700]; *Court Book*, B/5, f51v, 10 March 1614), yet the East India Company continued to employ him. He piloted Keeling's departing fleet in 1615 (*Court Book*, f365, 11 February 1614/15).

35. Johnson and Bell were committees of long standing; elected in 1607, Mountney served as "husband" of the Company for many years (Birdwood, 304).

36. Jardine and Brotton, 63, 70. I thank my colleague Rebecca Olson for her counsel on tapestries (see Olson).

CHAPTER 2

1. On the clash in the Red Sea, see Chapter 5.

2. On the "established tradition of individualism within the [Tudor] maritime community" (85), see Fury, esp. chap. 3.

3. Saris reported that "pieces in great quantity will not sell at any high rates . . . by reason the sailors are permitted to bring so many, who sell them so cheap that the country is both glutted and the commodities embased" (*LR*, 1:21).

4. "You shall also understand that in the Sixth Voyage we give our factors no liberty for any private trade. . . . You had some liberty granted by the Fourth Voyage to adventure some small matter in private. . . . But henceforth no private adventure to any factor will be permitted" (Birdwood, 310).

5. As the committees advised the Sixth Voyage's chief merchant, Lawrence Femell, "They are not to require their wages any more in the country but here in England" (Birdwood, 324).

6. Thus to Femell: "And although by accidental succession of place may fall upon some one of you whose wages is but small, yet we will not yield to any succession of salary or increase of wages, but retain that power in ourselves to reward where we shall find the same convenient" (Birdwood, 327; cf. 343).

7. Thus the Sixth Voyage commission dictates, "Some of the principals in each ship may confer their observations together at convenient times once or twice every week at the least, to the end [that] if any have forgotten what another hath observed, the same may be added, so as a perfect discourse may be set down" (Birdwood, 331).

8. *Court Book*, B/5, 308 13 December 1614; Satow, lxvii.

9. On the First Voyage, e.g., "Forasmuch as the days of man's life are limited, and . . . the end only known unto God," at Lancaster's demise, John Middleton was to succeed him, William Brund to succeed Middleton, John Hayward to succeed Brund (Birdwood, 7–8).

10. On King James's cult of *arcana imperii* or "mysteries of state," see Goldberg, esp. chap. 2, "State Secrets."

11. *Couchant*: lying down, open.

12. Farrington, *Catalogue*, 147, 502, 657; Birdwood, 329; Barbour, *Journals*, 8–9.

13. See Barbour, "Power."

14. *Articles*, D4, item 19.

15. Birdwood, 315–16; Barbour, *Journals*, 10–11; Markham, *Hawkins*, 392.

16. Having learned that "your men were faint hearted and yielded without resistance," the committees found it "a great neglect in you to be so secure as not to arm and animate your men thoroughly, being in the midst of dangers, and committing so much goods to their charge" (Birdwood, 315–16).

17. Huntingford, 37, 103; Barbour, *Journals*, 18, 151–54.

18. Pursuant to the "advice of Hawkins and the rest, if anything be presented to the king, prince, or great potentate, it is to be done (as you know) with state and comeliness" (Birdwood, 336).

19. "Here are nothing esteemed but of the best sorts: good cloth and fine, and rich pictures . . . so that they laugh at us for such as we bring." Foster, *Roe*, rev. ed., 77; see Barbour, *Orientalism*, chap. 5.

20. See Keay.

21. See Saris (hereafter cited as "S"). Satow presents only the latter portion of the journal.

22. Purchas (hereafter cited as "P"), 3:115–304; Downton, "Journal 1" (hereafter cited as "D"); Downton, "Journal 2"; Greene (hereafter cited as "G"); Foster, ed., *Jourdain* (hereafter cited as "J"); Danvers and Foster (hereafter cited as "*LR*").

23. Jenner, *ODNB*; http://www.oxforddnb.com.ezproxy.proxy.library.oregonstate.edu/view/article/19 683; Bergeron, ed., 961–62, 968–76.

24. Makepeace, *ODNB*; http://www.oxforddnb.com.ezproxy.proxy.library.oregonstate.edu/view/article/18673; Foster, *Middleton*, xv–xvi.

25. Foster, *Middleton*, 5; *Last East-Indian Voyage*, 1–64.

26. The factor Edmund Scott offers close but not identical figures (Foster, *Middleton*, 85, 111).

27. Foster, *Downton*, xiii–xiv, 2; *LR*, 1:86.

28. Downton, "Diary," f35; Foster, *Downton*, xxxii.

29. Foster, *Downton*, xxxii; *Court Book*, IOR B/5, 60 14 March 1614 .

30. Thus they counseled Femell, "Almighty God out of his mercy in Jesus Christ hath promised not only to hear us when we call upon him, but also to grant us his spirit of grace to strengthen us and assist us in all actions which Satan or the world can enforce against us" (Birdwood, 323).

31. Foster, *Downton*, xv; *LR*, 3:79.

32. *LR*, 1:155 (24 February 1612), 259 (20 June 1613).

33. See Moreland; and Chaudhuri, 37, 49–50.

34. Markham, *Lancaster*, 147; Purchas, 3:115, 194. The master's mate Thomas Love's journal, shy on detail, starts on 4 April; a terse, anonymous *Peppercorn* journal on 1 April. The initial leaves of Downton's manuscript and the entirety of Middleton's are lost.

35. Marlowe in Barbour, *Journals*, 75.

36. Foster, *Roe* (1899), 7.

37. On the disputed stagings, see Barbour and Klein; Barbour, *Journals*, 23–28, 243–45. On Molyneux's reassignment from the *Dragon* to the *Trades Increase*, Barbour, *Journals*, 7–9, 18; Birdwood, 329. On 8 January 1610, the *Court Book* (B/3) indicates that the *Dragon*'s purser, John Lancellott, was reassigned to the new flagship (f165v). Other mariners surely shared the trajectory.

38. *Fret*: "A sudden disturbance (of weather); a gust, squall (of wind); in early use also, agitation of waves" (*OED*).

39. Lancaster in Birdwood, 136–37; Foster, *Middleton*, 9; crew figures in Farrington, *Catalogue*, 168. On Keeling, see Barbour, *Journals*, 16, 188–89.

40. Captain Rowles "told the general he had many men sick of the scurvy down and many others infected; and . . . said that if the general . . . touched not at the Cape, that they would go to their cabins and die, for they knew that they were but dead men" (J, 11). On the stay, see J, xx, 13–19.

41. Peter Schoonees describes them as an early postal system. I thank Jaco Boshoff of the Iziko Museums for the reference.

42. Strachey, 18, 32–33. Synonymous with "colony" in seventeenth-century parlance, "plantation" encodes the hopeful transfer of English flora to other lands.

43. On English appropriation of Roman triumphalism, see Miller.

44. Harrison, plates F, G, H. For discussion, see Barbour, *Orientalism*, 70–80.

45. On the Turkish occupation, see Stookey, 127–46; and Chew, 553.

46. See Keay.

47. See "Introduction to Mocha Factory Records," *Factory Records*, 7–9.

48. Birdwood, 436. With incidental variations, Purchas published this letter and the sultan's seal in the Saris narrative (P, 3:384–85).

49. Compare Ambassador Lello's account to Thomas Dallam in Constantinople: "When I come to his gates I shall be taken off my horse and searched, and led betwixt two men holding

my hands down close to my sides, and so led into the presence of the Grand Signior, and I must kiss his knee or his hanging sleeve" (Bent, 65).

50. Ja'far Basha spoke accurately of his need to please Achmed I. Describing Middleton's trials in Arabia Felix, Purchas writes, "The treacherous [Regib] *Aga* was removed, *Ider Aga* placed in his room: and since, *Jeffar Bassa* is also reported to have lost his head" (*Pilgrimage*, 583).

51. Dabul, Diu, and Chaul—port cities on the Malabar (west) coast of India; Cochin—Vietnam; Ormus—Hormuz, Gulf of Oman.

52. *Ethiopia*: in the seventeenth century, the term often signified Africa in general.

CHAPTER 3

1. D in P, 3:214; Greene names the governor or "mir" (G, f2v, 11 February 1610/11).

2. "Once men of status with a share of power over others, they now had to accustom themselves to insignificance and powerlessness in an alien society" (Colley, 291).

3. Greene, f1, 15 November 1610 (hereafter cited as "G").

4. Downton, "Journal 1," f25v, 21 December 1610 (hereafter cited as "D"). Purchas omits the conditional clauses following "against us" (3:223).

5. *Asper*: a Turkish coin of small value.

6. *Ging*: crew, company, gang.

7. Middleton estimates 180 miles (M in P, 3:137), but Google Maps puts the distance, on a route resembling his, at about 435 kilometers (270 miles).

8. M in P, 3:135–36, 151; Pemberton's letter to Middleton details his escape and arrival at the great ship, "all spent with labour and want of drink, having drunk all my own water [urine] that nature could afford me" (*LR*, 1:56–57). Downton reports that Pemberton was utterly spent, "scarce able to speak through faintness," when he was rescued (D in P, 3:230).

9. See Chapter 2, note 49 on this practice.

10. *Shabunder*: from Persian *Shābhandar*, "lord of the haven," official in charge of the harbor and customs payments (Foster, *Jourdain*, 59n).

11. Cf. *Tamburlaine*'s boastful Bajazeth: "I have of Turks, Arabians, Moors and Jews / Enough to cover all Bithynia. / Let thousands die, their slaughtered carcasses / Shall serve for walls and bulwarks to the rest" (Marlowe, part 1, 47: 3.3.136–39).

12. *Jelba*: an Arabian transport vessel for hire.

13. *Scale*: synecdoche for the market.

14. The letter refers to Arabs boarding the flagship. The *LR* transcript, "in the presence of the Aga," errs. Regib Aga would not have submitted himself to potential captivity aboard the *Trades Increase*. Downton's copy of Middleton's letter offers "in view of the Arabs" (D, f36v, 25 March 1611); Thornton's 26 March 1611 letter repeats Middleton's request "that I should set him free before the Arabians" (*LR*, 1:83).

15. Pemberton's veiled allusion to Femell, "Some that hurts were as big as their bodies," links the cape merchant's bulk to his hesitant nature (*LR*, 1:84); Downton describes Femell's "fatness" as "unwieldy" (D, 41v, 13 May 1611).

16. Hewitt, Campbell, and Schaffelke, 326–37.

17. *Nohuda*: captain or master of a vessel; Middleton provides his name (M in P, 3:152, 154).

CHAPTER 4

1. Of Allee, Purchas evidently mistook the manuscript's "captive" (D, f44v, 2 June) for "captain" (P, 3:241).

2. *Cannanor* (today's Kannur), on India's southwest coast. Downton indicated that the pact extended to Cape Comorin, the southern tip of India. He also registered its failure: "Whether the Basha thought his hopes or advantage therein to be the greater, or whether the Governor Regib Aga thought not fit to acquaint the Basha thereof, I know not; but they made no mention of allowances of the said business" (D, f47, 1 July 1611).

3. Saris, "Journal," f51v–f52, 18 February 1612 (hereafter cited as "S"); cf. *LR*, 1:129. This counsel is seconded by John Staunton's letter surviving only in Saris's copy: "Though happily you shall have procured the Grand Signior's letter of protection to the Bashaw, yet by no means rely thereon, for they have command not to accept them" (S, f52v).

4. Middleton describes frigates as "men of war" (3:172). Originally applied to light, swift boats with oars or sails (*OED*, #1), the term denoted vessels of various sizes. Jourdain mentions one carrying over fifty men (J, 178).

5. As Foster notes, Bangham "proved himself so intelligent and trustworthy that on his return to England in 1614 he was made a factor and sent out again. . . . Roe speaks of him as the best linguist in the Company's service in India" (J, 133n; Foster, *Roe*, 82n).

6. Finch died in Baghdad in October 1613. On Finch, see Foster, *Travels*, 122–87 (Finch's narrative); Foster, *Jourdain*, 140n; Barbour, *Journals*, 12–13.

7. Markham, *Hawkins*, 393, 395–97; Foster, *Travels*, 64, 74, 76–78.

8. Coverte describes the scene: "The merchants had some £10,000 lying between the mainmast and the steerage, whereof the general bid the company to take what they would, . . . some more, some less, and so we left the ship" (24).

9. On Hawkins's wife, Mariam Khān, see Malieckal; Robertson; and Sen.

10. Moreland, *Floris*, 14; see also Purchas, 3:304–42.

11. This Jaddow may be the intermediary who subsequently assisted Sir Thomas Roe. See index in Foster, *Roe*; and Barbour, *Orientalism*, 161.

12. Downton puts the reunion on 15 October, Jourdain and Greene, 14 October.

13. On the ethnic diversity of East India Company crews and workers, see Barbour, "Multinational."

14. In a note on Jourdain's account of the grounding, Foster mentions Greene's entry but mistakenly (and unfairly) asserts that "Downton does not mention the grounding of the *Peppercorn*" (J, 180n)—as if the lieutenant general were loath to recount an incident that might impugn his seamanship.

15. Birdwood, 350–51; cf. royal letters to the emperor, 348–50.

16. As Greene explicated, Mukarrab Khān "agreed upon the price of our English commodities, for which they would pay us in callicoes and pintadoes of diverse sorts" (G, f10v, 7 December).

17. *Firmaen*: an order, patent, or passport; a formal grant of privileges (*LR*, 1:336).

18. *Maund*: a variable measure of weight (J, 182n); *kintall*: a hundredweight, or 112 pounds.

19. *Cared not*: was untroubled, not displeased.

20. On Abdala Khān, see Foster, *Roe*, 170.

CHAPTER 5

1. Saris, "Journal," f51v–f52v, 18 February 1612 (hereafter cited as "S"). Purchas's edition of Saris's journal ("S in P") mentions but does not reproduce Middleton's letter and omits intracorporate disputes detailed in Saris's manuscript.

2. On the clash in the Red Sea, see Satow, xviii–xxiv; and Barbour, "Praxis," 1–29.

3. Saris and his brother John both invested in the Eighth Voyage, Middleton in the Third and Sixth Voyages (Rabb, 342, 372); Middleton's letter in Foster, *Jourdain*, 222.

4. "Instructions left by Middleton at Bantam," Foster, *Middleton*, 196.

5. See Satow, 212–30; on the document's dating, ix; on Saris's knowledge of Malayan, 45.

6. Though Saris may not have known this, Regib Aga was also a "Greek by nation, benegado [renegado]" (J, 77).

7. Cocks's letter to Smythe seconded Saris's optimism: "He was royally received and feasted by the governor, . . . and afterwards richly vested and conveyed through the town with drums and music to the captain's house and there newly feasted, and towards night returned aboard with promise of settling a Factory, to our own contents, being sorry for the injury formerly offered to Sir Henry Middleton, desiring it might be forgotten; and that upon his head be it if ever hereafter the like were offered again" (*LR* 1:218–19).

8. D, f88v, 19 July 1612; cf. D in P, 3:290. Foregrounding England's inaugural voyage to Japan, Satow published only the post-Java half of Saris's journal.

9. Minutes of the award meeting note that the book "recorded particularly the many discoveries made by this company, together with the great benefit which this kingdom reapeth thereby" (Pennington, 1:366–67); see also 1:49–50.

10. The East India Company's Captain Andrew Shilling finally succeeded in establishing a factory in Mocha in May 1618, but the ensuing trade was infrequent and beset by piracy. The factory did not fulfill Saris's hopes until Europe's appetite for coffee fueled annual voyages from England to Mocha in the eighteenth century (Factory Records, IOR G/17, 7–9).

11. Not in Purchas's redaction, however. Here is the full entry: "The fifteenth Sir Henry came aboard the *Clove*" (S in P, 3:393).

12. Jourdain puts their number at forty (J, 208), Saris at twenty-one (S, f76v, 28 April).

13. *Ties*: "runners of thick rope . . . used in hoisting topsails" (Foster; J, 211n).

14. On Saris's difficulties in London, see Satow, lvii–lxxiv.

15. On Khwāja Abū-l Hassan, see Foster, *Jourdain*, 154n.

16. "Asab Bey, an excellent anchorage opposite to Mocha" (Foster's note, J, 210). Saris counted "11 sail of junks or India ships of several places" riding with the *Hector* and *Trade* when he rejoined them (S, f76, 27 April).

17. *Half-deck*: "elevated deck aft of the mainmast and below the quarter-deck; *waist*: the lowest open-air deck of the ship, between the half-deck and the forecastle" (*OED*).

18. As Captain John Smith explains, "The master and his mates are to direct the course, command all the sailors, for steering, trimming, and sailing the ship" (Smith, 34). While boatswains were his enforcers, a domineering physicality advantaged the master as well.

19. *Falchion*: "a broad, slightly curved sword; *brewer's bung*: a large awl-like instrument with handles to rotate so to carve a bung hole in a cask; *naked*: unsheathed" (*OED*).

20. *Nohuda* (*Nākhudā*): "ship-master" or captain (Foster, *Jourdain*, 226n).

21. The *Court Book* entry of 10 March 1615 suggests that Middleton's salary exceeded Saris's by £1,100 (Satow, lxxiii).

22. *Cables*: thick ropes attached to anchors; cf. hawser.

23. *Rummaging*: "removing and clearing of things in the ship's hold" (Manwayring, 87).

24. S, f92, 3 July 1612.

25. Foster, *Lancaster*, xix–xxiii, xxx, 31–74, 107, 135; Barbour, "Praxis," 12–13.

26. See Colley on English vulnerability and imperial tactics in India, esp. chap. 8.

CHAPTER 6

1. On Lancaster's presentation of Queen Elizabeth's letter and negotiations with the king, see Foster, *Lancaster*, 90–101.

2. The letter accompanied the "Instructions given by us the Governor and Committees" of the East India Company "unto Lawrence Femell, our principal factor, and the rest of the factors now employed in this Sixth Voyage" (Birdwood, 319).

3. "I was credibly informed that Mr. Peacock, contrary to the trust reposed in him, had carried letters of Sir *Henry's* from Asab [Bey] to Mr. Fowler at Priaman or Tiku, given a copy of our cargazone [cargo] to the knight and acquainted him continually what in counsel was concluded upon by us, to the better enabling of Sir *Henry* to effect what he so often had vowed against the benefit of this Eighth Voyage. . . . I reproved him before them all [the voyage's other merchants]. They all much blamed him, so as he seemed to be sorry" (S, f109–109v, 23 November 1612).

4. On the voyage of the *James*, see Purchas, 4:77–88; and Chapter 7.

5. Barbour, *Journals*, 145, 268n37.

6. Cf. Downton: "No further trade can be here had . . . without the letter of allowance from the King of Achin, their sovereign lord, which will not be obtained without great charge in presents or otherwise" (D, f94, 11 November).

7. On David Middleton's voyage, see Purchas, 3:90–115.

8. This report was erroneous. The *James* reached Bantam before its (initial) fleet mates in the Tenth Voyage. To clarify the numbering: the Ninth Voyage involved one ship, the *James*, which separated from three others outbound on the Tenth—the *Dragon*, *Hosiander*, and *Solomon* (Birdwood, xiv). On the Tenth Voyage, see Foster, *Best*.

9. See Moreland, *Floris*.

10. On Castleton's voyage, see Purchas, 3:343–54.

11. A boat from the Tenth Voyage sank "upon the bar of Pasaman," reported Thomas Best in October 1613, "the country people very kind unto them, and took great pains to help them, both to save their boat and goods" (Foster, *Best*, 68).

12. *Careful of*: attentive to.

13. Jourdain puts the figure at thirty bahars (J, 236). *Bahar*: widely used in the Indian Ocean, a weight of about 400 pounds. Greene reports that in the Sumatran city of Andripura, "they measure . . . 200 Cattees for a Bahar, which doth weigh in . . . our English weight 366 lbs" (G, f19, 14 November).

14. The stone archways supporting London Bridge corralled the Thames into a phalanx of tidal rapids. "'Shooting the bridge' was dangerous, even for experienced watermen, and impossible at low tide" (Chalfant, 119).

15. *Chain pumps*: "These . . . are soonest mended if anything fail, having spare esses, if any chance to give way: these have a chain full of bars and a wheel, which makes it deliver so much" water upward and overboard in buckets (Manwayring, 79).

16. Barbour, *Journals*, 188.

17. *Keelson*, internal keel (J, 238n), "the lowest piece of timber within the ship's hold" (Manwayring, 57).

18. Sighting a shoal "right in the fairway" as they sailed out, Robert Bonner of the Tenth Voyage wrote on 7 August 1613, "We sent our boat to it, and found it but two fathom and a half, being a rock of two cables length long. This is the unlucky rock whereon the princely *Trade* received her destruction, as we understand by those people" of Tiku (Foster, *Best*, 205).

19. The "buzzard," a lesser hawk unfit for falconry, gave its name to an ineducable, obstinate, or blundering person (J, 240n).

CHAPTER 7

1. Farrington, *Trading*, 34; cf. Moreland, xxiii.

2. Ricklefs, 44; Foster, *Middleton*, 131.

3. On its early years, see Neill, 285–310; Barbour, "Multinational"; and Barbour, "Nation."

4. *LR*, 1:260, 20 June 1613; *Stew*: Jacobean slang for a house or district of prostitution.

5. Foster, *Middleton*, xxxvii–viii; Scott's text, 81–176; Neill, 300, 478n6.

6. In Foster, *Middleton*, 1–64.

7. On the settlement, see Factory Records: Java, 55; on the Dutch and others there, Ricklefs.

8. On the East India Company as a political body active both within and beyond the Jacobean state, see Stern, *Company-State*.

9. On the incident, see E. Scott, 112–24; Neill, 290–98; and Greenblatt, 11–15.

10. General Best reported, "At Bantam, the king hath expected to five and three-quarters per cent or more" in customs (*Court Book*, B/5, 123, 17 June 1614).

11. *Pecul*: "the Malay equivalent of the Chinese weight of 100 catties" (*LR*, 1:338). Saris puts the figure at 132 English pounds (S, f106).

12. On return to London, Spalding was compelled to answer for the charges of "enriching himself by indirect courses" as described here, and for leaving Bantam when "exceedingly pressed" by Middleton and Saris to remain, "whereas his stay might have been an especial means of saving a great part of the *Trades Increase*'s goods that were afterwards embezzled and stolen away" (*Court Book*, B/5, 194, 9 August 1614). He managed to exonerate himself, in part by dedicating his primer for those "who shall happily hereafter undertake a voyage to the East-Indies" (title page) to Governor Smythe. Adapted from a Dutch source, Spalding's *Dialogues* (1614) was the first Malay book printed in England (Farrington, *Trading*, 37).

13. On temperance as an imperial virtue, see Neill, 332–34. Purchas describes navigation as a "school of sobriety and temperance," for the sea "holds [men] in good temper, and is a correction house of the most dissolute; but the land makes them forget the sea and temperance altogether" (qtd. in Neill, 332).

14. On Ward see Foster, *Best*, 12n. Ward was the vessel's chief merchant.

15. *Admired*: was astonished by.

16. The commission is not extant (Moreland, 111n).

17. Davis had sailed as master with Sir Henry's brother David on the Third and Fifth Voyages, both performed with exemplary dispatch. On the Ninth Voyage, see Davis in Purchas, 4:77–88.

18. On dysfunctions aboard the *James*, "not a 'happy ship,'" see Moreland, 116; on disputes between Davis and Marlowe and the latter's cantankerous and inebriate ways, *LR* 2:64,

89, 312. Saris reported pervasive weakness of crewmen, nine deaths, and "great dissentions between the master, captain, and merchants" on the *James* during its four weeks of aborted departure for Coromandel (S, f111, 11 December 1612).

19. Cocks died eleven days later, his burial solemnized with fifteen rounds from the ships of the fleet (S, f109v, 26 November 1612).

20. On promotions and raises abroad, see Chapter 2, "The Shareholders Assert Their Authority."

21. Jones was likely Thomas Jones, a factor on the *James*; see Foster, *Jourdain*, 241n, and *LR*, 2:122.

22. *To grave*: "Graving a ship is bringing her to lie dry aground, and then to burn off the old filth and stuff . . . and so to lay on new" (Manwayring, 46).

23. Manwayring, 20–21.

24. *LR*, 1:289, 11 September 1613.

25. In Femell's commission, Frayne was named second in succession after Fowler, who died in Tiku (Birdwood, 326). It was he who repaid Camden the advance of 2,000 rials from the Eighth Voyage (S, f109v, 25 November 1612). Jourdain inherited Frayne's charge, giving "Sir Henry my word to stay after his [Frayne's] death with him as long as he stayed in the country" (J, 241).

26. Downton wanted to solemnize their parting with more rounds: "I gave him five shot, having no more pieces out nor ports uncaulked" (*LR*, 1:242).

27. "I fitted Capt. Hawkins and his family in a part of a house I had hired for the Eighth Voyage, he being much depressed and finding at sea but little courtesy" (S, f112, 23 December 1612).

28. On Towerson's return and death, see Foster, *Travels*, 69–70; on Mariam Khān, see Chapter 4, note 9.

29. Downton makes no mention of Thornton's death; Jourdain reports that Middleton delivered the news in Bantam on the evening of 9 February, after seeing off the *Peppercorn* (J, 242).

30. "Mr. Jourdain, in Captain Sharpeigh's absence," wrote Downton homeward bound, "is his [Middleton's] greatest help" (*LR*, 1:259–60).

31. Downton notes that Middleton sent home "all advice, by journal, invoice and letters, that then he might" in the *Solomon*, "which by haste for want of writers he could not again perform by me" (*LR*, 1:291), when the *Peppercorn* sailed days later.

32. I accept Foster's transcription of 200 (J, 302n) over Moreland's 100. The figure "2" is easily mistaken for "1" in Jacobean hand.

33. Returning from Japan, on 30 December 1613 Saris wrote flatly, "We had sight of the *Darling*, plying for Coromandel. . . . By them we first understood of the death of Sir Henry Middleton, and loss of the *Trades Increase*, etc." (Satow, 191).

34. Factory Records: Java 1595–1827, BL IOR, G/21.

CHAPTER 8

1. On Carmichael, see Foster, *Best*, xl.

2. Mun, *Discourse* (1621); Mun, *Treasure* (1664). Forman (qtd. phrase, 1) aptly links Mun's economic theories to a dramatic genre increasingly popular in the age of joint-stock investment, tragicomedy, whose plots translate else-tragic losses into eventual redemption.

3. On seventeenth-debates debates over whether monopolies serve public or private interests, see Stern on the "Great Case of Monopolies," *East India Company v. Thomas Sandys* (1682–84), in *Company-State*, 47–58.

4. See Chaudhuri, 209 (table 8) for a chart of East India Company profits through 1642.

5. *Doubt*: concern, suspicion.

6. Neill, 299–300. On Burre, see McKerrow, 56.

7. Jackson, 355; qtd. in Ogborn, 107.

8. See Ogborn's overview of the controversy, 107–20; and Wright, *Culture*, 453–57.

9. Gentleman, title page. *Buss*: a vessel of two to three masts; *Pink*: originally a sailing vessel of small size used for coasting and fishing; *Line-boat*: evidently a boat used for line-fishing (uncertain).

10. On long-standing concerns over the depopulation of countryside that multiplied legions of the urban poor, see McCormick.

11. A Levant Company complaint to the Privy Council on 2 April 1615 supports Kayll's allegations about the "decay" of trade there, "by reason of the late repair of the Hollanders to those parts, who through their cheap sailing in great ships, do not only gain the freights wherein the English shipping were heretofore employed, but also engross the commodities of those parts, and bring them in their own shipping into his Majesty's dominions, to the great damage and hindrance of the said Company" (*Acts of Privy Council*, 98).

12. On Dutch influence at court, see Neill, 313–30; on the negotiations, see Ogborn, 110–16, 120–29.

13. Cf. Stern and Wennerlind, who pose "two central propositions: first, that mercantilist projects served to augment the power and wealth of a variety of political communities, not merely the monarchy and the nation-state; and second, that the statist programs articulated by many early modern writers, so often taken as emblematic of mercantilism, were deeply circumscribed in practice by the limited ambition, authority, and power of that state" (12).

14. See Klein, *Changes*. Cf. historian Christopher R. Browning: "The looming effects of human-caused climate change . . . will be inescapable. Desertification of continental interiors, flooding of populous coastal areas, and increased frequency and intensity of extreme weather events, with concomitant shortages of fresh water and food, will set in motion both population flight and conflicts over scarce resources that dwarf the current fate of Central Africa and Syria" (17).

15. On the East India Company's anxieties about women, see Barbour, "Desdemona"; Robertson; and Sen, "Sailing."

16. See Fury, 140, 159.

17. See 2 Samuel 14–17. "And he said, be it far from me, O Lord, that I should do this: is not this the blood of the men that went in jeopardy of their lives? therefore he would not drink it" (2 Samuel 17, KJV).

18. Withington, 141; see also 230.

19. A believer in "the mystery of the King's power," James advised in *Basilikon Doron*, "Encroach not upon the prerogative of the Crown. . . . If there fall out a question that concerns my prerogative or mystery of state, deal not with it" (ed. McIlwain, 333, 332).

20. Purchas, *Pilgrimage*, 484.

21. Qtd. from *Court Minutes* (27 February 1622) in Foster, *Roe*, lxii (emphasis added).

22. Ogborn, 111. Also a member of the Levant, Virginia, Muscovy, Merchant Adventurers, French, and Northwest Passage companies, Maurice Abbot went on to become deputy governor and, in 1624, governor of the East India Company for many years. As a member of

Parliament, he was a vocal advocate of the eastern trade. He was knighted on the accession of Charles I and served as lord mayor of London in 1638 (Birdwood, 164n; Thrush, accessed 25 November 2018).

23. *Court Book*, B/5, 400, 29 March 1615; Sainsbury, 398 (#947); Ogborn, 114–15.

24. *Acts of Privy Council*, 108, 99.

25. Kelsey, accessed 25 November 2018; Schoenbaum, 181, 300.

26. Digges, *Circumference*, cited in Ogborn, 116; on Digges, see also Withington, 227–31.

27. See Strong, 71–86; and Coryat, 1:31–32.

28. Barbour, *Orientalism*, 117.

29. Digges, *Defence*, title page. Ogborn errs in stating that Digges placed "his own name prominently on the title page" (116).

30. Withington mistakenly identifies Kayll's pamphlet by Digges's variant title, *The Increase of Trade* (228).

31. On texts that obsolesce themselves, see Fish.

32. On Jacobean Romanism, see, e.g., Goldberg, 117–41; Barbour, *Orientalism*, 70–80.

33. Digges, 22, a reassembled paraphrase offered as a quotation; cf. *Increase*, 15, 19.

34. See Foster, *Best*; and Foster, *Downton*. The emperor wrote, "In the roadstead of the port of Surat a fight took place between the English, who had taken shelter there, and the Viceroy. Most of his ships were burnt by the English fire" (Beveridge, 1:274).

35. Covert may not be a consistently credible witness, yet Jourdain likewise declares Grove's "villainy . . . both at sea and aland, . . . shameful" (J, 134–40).

36. See E. N. Wood, *Origin*.

37. Appleby, 2; Fury, 172.

38. *Rumney-Marsh*: Romney Marsh, a wetland area in Kent and East Sussex that was malarial in the early modern period.

39. *Purgamenta urbium*: refuse of the city. Raleigh cites the phrase to describe feckless common soldiers (*Cabinet-Council*, 61). Compare Falstaff's "food for powder, food for powder. They'll fill a pit as well as better. Tush, man, mortal men, mortal men" (*1 Henry IV*, 4.2.64–66).

40. *Tyburn*: Middlesex gallows site. *Wapping*: site near the Tower of London where pirates were executed.

41. Mun, *Discourse*, 35–36, qtd. in McCormick, 29. Where Downton's June 1613 letter observed that East Indian voyages foster insubordination, Mun maintained to the contrary that the East India Company made sound mariners of the poor: "Thus is the kingdom purged of desperate and unruly people, who being kept in awe by the good discipline at sea, do often change their former course of life" (Mun, *Discourse*, 36–37).

42. *Hot drinks*: those with high alcohol content, like *raki*.

43. Birdwood, 167. On cultural materialism, see, e.g., Williams, whose call for the study of "Language in history: that full field" informs my interest in the writing practices of the East India Company (*Writing*, 189).

44. See Spang; Fischer; and Bowles.

BIBLIOGRAPHY

Acts of the Privy Council of England, 1615–16. London: HMSO, 1925.

Akhimie, Patricia, and Bernadette Andrea, eds. *Travel and Travail: Early Modern Women, English Drama, and the Wider World*. Lincoln: University of Nebraska Press, 2019.

Andrea, Bernadette, and Linda McJannet, eds. *Early Modern England and Islamic Worlds*. New York: Palgrave Macmillan, 2011.

Andrews, Kenneth. *Elizabethan Privateering: English Privateering During the Spanish War 1585–1603*. Cambridge: Cambridge University Press, 1964.

———. "Sir Robert Cecil and Mediterranean Plunder." *English Historical Review* 87: 344 (1972), 513–32.

Annis, P. G. W., ed. *Ingrid and Other Studies: Maritime Monographs and Reports No. 36*. Greenwich: National Maritime Museum, 1978.

Appleby, John H. "Woodall, John." In *Oxford Dictionary of National Biography*.

Articles of Peace, Entercourse, and Commerce. London: Robert Barker, 1605.

Barbour, Philip L., ed. *The Complete Works of Captain John Smith (1580–1631)*. 3 vols. Chapel Hill: University of North Carolina Press, 1986.

Barbour, Richmond. *Before Orientalism: London's Theatre of the East, 1576–1626*. Cambridge: Cambridge University Press, 2003.

———. "Command Performances: Early English Traders in Arabia Felix." In Schülting, Müller, and Hertel, 43–66.

———. "Corporate Praxis and the Legacy of Privateering: The Jacobean East India Company." *Clio* 41: 1 (Fall 2011), 1–29.

———. "Desdemona and Mrs. Keeling." In Akhimie and Andrea, 19–40.

———. "'The *English* Nation at *Bantam*': Corporate Process in the East India Company's First Factory." *Genre* 48: 2 (July 2015), 159–92.

———. "A Multinational Corporation: Foreign Labor in the London East India Company." In Singh, 129–48.

———. "Power and Distant Display: Early English 'Ambassadors' in Moghul India." *Huntington Library Quarterly* 61: 3–4 (2000), 343–68.

———. *The Third Voyage Journals: Writing and Performance in the London East India Company, 1607–10*. New York: Palgrave Macmillan, 2009.

Barbour, Richmond, and Bernhard Klein. "Drama at Sea: A New Look at Shakespeare on the *Dragon*, 1607–08." In Jowitt and McInnes, 150–68.

Bawlf, Samuel. *The Secret Voyage of Sir Francis Drake 1577–1580*. London: Penguin, 2003.

Beeching, Jack, ed. *Voyages and Discoveries*, by Richard Hakluyt. London: Penguin, 1972.

Bent, J. Theodore, ed. *Early Voyages and Travels in the Levant*. London: Hakluyt Society, 1893.

Bergeron, David M., ed. *The Manner of his Lordship's Entertainment* and *The Triumphs of Truth*. In Taylor and Lavagnino, 959–76.

Bernhard, Virginia. *A Tale of Two Colonies: What Really Happened in Virginia and Bermuda?* Columbia: University of Missouri Press, 2011.

Beveridge, Henry, ed. *The Tuzuk-I-Jahāngīrī, or Memoirs of Jahāngīr*. Translated by Alexander Rogers. 2 vols. 2nd ed. Delhi: Munshiram Manoharlal, 1968.

Bevington, David, and others, eds. *The Cambridge Edition of the Works of Ben Jonson*. 7 vols. Cambridge: Cambridge University Press, 2012.

Birdwood, George, ed. *The Register of Letters &c. of the Governour and Merchants of London trading into the East Indies 1600–1619*. London: Quaritch, 1893.

Bowles, Samuel. *The Moral Economy: Why Good Incentives Are No Substitute for Good Citizens*. New Haven, CT: Yale University Press, 2016.

Bradshaw, Samuel. "The unhappie Voyage of the Vice-Admirall, the Union." In Purchas, 3:74–78.

Browning, Christopher R. "The Suffocation of Democracy." *New York Review of Books* 65: 16 (25 October 2018), 14–17.

Bruce, John. *Annals of the Honorable East-India Company*. Vol. 1. London: Cox, Son, and Baylis for East India Company, 1810.

Burnell, Arthur Coke, ed. *The Voyage of John Huyghen van Linschoten to the East Indies*. 2 vols. London: Hakluyt Society, 1885.

Camden, William. *Britain*. Translated by Philemon Holland. London: F. Collins for A. Swalle, 1610.

Campbell, Thomas P. *Henry VIII and the Art of Majesty: Tapestries at the Tudor Court*. New Haven, CT: Yale University Press, 2007.

Chalfant, Fran C. *Ben Jonson's London: A Jacobean Placename Dictionary*. Athens: University of Georgia Press, 1978.

Chaudhuri, K. N. *The English East India Company: The Study of an Early Joint-Stock Company 1600–1640*. New York: Kelley, 1965.

Chew, Samuel. *The Crescent and the Rose*. Oxford: Oxford University Press, 1935; repr. New York: Octagon, 1965.

Christensen, Ann C. *Separation Scenes: Domestic Drama in Early Modern England*. Lincoln: University of Nebraska Press, 2017.

Colley, Linda. *Captives: Britain, Empire and the World 1600–1850*. London: Pimlico, 2003.

Coryat, Thomas. *Coryat's Crudities*. 2 vols. Glasgow: MacLehose and Sons, 1905.

Court Book of the East India Company, 31 December 1606–26 January 1610. BL IOR B/3.

Court Book of the East India Company, December 1613–10 November 1615. BL IOR B/5.

Coverte, Robert. *A True and Almost Incredible Report*. London: Hall for Archer and Redmer, 1612.

Danvers, Charles, and William Foster, eds. *Letters Received by the East India Company from Its Servants in the East*. 6 vols. London: Sampson Low, 1896–1902; repr. Amsterdam: N. Israel, 1968. Cited as *LR* in the text.

Darwin, John. *Unfinished Empire: The Global Expansion of Britain*. New York: Bloomsbury, 2012.

Digges, Dudley. *Of the Circumference of the Earth: Or, A Treatise of the North-East Passage*. London, 1612.

———. *The Defence of Trade*. London: Stansby for Barnes, 1615.

Downton, Nicholas. "Diary of January 1610." BL Egerton MS 2100, ff35–36.

———. "Journal 1, 19 April 1610–19 November 1613." Cited as "D" in the text. BL IOR L/MAR/A/11.

———. "Journal 2, 23 July 1610–30 September 1613." BL Cotton MS Otho E 8, ff244–57.

East India Company Factory Records c1595–1858. BL IOR G/17.

East India Company Factory Records: Java, 1595–1827. BL IOR G/21.

Fagles, Robert, trans. *Virgil: The Aeneid.* London: Penguin, 2006.

Farrington, Anthony. *A Catalogue of East India Company Ships' Journals and Logs.* London: British Library, 1999.

———. *Trading Places: The East India Company and Asia 1600–1834.* London: British Library, 2002.

Fischer, Liliann, ed. *Rethinking Economics: An Introduction to Pluralist Economics.* New York: Routledge, 2018.

Fish, Stanley E. *Self-Consuming Artifacts: The Experience of Seventeenth Century Literature.* Berkeley: University of California Press, 1972.

Forman, Valerie. *Tragicomic Redemptions: Global Economics and the Early Modern English Stage.* Philadelphia: University of Pennsylvania Press, 2008.

Foster, William, ed. *Early Travels in India 1583–1619.* Oxford: Oxford University Press, 1921.

———, ed. *The Embassy of Sir Thomas Roe to India 1615–19.* London: Hakluyt Society, 1899; repr. Kraus: Nendeln/Liechtenstein, 1967. Rev. ed. London: Oxford University Press, 1926.

———. *John Company.* London: John Lane, 1926.

———, ed. *The Journal of John Jourdain, 1608–1617.* Cambridge: Hakluyt Society, 1905. Cited as "J" in the text.

———, ed. *The Voyage of Nicholas Downton to the East Indies 1614–15.* London: Hakluyt Society, 1939.

———, ed. *The Voyage of Sir Henry Middleton to the Moluccas, 1604–1606.* London: Hakluyt Society, 1943.

———, ed. *The Voyage of Thomas Best to the East Indies, 1612–1614.* London: Hakluyt Society, 1934.

———, ed. *The Voyages of Sir James Lancaster to Brazil and the East Indies 1591–1603.* London: Hakluyt Society, 1940.

Furber, Holden. *Rival Empires of Trade in the Orient, 1600–1800.* Minneapolis: University of Minnesota Press, 1976.

Fury, Cheryl. *Tides in the Affairs of Men: The Social History of Elizabethan Seamen, 1580–1603.* Westport, CT: Greenwood Press, 2002.

Gentleman, Tobias. *England's Way to Win Wealth.* London: Nathaniel Butter, 1614.

Gillies, John, and Virginia Mason Vaughan, eds. *Playing the Globe: Genre and Geography in English Renaissance Drama.* Madison, WI: Fairleigh Dickinson University Press, 1998.

Goldberg, Jonathan. *James I and the Politics of Literature: Jonson, Shakespeare, Donne, and Their Contemporaries.* Baltimore: Johns Hopkins University Press, 1983.

Goodwin, Peter. *The Construction and Fitting of the English Man of War 1650–1850.* London: Naval Institute Press, 1987.

Greenblatt, Stephen. *Learning to Curse: Essays in Early Modern Culture.* London: Routledge, 1990.

Greene, Benjamin. "Journal, 15 November 1610 to 22 December 1612." Cited as "G" in the text. BL IOR L/MAR/A/12.

Hakluyt, Richard. *The Principal Navigations, Voyages, Traffics and Discoveries of the English Nation.* 3 vols. London: Bishop, Newberie and Barker, 1598–1600.

Harrison, Stephen. *The Archs of Triumph Erected in Honor of the High and Mighty Prince James the First of That Name, King, of England and the Sixt of Scotland.* London: John Windet, 1604.

Hewitt, Chad L., Marnie L. Campbell, and Britta Schaffelke. "Introductions of Seaweeds: Accidental Transfer Pathways and Mechanisms." In Johnson, *Seaweed Invasions,* 326–37.

Hinton, R. W. K. *The Eastland Trade and the Common Weal in the Seventeenth Century.* Cambridge: Cambridge University Press, 1959; repr. Hamden: Archon, 1975.

Huntingford, G. B. W., trans. and ed. *The Periplus of the Erythraean Sea.* London: Hakluyt Society, 1980.

Innes, A. D. *The Maritime and Colonial Expansion of England Under the Stuarts.* London: Sampson Low, 1932.

Jackson, William A., ed. *Records of the Stationers' Company, 1602–1640.* London: Bibliographical Society, 1957.

Jardine, Lisa, and Jerry Brotton. *Global Interests: Renaissance Art Between East and West.* Ithaca: Cornell University Press, 2000.

Jenner, Mark S. R. "Myddelton, Sir Hugh." In *Oxford Dictionary of National Biography.* Accessed 17 August 2015. http://www.oxforddnb.com.ezproxy.proxy.library.oregonstate .edu/vi ew/article/19 683.

Johnson, Craig, ed., *Seaweed Invasions: A Synthesis of Ecological, Economic and Legal Imperatives.* Berlin: Walter de Gruyter, 2007.

Jourdain, John. "Journal, 25 March 1608–19 June 1617." BL Sloane Ms 868.

"Journal kept on the *Peppercorn,* 1 April 1610–29 January 1611." BL IOR L/MAR/A/9.

Jowitt, Claire, and David McInnes, eds. *Travel and Drama in Early Modern England: The Journeying Play.* Cambridge: Cambridge University Press, 2018.

Kantorowicz, Ernst H. *The King's Two Bodies: A Study in Mediaeval Political Theology.* Princeton, NJ: Princeton University Press, 1957.

[Kayll, John]. *The Trades Increase.* London: Okes for Burre, 1615.

Keay, John. *The Spice Route: A History.* Berkeley: University of California Press, 2006.

Kelsey, Sean. "Digges, Sir Dudley." In *Oxford Dictionary of National Biography.*

Klein, Naomi. *This Changes Everything: Capitalism vs. the Climate.* New York: Simon and Schuster, 2014.

———. *The Shock Doctrine: The Rise of Disaster Capitalism.* New York: Picador, 2007.

Knolles, Richard. *The Generall Historie of the Turkes.* London: Adam Islip, 1603.

Knowles, James. "Cecil's Shopping Center." *Times Literary Supplement,* no. 4897 (7 February 1997), 14–15.

———, ed. *The Entertainment at Britain's Burse.* In Bevington, 3:357–68.

Larkin, James F., and Paul L. Hughes, eds. *Stuart Royal Proclamations.* Vol. 1, *Royal Proclamations of King James I.* Oxford: Clarendon Press, 1973.

The Last East-Indian Voyage. London: T. P. for Walter Burre, 1606.

Lavery, Brian. *The Ship of the Line.* Vol. 1, *The Development of the Battlefleet 1650–1850.* London: Naval Institute Press, 1983.

Lawson, Philip. *The East India Company: A History.* London: Longman, 1993.

Love, Thomas. "Journal kept on the *Trades Increase* and *Peppercorn,* 4 April 1610–4 December 1611." BL IOR L/MAR/A/10.

MacLean, Gerald. *Looking East: English Writing and the Ottoman Empire Before 1800.* New York: Palgrave Macmillan, 2007.

MacClure, Norman Egbert, ed. *The Letters of John Chamberlain.* 2 vols. Philadelphia: American Philosophical Society, 1939.

Makepeace, Margaret. "Sir Henry Middleton." In *Oxford Dictionary of National Biography.*

Malieckal, Bindu. "Mariam Khan and the Legacy of Mughal Women in Early Modern Literature of India." In Andrea and McJannet, 97–122.

Malynes, Gerard. *A Treatise of the Canker of Englands Commonwealth.* London: Field for Johnes, 1601.

Manwayring [Manwaring], Henry. *The Seaman's Dictionary.* London: Bellamy, 1644; repr. Menston: Scholar Press, 1972.

Markham, Clements R., ed. *The Hawkins' Voyages During the Reigns of Henry VIII, Queen Elizabeth, and James I.* London: Hakluyt Society, 1878.

———, ed. *The Voyages of Sir James Lancaster, Kt., to the East Indies.* London: Hakluyt Society, 1878.

Marlowe, Christopher. *Tamburlaine Parts One and Two.* 2nd ed. Edited by Anthony B. Dawson. London: A&C Black, 1997.

McCormick, Ted. "Population: Modes of Seventeenth Century Demographic Thought." In Stern and Wennerlind, 25–45.

McGowan, A. P. "William Burrell (c.1570–1630) a Forgotten Stuart Shipwright." In Annis, *Ingrid and Other Studies,* 91–101.

McIlwain, Charles H., ed. *The Political Works of James I.* Cambridge, MA: Harvard University Press, 1918.

McKerrow, R. B., ed. *A Dictionary of Printers and Booksellers in England, Scotland and Ireland, and of Foreign Printers of English Books 1557–1640.* London: Bibliographical Society, 1910; repr. Mansfield Centre, CT: Martino, 2005.

Miller, Anthony. "Domains of Victory: Staging and Contesting the Roman Triumph in Renaissance England." In Gillies and Vaughan, 260–87.

Misselden, Edward. *Free Trade, or the Means to Make Trade Flourish.* London: Legatt for Waterson, 1622.

Moreland, W. H., ed. *Peter Floris His Voyage to the East Indies in the "Globe" 1611–1615.* London: Hakluyt Society, 1934.

Morgan, Basil. "Smythe, Sir Thomas (c. 1558–1625)." In *Oxford Dictionary of National Biography.*

Mun, Thomas. *A Discourse of Trade, from England unto the East Indies.* London: Okes for Pyper, 1621.

———. *England's Treasure by Foreign Trade.* London: Clark, 1664.

Neill, Michael. *Putting History to the Question: Power, Politics, and Society in English Renaissance Drama.* New York: Columbia University Press, 2000.

Niebuhr, Reinhold. *Moral Man and Immoral Society: A Study in Ethics and Politics.* New York: Scribners, 1932, 1960.

Ogborn, Miles. *Indian Ink: Script and Print in the Making of the English East India Company.* Chicago: University of Chicago Press, 2007.

Olson, Rebecca. *Arras Hanging: The Textile That Determined Early Modern Literature and Drama.* Newark: University of Delaware Press, 2013.

Oxford Dictionary of National Biography. Oxford: Oxford University Press, 2004; online ed., 2008.

Parry, J. H. *The Age of Reconnaissance: Discovery, Exploration and Settlement 1450 to 1650*. Berkeley: University of California Press, 1963.

Pennington, L. E., ed. *The Purchas Handbook: Studies in the Life, Times and Writings of Samuel Purchas 1577–1626*. 2 vols. London: Hakluyt Society, 1997.

Perrin, W. G., ed. *The Autobiography of Phineas Pett*. London: Navy Records Society, 1918.

———, ed. *Boteler's Dialogues*. London: Navy Records Society, 1929.

Pilling, David. *The Growth Delusion: Wealth, Poverty, and the Well-Being of Nations*. New York: Tim Duggan, 2018.

Pincus, Stephen. "Rethinking Mercantilism: Political Economy, the British Empire, and the Atlantic World in the Seventeenth and Eighteenth Centuries." *William and Mary Quarterly* 69: 1 (January 2012), 3–34.

Prockter, Adrian, and Robert Taylor, eds. *The A to Z of Elizabethan London*. Lympne Castle, Kent: Harry Margary; London: Guildhall Library, 1979.

Purchas, Samuel, ed. *Hakluytus Posthumus, or, Purchas His Pilgrimes*. 20 vols. Glasgow: MacLehose, 1905–7. Cited as "P" in the text.

———. *Purchas His Pilgrimage*. 4th ed. London: William Stansby, 1626.

Rabb, Theodore K. *Enterprise and Empire: Merchant and Gentry Investment in the Expansion of England, 1575–1630*. Cambridge, MA: Harvard University Press, 1967.

Raleigh, Walter. *The Cabinet-Council containing the Chief Arts of Empire and Mysteries of State*. London: Newcomb for Johnson, 1658. Pub. John Milton.

———. *Excellent Observations and Notes, Concerning the Royall Navy and Sea-Service*. In Raleigh, *Judicious and Select Essayes and Observations*. London, 1650.

Ricklefs, M. C. *A History of Modern Indonesia c. 1300 to the Present*. Bloomington: Indiana University Press, 1981.

Robertson, Karen. "A Stranger Bride: Mariam Khan and the East India Company." In Akhimie and Andrea, 41–63.

Rodger, N. A. M. *The Safeguard of the Sea: A Naval History of Britain 660–1649*. New York: W. W. Norton, 1997.

———. *The Wooden World. An Anatomy of the Georgian Navy*. New York: W. W. Norton, 1996.

Sainsbury, W. Noel, ed. *Calendar of State Papers, Colonial Series, East Indies, China and Japan, 1513–1616*. London: Her Majesty's Stationery Office, 1862; repr. Vaduz: Draus, 1964.

Saris, John. "Journal of Captain John Saris in the *Clove*," 3 April 1611–17 November 1613. Cited as "S" in the text. BL IOR L/MAR/A/14.

Satow, Ernest, ed. *The Voyage of Captain John Saris to Japan, 1613*. London: Hakluyt Society, 1900; repr. Nendeln/Liechtenstein: Kraus, 1967.

Schoenbaum, S. *William Shakespeare: A Compact Documentary Life*. Rev. ed. New York: Oxford University Press, 1987.

Schoonees, Pieter. *Inscriptions on Padrões, Postal Stones, Tombstones and Beacons*. Cape Town: South African Cultural History Museum, 1991.

Schülting, Sabine, Sabine Lucia Müller, and Ralf Hertel, eds. *Early Modern Encounters and the Islamic East: Performing Cultures*. Farnham, Surrey: Ashgate, 2012.

Scott, Edmund. *An Exact Discourse of the Subtilties, Fashions, Policies, Religions, and Ceremonies of the East Indians*. London: Burre, 1606. In Foster, *Middleton*, 81–176.

Scott, William Robert. *The Constitution and Finance of the English, Scottish, and Irish Joint Stock Companies to 1720*. Cambridge: Cambridge University Press, 1912.

Sen, Amrita. "Sailing to India: Women, Travel, and Crisis in the Early Seventeenth Century." In Akhimie and Andrea, 64–80.

———. "Traveling Companions: Women, Trade, and the Early East India Company." *Genre* 48: 2 (July 2015), 193–214.

Shakespeare, William. *The Complete Works*. Edited by Stephen Orgel and A. R. Braunmuller. 2nd ed. New York: Penguin, 2002.

Singh, Jyotsna, ed. *A Companion to the Global Renaissance: English Literature and Culture in the Era of Expansion*. Oxford: Wiley Blackwell, 2009.

Shepherd, Francis. *London: A History*. Oxford: Oxford University Press, 1998.

Skilliter, S. A. *William Harborne and the Trade with Turkey 1578–1582*. Oxford: Oxford University Press for British Academy, 1977.

Smith, John. *A Sea-Grammar*. London: Haviland, 1627; repr. Amsterdam: Da Capo, 1968.

Spalding, Augustine. *Dialogues in the English and Malayan Languages*. London: Kingston for Welby, 1614.

Spang, Rebecca L. "Want a Reformation? Rethinking the Discipline of Economics." *Times Literary Supplement*, no. 5993 (9 February 2018), 12–13.

Spence, Richard T. *The Privateering Earl*. Phoenix Mill: Sutton, 1995.

Stern, Philip J. *The Company-State: Corporate Sovereignty and the Early Modern Foundations of the British Empire in India*. Oxford: Oxford University Press, 2011.

Stern, Philip J., and Carl Wennerlind, eds. *Mercantilism Reimagined: Political Economy in Early Modern Britain and Its Empire*. Oxford: Oxford University Press, 2014.

Stevens, Henry, ed. *The Dawn of British Trade to the East Indies as Recorded in the Court Minutes of the East India Company 1599–1603*. New York: Burt Franklin, 1970; orig. pub. 1886.

Stone, Lawrence. *Family and Fortune: Studies in Aristocratic Finance in the Sixteenth and Seventeenth Centuries*. Oxford: Clarendon Press, 1973.

Stookey, Robert W. *Yemen: The Politics of the Yemen Arab Republic*. Boulder, CO: Westview Press, 1978.

Strachan, Michael, and Boies Penrose, eds. *The East India Company Journals of Captain William Keeling and Master Thomas Bonner, 1615–1617*. Minneapolis: University of Minnesota Press, 1971.

Strachey, William. "A True Repertory of the Wreck and Redemption of Sir Thomas Gates, Knight." In Wright, *Voyage*, 1–101.

Stromberg, Joseph. "Starving Settlers in Jamestown Colony Resorted to Cannibalism." *Smithsonian*, 30 April 2013. http://www.smithsonianmag.com/history-archaeology/Starving -Settle rs-in-Jamesto wn-Colony-Resorted-to-Eating-A-Child-205472161.html.

Strong, Roy. *Henry, Prince of Wales and England's Lost Renaissance*. London: Thames and Hudson, 1986.

Taylor, Gary, and John Lavagnino, eds. *Thomas Middleton: The Collected Works*. Oxford: Clarendon Press, 2007.

Thrush, Andrew. "Abbot, Sir Maurice." In *Oxford Dictionary of National Biography*.

Turner, Henry S. *The Corporate Commonwealth: Pluralism and Political Fictions in England, 1516–1651*. Chicago: University of Chicago Press, 2016.

———. "Corporations: Humanism and Elizabethan Political Economy." In Stern and Wennerlind, 153–76.

Van Linschoten, John Huighen. *John Huighen Van Linschoten, His Discours of Voyages unto the Easte and Weste Indies*. London: John Wolfe, 1598.

Wernham, R. B. *The Making of Elizabethan Foreign Policy, 1558–1603.* Berkeley: University of California Press, 1980.

Williams, Raymond. *Marxism and Literature.* Toronto: Oxford University Press, 1977.

———. *Problems in Materialism and Culture: Selected Essays.* London: Verso, 1997.

———. *Writing in Society.* London: Verso, 1983.

Williamson, James A., ed. *The Observations of Sir Richard Hawkins.* London: Argonaut, 1933; repr. New York: Da Capo, 1970; orig. pub. London: John Haggard, 1622.

Withington, Phil. *Society in Early Modern England: The Vernacular Origins of Some Powerful Ideas.* Cambridge: Polity, 2010.

Wood, Alfred C. *A History of the Levant Company.* New York: Barnes and Noble, 1935.

Wood, Ellen Meiksins. *The Origin of Capitalism.* New York: Monthly Review Press, 1999.

Woodall, John. *The Surgeon's Mate.* London, 1617.

Woodman, Richard. *The History of the Ship.* 2nd ed. London: Lyons Press, 2002.

Wright, Louis B., ed. *A Voyage to Virginia in 1609: Two Narratives; Strachey's "True Repertory" and Jourdain's "Discovery of the Bermudas."* Charlottesville: University Press of Virginia, 1964.

———. *Middle Class Culture in Elizabethan England.* Chapel Hill: University of North Carolina Press, 1935.

———. *Religion and Empire: The Alliance Between Piety and Commerce in English Expansion, 1558–1625.* New York: Octagon, 1965; orig. pub. by University of North Carolina Press, 1943.

INDEX

Index

ACKNOWLEDGMENTS

Long in the making, this book holds debts to a substantial number of friends, colleagues, fellow early modernists, librarians, and institutions in the United States and the United Kingdom. My interest in the East India Company as a foundational institution of global capitalism took shape in conversations with the late Patrick Condon and the late William Netzer, my flatmates in the 1980s, whose intellectual companionship prompted me to interrogate corporate and maritime history. The compelling story of the East India Company's Sixth Voyage (1610–13)—with the six-month captivity of its general in Yemen, and the grievous loss in Java of Jacobean England's greatest merchant ship on its premiere voyage—seized my attention as I worked on another book at the British Library's Oriental and India Office, Bankside. The staff there, and subsequently in the Asian and African Studies Collection at the St. Pancras facility, proved impeccably helpful. I would single out Richard Morel, who took pains to facilitate my archival research, and Margaret Makepeace for her illuminating counsel. Repeated fellowship support from the Huntington, including a grant for study in London, was invaluable. The staff at the Huntington is superb; I thank in particular Susan Green, Laura Stalker, and Stephen Tabor. Among the most welcome outcomes of my seasons there is the friendship of Anthony Parr, whose erudition in the literatures of theater and travel, generous perusal of the opening chapters, and advocacy of lucid, story-driven exposition helped me frame the book more incisively. I am deeply grateful to Bernhard Klein, my coauthor for a recent book chapter, whose work on oceanic history, the drama of voyaging, and ship biographies as tools of cultural and material inquiry informs this book in fundamental ways. I thank Richard Strier for encouraging me, a literary scholar, to write a generational study of the East India Company. I am honored to thank many others for their interest and support, notably the late Paul Alpers, Joel Altman, Bernadette Andrea, John Michael Archer, David

Baker, Peter Betjemann, A. R. Braumuller, Daniel Carey, Ann Christensen, Nandini Das, Stephen Deng, Matthew Dimmock, Susan Frye, Mary Fuller, Christopher Hodgkins, Claire Jowitt, Gerald MacLean, Mark Netzloff, Su Fang Ng, Rebecca Olson, Stephen Orgel, Karen Robertson, Sabine Schülting, Timon Screech, Barbara Sebek, Amrita Sen, Jyotsna Singh, Philip Stern, and Michael Witmore. I thank Oregon State University's Center for the Humanities for internal fellowship support, the Center's current and former directors Christopher Nichols and David Robinson for their heartening feedback and counsel, and the Office of Research for funds to study in London. I remain particularly indebted to the National Endowment for the Humanities, which awarded the project a major grant in 2013.

My deepest gratitude goes, as ever, to my partner, Nancy Staton Barbour. Her keen insights, theoretical expertise, lucid argumentation, and gifted eye for effective strategies of exposition have enriched this study, in granular detail and overall scope, immeasurably. Like the two before it, this book is lovingly dedicated to her.

The Loss of the "Trades Increase" expands upon some material I have treated before. Portions of the introduction appeared in "Corporate Praxis and the Legacy of Privateering: The Jacobean East India Company," *Clio* 41: 1 (Fall 2011), 1–30, and "'The *English* Nation at *Bantam*': Corporate Process in the East India Company's First Factory," *Genre* 48: 2 (July 2015), 159–92. The latter essay also contributed to Chapters 5 and 7. Portions of Chapter 3 appeared in "Command Performances: Early English Traders in Arabia Felix," in Sabine Schülting, Sabine Lucia Müller, and Ralf Hertel, eds., *Early Modern Encounters with the Islamic East: Performing Cultures* (Farnham: Ashgate, 2012), 43–66. Portions of Chapters 7 and 8 appeared in "A Multinational Corporation: Foreign Labor in the London East India Company," in *A Companion to the Global Renaissance: English Literature and Culture in the Era of Expansion*, ed. Jyostna Singh (Oxford: Wiley-Blackwell, 2009), 129–48.

Lightning Source UK Ltd.
Milton Keynes UK
UKHW010656280121
377821UK00008B/69/J

9 780812 252774